Advancing Comparative Area Studies

Advancing Comparative Area Studies

Analytical Heterogeneity and Organizational Challenges

Edited by

ARIEL I. AHRAM
PATRICK KÖLLNER
RUDRA SIL

OXFORD
UNIVERSITY PRESS

Oxford University Press is a department of the University of Oxford.
It furthers the University's objective of excellence in research, scholarship,
and education by publishing worldwide. Oxford is a registered trade mark of
Oxford University Press in the UK and in certain other countries.

Published in the United States of America by Oxford University Press
198 Madison Avenue, New York, NY 10016, United States of America.

© Oxford University Press 2025

All rights reserved. No part of this publication may be reproduced, stored in a retrieval system, transmitted, used for text and data mining, or used for training artificial intelligence, in any form or by any means, without the prior permission in writing of Oxford University Press, or as expressly permitted by law, by license or under terms agreed with the appropriate reprographics rights organization. Inquiries concerning reproduction outside the scope of the above should be sent to the Rights Department, Oxford University Press, at the address above.

You must not circulate this work in any other form
and you must impose this same condition on any acquirer

Library of Congress Cataloging-in-Publication Data
Names: Ahram, Ariel I. (Ariel Ira), 1979- editor | Köllner, Patrick, 1968- editor |
Sil, Rudra, 1967- editor
Title: Advancing comparative area studies : analytical heterogeneity and organizational challenges/
edited by Ariel I. Ahram, Patrick Köllner, Rudra Sil.
Description: New York, NY : Oxford University Press, 2025. |
Includes bibliographical references and index.
Identifiers: LCCN 2025006791 (print) | LCCN 2025006792 (ebook) | ISBN 9780197809372 paperback |
ISBN 9780197809365 hardback | ISBN 9780197809402 |
ISBN 9780197809389 epub
Subjects: LCSH: Area studies—Comparative method
Classification: LCC D16.25 .A224 2025 (print) | LCC D16.25 (ebook) |
DDC 909—dc23/eng/20250404
LC record available at https://lccn.loc.gov/2025006791
LC ebook record available at https://lccn.loc.gov/2025006792

DOI: 10.1093/oso/9780197809365.001.0001

Paperback Printed by Integrated Books International, United States of America
Hardback Printed by Bridgeport National Bindery, Inc., United States of America

The manufacturer's authorized representative in the EU for product safety is Oxford
University Press España S.A., Parque Empresarial San Fernando de Henares,
Avenida de Castilla, 2 – 28830 Madrid (www.oup.es/en).

Contents

Contributors	ix
Prologue *Timothy J. Power*	xv

1. Introduction: Extending the Horizons
   of Comparative Area Studies   1
   Patrick Köllner, Rudra Sil, and Ariel I. Ahram

PART I COMPARATIVE AREA STUDIES AND THE PROSPECTS FOR INTERPRETATION ACROSS CONTEXTS

2. Communicating Across Contexts: How Translation
   Can Benefit Comparative Area Studies   29
   Erica S. Simmons and Nicholas Rush Smith

3. Comparative Area Studies and Interpretivism:
   Toward an Interpretive-Comparative Research Approach   47
   Anna Fünfgeld

PART II HOW COMPARATIVE AREA STUDIES BENEFITS, AND BENEFITS FROM, VARIED STRATEGIES OF CAUSAL ANALYSIS

4. Causal Explanation with Ideal Types: Opportunities
   for Comparative Area Studies   75
   Ryan Saylor

5. Advancing Theory Development in Comparative
   Area Studies: Practical Recommendations for
   Evaluating the Equifinality of Causal Mechanisms   105
   Marissa Brookes and Jesse Dillon Savage

vi CONTENTS

6. The Best of Two Worlds?: Generalizing
and Individualizing through Multi-Method
Research in Comparative Area Studies 129
Matthias Basedau and David Kuehn

PART III RETHINKING THE SITES AND SPACES OF COMPARISON

7. Crossing the Boundaries of Comparison:
Comparative Area Studies and Comparative
Historical Analysis 159
Amel Ahmed

8. Comparison as Ontology, Region as Concept:
On the Synergies of Comparative Area Studies 181
Erik Martinez Kuhonta

9. The Contextualized Comparative Sector Approach:
Comparative Area Studies at the Sectoral Level of Analysis 205
Roselyn Hsueh

PART IV COMPARATIVE AREA STUDIES AND THE PROMISE OF GLOBAL IR

10. The Promise of Comparative Area Studies
for the Study of Human Rights 231
Eileen Doherty-Sil

11. Revisionist (Eurasian) Powers and the West:
A Comparative Area Studies Bridge Between
International Relations Theory and Area Expertise 255
Nora Fisher-Onar

PART V ORGANIZATIONAL CHALLENGES AND INSTITUTIONAL FRAMEWORKS FOR COMPARATIVE AREA STUDIES

12. Comparative Area Studies: Programs, Departments,
Constraints, Opportunities 281
Sara Wallace Goodman and Thomas B. Pepinsky

CONTENTS vii

13. Comparative Area Studies in the Great Brain Race:
Institutional Legacies and Programmatic Innovation
in the Global Age 303
Ariel I. Ahram and Connie Stovall

Epilogue 333
Amrita Narlikar

Index 337

Contributors

Amel Ahmed is Associate Professor of Political Science at the University of Massachusetts, Amherst. Her main area of specialization is democratic studies, with a special interest in elections, voting systems, legislative politics, party development, and voting rights. She examines these issues in historical and comparative perspective, and her work combines a regional focus on Europe and the United States. She is author of *Democracy and the Politics of Electoral System Choice: Engineering Electoral Dominance* (Cambridge University Press, 2013) and *The Regime Question: Foundations of Democratic Governance in Europe and the United States* (Princeton University Press, 2025). She has also written extensively on issues of research methods and the epistemological foundations of social scientific inquiry. Her work has appeared in journals including *Comparative Political Studies, Perspectives on Politics, Journal of Politics, Polity,* and *Studies in Comparative International Development*.

Ariel I. Ahram is Professor in the Virginia Tech School of Public and International Affairs and a nonresident Associate of the German Institute for Global and Area Studies. He earned a BA in history and Islamic studies from Brandeis University and an MA in Arab studies and PhD in government from Georgetown University. He is the author of *War and Conflict in the Middle East and North Africa* (Polity, 2020) and *Break All the Borders: Separatism and the Remaking of the Middle East* (Oxford University Press, 2019). He has written extensively on issues of research methods, including the theory and method of comparative area studies and the linking of qualitative and quantitative methodology. His work has appeared in the journals *Political Research Quarterly, Qualitative Research, World Development, Theory & Society, International Journal of Middle East Studies, Survival, Middle East Journal,* and *Terrorism & Political Violence,* among others.

Matthias Basedau is Director of the GIGA Institute for African Affairs and Adjunct Professor of Political Science at the University of Hamburg, Germany. His main fields of interest are the causes of violent conflict, especially ethnicity, natural resources, political institutions, and religion. His most recent book is the coauthored monograph *Religious Minorities at Risk* (with Jonathan Fox and Ariel Zellman, Oxford University Press, 2023). He also takes keen interest in reflecting on comparative area studies. His work has been published in journals like the *American Journal of Political Science, Democratization, European Political Science Review, Journal of Conflict Resolution, Journal of Peace Research, Party Politics, Political Geography,* and *Political Research Quarterly*.

X CONTRIBUTORS

Marissa Brookes is Associate Professor and Director of Graduate Studies in the Department of Political Science at the University of California, Riverside and Faculty Co-Director of the UCR Inland Empire Labor and Community Center. Her research focuses on labor movements, transnational activism, the political economy of labor, and qualitative methodology. Her book *The New Politics of Transnational Labor: Why Some Alliances Succeed* (Cornell University Press, 2019) analyzes the causes of success and failure in transnational labor campaigns. Her work has also been published in outlets such as *Comparative Political Studies, PS: Political Science and Politics, Development and Change, Labor Studies Journal*, and *Qualitative and Multi-Method Research.*

Jesse Dillon Savage is Associate Professor in Global Politics at Trinity College Dublin, University of Dublin. His primary areas of research are in international relations theory and international security. His book *Political Survival and Sovereignty* was published by Cambridge University Press in 2020. His research has also been published in *International Studies Quarterly, Journal of Peace Research, Journal of Conflict Resolution,*and the *European Journal of International Relations.*

Eileen Doherty-Sil is Senior Lecturer in Political Science and Faculty Director of the core curriculum at the Joseph H. Lauder Institute of Management & International Studies of the University of Pennsylvania. At the Lauder Institute, she is part of the leadership team focusing on interdisciplinary curricular development in support of the university's MBA/MA Joint Degree Program in International Studies. Her teaching and research interests encompass international relations theory as well as global human rights, especially the role of business and international human rights law. She previously coedited and contributed to *Beyond Boundaries? Disciplines, Paradigms and Theoretical Integration in International Studies.*

Nora Fisher-Onar is Associate Professor of Global Studies at the University of San Francisco. Her research interests include international relations theory, comparative politics/area studies (Middle East, Europe, Eurasia), foreign policy analysis, political ideologies, gender, and history/memory. She is author of *Contesting Pluralism(s): Islamism, Liberalism and Nationalism in Turkey and Beyond* (Cambridge University Press, 2025) and lead editor of *Istanbul: Living with Difference in a Global City* (Rutgers University Press, 2018). She has published extensively in journals like the *Journal of Common Market Studies, Conflict and Cooperation, Millennium, Theory and Society, Qualitative and Multi-Method Research, Women's Studies International Forum*, and *Middle East Studies*. Fisher-Onar also contributes policy commentary to *Foreign Affairs*, the *Guardian, OpenDemocracy*, and the *Washington Post* (*Monkey Cage* blog), as well as for bodies like Brookings, Carnegie, and the German Marshall Fund (GMF). At the GMF, she has served as a Ronald Asmus Fellow, Transatlantic Academy Fellow, and Non-Residential Fellow.

Anna Fünfgeld is a postdoctoral researcher and member of the Cluster of Excellence 'Climate, Climatic Change and Society' (CLICCS) at the University of Hamburg. She is a nonresident Associate of the German Institute for Global and Area Studies and obtained her doctorate from the University of Freiburg. Her research focuses on energy and climate politics, infrastructure studies, natural resource conflicts, social movements, and the far right in Southeast Asia, South America, and Germany. She has taught graduate and undergraduate courses on research methods and acted as methodology coordinator of the interdisciplinary Southeast Asian Studies Program at Freiburg University. Her work has been published in journals such as *The Indonesian Quarterly, Earth System Governance, Energy Research & Social Science, and Pacific Affairs.*

Sara Wallace Goodman is Professor of Political Science at the University of California, Irvine. Her research examines citizenship and the shaping of political identity through immigrant integration, with regional expertise in both Europe and the United States. She is the author of *Citizenship in Hard Times: How Ordinary People Respond to Democratic Threat* (Cambridge University Press, 2022), coauthor of *Pandemic Politics* (Princeton University Press, 2022), and author of *Immigration and Membership Politics in Western Europe* (Cambridge University Press, 2014), which received the Best Book Award from the European Politics and Society section of the American Political Science Association. Her work has also appeared in journals including *Journal of Politics, World Politics, Comparative Political Studies, International Organization,* and other venues.

Roselyn Hsueh is Professor of Political Science at Temple University, Philadelphia, where she codirects the Certificate in Political Economy. She is the author of *Micro-Institutional Foundations of Capitalism: Sectoral Pathways to Globalization in China, India, and Russia* (Cambridge University Press, 2022), *China's Regulatory State: A New Strategy for Globalization* (Cornell University Press, 2011), and scholarly articles and book chapters on states and markets, comparative regulation and governance, and development and globalization. Various peer-reviewed journals including *Comparative Political Studies, Governance,* and *Review of Policy Research* have published her work. News and policy outlets such as the BBC, *Foreign Affairs, Foreign Policy,* and the *New York Times* have featured her research and writing. The Fulbright Global Scholar Award and other prestigious fellowships have funded her research. She held the Hayward R. Alker Postdoctoral Fellowship at the University of Southern California and earned her BA and PhD from the University of California, Berkeley.

Patrick Köllner is Vice President of the German Institute for Global and Area Studies, Director of the GIGA Institute for Asian Studies, and Professor of Political Science at the University of Hamburg. His research has focused on the formal and informal organization of political parties in Japan and in comparative perspective, the politics and external relations of the two Koreas, Australia and New Zealand's relations with China and the Pacific, and think tanks in comparative perspective. He has published in journals such as the *British Journal of Politics and International Relations, Democratization, Journal of Civil Society, Journal of East Asian Studies, Japanese Journal of Political Science, Pacific Affairs, Pacific Review, Political Science,* and *Politische Vierteljahresschrift.* He has edited or coedited more than twenty books and yearbooks, including most recently (with Delphine Allès and Christophe Jaffrelot) *Order and Agency in the Indo-Pacific* (Palgrave Macmillan, 2025).

David Kuehn is Senior Research Fellow at the GIGA Institute for Asian Studies, Hamburg, Germany. His substantive research focuses on the political role of the military in authoritarian regimes, new democracies, and periods of regime transition. He has also published extensively on issues related to social scientific research methods with a focus on multi-method research. His most recent book is the coauthored monograph *Dictators' Endgames* (with Aurel Croissant and Tanja Eschenauer-Engler, Oxford University Press, 2024). His work has appeared in journals such as *Democratization, European Political Science Review, Journal of Democracy,* and *Sociological Methods and Research.*

Erik Martinez Kuhonta is Associate Professor of Political Science at McGill University and the 2024-25 John H. McArthur Fellow of the Asia-Pacific Foundation of Canada. He is a comparativist and Southeast Asianist who writes on political development, democracy, political economy, and qualitative methods. Kuhonta is author of *The Institutional Imperative: The Politics of Equitable Development in Southeast Asia* (Stanford University Press, 2011), which was short-listed for the Canadian Political Science Association Prize in Comparative Politics. He has published articles in *Comparative Political Studies, Pacific Affairs, Contemporary Southeast Asia, Asian Survey,* and the *Pacific Review.* He has coedited *Party System Institutionalization in Asia: Democracies, Autocracies, and the Shadow of the Past* (Cambridge University Press, 2015) and *Southeast Asia in Political Science: Theory, Region, and Qualitative Analysis* (Stanford University Press, 2008).

Amrita Narlikar is Distinguished Fellow at the Observer Research Foundation, New Delhi, and Honorary Fellow at Darwin College, University of Cambridge. Between 2014 and 2024 she served as President of the German Institute for Global and Area Studies and Professor of Political Science at the University of Hamburg. She recently coedited the *How Not to Guide for International Relations,* published as a special issue of *International Affairs* to mark the journal's centenary anniversary in 2022. Her books include (coauthored) *Strategic Choices, Ethical Dilemmas: Stories from the Mahabharat* (Penguin Random House India, 2023), *Poverty Narratives and Power Paradoxes in International Trade Negotiations and Beyond* (Cambridge University Press, 2020), (coauthored) *Bargaining Together with a Rising India: Lessons from the Mahabharata* (Oxford University Press, 2014), and (coedited) *The Oxford Handbook on the World Trade Organization* (Oxford University Press, 2012). Her current research deals with questions of geoeconomics, multilateralism, and global (and regional) order.

Thomas B. Pepinsky is the Walter F. LaFeber Professor of Government and Public Policy at Cornell University, where he is also the Director of the Southeast Asia Program and Associate Director of the Modern Indonesia Project. He is also a Nonresident Senior Fellow at the Brookings Institution. A comparative political economist with a special interest in Southeast Asia, he is the coauthor of, most recently, *Pandemic Politics: The Deadly Toll of Partisanship in the Age of COVID* (Princeton University Press, 2022). His current research focuses on the political economy of identity in Southeast Asia and around the world.

Timothy J. Power is Professor of Latin American Politics at the University of Oxford, where he currently serves as Head of the Social Sciences Division. He previously directed the Oxford School of Global and Area Studies and, before that, the Latin American Centre. His research concerns comparative political institutions as well as Brazilian politics and government. His most recent book (with Paul Chaisty and Nic Cheeseman) is *Coalitional Presidentialism in Comparative Perspective* (Oxford University Press, 2018). His articles have appeared in *Comparative Political Studies, Journal of Politics, European Journal of Political Research, Comparative Politics, Political Research Quarterly, Democratization, Electoral Studies, Party Politics*, and many other journals.

Ryan Saylor is Associate Professor of Political Science at the University of Tulsa, where he teaches courses on bureaucratic reform, state building, Latin American politics, and African politics. He is author of *State Building in Boom Times: Commodities and Coalitions in Latin America and Africa* (Oxford University Press, 2014). His new book manuscript analyzes how creditors spurred the professionalization of tax collection and bureaucratic administration in seventeen European countries between 1600 and 1900. His articles have appeared in journals such as *Sociological Methods & Research, Theory and Society*, and *World Politics*. He coordinated a symposium on comparative area studies that appeared in *Qualitative and Multi-Method Research* in 2020.

Rudra Sil is Professor and Director of Graduate Studies in the Department of Political Science at the University of Pennsylvania, where he also serves as the SAS Director of the Huntsman Program in International Studies & Business. His scholarly interests encompass comparative politics, qualitative methodology, international development, labor politics, Russian and East European studies, and Asian studies. He is author, coauthor or coeditor of seven books. These include *Managing "Modernity": Work, Community, and Authority in Late-Industrializing Japan and Russia* (University of Michigan Press, 2002) and *Beyond Paradigms: Analytic Eclecticism in the Study of World Politics* (Palgrave Macmillan, 2010), coauthored with Peter Katzenstein. He is also author of three dozen papers, including articles published in such journals as *Comparative Political Studies, International Studies Quarterly, Perspectives on Politics*, and *Europe-Asia Studies*. Sil is also an elected board member of the Committee on Concepts and Methods of the International Political Science Association.

Erica S. Simmons is Associate Professor of Political Science and International Studies at the University of Wisconsin–Madison, where she holds the Political Science Department Board of Visitors Professorship. She is the author of *Meaningful Resistance: Market Reforms and the Roots of Social Protest in Latin America* (Cambridge

University Press, 2016) which was awarded the 2017 Charles Tilly award for distinguished contribution to scholarship on collective behavior and social movements. Simmons also writes on qualitative methods, coediting (with Nicholas Rush Smith) *Rethinking Comparison: Innovative Methods for Qualitative Political Inquiry* (Cambridge University Press, 2021), and coauthoring articles in *Comparative Politics, PS: Political Science and Politics*, and *Qualitative and Multi-Method Research*. Her work has also appeared in *World Politics, Comparative Political Studies*, and *Theory and Society*, among others.

Nicholas Rush Smith is Associate Professor of Political Science at the City University of New York–City College and a Senior Research Associate in the Department of Sociology at the University of Johannesburg. His research utilizes qualitative methods to examine how democratic states use violence to produce order and why citizens sometimes use violence to challenge that order. His first book, *Contradictions of Democracy: Vigilantism and Rights in Post-Apartheid South Africa* (Oxford University Press, 2019), explored these themes through the lens of crime, policing, and vigilantism in South Africa. With Erica S. Simmons, he has also written about the intersection of comparative and ethnographic methods, coediting *Rethinking Comparison: Innovative Methods for Qualitative Political Inquiry* (Cambridge University Press, 2021), among other publications.

Connie Stovall is Director for Research Impact & Intelligence at Virginia Tech, and her team collaborates with campus stakeholders to translate information to insights. She utilizes bibliometrics, other institutional data, and visualization tools such as Tableau and VosViewer to help identify research competencies, to understand collaboration networks, and to demonstrate impact. She earned her master of library and information science at the University of Alabama.

Prologue

Timothy J. Power

The publication of the present collection, following on the influential 2018 volume *Comparative Area Studies: Methodological Rationales and Cross-Regional Applications*, is yet another step forward in the consolidation of an exciting new scholarly movement toward comparative area studies (CAS). The present book explores the ideational, epistemological, theoretical, and methodological aspects of CAS. It provides an opportune moment to reflect not only on the important intellectual ramifications of the turn to CAS, but also on its implications for our everyday professional lives. How might we translate some of the insights and requirements of CAS into fresh ideas for restructuring the (often rigid) institutional architecture of our universities and research centers?

This volume's coeditors have kindly asked me to reflect on the nexus between CAS and the institutional architecture of area studies and have encouraged a personal "take" on the key issues. As a longtime area studies scholar (in the politics of Latin America) and more recently as a university administrator, I have often thought that the conventional institutional incarnations of area studies were sorely in need of a shakeup. CAS, as an authentic intellectual impetus (as opposed to, say, an emerging budget constraint or a stern letter from a university bureaucrat), and one that originated within the area studies community itself, provides us with exactly the right kind of incentive for us to look ourselves in the mirror. I say this from a position that is decidedly non-neutral; it is no secret that my own university's area studies community has been strongly influenced by dialogue with leading practitioners of CAS in different parts of the world and by one of its leading institutional champions, the German Institute for Global and Area Studies. My reflections are also shaped strongly by an area studies environment in which social sciences are prominent. In Oxford, the Oxford School of Global and Area Studies (OSGA) is a department in the Social Sciences Division and encompasses seven regional centers (for Africa, China, Japan, Latin America, the Middle East, Russia and Eastern Europe, and South Asia). All

xvi PROLOGUE

seven centers employ historians, but they tend to be dominated by specialists in anthropology, political science, sociology, economics, and development.

My comments are directed to universities where the number of established area studies communities (e.g., regionally focused centers, institutes, or programs) is greater than one. For universities in which two or more area studies programs are already institutionally linked in some nontrivial way, the CAS agenda has the potential to spark fascinating conversations. In particular, CAS provides an intellectual justification for emplacing greater "connective tissue" between area studies programs. By connective tissue, I do not advocate the merging of area studies units or the erasure of sensible boundaries between them, as this would blatantly contradict the emphases on "context" and "difference" that form the bedrock of the area studies tradition. Rather, I am thinking of an intensification of inter-unit engagement, a continuous multilateral cultivation of inherent strengths. To borrow the language of the Treaty of Rome, we should strive for an "ever closer union" that benefits area studies everywhere, all the time.

Why is such integration potentially valuable to all of us? There are many reasons, but I will name five here. Not all are related to the substantive intellectual content of CAS, but all are compatible with it. First, although the editors of this volume are correct that the area studies "wars" of the 1990s (i.e., disciplines against area studies) have now receded, the tensions that sparked them have not fully disappeared. One can still often perceive a double standard in academic politics, under which area studies programs are continually asked to justify their relevance but traditional disciplines are not. Being placed in a reactive position is tiresome, leading many area studies colleagues to wonder how one can "defend" the area studies tradition without sounding "defensive." The CAS project infuses rich substantive content and persuasive arguments into this debate. For example, the present volume injects area studies forcefully into ongoing debates about epistemology and methodology that are relevant to both the positivist and the interpretivist traditions, pushing forward the analytical frontiers within both. In this sense, CAS lends agency to area studies and moves it away from a predominantly defensive position.

Second is the fact that university administrators continue to advocate for economy of scale and value for money. They often oppose duplication of administrative efforts and encourage closer cooperation between programs. This in and of itself is no reason to federate or integrate. However, my experience is that when integration happens, it can provide unexpected intellectual payoffs even to those who were initially skeptical. Our area centers in Oxford were independent prior to 2004, when a department of area studies was created (now called OSGA). The creation of an institutional umbrella gradually propelled greater collaboration among our area studies specialists, including joint research, joint teaching, and the introduction of cross-regional degree programs at the MA and PhD levels. OSGA is now a community of approximately two hundred faculty and graduate students spread across seven regional centers, all of which retain their own masters programs in addition to the new shared ones. The "central government" of OSGA resembles a federal council, one that is driven by a shared concern for the position of area studies within the Social Sciences Division and within the university. This process of federation has not been easy—far from it—but our improved intellectual life is a persuasive example of a beneficial byproduct of university reorganization. Timing is key. We were advantaged by the creation of an umbrella institution just prior to the crystallization of the CAS agenda, which then reinforced our new structure by infusing it with creative intellectual content.

Third, integration of area studies programs in universities is a sensible insurance policy against volatility in the relative salience of countries and regions. Academics with longer careers are undoubtedly familiar with these cycles: the country that today is "hot" tomorrow is not. Funding, visibility, and student numbers often parallel these trends, exposing individual area programs to dangerous downturns. For example, the country where I have conducted most of my research, Brazil, sparked great interest during the "Brazilian Miracle" of 1968–1973 and then again during the commodity boom and social inclusion of 2004–2012, but these periods of salience were bookmarked by downturns in the fortunes of Brazilian studies. Attention to MENA countries and Arabic language has risen and fallen in tandem with international conflicts; in Asian studies, the catalytic role played by Japan circa 1990 had been taken by China circa 2020; other examples abound. But if area studies programs are federated into umbrella institutions, this volatility can be softened: the goal of area studies administrators should always be to govern in a countercyclical manner. CAS helps smooth the cycles.

Fourth, as this volume and its predecessor make clear, globalization is not a threat but rather an opportunity for area studies. The questions that we ask about inequality, ethnicity, climate change, human development, and regime dynamics are increasingly planetary ones. They benefit from cross-regional and cross-unit analysis and dialogue. A twenty-first-century form of area studies is one in which scholars tackle overarching global issues and examine how these refract differently within "areas," socially constructed though these may be. The active comparison of these refractions, promoted and nourished by umbrella institutions, is yet another way to generate the connective tissue that is needed between area studies programs. Within OSGA, we often refer to "global questions, regional expertise" as an appropriate framing device for an institution that claims space in both global and area studies.

Fifth, integration of area studies programs creates a vibrant intellectual space for the methodological innovations of CAS and can help to translate these into new pedagogical initiatives. In 2021, OSGA launched its first MA-level degree in comparative area studies, which is called "MPhil in Global and Area Studies." The objectives of the degree program—the brainchild of the former head of OSGA, Christopher Gerry—are to allow students to work on key thematic global challenges from a comparative area studies perspective, and to equip them with the conceptual and theoretical expertise to interrogate the notions of "area," "comparative area," and the implications for disciplinary enquiry. The idea is to facilitate an interdisciplinary approach to comparative study across two or more regions and foster a critical approach to area studies. Students take a seminar titled Contending Approaches to Area Studies (heavily influenced by *Comparative Area Studies: Methodological Rationales and Cross-Regional Applications*), take methods options for social sciences and humanities; complete an area studies "immersion" (which can be fieldwork, study abroad, or an internship); take at least one thematic course spanning two or more regions; and complete a thirty-thousand-word thesis. This is an example of postgraduate training that actively embraces the CAS agenda and uses it to inform a two-year curriculum of studies.

Area studies are in need of greater harmony between academic content and institutional architecture. Federated, integrated, umbrella institutions provide the hardware: the intellectual agenda of comparative area studies provides the software. The combination of the two can help us navigate between the Scylla of universalism (the belief that the "world is flat" and humans are interchangeable robots) and the Charybdis of exceptionalism (the belief that each of "our" areas is unique and cannot be compared). In Greek mythology, Charybdis was a deadly whirlpool, which is perhaps an appropriate metaphor for the parochialism that has sometimes impeded the progress of area studies. In this volume and its predecessor, the editors have provided us with an anti-exceptionalist manifesto that has begun to stimulate salutary dialogue throughout the area studies community. I look forward to seeing this volume in our classrooms.

1

Introduction

Extending the Horizons of Comparative Area Studies

Patrick Köllner, Rudra Sil, and Ariel I. Ahram

Comparative Area Studies: A Brief Review

The role of area studies in social science disciplines—and in political science in particular—cannot be taken for granted. Academic debates in the 1990s, most notably among political scientists in the United States (but less so elsewhere; cf. Middell 2019a, 6–7),[1] saw some openly question the rigor and relevance of "traditional" area studies for the advancement of social scientific analyses. Political scientists' retreat from area studies was a part of a wider push to separate social sciences from the more humanities-oriented fields like literature and history. Area studies, in this sense, were just part of the wedge used to divide areas of inquiry that were previously closely tied.

Recently, the discussion about the future of area studies has taken a more pragmatic turn. There are new friendly critiques and constructive engagements between the area studies and social science disciplines (Anderson 2016; Chansa-Ngavej and Lee 2017; Duller 2015; Houben 2017, 2020; Hutt 2019; Lees 2006; Mielke and Hornidge 2017; Milutinovic 2019; Woods 2016). Discussions of methodology have been more cognizant of the relevance of local knowledge and area expertise, whether in support of natural experiments (Dunning 2012, 313–337) or statistical models in multimethod research (Basedau and Kuehn, this volume). And, as approaches such as qualitative comparative analysis (QCA) and comparative historical analysis (CHA) have sought to distinguish more fine-grained causal configurations and encourage complex forms of process-tracing across different settings, it is increasingly evident that area-specific knowledge is necessary

---

[1] On the varied histories of area studies see the contributions to Part 1 of Middell (2019b), especially Marung (2019). See also Naumann et al. (2019) and Beissinger (2020).

Patrick Köllner, Rudra Sil, and Ariel I. Ahram, *Introduction*. In: *Advancing Comparative Area Studies*. Edited by: Ariel I. Ahram, Patrick Köllner, and Rudra Sil, Oxford University Press. © Oxford University Press (2025).
DOI: 10.1093/oso/9780197809365.003.0001

to identify the relevant variables and assess their significance in any given case (Sil 2020).

For their part, area specialists in the social sciences have become more attentive to disciplinary trends and policy-relevant discussions, while still contributing new stocks of knowledge that can "hold theory and method accountable to reality" (Beissinger 2020, 146; see also 134–136). As in the past, when area specialists developed new concepts and theoretical propositions that shaped research agendas across disciplines (Sil 2020), area studies are again helping to propel the development of new fields of scholarly enquiry that transcend or cut across existing disciplinary structures, such as international studies (Curran 2019) and transregional studies, with the latter focusing on connections between regions, flows transcending them, and the societal transformation resulting from such entanglements (Middell 2019a, 10, 11).

Proponents of interpretive analysis, too, have sought to lay out just how and where immersive qualitative research, despite being context-specific, generates important interventions into theoretical and methodological debates in the social sciences (Schatz 2009; Schaffer 2021). In effect, the latest trends apparent within the disciplinary structures of the social sciences include renewed awareness of the indispensable value of area-specific knowledge even as new concepts and methods continue to emerge, while area specialists in the social sciences are engaging more explicitly and pragmatically with theories, concepts, and approaches in their respective disciplines, increasingly with an eye to relevant research being conducted in other regions.

In institutional terms as well, regionally focused social scientific research also appears to be enjoying new energy and impetus in many parts of the world. In the United Kingdom, as Timothy Power notes in his prologue to this volume, Oxford University's School of Global and Area Studies (OSGA) continues to house seven vibrant regional centers in which the majority of scholars are attached to social science disciplines. The University of East Anglia launched a new journal in 2020, *New Area Studies*, speaking to the need for studies that are "rooted in space, place and community, but moving beyond the traditional constraints of national boundaries" while they analyze "the ways in which our globalized world is still shaped by local issues and fully engage with its most pressing problems" (University of East Anglia, n.d.). These efforts seek to draw social sciences back to the humanities fields (Hodgett 2019; Rhodes and Hodgett 2021). Elsewhere in Europe, the German Institute for Global and Area Studies (GIGA) has hosted speakers, conferences, and webinars that regularly feature social scientists who specialize in major world regions.

Even in the United States, where government funding for area studies has declined, private foundations and (problematically) national security agencies stepped in to fill some of the void. The vast majority of books published in the field of comparative politics continue to showcase expert knowledge focused on a single country or area (Köllner et al. 2018, 17). In the Global South as well, while many countries may not be in a position to finance multiple area studies centers, we are seeing increasing resources being devoted to the creation and dissemination of knowledge about their immediate areas, as evident in the Institute of Southeast Asian Studies in Singapore and the Africa Institute of South Africa. Moreover, some US-based but globally oriented area studies associations as well as organizations such as the International Institute for Asian Studies in Leiden have stepped up their efforts to bring different area studies communities into communication with each other via conferences and other platforms. These are just a few indications that, despite some initial fears (or hopes) about the obsolescence of area studies, the latter have survived and adapted to evolving conditions across varied institutional settings worldwide (Beissinger 2020; Sil 2020, 259–262).

One aspect of the pragmatic turn that has supported the revitalization of area studies, we submit, is the increased compatibility of area-focused qualitative inquiry and comparative analysis that cuts across areas and regions. This was not always the case. For much of the latter half of the twentieth century, area specialists often expressed skepticism of case studies produced in the service of macro-comparative analyses but not always by scholars with the training and experience to appreciate complexities on the ground or contentious aspects of historiography (Lustick 1996). From the other side, comparativists in the social sciences questioned the relevance of seemingly idiosyncratic single-country narratives for theoretical and methodological issues of interest to disciplines such as political science (Lees 2006). Over the last two decades, however, the effort to preserve and update space for qualitative research in the face of evolving techniques of quantitative analysis has created a new environment in which investment in area expertise and qualitative comparative analysis not only coexist but rely on each other to produce scholarship that has greater relevance beyond a single area and greater resonance in disciplinary debates. Comparative area studies (CAS) plays a crucial role in this context, supporting the revitalization of area studies and expanding the scope for context-sensitive contextualized comparisons that speak to theoretical and practical problems of interest to social scientists.

While the term "comparative area studies" has been used loosely at times, a more purposeful and institutionalized effort to define and promote CAS emerged from the German Institute for Global and Area Studies (GIGA) in Hamburg in the mid-2000s (Basedau and Köllner 2006; 2007). Since that time, the effort has expanded steadily and significantly, supported by the work of individual scholars on both sides of the Atlantic who were not necessarily using the label of "CAS" but were engaging in cross-regional comparisons in creative ways that bear a family resemblance to one another. These synergies and convergences are what eventually led to the publication by Oxford University Press of our first volume, *Comparative Area Studies: Methodological Rationales and Cross-Regional Applications* (Ahram et al. 2018). This book laid out in detail the distinctive features and value added of CAS—with one eye on its place within ongoing methodological debates and another on the novel findings that have emerged from the actual practice of CAS-style studies on a wide range of issues of interest to political scientists and social scientists writ large. We define CAS as a self-conscious effort to

(i) balance deep sensitivity to context in each of the locales being examined with the use of some variant of the comparative method to surface causal linkages that are portable across world regions; and (ii) engage ongoing research and scholarly discourse in two or more area studies communities against the backdrop of more general concepts and theoretical debates within a social science discipline. (Köllner et al. 2018, 3)

As we conceive of it, CAS is designed not to decenter but leverage the strengths of the area studies approach, taking advantage of skills, experiences, networks, and intuitions that a trained area expert possesses. At the same time, in order to explore the possibility of findings from a single case study or an intraregional comparison that may be portable to other areas or may at least find interesting contrasts in cases drawn from other regions, CAS recognizes the potential utility of some approximation of the comparative method. However, CAS emphasizes a style of qualitative comparative analysis different from the standard Mill-type controlled comparison, where the logic of case selection is privileged over area expertise, or intraregional comparison that relies upon deep familiarity of a specific region, where area expertise is paramount, even if sometimes at the expense of strict adherence to principles of case selection. CAS differentiates itself with its emphasis on *contextualized* comparison, reflected in due consideration of the spatial and temporal contexts within which phenomena of interest take place as well as engagement with relevant discourses and parallel debates unfolding in different area studies communities. In the first volume, we built on the earlier references to "contextualized comparison" by Richard Locke and Kathleen Thelen (1995) and by Paul Pierson (2003):

> Cross-regional contextualized comparison is distinguished by the fact that, while cases are selected from different areas to afford a degree of control on key variables, there is also a self-conscious effort to adjust the operationalization of concepts, the calibration of measures, and the coding of observations for each case in light of contextual attributes deemed significant by the relevant country- or area-specialists. (Sil 2018, 233)

By context, we mean the distinctive set of background conditions and circumstances and shared understandings that exist among a specific set of actors within a clearly bounded time period and local setting. Tulia Falleti and James Mahoney (2015, 212) state: "Both events and occurrences take place against the backdrop of—and interact with—temporal and spatial contexts. The contexts in which events and occurrences occur provide them with meaning and shape their causal effects." Without some attention to contextual specificities of a case, it may be extremely difficult to produce a narrative about that case that will be viewed as compelling, if not convincing, in the eyes of area experts who regularly participate in scholarly debates with others who are also area experts. Moreover, as Erica Simmons and Nicholas Rush Smith (2021b), argue, an "ethnographic sensibility" can enrich comparisons by providing a deeper and more complex understanding of the ways in which actors in a specific setting might assign meaning to their experiences in the process of formulating their ideas and interests. On the flip side, inadequate attention to context potentially undercuts comparative analysis, making it difficult to properly code observations and measure variables across very different settings, or to trace the varying effects of certain factors or mechanisms across different spatiotemporal contexts (Falleti and Lynch 2009; Saylor 2013; Schatz and Maltseva 2012; Sil 2018).

Yet, even as CAS avoids the contextual excision that is too common in large-N cross-national comparison (Ahram 2011), it remains focused on what Thomas Pepinsky calls elsewhere the core macro-scale social phenomena of political inquiry, such as regimes of representation, political order, economic growth, policy processes, and social movements (Pepinsky 2019). At the same time, CAS lenses see the social world not as plain but as highly textured. The social world consists of complex, heterogeneous entities encompassing many intertwined processes, many of which are big, slow-moving, and sometimes invisible (Mahoney and Rueschemeyer 2003). Some of these processes might initially surface in one country or in particular locales within it, and only later make an appearance in other countries. Indeed, this is why the promise of CAS has been bolstered by renewed interest in theoretically informed single-country studies (Pepinsky 2019) and by subnational comparison (Frazier 2019, 2022; Sellers 2019; Snyder 2001; Giraudy et al. 2019), alongside the long-standing interest in paired cross-national comparison (Gisselquist 2014; Slater and Ziblatt 2013; Tarrow 2010).

CAS is intended in part to provide a shared platform upon which these varied forms of qualitative research can combine fruitfully to generate novel macro-level findings alongside fine-grained, textured interpretations of local-level phenomena. This provides a path for area studies and qualitative social scientific research to support one another and demonstrate their continuing relevance, instead of receding to the margins in the face of advanced techniques of statistical analysis or experimental methods geared toward exploration of micro-level behaviors (Woods 2016). And, in contrast to an earlier era, when area specialists and scholars producing cross-area comparisons may have engaged in duels with one another, both appear to have now gravitated to a position where they can "jointly affirm that their research output, far from being esoteric or idiosyncratic, has much to tell us about how global, regional, national, and local factors shape political outcomes worldwide" (Sil 2020, 269).

It also bears emphasizing that CAS is predicated on the assumption that terms like "area" and "region" are social constructs. As we have previously noted (Köllner et al. 2018, 7), "We view past, present and future conceptualizations of areas and regions as tentative social constructions subject to revision and contestation." Sometimes "areas" or "regions" may cohere with geographic or cultural boundaries that makes them more readily recognizable on a map. At other times, they are more a reflection of assumptions and objectives of a community of scholars at a given point in time. That being said, Christopher Antweiler (2020, 93) reminds us that "overstated critiques entail the danger that the 'spatial turn' in social science and in cultural studies shifts again to an 'aspatial turn.'" While it is true that our understanding of "areas" must guard against the "spatial determinism of geo-ecological or geopolitical traditions," it is also true that spatial features are nonetheless "a condition enabling and constraining human action." Thus, "areas" are best understood as "an amalgam of physical surfaces plus spatialised social relations, supplemented by culturally mediated and often politically charged conceptualizations of these spatials features" (Antweiler 2020, 93).

In sum, the first volume (Köllner et al. 2018) made the case for CAS and discussed what it brought to the table in terms of (1) theory development based on deep engagement with the context conditions of cases studied within and across regions; (2) underappreciated but still portable inferences derived from exploring similarities and differences across cases and regions selected for reasons beyond the requirements of controlled comparison; (3) novel insights drawn from contextualized comparisons about our understanding of the individual countries or locales being treated as "cases"; and, most important, (4) the expanded scope for dialogue and collaboration across area studies communities and between them and broader disciplinary audiences in the social sciences. The volume discussed the compatibility of different strategies and scales of CAS—from inter- and cross-regional studies down to subregional and subnational comparisons—and reflected on the trade-offs these entailed. It also considered a number of methodological and practical challenges in the execution of CAS in various settings, but also offered exemplary illustrations of CAS in action in relation to a wide range of substantive issues—the genesis of electoral systems, the dynamics and diffusion patterns of the Arab Spring, pathways of transregional production networks, anticorruption campaigns in autocracies, natural resource booms and state formation, as well as separatist movements and the organizational basis for rebellion. These studies collectively demonstrate a fundamental premise of CAS, that "the quest for social science theory and the pursuit of area-specific knowledge have never constituted a zero-sum game" (Sil 2018, 230). Yet, importantly, CAS was never intended to serve as a new model or gold standard for qualitative research in the social sciences. As we previously noted (Köllner et al. 2018, 5):

None of this implies that CAS is intrinsically superior to work done by area specialists on their respective areas, or that CAS represents a cutting-edge approach that should replace or subsume other approaches. The aims of this volume are more modest: to create more space in the academic division of labor for small-N qualitative studies that consciously take into account local context and area-specific scholarly discourse while leveraging some version of the comparative method to generate distinctive theoretical insights into phenomena not confined to a single region.

Extending the Horizons: The Rationale for "CAS 2.0"

Since its publication in 2018, the first volume on CAS has been the subject of discussions among both qualitative researchers and scholars working on various world regions. Core arguments in the volume were discussed at conferences of the American Political Science Association (APSA), the European Consortium for Political Science, the International Studies Association, the German Political Science Association, and the 2017 Crossroads Asia conference "Area Studies' Futures." In addition, a symposium published in 2020 in *QMMR*, the newsletter of the APSA Section on Qualitative & Multi-Method Research, pooled a set of constructive critiques, spirited defenses, and creative extensions of CAS as presented in the first volume (Ahmed 2020; Brookes 2020; Fisher-Onar 2020; Hsueh 2020; Pepinsky 2020; Saylor 2020). Four of the participants in that symposium had not previously been part of the discussions on CAS and subsequently accepted our invitation to contribute to the present volume in order to explore ways in which their own research agendas could profit from creative adaptations of the CAS framework.

During this period, the editors of the first volume received dozens of invitations to give presentations on CAS at leading research universities in North America and Europe, while conferences held in Africa, South America, and Southeast Asia organized panels and lectures discussing the potential of CAS for the purpose of better understanding developments across regions of the Global South. Oxford University Press also received—and responded positively to—a request to translate the entire first volume into Chinese, while the main international relations journal of the People's Friendship University in Russia (RUDN) published a positive review of CAS (Agazade 2020) alongside a summary version of CAS and its utility for studying the Global South (Sil and Ahram 2020).

These discussions reveal both a much deeper and a much wider level of interest than anticipated in what we had to say about area studies and about the utility of CAS. They also suggest a growing desire among new audiences to push CAS toward more expansive and creative discussions of how CAS's methodological and epistemological assumptions might be stretched to accommodate new kinds of problematics. Although initially anchored within comparative politics, scholars housed in other disciplines and subfields have raised the prospects of extending CAS to generate different approaches to empirical puzzles normally seen as part of the international relations (IR) subfield and to engage in more sustained dialogue with concepts and approaches employed in cognate fields such as anthropology, geography, and sociology.

CAS has also been creating opportunities for more inclusive conversations with (and among) researchers based in different regions of the Global South, which was particularly evident at a panel chaired by Tim Power (who has authored the prologue to this volume) at a recent conference of the Latin American Studies Association held in Ghana (LASA/Africa). At the same time, sobering conversations highlighted the need for more serious and more concrete consideration of the practical and organizational issues that can affect (or even limit) the prospects for CAS in different organizational and institutional settings. These include issues related to the resources, training, and coordination required to fully realize the potential of the CAS framework while maintaining the quality and utility of the research that comes out of it.

These new challenges and possibilities excited us enough to start plotting a second volume, although this was not something we had planned on at the time the first was published. We began with invitations to the contributors to the aforementioned QMMR symposium, each of whom has contributed a chapter to this volume. We also corresponded with discussants and commentators who had been present at various conference panels to identify others who might be interested in being potential contributors. And, in our own presentations of the first volume at various universities and institutes, we encountered still other scholars eager to engage with us and bring their own work under the CAS umbrella.

With a critical mass of scholars emerging almost effortlessly, we set out to solicit concrete proposals for papers that were initially scheduled to be presented in April 2021 at a workshop hosted by the GIGA in Hamburg, where first drafts of the papers would be presented, critiqued, and discussed. The global pandemic, however, put those plans on hold. Rather than delay the project, however, we organized a series of monthly webinars where the first draft of each chapter was thoroughly discussed with the aim of encouraging substantial revision. In April 2022 we were finally able to gather in Hamburg to subject the new chapter drafts to yet another round of critique and interrogation. The resulting versions are the chapters assembled in this volume, with fifteen of the seventeen contributors (not counting the editors) not having participated in the making of the first (2018) CAS volume.

One of the questions we asked all authors to keep in mind in preparing their chapter for this volume concerned the extent of CAS's epistemological flexibility. While we were always clear about the pluralist impulses behind CAS, and while we distinguished contextualized comparison aimed at "middle range" theorizing[2] from controlled comparison aimed at general explanatory propositions, we did not specifically address whether CAS is able to accommodate epistemologies that go beyond positivism and empiricism. In fact, even as we emphasized the significance of spatial context, we sought to guard against the impression that hermeneutic projects were inherently superior to the search for causal inference (Köllner et al. 2018, 15). Thus, many of the methodological discussions in the 2018 volume tended to veer in the direction of addressing logics of causal explanation and analysis rather than constitutive or interpretive analysis. And the majority of empirical applications showcased there were designed to illustrate how CAS made important contributions in nomothetically inclined causal analysis on key problems.[3] This volume consciously expands the epistemological breadth of CAS so as to cover more of the vast chasm between nomothetic causal generalizations at one end of the spectrum and

---

[2] By "middle range" theorizing, we mean—adapting the use of the phrase by Merton (1949)—causal propositions structured around specific mechanisms and causal links that are portable, but for the limited purpose of examining a subset of possible cases in line with their value for theoretical and/or practical insights in relation to a problem manifested in more than one place.

[3] One chapter in the first volume (Chen 2018) did incorporate some ethnographic research but did not address the epistemological implications of doing so; it mostly engaged in showing how social relations and practices could cross regions from one location to another via migration. More generally, while some scholars, including the philosopher von Wright ([1917] 2004, 55), draw a clear distinction between causal explanation and causal analysis, and still others have a more flexible view of "causal stories" cast at different levels of generality (Abbott 2004), in general, "causal analysis" has been employed as a general term to capture any analysis that seeks to explain a certain outcome or variation in terms of prior causes or to offer an explanandum based on causal inferences relating to some set of factors or explanans.

idiographic context-bound research at the other. In between those two endpoints lies a significant space within which CAS can support "soft" positivist analyses of emergent variation as well as post-positivist efforts to apply techniques of interpretive analysis to illuminate the distinctiveness of particular contexts.

Toward the more nomothetic end, the virtues of CAS are perhaps most evident in the connection to efforts within economics to better understand long-term trajectories of economic change across regions. Historically, even as formal models and game theory proceeded from universal rationalist assumptions to offer powerful covering laws about economic behavior, it was understood that area knowledge often underpinned much of the discipline's empirical and theoretical work (Beissinger 2020). Development economics, for example, was a prominent branch of economics in the Cold War period that was closely tied to deep knowledge about developing areas (Vitalis 2016). Similarly, although often unacknowledged, area expertise informed the efforts within the new institutionalist economics to trace the relationship between regionally specific institutional structures and the long-run economic divergence between Europe, Asia, the Middle East, and Africa (North 1994; North and Thomas 1973; Kuran 2018; Lin 1995; Greif 1993).

Over time, however, departments of economics at leading research institutions have moved away from research on regional or developmental economics, with the most vaunted studies rarely making mention of proper nouns—specific countries or places from which a study is derived or to which it applies (Kurzman 2017). The ascent of behavioral economics has emphasized randomized control trials and "evidence-based" policymaking, which have rapidly diffused across other social science disciplines, especially political science (Baldassari and Abascal 2017; Dunning et al. 2019). The approach is certainly powerful and has produced some important breakthroughs, at least when it comes to understanding economic behavior within the Western, educated, industrialized, rich, and democratic (WEIRD) countries where most experiments are conducted in economics (Apicella et al. 2020; Henrich et al. 2010).

Yet, when it comes to understanding variations across regions and the challenges of economic development, recent Nobel laureates working at the cutting edge of behavioral economics have recognized that the field is poorer for allowing qualitative cross-country comparison to become so marginalized amid the growing popularity of field experiments. In effect, as we think of what CAS can contribute closer to the nomothetic end of the epistemological spectrum, we agree with Timur Kuran (2012), who has intriguingly suggested reconnecting economics with area studies, with an emphasis on structured cross-regional analytical comparison. While this is not the main task of this volume, at least one chapter (Hsueh, this volume) analyzes how CAS can help explain varying economic outcomes through cross-regional comparisons cast at the sectoral level.

Moving further toward the opposite end, the idiographic pole, the emphasis shifts to how CAS might support work based on post-positivist epistemologies such as those that underpin the exploration of meaning-making that actors engage in within their local contexts. While such an approach is sometimes seen as inconsistent or at least orthogonal to standard small-N comparative analysis, recent works remind us that "comparison" itself can be understood and practiced in any number of ways. Notably, two of the authors featured in this volume, Simmons and Smith, have made the case elsewhere for "comparative ethnography" (Simmons and Smith 2019) and, in later work, have pooled various styles of comparative inquiry that encompass diverse modes of comparison connected to different sorts of interpretive analysis (Simmons and Smith 2021b, 2021c). Others explicitly call for interpretivists to "embrace creatively comparative work that uses the dilemmas of situated agents as its empirical starting point" and argue that "a comparative focus on dilemmas enables the use of a kaleidoscope of different analytical lenses and tools to explore complex specificness in context" (Boswell et al. 2019, 5, 17).

This aligns well with recent calls for revitalization of the comparative project in anthropology and historical sociology, particularly in relation to the analysis of such complex sociocultural phenomena as civilization, social inequality, nationalism, and religion. Along these lines, there is growing appetite for site-focused qualitative comparisons that eschew standard diktats of structured comparison in order to illuminate the co-constitution of local and global forces (Riofrancos 2021). At the same time, according to Peter van der Veer (2016, 9, 28), comparison does not promise unified theories but enhances "the intensive study of fragments of social life," which in turn allows the analyst to creatively interpret and translate these fragments across diverse conceptual and semantic universes. Reflecting these varied and sensible understandings of social knowledge, this iteration of CAS aims to stretch our understandings of "comparison" to accommodate different scales, purposes, and problematics, while simultaneously encouraging interpretivists to consider the prospect of novel insights emerging from translating their findings across varied local contexts.

The chapters assembled in this volume collectively aim to pursue several broad objectives. While these objectives may well be intertwined in practice, each represents a focal point for one of the five parts of the book: Part I focuses on the flexibility of CAS's epistemological underpinnings, particularly in relation to its ability to accommodate interpretive analysis. Part II showcases creative strategies for leveraging CAS for causal analysis without sacrificing the commitment to context. Part III features efforts to rethink the logic, scale, and purpose of comparison in different ways in relation to different temporal, spatial, and institutional contexts. Part IV is intended to promote CAS's role in deepening the interface between comparative politics and IR, keeping in mind both new puzzles emerging in IR and the critiques offered by global IR. And Part V considers the significance of organizational challenges and varied institutional frameworks in simultaneously maintaining the capacity for in-depth area studies while encouraging the scope for cross-regional collaborations and knowledge cumulation in the social sciences.

The first of the two chapters in Part I, "Communicating Across Contexts: How Translation Can Benefit Comparative Area Studies," is authored by Erica S. Simmons and Nicholas Rush Smith, who expand on the meaning and practice of "translation" as a way of creating equivalence in concepts, meanings, and observations in different settings (see also Simmons and Smith 2021a, 21–22). Regardless of the methods used, they argue, much of political science research aims to produce causal arguments that are applicable across a population of cases. Yet Simmons and Smith find this endeavor to be premised on a narrow understanding of the portability of political science research. Through a process analogous to linguistic translation, they make the case for comparing for the sake of facilitating the translation of ideas to render them intelligible in a different context, even as the context may change the ways in which an idea or political practice is interpreted or enacted. This process then allows scholars to reflect back on the categories, concepts, and assumptions on the basis of which a piece of research is initiated, potentially opening the door to both new causal pathways and creative efforts to redescribe or reconceptualize political phenomena. The process points to new possibilities for comparative area studies, in particular

14 ADVANCING COMPARATIVE AREA STUDIES

as it develops a clear logic for comparisons that are both deeply grounded in particular times and able to shed light on phenomena in other regions.

The second chapter in Part I, by Anna Fünfgeld, is titled "Comparative Area Studies and Interpretivism: Towards an Interpretive-Comparative Research Approach." While comparisons based on interpretive case studies may not be difficult to find, Fünfgeld argues that methodological discussions of such comparisons tend to be circumscribed by a positivist epistemology favoring systematic, controlled comparison. This mismatch between epistemology and purpose presents special challenges for scholars interested in conducting interpretive comparisons. Based on insights from her own interpretive, cross-regional comparison of energy transformations in Indonesia and Brazil, Fünfgeld makes a compelling case for why interpretive-comparative research requires a different approach to case selection, to the formulation of research questions, and even to the style of writing used and the structuring and publishing of texts. Since some area studies traditions tend to resemble interpretive approaches, especially in terms of sensitivity to context, CAS provides a helpful setting within which to identify the shared aims, strategies, and value of interpretive-comparative research.

If Part I stretches the epistemological boundaries of CAS in the direction of interpretive scholarship, Part II continues to investigate the ways in which CAS presents new opportunities for deploying contextualized comparison in the service of causal analysis. In Chapter 4, "Causal Explanation with Ideal Types: Opportunities for Comparative Area Studies," Ryan Saylor explores the ways in which Weberian ideal types can assist researchers engaging in cross-regional research while remaining sensitive to context within and between world regions. Ideal-typical claims here resemble theoretical models encompassing causal propositions valid across cases, which also permits researchers to identify other factors accounting for the outcome in a particular case. The determination of the factors pertinent to a case-specific outcome but extraneous to the ideal type is one strategy for weighing and adjusting for context without diluting the significance of a broader causal claim applicable to cross-regional research. Saylor's chapter describes what ideal types are, shows how ideal types are useful for achieving causal explanation, offers practical guidance for building and using ideal types, and illustrates their vitality through two seminal works that have had lasting influence in their respective fields—sociology and political science.

Chapter 5, by Marissa Brookes and Jesse Dillon Savage, is titled "Advancing Theory Development in Comparative Area Studies: Practical Recommendations for Evaluating the Equifinality of Causal Mechanisms." This chapter also aims to refine the ways through which CAS can help to test whether causal explanations travel across cases situated in different areas, while also enabling refinement of case-specific explanations through the careful consideration of context that is the hallmark of classic area studies. In contrast to much CAS analysis that emphasizes the congruence of variables, Brookes and Dillon Savage argue that CAS would benefit from more careful attention to the identification and interpretation of causal mechanisms. They call for closer attention to apparent equifinality in causal mechanisms, while holding variables constant. Accordingly, the chapter suggests a three-step approach for analyzing different mechanisms in cases featuring the same X_1/Y_1 relationship in a CAS study: selecting at least one additional X1/Y1 case study, reconsidering the conceptualization of the causal mechanisms across cases, and interpreting equifinality in light of the necessity or sufficiency of X1 for Y1.

The final chapter in Part II is Matthias Basedau and David Kuehn's "The Best of Two Worlds? Generalizing and Individualizing through Multi-Method Research in Comparative Area Studies." This chapter highlights the promising linkages between CAS and multi-method research (MMR) using qualitative and quantitative forms of analysis. The authors argue that MMR can help CAS's effort to combine context-sensitive, in-depth knowledge with the advancement of rigorous conceptual, methodological, and theoretical scholarship in three ways. First, MMR designs offer a systematic methodological framework to reach both *individualizing* and *generalizing* research objectives, something that many CAS studies also aspire to. Second, MMR makes it more possible for CAS studies to develop a uniform conceptual and theoretical framework that is both applicable across a broader population and sufficiently sensitive to individual contexts. Finally, MMR designs allow for the integration of deductive and inductive steps, each performing distinct functions and taking advantage of distinct methodological instruments in the research process.

Part III pushes CAS to consider units of analysis apart from nation-states or other discrete administrative boundaries. A handful of scholars have deployed CAS in studies that compare cities (Frazier 2022) or regional organizations (Rüland and Carrapatoso 2022) instead of countries. Others have more broadly pointed to the need to find ways to compare how sites within and across regions might differently reflect the impact of global processes (Riofrancos 2021) or help refine the understanding and application of transnational concepts across regional contexts (Jokela-Pansini 2019). The three chapters in this part of the book explore different ways of thinking about the logic of comparison and the integration of knowledge that originates in the study of transnational spaces and subnational sectors within and across regions.

In Chapter 7, "Crossing the Boundaries of Comparison: Comparative Area Studies and Comparative Historical Analysis," Amel Ahmed shows how the venerable tradition of the *Annales* school of historical research can guide the progress of CAS. In particular, Ahmed emphasizes the school's emphasis on spatiotemporal context, scope conditions, and midrange theorizing as necessary conditions for causal explanation. While the *Annales'* direct progenitor is comparative historical analysis (CHA) and associated historical sociology (Mahoney 2003; Wood and Williamson 2007), CAS, too, can be counted among the descendants of *Annales*. CAS and CHA offer complementary tools for comparative analysis and an opportunity to bring together features of the *Annales* tradition that have been divided between different research communities. They serve as intellectual anchors for approaches that embrace pragmatic hermeneutics and understand social scientific inquiry as the terrain of conceptual clarification and bounded explanation within and across spatiotemporal contexts.

The following chapter, by Erik Martinez Kuhonta, is titled "Comparison as Ontology, Region as Concept: On the Synergies of Comparative Area Studies." This chapter seeks to promote creativity and knowledge accumulation by encouraging greater dialogue between comparative analysis, area studies, and concept formation. Kuhonta begins by examining the problematic social concept of "region." He asks how discourse and practice make regions into social realities. Close analysis of the construction of Southeast Asia shows that grappling with contrasts and similarities within this region can actually provide fresh insights into both intra and interregional comparative analytics. This exercise of comparison cast at different levels of abstraction facilitates not only deeper understanding of a given region but also spurs concept formation and theory building because the very act of comparison points to broader questions. To illuminate how deep area knowledge can yield the formation of general concepts, Kuhonta shows how the portable concept of the "plural society" can be traced to in-depth knowledge of and comparisons within Southeast Asia. The concept of the plural society reveals how variations observed within the region of Southeast Asia can be scaled up to shed light on broader cross-regional comparisons and support cross-regional collaboration under the rubric of CAS. Ultimately, Kuhonta concludes, comparison as an ontological prior anchors the vision of comparative area studies and scholarly efforts to link theory with region.

In Chapter 9, "The Contextualized Comparative Sector Approach: Comparative Area Studies at the Sectoral Level of Analysis," Roselyn Hsueh shows that problems revolving around political economy of development also might benefit from creatively rethinking the units of comparison and by taking contextualized regional comparisons to the sectoral level. An integrated middle-range theoretical approach of the sort promoted by CAS transcends the standard assumptions in comparative analyses regarding the significance of similarities and differences in cross-national comparisons. When comparing large, complex economies, Hsueh argues, CAS might be most productive when focused on dynamics of sectoral production and the organization of sector-specific institutions within economies situated in different regions. Such an approach also permits the scholar to adjudicate between, or integrate elements of, competing causal factors in the study of states and markets. Recent scholarship on emerging economies and regional powers of the Global South demonstrates the analytical power and theoretical value of scaling cross-regional contextualized comparison at the sectoral level.

Part IV explores the ways in which CAS can contribute to the interface between cross-regional comparison and new perspectives in IR. The field of IR, whether as a part of political science or a stand-alone discipline, has been historically characterized by recurrent confrontations between emergent paradigms (most recently framed around realism, liberalism, and constructivism, although many other schools and "isms" have coexisted alongside these). More recently, however, these debates have given way to calls for more "analytically eclectic" efforts to pose more open-ended questions and develop complex causal stories that selectively combine logics, mechanisms, and data points drawn from contending paradigms (Sil and Katzenstein 2010). These eclectic efforts include sustained attention to regional and local-level attributes that regularly interact with systemic or global forces to generate different patterns and outcomes. Indeed, discrete institutional orders formed in various world regions often mediate the impact of global and international forces and give rise to distinctive policy challenges and calculations in relation to such typical IR domains as security and political economy (Katzenstein 2005). For IR scholars who take seriously the significance of regional settings, CAS's emphasis on cross-regional contextualized comparison is a natural fit for illuminating hidden dynamics and generating novel arguments about the sources of cross-regional and intraregional variation.

Over the past decade, IR has also seen the rise of fresh critiques and creative interventions launched from scholars outside of the "mainstream"—particularly those studying and/or situated in non-Western regions. This is most evident in the emergence and rapid diffusion of what is called "global IR," a conscious movement intended to decenter Western-centric assumptions underlying mainstream IR theories in favor of a more holistic and deeper appreciation of the varied experiences across non-Western regions, particularly those across the Global South (Acharya and Buzan 2019; Kang 2020; Tickner and Smith 2019). Global IR has spawned a plethora of narratives focused on—and often produced within—non-Western areas that are not easily accommodated within dominant theoretical traditions or methodological approaches of "mainstream" IR.

Yet, as Michael Barnett (2021) has argued, global IR has for the most part been largely oppositional in content, driven more by its starkly critical posture rather than by a concerted effort to construct alternative analytic framework. As a result, global IR has been characterized by some as following a "hub and spoke" pattern whereby emerging nodes of IR scholarship in the global periphery tend to engage not with each other but with established nodes of IR scholarship in the core (Risse et al. 2022). These observations suggest that global IR, while opening the door to dialogue between IR and various area studies communities, needs to take the next step, which is to encourage dialogue across non-Western areas and cumulate insights from different regions to generate alternative theoretical frameworks and new research agendas. This is precisely where CAS can prove a useful ally, as both of the chapters in Part IV suggest (Sil and Ahram 2020).

In Chapter 10, "The Promise of Comparative Area Studies for the Study of Human Rights," Eileen Doherty-Sil acknowledges that global IR has done much to correct for the disproportionate attention to Western history in mainstream IR while bringing to the fore new voices and experiences from non-Western societies. In order to move beyond critiquing mainstream IR to generating compelling alternatives to it, however, global IR has much work to do—and much to gain from sustained engagement with area specialists along with cross-regional contextualized comparison of the sort encouraged by CAS. Focusing on the varied trajectories of human rights practice, the author contends that CAS provides new opportunities to formulate novel middle-range arguments that are both portable and capable of providing compelling alternatives to Eurocentric conceptions and standards of global human rights. Dorothy-Sil goes on to focus on three specific human rights puzzles to show how CAS can help mediate between ardent proponents of universalist and particularist visions of human rights, while encouraging more open-ended cross-regional studies. First, what explains the stark cross-regional variation in International Criminal Court membership as well as the existence of outlier cases within geographic regions? Second, why are treaty-based regional human rights courts prevalent in some regions but not in others? Third, what explains the emergent cross-regional and intraregional variations when it comes to the ratification of human rights treaties? Such problems gain from efforts to leverage regional expertise to understand the dynamics in particular cases while also relying on cross-regional contextualized comparison to aggregate insights and construct middle-range theoretical arguments about patterns of human rights practices across and within regions.

In the following chapter, "Revisionist (Eurasian) Powers and the West: A Comparative Area Studies Bridge Between International Relations Theory and Area Expertise," Nora Fisher-Onar begins with the premise that mainstream IR has difficulty in making comparative sense of attitudes and behaviors in revisionist powers within (or beyond) greater Eurasia. She sees this as a function of the "hub and spoke" structure of knowledge production in IR, which tends to sequester non-Western expertise and instead interpret complex phenomena through the more familiar lens of Western (mainly European) historical experiences. As a result, analysts tend to either ignore or to reify historical and cultural factors in shaping revisionist powers' domestic and foreign policy behavior, leaving behind a host of blind spots that lead to the misreading of the objectives, assumptions, and behaviors of regional powers, particularly those that have descended from former empires and do not automatically accept the status quo global order. Fisher-Onar sees CAS as offering a framework that overcomes such blind spots and identifies theoretically significant "family resemblances" across these "former empires turned revisionist powers" (FERPs), focusing on the Eurasian cases of China, Iran, Turkey, and Russia. The chapter leverages cross-regional contextualized comparison of the sort encouraged by CAS to capture three categories of family resemblances among FERPS—structural, agential, and processual—that combine to illuminate historical, sociological, political, and foreign policy similarities and differences across these powers, which are typically thought to be situated in different regions but are in fact situated within the wider geographic space of Eurasia. The result is a framework for more nuanced analysis of complex, real-world phenomena, including the roles and behaviors of revisionist (Eurasian) powers in an age of growing multipolarity.

Part V engages with the organizational and institutional factors that affect the scope and impact of CAS. Throughout the many conversations that the contributors to this volume have held with each other, there has been an important practical matter lurking in the background: Can the existing institutional architecture for training researchers to study phenomena within particular regions be adapted to simultaneously facilitate cross-regional research projects—without undermining the quality of area-specific training or delimiting the sorts of problems that area specialists engage in? This is not a question that can be definitively answered, especially considering the very different kinds of institutional trends that are already in evidence in different regions of the world—often with quite different implications for the study of particular regions or for the future of area studies writ large. Yet, in promoting CAS for its potential intellectual and methodological payoffs, it is incumbent upon us to consider how—and how well—this can be done without trading away the deep insights and distinctive findings that often come from a focused, close-range examination of particular places in their respective regional contexts.

In Chapter 12, "Comparative Area Studies: Programs, Departments, Constraints, Opportunities," Sara Wallace Goodman and Thomas B. Pepinsky examine the organizational and institutional foundations of contemporary area studies in the United States and around the world. Comparing European studies and Southeast Asian studies, the authors view the present organization of area studies as hampered by the contestedness of world regions as analytical constructs. This core problem manifests in the fact that the institutional structures that encourage deep area knowledge (a prerequisite for comparative area studies) are not designed to support the kind of cross-regional comparative work that is essentially to CAS. Thus, for CAS to advance, scholars should embrace the internal critiques of traditional area studies and support new institutional models that encourage cross-regional work while maintaining the deep substantive engagement seen in traditional area studies. In effect, CAS requires not only continued investment in area studies and space for contextualized comparison but also institutional

INTRODUCTION 21

innovation that it can balance the requirements of deep area research with the possibilities for cross-regional comparative analysis.

The final chapter, titled "Comparative Area Studies in the Great Brain Race: Institutional Legacies and Programmatic Innovation in the Global Age," is by Ariel I. Ahram and Connie Stovall. The authors examine institutional arrays (centers, departments, institutes, etc.) that support or inhibit creative collaboration between area studies and social sciences, and pay particularly close attention to the effect of what Aaron Wildavsky (2012) dubs the "great brain race" in higher education—efforts to attract students, faculty, and funding from around the world and, in turn, to offer globally relevant curricula, training, and research. Ahram and Stovall note one unfortunate trend: even as universities seek to compete around the globe, traditional modes of area studies face pronounced intellectual and especially fiscal challenges, while many chief internationalization officers overlook or dismiss area studies in their strategic planning. The chapter presents original data on administrative interaction, curricular overlap, and collaborative research among area studies centers and social science departments in the United States. It shows that some American universities are uniquely poised to adopt and implement CAS's rubric of cross-regional comparison, not just for individual scholars but as a broader program for international studies. Such programing builds on existing infrastructure while facilitating new connectivity and linkage between interdisciplinary area studies centers and between those centers and social science departments.

The above chapters are bookended by two short but important essays by Timothy J. Power and by Amrita Narlikar, two renowned scholars who have played vital roles in the development of area studies and comparative research – Power as the former Head of OSGA at the University of Oxford and Narlikar as the past President of the Hamburg-based GIGA. Power's prologue and Narlikar's epilogue both point to the benefits of area studies centers and programs pooling their research efforts and intellectual output so that the whole may be greater than the sum of its parts. As Power puts it, CAS can provide the intellectual justification for the "connective tissue" required to support "the intensification of inter-unit engagement" among area studies programs without erasing "sensible boundaries" that permit area specialists to cultivate in-depth expertise. And, while this volume does not explicitly address the implications of CAS for policy, Narlikar sees the novel insights generated by CAS as having the potential to offer both "a feast of ideas at our hand for intellectual debate as well as policy-relevant findings." This volume, we know, is not yet close to realizing this potential; but perhaps it has taken some important steps to move beyond the preliminary vision for CAS as laid out in our 2018 book.

Bibliography

Abbott, Andrew. 2004. *Methods of Discovery: Heuristics for the Social Sciences.* New York: Norton.

Acharya, Amitav, and Barry Buzan. 2019. *The Making of Global International Relations: Origins and Evolution of IR at Its Centenary.* Cambridge: Cambridge University Press.

Agazade, M. M. 2020. Book review: Ahram, A.I., Köllner, P. & Sil, R. (Eds.). (2018). *Comparative Area Studies: Methodological Rationales and Cross-Regional Applications.* Oxford University Press, 321 p. *Vestnik RUDN: International Relations* 20 (2): 408–410.

Ahmed, Amel. 2020. The Utility of Comparative Area Studies for Historical Analysis. *Qualitative & Multi-Method Research* 17–18 (1): 7–10.

Ahram, Ariel I. 2011. The Theory and Method of Comparative Area Studies. *Qualitative Research* 11 (1): 69–90.

Ahram, Ariel I., Patrick Köllner, and Rudra Sil, eds. 2018. *Comparative Area Studies: Methodological Rationales and Cross-Regional Applications.* New York: Oxford University Press.

Anderson, Lisa. 2016. Middle East Studies for the New Millennium: Infrastructures of Knowledge. In Seteney Shami and Cynthia Miller-Idriss, eds. *Middle East Studies for the New Millennium.* New York: NYU Press, 432–446.

Antweiler, Christopher. 2020. Southeast Asia as a Litmus Test for Grounded Area Studies. *International Quarterly for Asian Studies* 51 (3–4): 79–98.

Apicella, Coren, Ara Norenzayan, and Joseph Henrich. 2020. Beyond WEIRD: A Review of the Last Decade and a Look Ahead to the Global Laboratory of the Future. *Evolution and Human Behavior* 41 (5): 319–329.

Baldassarri, Delia, and Maria Abascal. 2017. Field Experiments Across the Social Sciences. *Annual Review of Sociology* 43: 41–73.

Banerjee, Abhijit V., and Esther Duflo. 2009. The Experimental Approach to Development Economics. *Annual Review of Economics* 1: 151–178.

Banerjee, Abhijit V., and Esther Duflo. 2014. Under the Thumb of History? Political Institutions and the Scope for Action. *Annual Review of Economics* 6: 951–971.

Barnett, Michael. 2021. International Progress, International Order, and the Liberal International Order. *Chinese Journal of International Politics* 14 (1): 1–22.

Basedau, Matthias, and Patrick Köllner. 2006. Area Studies and Comparative Area Studies: Opportunities and Challenges for the GIGA German Institute of Global and Area Studies. Discussion paper. Hamburg: GIGA German Institute of Global and Area Studies. https://www.researchgate.net/publication/228541318_Area_Studies_and_Comparative_Area_Studies_Opportunities_and_Challenges_for_the_GIGA_German_Institute_of_Global_and_Area_Studies (accessed September 9, 2022).

Basedau, Matthias, and Patrick Köllner. 2007. Area Studies, Comparative Area Studies, and the Study of Politics: Context, Substance, and Methodological Challenges. *Zeitschrift für Vergleichende Politikwissenschaft. Comparative Governance and Politics* 1 (1): 105–124.

Beissinger, Mark R. 2020. Disciplinarity, Interdisciplinarity and the Plurality of Area Studies: A View from the Social Sciences. In Zoran Milutinovic, ed. *The Rebirth of Area Studies: Challenges for History, Politics and International Relations in the 21st Century.* London: I.B. Tauris, 129–150.

Boswell, John, Jack Corbett, and R. A. W. Rhodes. 2019. *The Art and Craft of Comparison.* Cambridge: Cambridge University Press.

Brookes, Marissa. 2020. The Sweet Spot in Comparative Area Studies: Embracing Causal Complexity Through the Identification of Both Systematic and Unsystematic Variables. *Qualitative & Multi-Method Research* 17–18 (1): 20–22.

Chansa-Ngavej, Vee, and Kyu Young Lee. 2017. Does Area Studies Need Theory? Revisiting the Debate on the Future of Area Studies. *Korean Journal of International Studies* 15 (1): 85–101.

Chen, Calvin P. 2018. Organizing Production Across Regions: The Wenzhou Model in China and Italy. In Ariel I. Ahram, Patrick Köllner, and Rudra Sil, eds. *Comparative Area Studies: Methodological Rationales and Cross-Regional Applications.* New York: Oxford University Press, 204–221.

Curran, Sara R. 2019. Global Studies Versus International Studies. In Mark Juergensmeyer, Saskia Sassen, Manfred B. Steger, and Victor Faessel, eds. *The Oxford Handbook of Global Studies.* New York: Oxford University Press, 199–210.

Duller, Matthias. 2015. History of Area Studies. In James D. Wright, ed. *International Encyclopedia of the Social & Behavioral Sciences.* 2nd ed. Oxford: Elsevier, 949–954.

Dunning, Thad. 2012. *Natural Experiments in the Social Sciences: A Design Based Approach.* New York: Cambridge University Press.

Dunning, Thad, Guy Grossman, Macartan Humphreys, Susan D. Hyde, Craig McIntosh, and Gareth Nellis, eds. 2019. *Information, Accountability, and Cumulative Learning: Lessons from Metaketa I.* Cambridge: Cambridge University Press.

Falleti, Tulia G., and Julia F. Lynch. 2009. Context and Causal Mechanisms in Political Analysis. *Comparative Political Studies* 42 (9): 1143–1166.

Falleti, Tulia G., and James Mahoney. 2015. The Comparative Sequential Method. In James Mahoney and Kathleen Thelen, eds. *Advances in Comparative-Historical Analysis.* Cambridge: Cambridge University Press, 211–239.

Fisher-Onar, Nora. 2020. Making Sense of Multipolarity: Eurasia's Former Empires, Family Resemblances, and Comparative Area Studies. *Qualitative & Multi-Method Research* 17–18 (1): 15–19.

Frazier, Mark W. 2019. *The Power of Place: Contentious Politics in Twentieth-Century Shanghai and Bombay.* New York: Cambridge University Press.

Frazier, Mark W. 2022. The Challenges of China-India Comparative Urban Studies. *International Journal of Asian Studies* 19 (2): 319–332.

Giraudy, Agustina, Eduardo Moncada, and Richard Snyder, eds. 2019. *Inside Countries: Subnational Research in Comparative Politics.* New York: Cambridge University Press.

Gisselquist, Rachel M. 2014. Paired Comparison and Theory Development: Considerations for Case Selection. *PS: Political Science & Politics* 47 (2): 477–484.

Greif, Avner. 1993. Contract Enforceability and Economic Institutions in Early Trade: The Maghribi Traders' Coalition. *American Economic Review* 83 (3): 525–548.

Henrich, Joseph, Steven J. Heine, and Ara Norenzayan. 2010. The Weirdest People in the world? *Behavioral and Brain Sciences* 33 (2–3): 61–83.

Hodgett, Susan. 2019. Twenty-First-Century Area Studies: Blurring Genres, Evolutionary Thought and the Production of Theory. In Zoran Milutinovic, ed. *The Rebirth of Area Studies: Challenges for History, Politics and International Relations in the 21st Century.* London: I.B. Tauris, 19–53.

Hornidge, Anna-Katharina, and Katja Mielke. 2017. Concluding Reflections: The Art of Science Policy for 21st Century Area Studies. In Katja Mielke and Anna-Katharina Hornidge, eds. *Area Studies at the Crossroads: Knowledge Production After the Mobility Turn.* New York: Palgrave Macmillan, 327–344.

Houben, Vincent. 2017. New Area Studies, Translation and Mid-Range Concepts. In Katja Mielke and Anna-Katharina Hornidge, eds. *Area Studies at the Crossroads.* New York: Palgrave Macmillan, 195–211.

Houben, Vincent. 2020. New Area Studies as an Emerging Discipline. The Way Ahead for Southeast Asian Studies. *International Quarterly for Asian Studies* 51 (3–4): 51–58.

Hsueh, Roslyn. 2020. Synergies of CAS: New Inquiries, Theory Development, and Community. *Qualitative & Multi-Method Research* 17–18 (1): 10–11.

Hutt, Michael. 2019. Area Studies and the Importance of "Somewhere." *South East Asia Research* 27 (1): 21–25.

Jokela-Pansini, Maaret. 2019. Multi-Sited Research Methodology: Improving Understanding of Transnational Concepts. *Area* 51 (3): 516–523.

Kang, David. 2020. International Order in Historical East Asia. *International Organization* 74 (1): 65–93.

Katzenstein, Peter J. 2005. *A World of Regions: Asia and Europe in the American Imperium.* Ithaca, NY: Cornell University Press.

Köllner, Patrick, Rudra Sil, and Ariel I. Ahram. 2018. Comparative Area Studies: What It Is, What It Can Do. In Ariel I. Ahram, Patrick Köllner, and Rudra Sil, eds. *Comparative Area Studies: Methodological Rationales and Cross-Regional Applications.* New York: Oxford University Press, 3–26.

Kuran, Timur. 2012. Synergies Between Middle Eastern Economic History and the Analytic Social Sciences. *International Journal of Middle East Studies* 44 (3): 542–545.

Kuran, Timur. 2018. Islam and Economic Performance: Historical and Contemporary Links. *Journal of Economic Literature* 56 (4): 1292–1359.

Kurzman, Charles. 2017. Scholarly Attention and the Limited Internationalization of US Social Science. *International Sociology* 32 (6): 775–795.

Lees, Charles. 2006. We Are All Comparativists Now: Why and How Single-Country Scholarship Must Adapt and Incorporate the Comparative Politics Approach. *Comparative Political Studies* 39 (9): 1084–1108.

Lin, Justin Yifu. 1995. The Needham Puzzle: Why the Industrial Revolution Did Not Originate in China. *Economic Development and Cultural Change* 43 (2): 269–292.

Locke, Richard M., and Kathleen Thelen. 1995. Apples and Oranges Revisited: Contextualized Comparisons and the Study of Comparative Labor Politics. *Politics & Society* 23 (3): 337–368.

Lustick, Ian S. 1996. History, Historiography and Political Science: Multiple Historical Records and the Problem of Selection Bias. *American Political Science Review* 90 (3): 605–618.

Mahoney, James. 2003. Knowledge Accumulation in Comparative Historical Research. In James Mahoney and Dietrich Rueschemeyer, eds. *Comparative Historical Analysis in the Social Sciences.* Cambridge: Cambridge University Press, 131–174.

Mahoney, James, and Dietrich Rueschemeyer. 2003. Comparative Historical Analysis: Achievements and Agendas. In James Mahoney and Dietrich Rueschemeyer, eds. *Comparative Historical Analysis in the Social Sciences.* Cambridge: Cambridge University Press, 3–38.

Marung, Steffi. 2019. Area Studies, Regionalwissenschaften, Aires Culturelles: The Respatialization of Area Studies from a Bird's-Eye View. In Matthias Middell, ed. *The Routledge Handbook of Transregional Studies.* New York: Routledge, 46–57.

Merton, Robert K. 1949. On Sociological Theories of the Middle Range. In Robert Merton, *Social Theory and Social Structure.* New York: Simon & Schuster, Free Press, 39–53.

Middell, Matthias. 2019a. Transregional Studies: A New Approach to Global Processes. In Matthias Middell, ed. *The Routledge Handbook of Transregional Studies.* New York: Routledge, 1–16.

Middell, Matthias, ed. 2019b. *The Routledge Handbook of Transregional Studies.* New York: Routledge.

Mielke, Katja, and Anna-Katharina Hornidge, eds. 2017. *Area Studies at the Crossroads: Knowledge Production after the Mobility Turn.* New York: Palgrave Macmillan.

INTRODUCTION   25

Milutinovic, Zoran, ed. 2019. *The Rebirth of Area Studies: Challenges for History, Politics and International Relations in the 21st Century.* New York: Bloomsbury.

Naumann, Katja, Torsten Loschke, Steffi Marung, and Matthias Middell, eds. 2019. *In Search of Other Worlds: Essays Towards a Cross-Regional History of Area Studies.* Leipzig: Leipziger Universitätsverlag.

North, Douglass C. 1994. Economic Performance Through Time. *American Economic Review* 84 (3): 359–368.

North, Douglass C., and Robert Paul Thomas. 1973. *The Rise of the Western World: A New Economic History.* Cambridge: Cambridge University Press.

Pepinsky, Thomas B. 2019. The Return of the Single-Country Study. *Annual Review of Political Science* 22: 187–203.

Pepinsky, Thomas B. 2020. What's the "Area" in Comparative Area Studies? *Qualitative & Multi-Method Research* 17–18 (1): 22–26.

Pierson, Paul. 2003. From Area Studies to Contextualized Comparison. In Grzegorz Ekiert and Stephen E. Hanson, eds. *Capitalism and Democracy in Central and Eastern Europe: Assessing the Legacy of Communist Rule.* New York: Cambridge University Press, 353–376.

Rhodes, R. A. W., and Susan Hodgett 2021. *What Political Science Can Learn from the Humanities: Blurring Genres.* Cham, Switzerland: Palgrave Macmillan.

Riofrancos, Thea. 2021. From Cases to Sites: Global Processes in Comparative Inquiry. In Erica S. Simmons and Nicholas Rush Smith, eds. *Rethinking Comparison: Innovative Methods for Political Inquiry.* Cambridge: Cambridge University Press, 107–126.

Risse, Thomas, Wiebke Wemheuer-Vogelaar, and Frank Havemann. 2022. IR Theory and the Core-Periphery Structure of Global IR: Lessons from Citation Analysis. *International Studies Review* 24 (3). https://doi.org/10.1093/isr/viac029.

Rüland, Jürgen, and Astrid Carrapatoso. 2022. Introduction: Issues of governance Beyond the Nation State. In Jürgen Rüland and Astrid Carrapatoso, eds. *Handbook on Global Governance and Regionalism.* Cheltenham: Edward Elgar, 1–20.

Saylor, Ryan. 2013. Concepts, Measures, and Measuring Well: An Alternative Outlook. *Sociological Methods & Research* 42 (3): 354–391.

Saylor, Ryan. 2020. Comparative Area Studies: A Route to New Insights. *Qualitative & Multi-Method Research* 17–18 (1): 1–7.

Schaffer, Frederick. 2021. Two Ways of Comparing. In Erica S. Simmons and Nicholas Rush Smith, eds. *Rethinking Comparison: Innovative Methods for Political Inquiry.* Cambridge: Cambridge University Press, 47–63.

Schatz, Edward. 2009. Ethnographic Immersion and the Study of Politics. In Edward Schatz, ed. *Political Ethnography: What Immersion Contributes to the Study of Power.* Chicago: University of Chicago Press, 1–22.

Schatz, Edward, and Elena Maltseva. 2012. Assumed to be Universal: The Leap from Data to Knowledge in the *American Political Science Review. Polity* 44 (3): 1–27.

Sellers, Jefferey M. (2019). From Within to Between Nations: Subnational Comparison Across Borders. *Perspectives on Politics* 17 (1): 85–105.

Sil, Rudra. 2018. Triangulating Area Studies, Not Just Methods: How Cross-Regional Comparison Aids Qualitative and Mixed-Method Research. In Ariel I. Ahram, Patrick Köllner, and Rudra Sil, eds. *Comparative Area Studies.* New York: Oxford University Press, 225–246.

Sil, Rudra. 2020. The Survival and Adaptability of Area Studies. In Dirk Berg-Schlosser, Bertrand Badie, and Leonardo A. Morlino, eds. *The Sage Handbook of Political Science.* Vol. 1. London: Sage, 255–271.

Sil, Rudra, and Ariel Ahram. 2020. Comparative Area Studies and the Study of the Global South, *Vestnik RUDN: International Relations* 20 (2): 279–287.

Sil, Rudra, and Peter J. Katzenstein. 2010. *Beyond Paradigms: Analytic Eclecticism in the Study of World Politics.* London: Palgrave Macmillan.

Simmons, Erica S., and Nicholas Rush Smith. 2019. The Case for Comparative Ethnography. *Comparative Politics* 51 (3): 341–356.

Simmons, Erica S., and Nicholas Rush Smith. 2021a. Rethinking Comparison: An Introduction. In Erica S. Simmons and Nicholas Rush Smith, eds. *Rethinking Comparison: Innovative Methods for Political Inquiry*. Cambridge: Cambridge University Press, 1–28.

Simmons, Erica S., and Nicholas Rush Smith. 2021b. Comparisons with an Ethnographic Sensibility: Studies of Protests and Vigilantism. In Erica S. Simmons and Nicholas Rush Smith, eds. *Rethinking Comparison: Innovative Methods for Political Inquiry*. Cambridge: Cambridge University Press, 231–250.

Simmons, Erica S., and Nicholas Rush Smith, eds. 2021c. *Rethinking Comparison: Innovative Methods for Political Inquiry*. Cambridge: Cambridge University Press.

Slater, Dan, and Daniel Ziblatt. 2013. The Enduring Indispensability of the Controlled Comparison. *Comparative Political Studies* 46 (10): 1301–1327.

Snyder, Richard. 2001. Scaling Down: The Subnational Comparative Method. *Studies in Comparative International Development* 36 (1): 93–110.

Tarrow, Sidney. 2010. The Strategy of Paired Comparison: Toward a Theory of Practice. *Comparative Political Studies* 43 (2): 230–259.

Tickner, Arlene B., and Karen Smith, eds. 2019. *International Relations from the Global South: Worlds of Difference*. New York: Routledge.

University of East Anglia, Faculty of Arts and Humanities. N.d. New Area Studies. https://newareastudies.com/ (accessed September 13, 2022).

van der Veer, Peter. 2016. *The Value of Comparison*. Durham, NC: Duke University Press.

Vitalis, Robert. 2016. The Lost World of Development Theory. *Perspectives on Politics* 14 (4): 1158–1162.

von Wright, Georg Henrik. [1971] 2004. *Explanation and Understanding*. Ithaca, NY: Cornell University Press.

Wildavsky, Ben. 2012. *The Great Brain Race: How Global Universities Are Reshaping the World*. Princeton, NJ: Princeton University Press.

Wood, William R., and John Williamson. 2007. Comparative Historical Sociology. In Clifton D. Bryant and Dennis L. Peck, eds. *21st Century Sociology: A Reference Handbook*. Thousand Oaks, CA: Sage, 118–128.

Woods, Dwayne. 2016. The Future of Comparative Politics Is Its Past. *Chinese Political Science Review* 1 (3): 412–424.

PART I

COMPARATIVE AREA STUDIES AND THE PROSPECTS FOR INTERPRETATION ACROSS CONTEXTS

2

Communicating Across Contexts

How Translation Can Benefit Comparative Area Studies

Erica S. Simmons and Nicholas Rush Smith

Introduction

The importance of making generalizable arguments is drilled into most political scientists during their graduate training.[1] For example, during our time in graduate school at the University of Chicago, one of the most memorable lessons on the importance of generalization came from a faculty member who routinely asked, "But how many cases can your argument explain? The more cases you can explain, the better your argument." This might be an extreme example, but this kind of thinking, and the ambition to explain as much about politics as we can with simple, general arguments that undergirds it, plays a powerful role in how we conduct our research and how we evaluate the research of our peers—doing social science without proper names, to paraphrase Adam Przeworski and Henry Teune's (1970, 29–30) famous dictum.[2]

Despite this common sense, not all research traditions think about generalization in the same manner. Rather, how we think about what it means to generalize—including its limitations and possibilities—is often shaped by the methods we use. For example, for statistically oriented scholars, the goal is often to maximize the number of cases to which a causal argument

---

[1] We are grateful to the participants in the October 2021 and May 2022 CAS 2.0 workshops, the Comparative Politics Colloquium at the University of Wisconsin–Madison, and the CAS panel at the 2022 Annual Meeting of the American Political Science Association for their feedback on early versions of this chapter. Portions of this chapter are drawn from a previously published paper (Simmons and Smith 2025) to elaborate arguments specifically relevant to Comparative Area Studies.

[2] To be sure, the goal of creating an argument that speaks to many different times and places appears in a variety of semantic forms. For example, political scientists talk about how arguments "travel," whether they are "portable" (and to where) and how they might "generalize." There are real differences in the meanings of these words and the work they do. Yet in ordinary language use in political science, each refers to the idea that an argument can be simply picked up and move, in the whole, to a new context that is different from the one (or ones) in which it was originally generated.

Erica S. Simmons and Nicholas Rush Smith, *Communicating Across Contexts*. In: *Advancing Comparative Area Studies*. Edited by: Ariel I. Ahram, Patrick Köllner, and Rudra Sil, Oxford University Press.
© Oxford University Press (2025). DOI: 10.1093/oso/9780197809365.003.0002

can be applied by increasing the number of observations studied, a process that inherently makes the relevant variables less precise in explaining any particular case (King et al. 1994). For qualitative case study work, the goal is often the inverse: identifying the scope conditions under which a set of causal processes work, a tactic that inherently limits the number of cases to which the argument might apply with the goal of developing "middle range" theories, rather than universal ones (see, e.g., Ahram et al. 2018).[3] Scholars who use experimental methods encounter similar challenges as they grapple with questions around the external validity of their findings based upon research conducted in specific circumstances (see Blair and McClendon 2021). This challenge also bedevils ethnographers whose work tends to rely on deep knowledge of context—context that will inherently be different in another place or time (Schatz 2009). A final group of scholars have argued in favor of a unified mixed-methods approach to explanation that brings together strengths from both qualitative and quantitative methods (Brady and Collier 2010), yet may end up developing incoherent and contradictory epistemologies in the process (Goertz and Mahoney 2012).

Despite these contrasting approaches, the goal is often the same: to generalize an argument as much as possible within the limits allowed by the method's epistemological assumptions. Furthermore, political scientists tend to share a fairly homogeneous view of the purpose of generalization: providing causal explanations of political phenomena that can account for the maximum number of cases within the scope allowed by the research design. We argue, however, that when we limit ourselves to these goals our ability to generate arguments about the political processes and outcomes that are at the core of our work as political scientists is severely constrained.

We propose an alternative approach to prevailing notions of generalization: translation (see also Friedman 2013, 39–42; Cheah 2013, 56–59; von Soest and Stroh 2018, 71–73; Cheesman 2021).[4] By translation we

---

[3] Scholars in this tradition might use the language of "portability" to describe how their arguments carry to other cases, but there is a similar underlying logic of direct reproduction across cases, as with statistical analyses.

[4] We thank Richard Beth for suggesting this term during a discussion of early versions of these ideas at a panel during the 2014 Annual Meeting of the American Political Science Association. To be clear, we are not the first political scientists to highlight the value of the translation metaphor (see esp. von Soest and Stroh 2018; Cheesman 2021). Where we attempt to advance these existing discussions is by developing the metaphor of translation into a portable logic that can be used for a variety of different research projects, to further explicate the value it can add to political science inquiry, and to show how to execute research projects where translation is the goal, in part by examining how translation is practiced by professional translators.

mean a recursive process of making sense of ideas or phenomena across two or more contexts with the goal of illuminating family resemblances among concepts, political practices, or causal processes. Much like translation of a word or text, the logic of methodological translation assumes that ideas, practices, and processes are comprehensible across different contexts. Importantly, however, they may not work in precisely the same manner. A word in translation, for instance, may not carry exactly the same meaning as its cognate in another language, but the meaning is typically still understandable and interpretable, which can facilitate communication and understanding—both of similarities and of divergences. We argue that scholars can think about political practices in translation in the same way. Furthermore, if we include this approach as one of many ways to think about how our arguments travel, we will expand what we can do and say as political scientists.

Translation requires deep understanding of the original and depends upon the process of interpretation—one must first make sense of the meaning of the word or phrase to be translated. Put differently, translation is premised upon a prior practice: interpretation (see especially Venuti 2019). Yet for an interpretation to be intelligible in another time or place, an additional step is required: translation. This implies a constant tacking back and forth between the original and the translation, a process that improves understanding of both and may expose the limits of language to express ideas in each instance. In this sense, the logic of translation does not assume mechanistic reproduction of a text when it is moved from the original context into the new one. Rather, one assumes that there will be fissures, gaps, and breaks in meaning between the original and translation. Scholars may not be able to bridge these gaps, even as ideas are made newly available across time and space. This seeming dilemma, however, presents an opportunity for political science insofar as translation can help bring these gaps to light and potentially make them new objects of inquiry in their own right while inviting discussion of new possibilities for understanding across context in the process.

When thinking through how the practice of translation might inform our understanding of generalization, one also sees that *who* does the work may be as important as *what* is being worked on (see Chakraborty 2021 for a discussion). Specifically, much as with linguistic translation, the goal of comparing for translation is to develop arguments that are recognizable in a different context, even as the context will change the ways in which an idea or political practice is interpreted or enacted. In this sense, translation is a practice that enables understanding across time and space. Yet it simultaneously assumes that there will be gaps or limits in that understanding, as there can be no perfect cognate between the original place from which a process is identified and the additional places to which the scholar seeks to translate it (e.g., Alter 2019). In this process, who the scholars are and how they interpret that which is being translated are crucial to the process. Different scholars— just as with different translators (Kaza 2017; D. Smith 2018)—interpret texts, ideas, or processes differently and therefore will choose to translate their findings in different ways and to different contexts. This makes translation for the social sciences a deeply human process—a fact that may lead to goals for social scientific inquiry that differ altogether from the prevailing goal in much political science of causal inference. As we suggest below, if we adopt the logic of translation, improving our understanding of concepts, developing new descriptions of political processes, or finding entirely new political problems might all be valid research "outputs."

To be clear, we do not argue that translation should replace current approaches to thinking about generalizability in political science. Instead, we want to offer translation as an additional way to think about how the arguments we develop help us better understand other times and places. It can serve as a central component in research designs—think about how differently we might design our projects if we were looking to develop new concepts that could be translated from our field site to others as opposed to requiring that we elevate causal identification as the central strategy—in how we think through our data, and in how we describe what, ultimately, our insights are. At the most basic level, adding the logic of translation as one of many ways we think about the goals of political science research allows us to be explicit about the levels of abstraction at work in our analytical thinking. If we allow ourselves to think about how our arguments or observations translate to other times and places and hold this up as a valued end for political science, we create additional possibilities for knowledge creation.

Below, we focus on how the logic of translation might help scholars think anew about generalization from the vantage of comparative area studies. Drawing on a series of separate studies about state building, each of which was conducted in a different region, we show how thinking about the degree to which war makes the state has helped scholars reconsider how multiple kinds of war have made multiple kinds of states in different regions and how these multiple kinds of wars and states have lent themselves to very different concepts of what it means to rule in the first place. In considering the relationship between war making and state making, we show how scholars have translated Charles Tilly's famous insights from Europe to other world regions, enabling them to develop different ideas about both how war makes the state and what kinds of states war makes in different places. In other words, translating findings from one area to another allows both explanatory *and* conceptual innovation, while not assuming mechanical reproduction or generalization across space. While the scholarship we discuss does hold to a general idea that wars make states, it also shows that not all wars make states in the same way, nor do rulers have the same goal of expanding territorial states when they wage war, nor do subjects enduring state making experience it in the same way. Translating similarities, differences, and contradictions across the different sites, we show, has allowed scholars to enrich our knowledge of how states are made and our concepts of what states are in the first place.

In this regard, the logic of translation has particular value for comparative area studies. These innovations help us better understand the regions through which they were developed and the regions from which the "original" insights emerged. However, before we consider how the logic of translation might be useful for area studies scholars, it is instructive to see how political scientists and area studies scholars already unwittingly practice translation, even without a name for it—something we turn to in the next section.

War Making and State Making in Translation

How might the practice of translation contribute to our knowledge of politics? And to what degree might a comparative area studies approach be particularly well suited to processes of translating knowledge? To answer these questions, we think it useful to begin by working inductively from specific examples to consider the ways in which ideas and claims about politics are already being translated across regions before drawing out general answers to these questions. To do so, we draw on a series of separate studies, each of which was conducted in a different region, to show how combining a comparative area studies approach with the practice of translation can help us better understand similar questions with which scholars wrestle across different regions. We focus on one of the most influential bodies of social science scholarship—the literature on war making and state making—and how scholars working across different regions have understood differently how states and war coproduce one another (see Hui 2017; Slater 2010; Schwartz 2023; and Herbst 2000). After outlining how scholars studying different regions have differently approached this relationship in this section, we turn in the next section to general lessons that flow from it.

By now, Tilly's classic dictum, "War made the state and the state made war" (Tilly 1975, 42) has influenced how multiple generations of scholars think about both how states came to be and what states are in the first place. However, as scholars have translated Tilly's arguments into places and times beyond the early modern Europe where Tilly developed them, the meaning of this central insight has changed. Scholars of other regions still consider the ways in which war makes the state. But they have reconsidered both *how* war makes the state and *what kinds* of states different wars make. They have also reconsidered what war and state making *mean* to individuals from different regions—both rulers and ruled—to show that scholars' prior assumptions about concepts may mean something very different in practice. In other words, in studying the relationship between war making and state making, scholars have developed both explanatory and conceptual novelty in ways that don't fit comfortably under a logic of generalization. And yet Tilly's basic insights about war making and state making are still central to these new contributions. While scholars still agree that war making and state making are related in many parts of the world, they disagree greatly about how and to what ends. And, in this disagreement, they have developed new concepts to describe state making and new descriptions of how state making is practiced and experienced.

Before seeing how Tilly's ideas translated elsewhere, though, we need to understand how he saw war making the state. Although not often identified as such, as someone who wrote extensively about the histories of many European countries in comparative perspective, Tilly was a classic area studies specialist. After all, he develops his seminal argument in the context of European political development over a thousand years—from AD 990 to 1990 (Tilly 1975, 1990). In seeking to explain what accounts for the variation over time and space in the kinds of states that prevailed in Europe, Tilly finds that war making played a central role. Most basically, international warfare forced rulers to increase revenue collection, which, in turn, forced them to develop the bureaucratic apparatus necessary to make the revenue collection possible. Variations in the structural conditions faced by rulers across different states determined how this process unfolded across Europe and why different types of states emerged there.

The primary way that scholars have translated Tilly's insights has been to examine the degree to which the processes he describes in Europe extend to other parts of the world. For example, in a study of Chinese state formation, Victoria Tin-bor Hui (2017, 269; see also Hui 2005) has found that Tilly's "bellocentrist paradigm is remarkably applicable to historical China."[5] While Tilly himself argued that European and Chinese state formation are not comparable, Hui (2017, 273) argues that his account of the dissimilarity between the two cases "is the most Eurocentric and unhistorical statement he ever made." For Hui, early modern Europe and China's Warring States era shared remarkable similarities in their basic international relations and the political problems that flowed therefrom: a set of small competitors vying for survival and supremacy against rivals forced the development of ever larger state and tax apparatuses to manage ever larger armies.

However, while rulers in the two regions shared basically similar political problems, they ended up producing rather different solutions—a large, unified state in the case of China and a series of competitor states in Europe. To account for this difference, Hui subtly reads the differing decisions leaders made and theorizes that such decisions need to be thought of as part of strategic interactions and strategic decisions on the parts of rulers. Put differently, even when faced with similar dilemmas, Hui (2017, 275–276) argues, leaders might make different decisions on how to respond, with different outcomes being the result. In this sense, Hui directly translates the problems European leaders faced to China but finds that China had a different "grammar" in how political processes unfolded because of the different decisions leaders made in similar contexts.

Dan Slater's (2010) argument in *Ordering Power* offers an additional approach to translating Tilly's ideas to Hui's. Slater looks to explain variation in postcolonial states in Southeast Asia. But he finds that Tilly's argument, as articulated in the European context, provides little leverage. External warfare does not explain the types of states we see in postcolonial Southeast Asia. Instead of simply looking elsewhere for theoretical guidance, however, Slater carefully translates Tilly's core concept—that war can lead to state making—to these new contexts. In doing so, Slater both shows how Tilly's

---

[5] Thanks are due to Roselyn Hsueh and Ryan Saylor for pointing us to Hui's work.

argument, when translated, helps to explain Southeast Asia, and develops new theoretical insights about contentious processes and state formation.

Slater's key conceptual move is that he thinks about Tilly's central state-building mechanism as conflict broadly understood, not external war alone. In Southeast Asia, Slater finds that *internal* conflict inspires elite collective action in response to build states. Here the argument closely resembles Tilly's (and Hui's)—conflict forces elites to act together to make a stronger state to respond to the conflict and defend against future conflict. The conflict, however, takes a different form than in Tilly's and Hui's work. The mechanisms at work are similar: just as with external conflict, some forms of internal conflict led to increased extraction of revenue.

We see this as a process of translation because it effectively draws on key meanings of war making, as Tilly used the concept, while making those meanings intelligible in a new context—one without external war as a driving force. But Slater also complicates the story with additional insights into when and where *internal* conflict creates the coalitions necessary for this increased extraction—a form of conflict largely absent from Tilly's account. By focusing on the kinds of coalitions that internal conflict creates, Slater shows how the combination of class and communal conflict works to forge the coalitions among elites necessary for them to be willing to contribute the resources to build the state's infrastructural power. Basically, when elites perceive the state as a requisite protection against a perceived foe, they are willing to invest in its development and allow it to strengthen. These insights not only translate Tilly to another place (Southeast Asia) but also translate it to another time—one in which external conflict is much less likely. Even in a changed world historical context, when translated across time and space, Tilly still helps us understand how and why states look the way they do. In this sense, in seeing how Tilly's insights about external conflict do not reproduce precisely in Southeast Asia, Slater does not seek to falsify Tilly, as might be expected in scholarship reliant on classic views of generalization. Instead, by translating Tilly's broad insights about conflict and state making through a Southeast Asian idiom, Slater tells us something new about this relationship: internal conflict can help build states too.

But it is not just changed world historical or geographical context that Tilly's argument informs. Surprisingly, it can help us better understand how internal wars often appear to weaken, as opposed to strengthen, states. Rachel Schwartz (2023) translates both Tilly's and Slater's contribution to Central America and, in the process, complicates the ways in which internal conflict shapes states. Schwartz highlights a conflict in the political science literature—on the one hand, Tilly's argument tells us that wars build states. On the other, the corrosive effect of civil war on state institutions has been well documented (e.g., Besley and Persson 2008; Thies 2005, 2006, 2010). Yet Slater shows us that internal conflict can, in fact, build strong states—but only when certain types of war prompt certain types of coalitions. Schwartz translates both Tilly and Slater to the contexts of civil war Guatemala and civil war Nicaragua to show that their insights apply, but in a highly unexpected way. Civil war can, indeed, help to build strong state institutions as coalitions emerge to combat an internal enemy. But those institutions are not the ones that Slater and Tilly had in mind. Instead, Schwartz shows how civil wars can build "undermining" institutions—strong institutions, for sure, but ones that distort routine state activities, thus creating the image of the "weak" state described by so much of the literature.

With this argument, Schwartz effectively translates at least three of Tilly's and Slater's insights to the context of civil war in Central America. First, internal conflict can drive a process of coalition formation that builds state institutions. Second, war still makes strong institutions. But those institutions may actually work to undermine the state itself. And, finally, state-building processes that happen during conflict can be durable. Neither Tilly's nor Slater's insights can be directly generalized to the processes Schwartz observed because Schwartz identified different institutional outcomes in her cases. But they can be translated. And in translating them we learn how war making and internal conflicts create types of states that had not been previously identified—a conceptual innovation.

If one form of translation can make political scientists rethink the concepts through which they order the world, another mode of translation involves seeing how familiar ideas may function differently in the specific context one studies. For example, in his influential study of state formation on the African continent, Jeffrey Herbst (2000) finds that Tilly's paradigm generalizes poorly. The two regions have radically different relationships between population and geography, Herbst argues, which profoundly shaped how rulers historically built institutions, limiting the scope of Tilly's arguments. In Europe, a high population density combined with a small land mass pushed rulers to maximize the amount of territory they could rule over. By contrast, in Africa, where there was generally a low population density spread across a huge landmass, rulers rarely extended large territory-based empires as in Europe because people who were threatened could more easily escape attempts at political incorporation than in dense Europe. So Tilly's argument generalizes poorly to the African continent, on Herbst's account.

While Tilly's argument may not generalize, however, certain aspects of it may allow it to translate, albeit in a way that usefully allows us to see differences in how people from different backgrounds order the world. Specifically, Herbst (2000, 45ff.) translates how these population and geography dynamics shaped local concepts of what it meant to rule in Europe and Africa. In population-rich and land-poor Europe, leaders tended to think of sovereignty in unified territorial terms: they ruled over the ground upon which populations were settled in a uniform and unbroken way across the breadth of their kingdom. The concept of sovereignty, on Herbst's account, was different in Africa. In land-rich areas with relatively few people where groups could evade permanent political incorporation, sovereignty was rarely conceived as homogeneous control over a designated territory, as in the prevailing European imagination. Rather, rulership was conceived in more dynamic terms, with power frequently radiating out from the center of a kingdom and weakening at its edges with potential gaps in rule along the way. This system resulted in ideas of rule that were different than in Europe. For example, depending upon the geography of people and power, in some places there could be multiple sovereigns ruling over a given territory or group, rather than a singular king, as in much of Europe. That is, when translating Tilly's bellicist paradigm to Africa, Herbst placed an analytical category—sovereignty—into local context and found that the concept operated very differently, often distinctly shaping local patterns of rule. In translating the idea of sovereignty to a new context, Herbst found a very different way the concept was imagined, enriching our vocabulary of what it means to rule.

This process of translating concepts can also usefully work in the opposite direction from the method used by Herbst. If Herbst shows how analytical concepts map poorly onto local understandings, an alternative way to translate is to take local experiences and map them back onto analytical concepts to reframe the categories through which scholars themselves see the world. Nicholas Rush Smith's (2019) study of vigilantism and democratic state formation in South Africa is an example of this process. Smith seeks to understand why South Africa has experienced high rates of vigilantism since the end of apartheid, despite massive institutional reforms of its state institutions. As part of his research, he also sought to understand how the young men who are threatened by vigilantism experience the state themselves. Through ethnographic fieldwork among young men involved in various forms of crime, Smith found that these young men deeply feared the police, not only because they feared arrest but because they feared the possibilities of extrajudicial execution. During his work, Smith heard constant rumors about particular units or particular officers that young men needed to avoid because they were reputed to be killers, extrajudicially murdering alleged young criminals when afforded the opportunity. That is, young men viewed certain police officers as having an uncannily similar modus operandi as the vigilante groups Smith was studying in other parts of his research.

Later, in reflecting on the experience these young men had of the state, he translated their fears back to the dominant theories of the state and realized that few theories captured these men's experiences. Reflecting particularly on Tilly's (1985) theory of the state as protection racket, Smith saw that for these young men, their experience of the state was something very different from what Tilly described. Where Tilly argues that the state provides a double-edged form of protection wherein it creates a threat and then charges for its reduction, for these young men, the state was not experienced as protective at all. Instead, it was merely a threat. Put analytically, in translating these men's experiences back to dominant ideas of the state, Smith could see the state as something very different from Tilly's vision: the state was essentially a large-scale vigilante group. In taking these local experiences and translating them back onto Tilly's theory of the state, Smith was able to creatively redescribe what the state is.

In sum, scholars can rely on a logic of translation to take insights developed by other authors—their entire arguments, or smaller portions of those arguments—and show them to be at work in new contexts, albeit in different ways. When we translate these existing arguments into new contexts, we show both their promise—their ability to inform how we think about other times and places, as well as the value in thinking about comparisons within and across regions—and their limitations, the ways in which the arguments must necessarily change to address the new circumstances. Doing so can provide explanations and new concepts through which we see processes at work in the first place. Neither explanations nor concepts necessarily sit comfortably under a logic of generalizability, but they nonetheless rely on the practice of taking ideas developed in one region and translating them across borders.

How Translation Can Reframe Comparative Area Studies' Contribution to Social Science Knowledge

In considering the previous examples, we are now in a position to abstract out and think through some broad lessons for how political scientists approach their work. For political scientists and, indeed, social scientists more broadly, the logics of translation can work in multiple ways not only to improve the arguments we develop but also to understand how they inform other times and places. When we use translation as a vehicle for reconsidering the logics of generalization, we allow ourselves to think about the practice as a craft, as opposed to something for which strict rules and guidelines are always useful. This can shift how we approach insights developed in one context to inform our understandings of political processes and practices in others. If we no longer feel like causal chains or connections need to be repeated in precisely the same way to claim that our insights are generalizable, we can think about how particular elements of arguments—component pieces, so to speak—might help us understand other times and places even as all of the original argument do not travel. What might this process look like? In thinking about the above examples from the state-making literature that builds on Tilly's original model, we propose five discrete outcomes that using the logic of translation might enable.

First, much as with literary translation, we can translate processes, structures, and conditions into new contexts in a fairly straightforward manner, as in Hui's comparative study of Europe and China. Here she showed a remarkable similarity between initial conditions in Europe and China that helped touch off processes of state building that led to relatively strong states. Much as with a novel in translation, her study hews as closely as possible to Tilly's "original" model of bellicose state making in identifying initial conditions. Importantly, though, as with a translator who has a subtle grasp of the differences among languages, she pays close attention to what did not translate perfectly—in this case, how European and Chinese rulers made strategic decisions to respond to similar dilemmas. And, much as with a novel in translation, the final result she finds is something importantly different from Tilly's original, a study that bears a clear hallmark of the original but is also its own independent, creative contribution. In this sense, translation can simultaneously allow for close reproduction and the necessary adaptation that comes from producing a work that is simultaneously new.

Second, thinking through the logic of translation can allow scholars to identify subtle but crucial differences in the underlying "grammar" of a process that shifts outcomes, as with Slater's study of contention and state building in Southeast Asia. Here Slater takes almost the opposite approach to Hui, finding that postcolonial Southeast Asia and Tilly's early modern Europe had radically differing initial conditions. Where external war defined politics in Europe, Slater shifts focus to show how internal war was predominant, as postcolonial states largely had their borders set for them but had to fight a variety of perceived internal enemies. This change in the underlying structure, Slater shows, had profound consequences for explaining different state-building trajectories across the region. Instead of decisions by individual leaders being important, as in Hui's argument, like Tilly, Slater focuses on the structural conditions that led to different outcomes. The key structural condition in Southeast Asia was contrasting patterns of internal war. Here translation takes the form of identifying an entirely new "grammar" through which to think about how processes carry across space.

Third, translating for new grammars might also require developing new conceptual vocabularies through which to think. Schwartz's work on Central America is a good example. While her study takes inspiration from Tilly and Slater in trying to understand how contention builds state institutions, she finds that neither Tilly's nor Slater's account of institutions effectively captures the nature of some state institutions in Central America. The institutions she studies are not strong or weak, in the sense used by Slater and Tilly. Instead, they are strong but resist regular institutional processes. In naming this institutional configuration "undermining," Schwartz translates for both explanatory and conceptual innovation. She finds that war makes the state in Central America but does not make states that we have had language to describe before—another contribution that the logic of translation enables.

Fourth, in addition to helping us build new concepts, the logic of translation can push us to rethink taken-for-granted concepts through which we see the world. Herbst's account of the differing ideas of sovereignty in Europe and Africa is a case in point. Herbst's ostensible goal is to explain why state formation in Africa differed from the Europe Tilly examined. To do so, however, he has to reconsider what it means to rule in the first place. By showing how Tilly's model mistranslates to Africa, Herbst also shows that this does not necessarily mean that state building somehow developed along a suboptimal path from Europe. Instead, state building—and particularly what it meant to rule in the first place—took its own form. Sovereignty in Africa was simply thought differently than in Europe, which shows how when we translate causal processes, we also need to translate concepts in context.

Finally, we can rethink how we ourselves describe politics by taking contextual experiences and translating them back to our received ideas. Here Smith's model of the state as a large-scale vigilante group is a case in point. By taking the specific experience of young black men in South Africa encountering the police and reflecting back on received concepts of the state, Smith is able to show the importance of challenging taken-for-granted experiences of politics and the concepts that flow therefrom. Put differently, Smith translates from local experience back to analytical concepts and shows the need to rethink those concepts depending upon the concrete experiences of people in local contexts.

In sum, the logic of translation can help area studies scholars simultaneously bridge contexts and differentiate among them. The practices outlined here are different from generalization because translation presumes a rootedness in context. The practices are not simply useful for idiographic studies, though, as translation assumes a certain level of legibility across context. Nor is translation the same as developing a middle-range theory because one may not be identifying exactly the same processes or outcomes across a sample of cases. Instead, the logic of translation points to a different path of developing something like a conversation across space and time in which processes, concepts, and experiences are iteratively thought next to one another with the hopes of enriching our understanding of each in light of their similarities and differences across different contexts.

Conclusions

Even as generalization is an important goal in political science research, as it is currently conceived it also has potentially serious limitations. In particular, as theories explain a larger number of cases, they lose their power to explain any one case. So there is a trade-off between the breadth of a theory and its depth. Some scholars have responded to this challenge by discarding the goal of universal arguments in favor of middle-range theories that explain a political phenomenon in a subset of cases with strictly delimited scope conditions. Here the goal is to improve the quality of explanations for specific cases by limiting the universe of cases to which a theory should apply. While this is a reasonable solution to the trade-off imposed by breadth and depth, the underlying challenge remains the same as with more maximizing methods: generalizing an argument as much as possible within the limits allowed by the method's epistemological assumptions still involves trading off between the universe of cases that can be explained and the understanding it provides about any particular case.

In this chapter, we propose the logic of translation as one possible response to this dilemma. If we allow ourselves to think about our contributions to general knowledge through a logic of translation, we can comfortably talk about how arguments travel without requiring that they work exactly the same way across time and space. By adding this logic to our understandings of what is possible and acceptable as political scientists, we can expand how we think about the goals of political science research. This, in turn, will expand the possibilities for the knowledge we can create, opening new lines of inquiry and new ways of approaching long-standing puzzles.

The promise is particularly compelling when it comes to comparative area studies. The logic of translation requires area-based, context-specific knowledge *and* the willingness to expand analytic horizons that are foundational to comparative area studies. The logic of translation helps us better understand and explain the methodological rationale for why these kinds of cross-regional comparisons are compelling and convincing. When we incorporate translation as a way to think about how our arguments move, we allow ourselves the flexibility to compare across regions without running roughshod over regional differences. These kinds of comparisons will help us better refine, develop, and expand our understanding of how politics works—both similarly and differently—throughout the world. The concept of translation, particularly when applied to comparative area studies, also clearly shows that the social sciences have much to learn from the humanities and that the idea of a boundary does a great disservice to our efforts to advance knowledge. When we seek to compare regions through deep, contextually rooted knowledge, we are leveraging humanistic and social scientific insights. Translation requires precisely this kind of approach.

Yet, even as we see these potential advantages, as we noted above, translation is a vexed practice. Those who translate texts professionally are faced with difficult trade-offs in their work that present no easy solutions. Words, phrases, or ideas that are common in one language may have no equal cognate in the other. This suggests that translation relies on the judgment of the translators, the imaginative resources upon which they are able to draw to represent a translated phrase, and that they are likely to be wrong in some sense however they choose to translate. Translation is, therefore, a human process fraught with peril.

When applied to political science, translation's vexed nature suggests a similar challenge: our arguments will run aground in some sense. Perhaps the argument doesn't explain particular cases especially well. Perhaps the argument is so limited as to account for only a handful of cases. Perhaps the theory is so broad as to miss the underlying causal dynamics in any particular case.

Yet thinking about the vexed nature of political science research does not necessarily mean despair. Just as translation is necessary for our understanding one another across context (however imperfectly), so too are attempts to carry our arguments and theories to other times and places. Still, this discussion suggests that we should adopt substantial modesty when we translate. More radically, though, it may suggest the need to rethink our goals in carrying arguments across contexts and perhaps to see the object of political analysis anew. It also reminds us of the humanity of our enterprise no matter what we imagine the goals of political science to be.

Bibliography

Ahram, Ariel I., Patrick Köllner, and Rudra Sil, eds. 2018. *Comparative Area Studies: Methodological Rationales and Cross-Regional Applications*. New York: Oxford University Press.

Alter, Robert. 2019. *The Art of Bible Translation*. Princeton, NJ: Princeton University Press.

Blair, Graeme, and Gwyneth McClendon. 2021. Conducting Experiments in Multiple Contexts. In Donald P. Green and James N. Druckman, eds. *Advances in Experimental Political Science*. Cambridge: Cambridge University Press, 411–428.

Brady, Henry E., and David Collier, eds. 2010. *Rethinking Social Inquiry: Diverse Tools, Shared Standards*. Lanham, MD: Rowman & Littlefield.

Besley, Timothy and Torsten Persson. 2008. Wars and State Capacity. *Journal of the American Economic Association* 6 2/3. 522–530

Chakraborty, Mridula Nath. 2021. Friday Essay: Is This the End of Translation? The Conversation. March 11, 2021. http://theconversation.com/friday-essay-is-this-the-end-of-translation-156375.

Cheah, Pheng. 2013. The Material World of Comparison. In Rita Felski and Susan Stanford Friedman, eds. *Comparison: Theories, Approaches, Uses*. Baltimore: Johns Hopkins University Press, 168–190.

Cheesman, Nick. 2021. "Unbound Comparison." In Erica S. Simmons and Nicholas Rush Smith, eds. *Rethinking Comparison: Innovative Methods for Qualitative Political Inquiry*. Cambridge: Cambridge University Press, 64–83.

Friedman, Susan Stanford. 2013. Why Not Compare? In Rita Felski and Susan Stanford Friedman, eds. *Comparison: Theories, Approaches, Uses*. Baltimore: Johns Hopkins University Press, 34–45.

Goertz, Gary, and James Mahoney. 2012. *A Tale of Two Cultures: Qualitative and Quantitative Research in the Social Sciences*. Princeton, NJ: Princeton University Press.

Herbst, Jeffrey Ira. 2000. *States and Power in Africa: Comparative Lessons in Authority and Control*. Princeton, NJ: Princeton University Press.

Hui, Victoria Tin-bor. 2005. *War and State Formation in Ancient China and Early Modern Europe*. New York: Cambridge University Press.

Hui, Victoria Tin-bor. 2017. How Tilly's State Formation Paradigm Is Revolutionizing the Study of Chinese State Making. In Lars Bo Kaspersen and Jeppe Strandsbjerg, eds. *Does War Make States?* Cambridge: Cambridge University Press, 268–295.

Kaza, Madhu. 2017. Editor's Note: Kitchen Table Translation. Aster(Ix) Journal. August 9, 2017. https://asterixjournal.com/note-translation/.

King, Gary, Robert Keohane, and Sidney Verba. 1994. *Designing Social Inquiry: Scientific Inference in Qualitative Research*. Princeton, NJ: Princeton University Press.

Przeworski, Adam, and Henry Teune. 1970. *The Logic of Comparative Social Inquiry*. New York: Wiley-Interscience.

Schatz, Edward. 2009. Ethnographic Immersion and the Study of Politics. In Edward Schatz, ed. *Political Ethnography: What Immersion Contributes to the Study of Politics*. Chicago: University of Chicago Press, 1–22.

Schwartz, Rachel. 2023. *Undermining the State from Within: The Institutional Legacies of Civil War in Central America*. New York: Cambridge University Press.

Slater, Dan. 2010. *Ordering Power: Contentious Politics and Authoritarian Leviathans in Southeast Asia*. New York: Cambridge University Press.

Smith, Deborah. 2018. What We Talk About When We Talk About Translation. Los Angeles Review of Books. January 11, 2018. /article/what-we-talk-about-when-we-talk-about-translation/.

Smith, Nicholas Rush. 2019. *Contradictions of Democracy: Vigilantism and Rights in Post-Apartheid South Africa*. New York: Oxford University Press.

Simmons, Erica S. and Nicholas Rush Smith. 2025. How Cases Speak to One Another: Using Translation to Rethink Generalization in Political Science Research. *American Political Science Review*. First View.

Theis, Cameron G. 2005. War, Rivalry, and State Building in Latin America. *American Journal of Political Science*. 49 (3): 451–465.

Theis, Cameron G. 2006. Public Violence and State Building in Central America. *Comparative Political Studies*. 39 (10): 1263–1282.

Theis, Cameron G. 2010. Of Rulers, Rebels, and Revenue: State Capacity, Civil War Onset, and Primary Commodities. *Journal of Peace Research*. 47 (3): 321–332.

Tilly, Charles. 1975. Reflections on the History of European State Making. In Charles Tilly and Gabriel Ardant, eds. *The Formation of National States in Western Europe*. Princeton, NJ: Princeton University Press, 3–83.

Tilly, Charles. 1985. War Making and State Making as Organized Crime. In Peter Evans, Dietrich Rueschemeyer, and Theda Skocpol, eds. *Bringing the State Back In*. New York: Cambridge University Press, 169–191.

Tilly, Charles. 1990. *Coercion, Capital, and European States, AD 990–1990*. Cambridge, MA: Basil Blackwell.

Venuti, Lawrence. 2019. *Contra Instrumentalism: A Translation Polemic*. Lincoln: University of Nebraska Press.

von Soest, Christian, and Alexander Stroh. 2018. Comparison Across World Regions: Managing Conceptual, Methodological, and Practical Challenges. In Ariel I. Ahram, Patrick Köllner, and Rudra Sil, eds. *Comparative Area Studies: Methodological Rationales and Cross-Regional Applications*. New York: Oxford University Press, 66–84.

3

Comparative Area Studies and Interpretivism

Toward an Interpretive-Comparative Research Approach

Anna Fünfgeld

Introduction

In the social sciences, many theoretical approaches and concepts have been developed based on interpretive research, often including the contrasting of various cases within the same or different world regions. Much of this research has been conducted by area specialists who expanded their regional focus to reflect upon universal sociopolitical questions. Political scientists like the Southeast Asianists Benedict Anderson ([1983] 2006) and James C. Scott (1998) have demonstrated how fruitful an interpretive-comparative approach can be for understanding and conceptualizing political and societal developments and practices beyond a specific society or world region. However, although many scholars deploy interpretive-comparative research, their epistemological approach is rarely explicitly explained (Simmons and Smith 2021, 7).[1] At the same time, controlled comparisons based on positivist ontologies continue to constitute the status quo approaches in comparative political science research and dominate the methodology training of graduate schools. Positivist and interpretive research are based on different ontological and epistemological assumptions, which is why the instructions on controlled comparison developed from a positivist research tradition are not applicable to interpretive approaches.

---

[1] Anderson's memoir *A Life Beyond Boundaries* (2016), in which the author dedicates a chapter to comparisons, constitutes an exception in this regard.

Anna Fünfgeld, *Comparative Area Studies and Interpretivism*. In: *Advancing Comparative Area Studies*. Edited by: Ariel I. Ahram, Patrick Köllner, and Rudra Sil, Oxford University Press. © Oxford University Press (2025). DOI: 10.1093/oso/9780197809365.003.0003

Recently, this discrepancy between, on one hand, the widespread use of interpretative-comparative research and, on the other hand, the dominance of positivist comparative approaches has received increasing scholarly attention. This responds to a lack of consideration of interpretive approaches toward comparison, both in comparative area studies (CAS) and in political science more generally. In light of the fact that only a few (Asian) area studies comparisons have applied methods of controlled comparison, Mikko Huotari and Jürgen Rüland (2014, 2018) suggest widening CAS's understanding of comparisons toward reflecting the diversity of existing approaches. They suggest, inter alia, adding interpretive approaches to the CAS toolbox (Huotari and Rüland 2014, 427–429; Huotari and Rüland 2018, 93–94, 96). More recently, political scientists like John Boswell, Jack Corbett, and R. A. W. Rhodes (2019) and Erica Simmons and Nicholas Rush Smith (2021, 11) have also stressed the need for "epistemological logics for additional strategies of comparative inquiry" (Simmons and Smith 2021, 11) apart from the blueprints for controlled comparison that already exist. Boswell, Corbett, and Rhodes (2019, 2) argue that the "conventional wisdom about when, how and why to compare severely limits how we study and understand the social world" and that "as a result, we are missing potentially rich and illuminating insights because our analysis is either too rigid, structured and systematic or too bespoke, detailed and idiographic." Noticing this gap, some authors have rethought the logic of comparison (Adcock 2006; Boswell et al. 2019; Yanow 2014). Simmons and Smith (2017) demonstrate the potential "ethnographic sensibility" or a "comparative ethnography" approach (Simmons and Smith 2019) yield for comparative political science research. They argue for increased attention to processes of meaning-making, the recognition of the limitations to control variation, and an openness to changing and adapting one's questions and goals throughout the research process (Simmons and Smith 2017, 127–128; Simmons and Smith 2019, 342, 352). The same authors' 2021 edited volume discusses alternative approaches to comparative research beyond mainstream controlled comparison typologies, including interpretive approaches (see Riofrancos 2021; Soss 2021).

This chapter contributes to these efforts, elaborating on how to approach interpretive comparisons. It reflects upon the meaning of comparison in interpretive research, its objectives and scopes, and the conduct of such research. I argue that CAS can provide a productive environment for thinking more systematically about interpretive-comparative methodology. Like interpretive approaches, area studies are characterized by their emphasis on societal and historical context factors, local concepts, and meaning-making processes. However, despite the widespread application of interpretivism in area studies, initial approaches to CAS (see Ahram et al. 2018) have been largely informed by a positivist epistemology. Thus, the chapter's objective is threefold: It aims to provide suggestions on how interpretive-comparative research might be conducted in a methodologically reflexive manner. Additionally, it seeks to contribute to the inclusion of interpretive approaches in the CAS framework. Last, given skepticism toward comparison in area studies communities (Huotari 2014, 11–12), it encourages interpretive area specialists to embark on the exciting and intellectually rewarding journey into the world of comparisons.

The chapter draws largely on my experience in conducting a cross-regional interpretive comparison, the challenges I faced due to lack of methodological guidance, and the ways I dealt with them. With this, I intend to develop a more general guideline on what to consider when conducting an interpretive CAS project and to propose ways to deal with the methodological challenges related to this undertaking. My research has addressed the question of how energy transformations are inhibited in Indonesia and Brazil. I have examined the political-economic structures and the discourses and practices that lead to the development and maintenance or contestation of hegemonic energy systems in both countries. The research project is based on several months of field research in both countries and at international climate conferences, (mostly) conducted between 2016 and 2019. Based on the single-case analyses and their comparison, I have demonstrated that there exist three major barriers to energy transformations in both countries: the political-economic structures; hegemonic, developmentalist discourses; and enforcement measures applied to realize energy-related infrastructures on the local level. The political-economic structures enable key actors to establish structural barriers that hinder transformation in the energy sector. In both countries, attempts were made to organize consent to the existing energy system based on developmentalist narratives and imaginaries. Where this has not succeeded due to local resistance from the population, infrastructure projects have been imposed through enforcement mechanisms. Based on my findings, I have developed a theoretical framework for the study of energy transformations from a critical political economy perspective. I argue that neither the theoretical development nor the deep understanding of the cases would have been possible in such a comprehensive way without the comparative character of the project.

50 ADVANCING COMPARATIVE AREA STUDIES

In the process of learning substantively about energy politics, I encountered directly those barriers that interpretive-comparative research faces in political science, given the discipline-specific hegemonic understanding of what it means to compare and how comparisons should be conducted. They included, for example, questions about case selection and research design, writing styles, the structuring of a text, and the presentation of results. The chapter discusses ways to deal with these issues while remaining consistent with the principles of interpretive research. It strives to bring interpretative-comparative research out of the defensive position in which it is sometimes trapped due to the dominance of positivist approaches. In doing so, it is important to reflect on the epistemological foundations of interpretative methods in order to make their strengths usable for comparative approaches. Thus, I start with a brief introduction to interpretive research and its scientific principles. This is followed by a discussion of common challenges related to interpretive-comparative research and ways to deal with them. I tackle questions of case selection and interpretive-comparative analysis, as well as specifics of writing, structuring, and publishing interpretive-comparative texts. The final section summarizes the recommendations and makes a case for more systematized approaches to interpretive CAS.

On Interpretivism

Interpretive research is mainly aimed at understanding and tracing meaning-making and the resulting social processes, practices, and institutions. It rests on a constructivist-postpositivist ontology that "sees concepts and categories as embodying and reflecting the point of view of their creators" (Yanow 2006, 6). In contrast, positivist conceptions of science are based on realist-objectivist assumptions about the world and aim for the unraveling of or approximation toward objective knowledge via the testing (verification or falsification) of assumptions (Hawkesworth 2006, 29–34). Epistemologically, the central dividing line between the two perspectives is whether objective truth can be revealed or at least approximated through the research process. Interpretivists generally deny this possibility and assume that distinct narratives of the same event may exist. Thus, they aim to understand how people make sense of their experiences and the world they live in, thereby focusing on (intersubjective) processes and effects of meaning-making (Schwartz-Shea and Yanow 2012, 4, 40). Interpretive approaches have emerged from distinct philosophical traditions in the humanities and social sciences (for an overview, see Yanow 2006). We can generally think of different interpretive approaches in terms of a continuum between more constructivist ones that are mainly concerned with understanding a certain "text"[2] as an end in itself and critical interpretive approaches that aim to interpret text in order to understand (sociopolitical) context.[3]

As interpretive ontological and epistemological assumptions differ from those of positivist approaches, the logic of doing research and the scientific criteria based on which they are being judged are also different. Positivist research standards such as validity, reliability, replicability, and a largely fixed definition of concepts from the beginning of the research process do not match an interpretive epistemology and operate in very different terms. They are based on the idea that the researcher's presence can be eliminated from the research process and that researchers are able to conduct their studies from an external standpoint that does not interfere with its outcomes (Schwartz-Shea and Yanow 2012, 80–81, 92–95).

The scientific criteria crucial for interpretive research are abduction, reflexivity, contextuality, and flexibility. Abduction refers to the "going back and forth" between theoretical approaches or concepts and empirical insights (Friedrichs and Kratochwil 2009, 709). In contrast to positivist approaches that rely primarily on a priori defined concepts that are derived from the literature in a deductive process, interpretive research is dedicated to understanding concepts people use in the field of inquiry, which are at least as important as concepts and definitions from the literature (Schwartz-Shea and Yanow 2012, 18).

Reflexivity as a scientific criterion refers to both the research process and the situatedness of the researcher therein. It requires transparency concerning how evidence has been generated and how it leads to knowledge claims (Schwartz-Shea and Yanow 2012, 18, 80–81). Moreover, checking one's own sense-making process also involves reflecting upon the researcher's participation in the field, their role and positionality, changes in field realities, and techniques of data analysis. This is especially crucial for interpretive research, as the researcher is the paramount research "instrument," and therefore influences the entire research process, from data collection to writing (van Maanen 1995). Evidence has no prior ontological existence outside the framework of the research process. There are no objects with

---

[2] "Text" not only refers to written words but also includes other forms of data such as spoken words, visual data, artifacts, social media posts, event field notes, and practices.

[3] I am grateful to Marie Østergaard Møller for pointing this out.

fixed characteristics that exist in an automated manner, but they are always the result of the demarcations we as researchers produce. Hence, interpretivists are not so much external observers but closely intertwined with the world of their research. Unlike positivist researchers who assume that data somehow "exists" in the field and just needs to be "collected," in interpretive approaches, data is rather "created"—through a specific research focus, a puzzle, assumptions, and the selection of research questions (Emerson et al. 1995, 1–16; Schwartz-Shea and Yanow 2012, 79). This, in turn, does not mean throwing away objectivity. Instead, interpretivist research strives for another bounded objectivity and "situated knowledge" (Haraway 1988).

Contextuality in interpretive research refers to generating a context-sensitive understanding of meaning-making. Concepts are created during (not before) fieldwork and analysis and need to be situated, which implies that differences between various sources are mapped in order to grasp multiple perspectives in an intertextual manner (Schwartz-Shea and Yanow 2012, 38, 50–51).

Contextuality also requires a certain flexibility from interpretive researchers, in the sense that they must respond to changing field realities (Schwartz-Shea and Yanow 2012, 71). In positivist research, changes are often perceived as failures of a research design that did not work out as expected and therefore requires redesigning the study and collecting additional evidence (e.g., Gerring 2007, 149). In interpretive research, changing research questions and assumptions is an integral part of the learning process. Abductive reasoning is based on the idea that researchers start with what they know or expect in their initial design, but this is open to changes based on a reiterative process of understanding right from the beginning. The prominent role of research participants' worldviews, knowledge, and agency in interpretive research therefore implies that the researcher needs to cede control over the research process and work with what is happening in the field with an attentive and flexible attitude (Schwartz-Shea and Yanow 2012, 72–74).

The Interpretive-Comparative (Area Studies) Approach: Challenges and Tentative Solutions

The central importance of abduction, reflexivity, contextuality, and flexibility in interpretive research must inevitably be reflected in interpretive comparisons as well. Thus, a relatively fixed and static research design, as is common in positivist approaches, is not feasible for interpretive research since it requires a definition or at least a more precise idea of which variables are important for answering the research question from the beginning of the research process. However, as systematic comparative approaches continue to be treated as the standard for political science comparisons, interpretive researchers often face the challenge of defending themselves against the expectations deriving from this literature. It may be helpful for interpretive researchers to think through these typologies and potentially important variables or conditions during the initial research phase. This contributes to their reflexivity and transparency concerning their own situatedness and prior knowledge and assumptions and thereby supports a more conscious research process and provides ideas on what data might be potentially interesting for the project. However, if rigidly applied, these approaches can be too limiting for interpretive research, follow fundamentally different epistemological assumptions, and severely limit interpretive understanding.

It is crucial to further develop the CAS approach so as to include interpretive research designs. The strength of area studies lies in their dedication to understanding social and political phenomena based on a comprehensive consideration of their context, which resembles the interpretive approach. Cross-regional studies, I argue, provide especially fruitful examples for rethinking comparison from an interpretive perspective. Area studies share important intellectual sensibilities with interpretivism. They are concerned with understanding local concepts and meaning-making and strive to be aware of processes of knowledge production. While there are various approaches to area studies, central features usually include a commitment to intensive language studies, in-depth field research, devotion to local histories, perspectives and interpretations, a general orientation toward grounded theory, and an openness to multi- or interdisciplinarity (Szanton 2003, 5). Area studies communities are by nature multidisciplinary. It is one of their strengths that they enable exchange across disciplinary borders and thereby allow for a more holistic understanding of the field of study. They have been perceived as an act of translation, "an effort to make the assumptions, meanings, structures, and dynamics of another society and culture comprehensible to an outsider" (Szanton 2003, 1). They may also challenge and critically inform outsiders' understanding of their own society (Anderson 2016, 132; Szanton 2003, 1–2) as well as other research contexts (see "Interpretive-Comparative Analysis: Modes, Objectives, and Cross-Understanding").

54 ADVANCING COMPARATIVE AREA STUDIES

Ultimately, interpretive CAS needs to be consistent with the fundamental epistemological assumptions of interpretive research. Taking interpretivism seriously in comparative research must result in new approaches to case selection and choice of the research topic, data analysis, and comparison of the cases. An interpretivist turn in CAS also requires rethinking practices of research production and publication. It should be noted that interpretive research often intermingles case selection, analysis, and presentation of results concurrently, rather than sequentially, as is standard in positivist work. The writing process in interpretivism is also closely intertwined with the analysis process, beginning with writing field notes and memos to final publication.

Case Selection: From Discomfort to Access, Context, and "Casing"

Most of the blueprints for case selection in small-N research have been developed from a positivist-realist perspective (e.g., George and Bennett 2005; Gerring 2007).[4] They have little to say about interpretive-comparative analysis or are actually incompatible with the interpretive scientific criteria described above. Applying standard rules of case selection, such as the "most different" or the "most similar" logic, requires researchers define the concepts relevant to their research before commencing it.[5] Researchers need to have a clear understanding of what their concepts and variables mean and how they are related to each other, as well as how this relationship can be tested. In contrast, in interpretive projects, concepts are developed abductively and informed by empirical insights and perceptions within the field context. Consequently, the idea of defining concepts and the relations between different variables or conditions at the beginning of the research process contradicts the interpretive logic that requires a high degree of contextuality and flexibility as prerequisites for understanding meaning-making (Yanow 2014, 132).

This discrepancy between my interpretive-comparative approach and mainstream approaches to controlled comparison in political science led

---

[4] There have been some recent efforts to bridge the gap between positivist and interpretive approaches (see Bennett and Checkel 2014).

[5] This also concerns other case selection types, which do not necessarily aim for representativeness, such as, for example the selection of "extreme," "deviant," or "influential" cases, as suggested by Gerring (2007, 88–91).

to a discomfort that accompanied me during the first one to two years of my research project. This came to the fore when I was asked on the basis of which comparative logic I had selected my cases. The case selection question was one of the standard questions in almost every colloquium, and each time it put me in a defensive position. The problem was not that I had not been thinking through my case selection sufficiently—in my opinion, I had good reasons to choose Indonesia and Brazil as my contexts of study. The problem was that it did not meet with what was presented as the standard typology of case selection models. Moreover, it appeared that the problem of case selection is ever more relevant in cross-regional comparative analysis. Intraregional comparisons are usually perceived as more "natural" than research contexts from different world regions. The fact that the research contexts I selected are not located within the same area and did not follow standard textbook prescriptions created a feeling that there was something fundamentally wrong with my work. It appeared not to meet what I was taught were the criteria of scientific rigor—at least in political science. In more open discussions about the problem, I was advised to look again into the standard literature on case studies and comparisons in order to pick a typology that might seem fitting to my selection. Other suggestions were to give it a different name, such as speaking of "contrasting" instead of "comparing" the cases, or to abandon my second case, Brazil, entirely due the differences in energy sector characteristics of the two countries. Consequently, I attempted to squeeze my research into the tight corset of standard case selection typologies. However, I always felt that this conflicted with my epistemological assumptions and generally perceived this ex post allocation of my case selection to one of the comparison types as contrived. Moreover, it struck me that the same problem has apparently plagued many other researchers as well and that for many of them, especially doctoral researchers, it has led to "moments of existential crisis" (Htun and Jensenius 2021, 196). It took a more intensive study of the methodology literature and some courage to let go of this discomfort and emancipate myself from the typical case selection criteria in the course of my research. Meanwhile, I am assured that, due to its specific epistemological assumptions and scientific criteria, interpretive-comparative research requires a different logic of case selection and comparison in general and that it is necessary to elaborate on new ways of thinking about comparisons.

Following the principle of transparency in interpretative research, I would first like to explain how my case selection came about before deriving some recommendations from it that may be helpful to other researchers in a similar situation: My research started from observations about new developments in Indonesia, where I had been previously researching local conflicts over coal mining. In 2016, when I went to Indonesia on an explorative research stay to evaluate possible foci in my research project, I observed that coal had gained importance for domestic electricity production. I learned that Indonesia was about to construct almost three hundred new coal-fired power plants at a time when the climate crisis had become more and more apparent. The Paris Agreement had just been signed, with countries pledging to reduce their greenhouse gas emissions. Indonesia has always agreed to these goals in the international arena and even presented itself to the international community as a climate pioneer. At the same time, I knew from previous research about the disastrous environmental and social consequences of coal mining in Indonesia. Technical explanations seemed insufficient. The puzzle with which I started my research was how these diverging approaches to energy and climate politics could be understood, how the hegemonic energy approach had been established, on which political-economic structures it is based, and which discourses and practices enforced or contested this hegemony.

Aside from my desire to continue working in Indonesia, I was interested in comparative methods. I wondered whether my preliminary assumptions about Indonesian energy politics were very particular and context-specific or if similar developments and phenomena existed in other parts of the world. Energy planning and the development of new sources are crucial for large countries with fast-growing energy demand. At the same time, the world faces a worsening climate crisis, and many countries have demonstrated vulnerability to a changing climate. Thus, the question of how societies respond to the climate crisis while also expanding energy use appeared to provide a potentially interesting comparison. I thought through various possibilities for comparison. One was the Philippines, located within the same region as Indonesia and sharing a similar archipelagic geography. The Philippines also relies on coal production and consumption. However, I dismissed this idea because of the country's smaller size and lesser importance for international climate politics, but also due to language challenges. The ability to speak or at least learn the main language spoken in my field research sites, I believed, was crucial for my case selection. A year prior to commencing my research project, I led a project that relied on translators for conducting interviews with people from Syria and Afghanistan. I wanted to avoid the difficulties related to this additional layer of interpretation. Therefore, I excluded other Southeast Asian countries due to the language barriers that appeared too difficult to overcome within a short amount of time. Another idea was comparing Indonesia to my home country, Germany. Access would have been easy, and just as in Indonesia, resistance against coal mining and demands for environmental and social justice in the energy sector were on the rise. Additionally, I thought about this selection as a small subversive act, trespassing the common dividing line between "Western industrialized" and "developing Global South" countries. However, I was discouraged choosing Germany by colleagues and by finding out that its energy challenges were also different (for example, Germany does not need to expand its energy generation, as demand has generally not been growing substantially). Thus, I considered my second focus and region of interest, South America, to decide whether I could identify a suitable case for comparison. As I was already fluent in Spanish and had been staying mostly in Spanish-speaking countries (and briefly also in Brazil) when I was in South America for a couple of months, I checked those countries first. Yet I was finally convinced that Brazil would be the best context for comparison. As in Indonesia, past Brazilian governments were eager to present the country as an international climate leader. Moreover, fossil fuels were rising, offshore oil was developed, and large energy projects like the Belo Monte hydro dam were realized despite widespread contestation. Additionally, initially, the Workers' Party government of Lula da Silva was generally perceived as progressive and oriented toward social justice, albeit with a clearer leftist political orientation than the government of Joko Widodo in Indonesia. Therefore, a comparison between fossil-fuel-oriented energy politics under governments pursuing an international climate leadership role and a pro-poor, social-justice-oriented domestic agenda appeared fitting and exciting to me—despite the differences of the two countries' energy characteristics (with Brazil having a much higher share of renewables). Furthermore, I assumed that based on my knowledge of Spanish, some basics in French, and my general dedication to learning new languages, I would be able to learn Portuguese sufficiently to conduct interviews.

In cross-regional comparisons, there is often an imbalance at the beginning in terms of the researcher's expertise regarding the two (or more) research contexts. There are regions in which the research feels more "at home" than others. Therefore, it is crucial to consider how to compensate for this imbalance and how access to the new research field can be organized. Thus, my considerations were not only about language skills but also prior knowledge of the context and contacts and other options to gain access. I started my field trip to Brazil with an intensive Portuguese language course. I contacted many people I wanted to talk to or who could function as gatekeepers in Portuguese, which I believe was crucial for receiving replies. However, my field research experience in Indonesia was also important for gaining access to the field. While I was still exploring there, trying out different ways of making contact and having to learn to orient myself in the technical details of the energy sector, I could draw on this experience in my Brazil field research. Last but not least, I was still surprised by how much easier it was to arrange interview appointments in Brazil. In particular, access to politicians and employees of state institutions in general was enormously difficult in Indonesia. In contrast, after only a few months of field research in Brazil, I had spoken to just about every institution or person I considered important, even former ministers. In Indonesia, despite multiple visits, research took more time and creativity. This shows again that these kinds of processes are never fully controllable for the researcher, and it is also not assured that field research goes better in an already familiar context than in a new context. Overall, my field research went much more smoothly in Brazil than in Indonesia. It opened my eyes to things I had not recognized in Indonesia and thus proved to be a fruitful context for comparison.

Altogether, my case selection was based on a mixture of topic- and research interest-related aspects and more personal and practical criteria such as an interest in and proximity to certain regions and my language proficiencies. Yet, while they may significantly contribute to accessing and understanding a particular research context, which is central to interpretive studies (Schwartz-Shea and Yanow 2012, 70–71) and area studies research alike, many case study methods books either do not consider these aspects or mention them only cursorily. Especially, in interpretive research, where the researcher is the main "instrument" of inquiry, ignoring personal and practical matters reduces transparency. Considering questions of access such as specific knowledge, language skills, funding opportunities, and the passion for or familiarity with a specific research context ought thus to be understood as an asset rather than a limitation for gaining insights and developing theory. They are as crucial for case selection as the specific puzzle or dilemma a researcher seeks to study. Thus, it is essential to select the setting of study based on theoretical as well as practical and personal considerations and to be explicit and transparent about them (Boswell et al. 2019, 43, 58–62, 144; Htun and Jensenius 2021, 191, 198–199; Soss 2021, 91). Accordingly, based on my topic of interest and research puzzle, the incongruence between international climate politics and domestic energy politics, my expertise and interest in the countries and wider regions, and questions of access, I chose what I thought would be my two contexts for comparison, Indonesia and Brazil.

However, I soon understood that choosing two countries for comparing a specific policy field does not make them my "cases." As Joe Soss (2018, 2021) made us aware, we actually do not "study a case" but are "casing a study." A case does not exist a priori. It is "something we make—an analytic construct that we develop through our efforts to theorize the phenomenon we study" (Soss 2021, 85). We construct cases by setting multiple boundaries of what we study. This is why I prefer referring to Indonesia and Brazil not as my cases but as the contexts of my research within which I cased my study. Similarly, Mala Htun and Francesca Jensenius (2021) propose selecting contexts instead of cases, especially when theory development constitutes a central goal of the research project. Other authors have also questioned the case approach and suggest speaking of "siting" a research, especially when studying topics related to translocal processes (Marcus 1995; Riofrancos 2021). This is a fruitful approach to contemporary universal questions and the challenges encountered in different parts of the globe within a specific context, such as the climate crisis and related debates about energy transformations. For example, I consider studying the barriers to energy transformations a contemporary universal question that concerns most societies. Thus, looking at how governments and people in Indonesia and Brazil have been dealing with the challenge of energy transformations I consider to be "siting" my research interest in these two specific contexts—albeit they are not directly connected to one another.

Casing is an ongoing research activity, emerging "as we strive to make sense of the particular in more abstract terms" (Soss 2021, 85). Thus, the selection of cases (and sometimes even contexts) for interpretive comparisons is always, to some degree, provisional (Boswell et al. 2019, 71). Researchers may conduct a "preliminary casing" in the research design phase to select what context they generally want to look at. However, in accordance with the abductive logic and the standards of flexibility and contextuality underlying interpretive research, the researcher actually "cases" their study throughout—the interconnected processes of field research, analysis, and writing (Soss 2021, 91). For example, I re-cased the research several times by shifting my focus and adapting my research questions accordingly. These changes were based on insights and interpretations in the field and contrasting within and between the cases as well as to theoretical concepts (see "Interpretive-Comparative Analysis: Modes, Objectives, and Cross-Understanding"). For example, while the international climate politics / domestic energy politics puzzle was the central dilemma guiding my research at first, I eventually only treated it as one among several aspects impacting domestic energy politics. Moreover, I narrowed my scope by focusing on electricity generation and production. In Indonesia, political conflict lines were pretty straightforward, with a powerful politico-business coal lobby on one side and a civil society movement demanding social and environmental justice on the other. This appeared to be a common story, more or less easy to assess. In Brazil, in contrast, societal contestation by local communities and domestic and international civil society organizations was targeting hydropower plant construction. In international discourses, hydropower is generally considered a clean and low-carbon source of energy. In Brazil, however, it is oftentimes portrayed as ecologically unsustainable and socially unjust. Thus, my focus shifted toward including demands for different kinds of energy transformations—not strictly sticking to a shift from fossil fuel to low-carbon or renewable forms of electricity generation, as this did not reflect the dividing lines and the discourses in Brazil. Re-casings like these accompanied my entire research project. They cannot be separated from the process of analysis but depend on and constitute a central part of it.

At the beginning of interpretive research projects, we cannot know what our study will finally be a case of (Htun and Jensenius 2021, 191; Soss 2021, 91). Thus, researchers cannot control their variables and base their case selection on them, nor should they seek to do so (Boswell et al. 2019, 59, 71). Boswell, Corbett, and Rhodes (2019, 60) claim that, for example, in interpretive research, researchers ought not to select cases because they are "typical" or "deviant"; rather, it would be an outcome of the research to understand how a case is typical or deviant. According to the same authors, "The whole point of immersive fieldwork in detailed case research is that it is potentially transformative, admitting and celebrating the prospect of surprise and discovery. How we understand and justify comparison, in these terms, needs to evolve as the project evolves" (Boswell et al. 2019, 57). In this sense, "contextualized comparisons" can reveal parallels between contexts that researchers commonly believe to be very different and, likewise, highlight differences in contexts found to be similar (Locke and Thelen 1995). Moreover, case selection potentially needs to be re-justified when using the same data for publications with different foci or merging them with another researcher's data for a joint publication (Boswell et al. 2019, 63, 70). Thus, interpretive research usually undergoes various re-casings (Soss 2021, 92). This ought not to be understood as a misconception or failure of the research design but as necessary for insightful research that is based on an abductive logic and requires from the researcher flexibility and considerations of context.

In sum, whereas positivist studies select cases at the beginning of the research process based on certain variables derived from the literature, casing is an ongoing process in interpretive-comparative research. What is selected at the beginning of the research process are the contexts in which certain phenomena are being studied. The selection of research contexts does not only depend on the research puzzle or general topic of interest but is also related to practical issues such as the specific skills of the researcher and other criteria of access. Within these contexts, researchers case their studies, which involves refining research questions and shifting the focus of the research project (or even changing the contexts). Thus, any specific template on how to select cases for interpretive comparisons would do injustice to these processes that require context-sensitivity and flexibility and severely limit the research process. However, this does not mean that the choice of context and the casing process can be arbitrary, and it is crucial that it happens in a transparent and reflexive manner. Re-casing requires the aforementioned willingness to flexibly address context-bound aspects of the research. In interpretative research, re-casing is part of the analysis process and does not precede it.

Interpretive-Comparative Analysis: Modes, Objectives, and Cross-Understanding

In interpretive research, comparing does not imply the isolation of certain features from their context. Instead, comparing preserves the singularities and specificities of each case and their respective concepts that are intended to emerge from the field or iteratively between local and situated meaning and theory, as explained before. Learning and understanding continue throughout the entire research process, and it is mostly about relating specific local meanings and interactions to the theoretical frame. Comparison therefore also implies that the researcher makes sense of the particularities of each case (Yanow 2014, 143–145). Thus, interpretive comparisons are generally concerned with relating the particular to the universal and vice versa while preserving the singularities and specificities of each context.

We can generally distinguish three modes of comparison: (1) within-case comparison, (2) case-theory comparison, and (3) case-to-case comparison. The first two of these apply to interpretive research in general, whereas the third one is specific for comparisons involving different research contexts and is especially important for CAS. Within-case comparison refers to the comparison of interpretations and meanings from different sources within one context and can be related to triangulation. It is an intertextual comparison toward identifying cross-references. The second mode of comparison refers to contrasting impressions and interpretations from a specific context to either the theoretical framework, theoretical concepts, or other prior knowledge and assumptions. Here it is central to be reflective and transparent about one's own expectations and how they were shaped by a specific geographic, demographic, and academic background (see the principles of reflexivity and transparency above) (Yanow 2014, 145–147). Both modes of comparison are crucial to the process of interpretation.

The third mode, case-to-case comparison, is an additional form of contrasting that is unique to studies based on a contrasting juxtaposition of two or more cases from different research contexts. Case-to-case comparisons include the contrasting of various processes, structures, discourses, practices, and the like, depending on the research questions and the theoretical framework applied (which, however, may be revised, altered, or completely overthrown based on empirical insights). Like the other two modes of comparison, case-to-case comparisons are present in all (often simultaneous) phases of the research process—from developing the preliminary research design over field research and data analysis sessions up to writing.

Any comparison can be generally oriented along three different logics, focusing primarily on differences or on similarities, or trying to do both at once. For example, in *Imagined Communities* (1983), Anderson focuses on similarities of nationalisms in different parts of the world, whereas in the essay "The Idea of Power in Javanese Culture" (1972) he elaborates on the differences between Western and Javanese concepts of power (thereby demonstrating the underlying rationality of Javanese thinking). In *Under Three Flags* (2005), in turn, he elaborates on both by emphasizing similarities while also contrasting global anarchism and local nationalisms. It is difficult to decide whether two country contexts are generally different or similar, as this depends on one's perspective and the topic under investigation. Therefore, researchers ought to consciously consider the focus of their comparison (Anderson 2016, 130).

Generally, case-to-case comparisons are suitable for developing and revising theories and concepts (Htun and Jensenius 2021, 191–193), enable generalizations beyond a single context (Boswell et al. 2019, 4), and translations between contexts (see Simmons and Smith in this volume). Beyond that, it is not only that exploring a phenomenon embedded in different contexts helps researchers to understand its underlying processes and features much better (Htun and Jensenius 2021, 197). We also learn from one specific context about another one. Thus, case-to-case comparisons facilitate what I term "cross-understanding." For example, during my field research in Brazil, I recognized that strategies of depoliticization played an essential role in how energy politics was treated in the public discourse and that this is potentially linked to the modes, levels, and intensity of opposition against hegemonic energy models. In Indonesia, depoliticization was not such an outstanding feature as in Brazil. However, after I became aware of it through my Brazil field research, I also started to see my Indonesia data from a different angle and indeed recognized that depoliticization also played a role in the Indonesian discourse, even if to a lesser degree as compared to Brazil. For example, in Brazil, electricity politics was generally often referred to as a technocratic issue for experts to deal with. In Indonesia, that was not generally the case, but certain electricity programs and especially the use of coal for electricity generation, for example, were presented as common sense and, thereby, the only way to tackle current energy challenges. Depoliticization turned out to be an essential component of the theoretical approach I developed in my research. Thus, case-to-case comparison also informed the development of my concepts and theoretical framework.

Cross-regional interpretive comparisons additionally not only yield the potential to rethink the use and meaning of concepts in specific empirical contexts but also across disciplines and areas. Thus, they can facilitate dialogue between theoretical debates and concepts developed in different area studies communities (Köllner et al. 2018, 3). This is also the

64   ADVANCING COMPARATIVE AREA STUDIES

case when concepts developed in one world region—such as John Furnivall's (1948) "plural society" (see Kuhonta's contribution to this volume)
or Scott's "weapons of the weak" (1985) and "moral economy" (1976)—are
being translated to another context. Likewise, in interpretive-comparative
studies, the direct contrasting of empirical and scholarly concepts can fruitfully inform concept formation. Therefore, an interpretive approach toward
assessing meaning-making can identify different applications of the same
terms as well as similar concepts referred to with different terminologies. As
they open up dialogues between empirical and theoretical concepts of different epistemic academic communities, cross-regional comparisons yield the
potential to contribute significantly to the further refining of social science
concepts (Köllner et al. 2018, 19; von Soest and Stroh 2018, 71–73).

Additionally, cross-regional interpretive comparisons are often also multi-
lingual. This may be challenging as the translation of terminologies between,
for example, Brazilian Portuguese terms, Indonesian ones, and theoretical concepts from literature in different languages adds additional layers
of interpretation. However, language-specific terminology and its application may also make a difference in meaning more evident and easier to
detect. Frederic Schaffer (2000), for example, identified important conceptual differences by examining the everyday meanings of *démocratie*
and *demokaraasi* in Senegal and comparing them to Western ideal-typical
understandings of democracy. Thus, just as an outsider's perspective often
allows us to encounter things we cannot see in more familiar contexts, the
juxtaposition of different concepts and terminology facilitates learning and
cross-understanding.

Interpretive comparison can also focus on dilemmas, problems, or challenges common to humans in different parts of the world and how people
and societies have responded to them differently (or similarly) in different
contexts. This requires conceptualizing a problem in universal terms and
paying specific attention to how people have understood and responded to
it in a specific context shaped by perceptions and historical legacies (Adcock
2006, 61–62). These problems can be small, everyday "dilemmas" actors
across very different contexts experience. They are often related to new ideas
or challenges that stand in contrast to conventional practices or beliefs. The
researcher's task is to identify them by understanding how actors rationalize
their actions, perceive their choices, and relate these choices to their beliefs.
Furthermore, research must identify similarities and differences between
dilemmas from potentially very different contexts and compare the actors'

strategies (Boswell et al. 2019, 12–13, 39–52, 148). The focus on responses to shared dilemmas and challenges societies across very different geographical and historical contexts' experience is also what makes the cross-regional and cross-temporal comparisons of Anderson's study on the commonalities of nationalisms in *Imagined Communities* (1983) and Scott's analysis of strategies of state control in *Seeing Like a State* (1998) so intriguing. They relate context-sensitivity and their understanding of particular societies, times, and processes to universal human questions.

In my research on Indonesian and Brazilian energy politics, the general problem I started with was concerned with understanding how societies responded to the global challenge of climate change while facing the need to expand energy supply that, in turn, at least in its current fossilized model, stands in stark contrast to climate protection. This is a question about beliefs and values, about inequalities between and within societies, and vigorously contested in various respects. It was my aim to understand the similarities and differences that exist in the responses to this overarching question in a context-sensitive manner, paying attention to its relations to the meaning-making of different groups within these societies. I compared two different contexts to each other and to the theoretical frame in order to develop the latter and understand how energy politics are negotiated, maintained, and contested in Indonesia and Brazil—two contexts with the common challenge of rising energy demand, growth aspirations, and prevailing inequalities. What I compared is, thus, how people make sense of those aspects, relate them to each other, what they aspire to, and how they judge, contest, and enforce certain policies and political structures. Through within-case, case-theory, and case-to-case comparison, I developed a theoretical framework largely based on the combination and refinement of concepts from different research traditions. I thereby drew on concepts from the literature as well as from my cases. The theoretical insights, in turn, have—in an abductive process—not only informed the theoretical framework but also contributed to understanding similarities and differences in meaning-making in distinct contexts. Thus, unlike positivist approaches, where the detection of similarities and differences constitutes the beginning of the research process, namely the selection of cases, in interpretive research they are important results (Yanow 2014, 149). In interpretive research, we would never assume that two contexts are entirely similar or entirely different. Rather they may share more or fewer commonalities depending on the specific phenomena under investigation (Boswell et al. 2019, 60).

In sum, interpretive comparisons are commonly concerned with relating universal phenomena to particular contexts. They juxtapose concepts from the literature and empirical concepts from different contexts in order to contribute to concept and theory development. Furthermore, assumptions about differences and similarities are not only crucial for case selection but an outcome of the comparison, which informs concept formation and theory-building.

Presenting Interpretive Comparisons: Writing, Structure, and Publishing

Presenting and communicating the results of interpretive-comparative research poses several challenges and requires a few critical decisions. These are particularly related to (1) developing one's own writing style, (2) the structuring of the text, and (3) publication-related challenges. Of course, the challenges and considerations mentioned below do not apply to all interpretive research. Some may mostly apply to cross-regional interpretive-comparative projects, while others may also apply to positivist CAS approaches. However, I believe it is critical for interpretive-comparative researchers to think through these issues.

First, interpretive and positivist comparative writing styles differ. While positivist comparative writings generally place more emphasis on clear structure and analytical expression, interpretive texts do often follow a more ethnographic approach. They are characterized by a rather narrative style and storytelling elements such as vignettes and extensive field notes. Boswell, Corbett, and Rhodes (2019, 117–118) refer to this as the distinction between a more evocative and a more linear style of writing and suggest deciding pragmatically upon the writing style depending on the type of publication and audience (Boswell et al. 2019, 124–131). During my writing process, I sought to combine both tendencies without appearing too contradictory. Of course, writing styles are also shaped by our academic socialization and standards and modes of expression related to our native language and other language proficiencies. For example, I was educated in a German academic context in the disciplines of political science, geography, and anthropology, where (only partly in anthropology though) structured, analytic expression still constitutes the standard form of writing. Additionally, my writing language, English, is not my mother tongue. Thus, it has been a long journey for me to integrate narrative forms of writing in my work. An additional challenge for writing is that in interpretive-comparative work, we need to find a good balance between depth and breadth (Boswell et al. 2019, 118). While interpretive research is generally oriented toward a context-sensitive understanding of meaning-making and therefore requires a certain depth, the authors' leeway is often limited due to external constraints such as the total number of words or characters permitted for certain papers and books. In interpretive-comparative work, this constitutes even more of a challenge as it requires an in-depth presentation of more than one case and often also includes a less terse, more descriptive narrative.

The second challenge for interpretive comparisons (and often also for positivist CAS research) is structuring the text, which may be ordered according to different research contexts or by theoretical themes (Boswell et al. 2019, 116–117). For my research, the structural question concerned whether to present my results in two separate chapters—each on one context, Indonesia or Brazil—or to discuss both countries in chapters structured according to my theoretical approach. I experimented with both formats, initially organizing the text thematically. However, I ultimately dropped this approach out of concern for my readers. Since my work is based on a cross-regional comparison, I assumed my readers might include (a) people interested in critical political economy theory, (b) people interested in energy and climate politics, and (c) people with particular interests in Indonesia or Brazil. Accordingly, a contextually organized structure makes it easier for readers to choose which chapters to read. In addition, a contextual structure, especially in monographs, offers the possibility of providing readers who are not so familiar with one of the cases easier access to the necessary contextual knowledge. In shorter texts such as journal papers or a comparison within the same region or context, a thematic structure may be more suitable.

The publishing and presentation of results constitute the third challenge, especially for cross-regional interpretive-comparative research because of its potentially heterogeneous audience. It is often impossible to decide about a focus audience, especially if there does not exist a research tradition combining a specific thematic focus with a particular theoretical approach or a certain research topic that is commonly studied in a specific context. The audience can thus be either geographically oriented, topic oriented, or theory oriented. This provides many opportunities for (single case) presentations and papers in different conferences and outlets.

However, the options for publishing a monograph or a paper based on a cross-regional comparison may also be more limited, as, for example, area-specific book series or journals cannot be considered. Moreover, as mentioned above, due to the importance of providing more contextual information, cross-regional comparisons often require a more extensive presentation of results, which may also be challenging due to external restrictions.

In sum, while researchers following a positivist approach tend to a more linear and analytical style of writing, interpretive CAS approaches are more ethnographic and narrative centered. However, writing styles may vary depending on the form of the text, the outlet where it is going to be published, and the potential audience for that venue, as well as one's academic socialization. While a narrative writing style is rich and illustrative, allows for greater transparency, and involves the reader in the process of understanding, the required depth and contextuality of the presentation also pose a challenge. This is largely due to external constraints on the structure and length of academic texts. For comparative work, this is even more challenging since two or more different contexts need to be presented. Especially for cross-regional studies, a context-oriented structure, that is, the separate presentation of the study contexts, is recommended, as they usually have a heterogeneous readership that may be familiar with only one of the contexts. Concerning publication options, researchers conducting cross-regional studies find themselves in an ambivalent situation. On the one hand, possibilities for publishing are more limited for comparative work. On the other hand, researchers can participate in different area studies' journals and conferences, presenting one of their research contexts.

Beyond these content-related challenges that apply to interpretive comparisons, practical constraints arise from the researcher's resources, especially time and money. For example, in the German academic system, PhD scholarships are usually provided for a maximum of three years, while most social science PhD students require five to six years to complete their research project (Deutsche Forschungsgemeinschaft 2021; Jaksztat et al. 2012). Extensive field research in more than one context requires comparatively more time, which renders interpretive-comparative research more difficult to be completed within a required time frame.

Conclusion

While interpretive comparisons are widespread, the methodology literature on how to conduct comparative studies in the social sciences has been dominated by approaches to controlled comparison that are based on a positivist epistemology. This mismatch constitutes a challenge for scholars interested in interpretive comparisons. The resulting discrepancies between the approaches appear to be even stronger for cross-regional CAS. CAS provides a fruitful environment for elaborating on the specifics and potentials of interpretive-comparative research—not least because many characteristics of area studies research resemble the scientific criteria of interpretive research. Based on insights gained through conducting an interpretive, cross-regional comparison of energy politics in Indonesia and Brazil, this chapter discusses how to deal with case selection, comparative analysis, and writing and presenting research results in accordance with an interpretive epistemology. It develops general recommendations to guide interpretive CAS projects, assisting researchers in addressing the specific challenges they face.

The purpose of this contribution is threefold: First, it provides methodological reflections on interpretive comparisons from an area studies perspective to empower interpretive researchers who may feel trapped in the tight corset of today's dominant political science principles of controlled comparison. It encourages them to stick to the epistemological principles of interpretivism when conducting comparisons, thereby embracing the potential for new insights stemming from a context-sensitive, flexible, and reflective research practice. A strengthening of methodological consciousness helps to concretize the possibilities and limits of generalization based on interpretive-comparative research and detect the contribution it can have in refining concepts and developing theoretical approaches while refraining from neglecting the particularities of each case.

Second, the chapter contributes to the further development of CAS toward including interpretive approaches. The resemblances of interpretive approaches and area studies concerning the centrality of context-sensitive understanding suggest that interpretivism ought to gain a firm foothold within the universe of different CAS approaches. Third, the chapter thereby seeks to encourage (interpretive) area specialists to conduct comparative studies. CAS can certainly benefit from the context-sensitive and reflective

70 ADVANCING COMPARATIVE AREA STUDIES

attitude of interpretivism, which encourages an openness to potentially initially strange, yet all the more exciting new insights. Templates for controlled comparison are unnecessarily limiting interpretive approaches that gain from and even require ceasing control over the research process to a certain degree in order to allow for potentially surprising new perspectives arising from a context-sensitive and flexible research attitude. Not least, as Anderson writes in his memoir *A Life Beyond Boundaries* (2016), good comparative research is often based on experiences of surprise and strangeness.

Bibliography

Adcock, Robert. 2006. Generalization in Comparative and Historical Social Science: The Difference That Interpretivism Makes. In Dvora Yanow and Peregrine Schwartz-Shea, eds. *Interpretation and Method: Empirical Research Methods and the Interpretive Turn.* Armonk, NY: M.E. Sharpe, 50–66.

Ahram, Ariel I., Patrick Köllner, and Rudra Sil, eds. 2018. *Comparative Area Studies: Methodological Rationales and Cross-Regional Applications.* New York: Oxford University Press.

Anderson, Benedict R. O'G. 1972. The Idea of Power in Javanese Culture. In Claire Holt, ed. *Culture and Politics in Indonesia.* Ithaca, NY: Cornell University Press, 1–70.

Anderson, Benedict R. O'G. [1983] 2006. *Imagined Communities: Reflections on the Origin and Spread of Nationalism.* Rev. ed. London: Verso.

Anderson, Benedict R. O'G. 2005. *Under Three Flags: Anarchism and the Anti-Colonial Imagination.* London: Verso.

Anderson, Benedict R. O'G. 2016. *A Life Beyond Boundaries.* New York: Verso.

Bennett, Andrew, and Jeffrey T. Checkel, eds. 2014. *Process Tracing: From Metaphor to Analytic Tool: Strategies for Social Inquiry.* Cambridge: Cambridge University Press.

Boswell, John, Jack Corbett, and R. A. W. Rhodes. 2019. *The Art and Craft of Comparison.* Cambridge: Cambridge University Press.

Deutsche Forschungsgemeinschaft. 2021. Sprint oder Marathon? Die Dauer von Promotionen in DFG-geförderten Verbünden. March 2021 (accessed May 23, 2022).

Emerson, Robert M., Rachel I. Fretz, and Linda L. Shaw. 1995. *Writing Ethnographic Fieldnotes.* Chicago: University of Chicago Press.

Friedrichs, Jörg, and Friedrich Kratochwil. 2009. On Acting and Knowing: How Pragmatism Can Advance International Relations Research and Methodology. *International Organization* 63 (4): 701–731.

Furnivall, John Sydendam. 1948. *Colonial Policy and Practice: A Comparative Study of Burma and Netherlands India.* Cambridge: Cambridge University Press.

George, Alexander L., and Andrew Bennett. 2005. *Case Studies and Theory Development in the Social Sciences.* Cambridge, MA: MIT Press.

Gerring, John. 2007. *Case Study Research: Principles and Practices.* Cambridge: Cambridge University Press.

Haraway, Donna. 1988. Situated Knowledges: The Science Question in Feminism and the Privilege of Partial Perspective. *Feminist Studies* 14 (3): 575–599.

Hawkesworth, Mary. 2006. Contending Conceptions of Science and Politics: Methodology and the Constitution of the Political. In Dvora Yanow and Peregrine Schwartz-Shea, eds. *Interpretation and Method: Empirical Research Methods and the Interpretive Turn.* Armonk, NY: M.E. Sharpe, 27–49.

COMPARATIVE AREA STUDIES AND INTERPRETIVISM 71

Htun, Mala, and Francesca R. Jensenius. 2021. Comparative Analysis for Theory Development. In Erica S. Simmons and Nicholas Rush Smith, eds. *Rethinking Comparison: Innovative Methods for Qualitative Political Inquiry*. Cambridge: Cambridge University Press, 190–207.

Huotari, Mikko. 2014. Introduction: Fostering Methodological Dialogue in Southeast Asian Studies. In Mikko Huotari, Jürgen Rüland, and Judith Schlehe, eds. *Methodology and Research Practice in Southeast Asian Studies*. Basingstoke: Palgrave Macmillan, 1–24.

Huotari, Mikko, and Jürgen Rüland. 2014. Introduction: Context, Concepts and Comparison in Southeast Asian Studies. *Pacific Affairs* 87 (3): 415–439.

Huotari, Mikko, and Jürgen Rüland. 2018. Context, Concepts, and Comparison in Southeast Asian Studies. In Ariel I. Ahram, Patrick Köllner, and Rudra Sil, eds. *Comparative Area Studies: Methodological Rationales and Cross-Regional Applications*. New York: Oxford University Press, 85–102.

Jaksztat, Steffen, Nora Preßler, and Kolja Briedis. 2012. Promotionen im Fokus: Promotions- und Arbeitsbedingungen Promovierender im Vergleich. December 2012 (accessed May 23, 2022).

Köllner, Patrick, Rudra Sil, and Ariel I. Ahram. 2018. Comparative Area Studies: What It Is, What It Can Do. In Ariel I. Ahram, Patrick Köllner, and Rudra Sil, eds. *Comparative Area Studies: Methodological Rationales and Cross-Regional Applications*. New York: Oxford University Press, 3–26.

Locke, Richard M., and Kathleen Thelen. 1995. Apples and Oranges Revisited: Contextualized Comparisons and the Study of Comparative Labor Politics. *Politics & Society* 23 (3): 337–367.

Marcus, George E. 1995. Ethnography in/of the World System: The Emergence of Multi-Sited Ethnography. *Annual Review of Anthropology* 24: 95–117.

Riofrancos, Thea. 2021. From Cases to Sites. In Erica S. Simmons and Nicholas R. Smith, eds. *Rethinking Comparison: Innovative Methods for Qualitative Political Inquiry*. Cambridge: Cambridge University Press, 107–125.

Schaffer, Frederic Charles. 2000. *Democracy in Translation: Understanding Politics in an Unfamiliar Culture*. Ithaca, NY: Cornell University Press.

Schwartz-Shea, Peregrine, and Dvora Yanow. 2012. *Interpretive Research Design: Concepts and Processes*. New York: Routledge.

Scott, James C. 1976. *The Moral Economy of the Peasant: Rebellion and Subsistence in Southeast Asia*. New Haven: Yale University Press.

Scott, James C. 1985. *Weapons of the Weak: Everyday Forms of Peasant Resistance*. New Haven: Yale University Press.

Scott, James C. 1998. *Seeing Like a State: How Certain Schemes to Improve the Human Condition Have Failed*. New Haven: Yale University Press.

Simmons, Erica S., and Nicholas Rush Smith. 2017. Comparison with an Ethnographic Sensibility. *PS: Political Science & Politics* 50 (1): 126–130.

Simmons, Erica S., and Nicholas Rush Smith. 2019. The Case for Comparative Ethnography. *Comparative Politics* 51 (3): 341–359.

Simmons, Erica S., and Nicholas Rush Smith. 2021. Rethinking Comparison: An Introduction. In Erica S. Simmons and Nicholas Rush Smith, eds. *Rethinking Comparison: Innovative Methods for Qualitative Political Inquiry*. Cambridge: Cambridge University Press, 1–28.

Soss, Joe. 2018. On Casing a Study Versus Studying a Case. *Qualitative and Multi-Method Research* 16 (1): 21–27.

Soss, Joe. 2021. On Casing a Study Versus Studying a Case. In Erica S. Simmons and Nicholas Rush Smith, eds. *Rethinking Comparison: Innovative Methods for Qualitative Political Inquiry*. Cambridge: Cambridge University Press, 84–106.

Szanton, David L. 2003. The Origin, Nature and Challenges of Area Studies in the United States. In David L. Szanton, ed. *The Politics of Knowledge: Area Studies and the Disciplines.* Berkeley: University of California Press, 1–33.

van Maanen, John. 1995. *Representation in Ethnography.* Thousand Oaks, CA: Sage.

von Soest, Christian, and Alexander Stroh. 2018. Comparisons Across World Regions: Managing Conceptual, Methodological, and Practical Challenges. In Ariel I. Ahram, Patrick Köllner, and Rudra Sil, eds. *Comparative Area Studies: Methodological Rationales and Cross-Regional Applications.* New York: Oxford University Press, 66–84.

Yanow, Dvora. 2006. Thinking Interpretively: Philosophical Presuppositions and the Human Sciences. In Dvora Yanow and Peregrine Schwartz-Shea, eds. *Interpretation and Method: Empirical Research Methods and the Interpretive Turn.* Armonk, NY: M.E. Sharpe, 5–26.

Yanow, Dvora. 2014. Interpretive Analysis and Comparative Research. In Isabelle Engeli and Christine R. Allison, eds. *Comparative Policy Studies.* London: Palgrave Macmillan, 131–159.

PART II

HOW COMPARATIVE AREA STUDIES BENEFITS, AND BENEFITS FROM, VARIED STRATEGIES OF CAUSAL ANALYSIS

4

Causal Explanation with Ideal Types

Opportunities for Comparative Area Studies

Ryan Saylor

Introduction

The comparative area studies initiative challenges researchers to under-take cross-regional research while remaining sensitive to contextual nuance within and between different world regions. Rudra Sil (2018, 233) advises scholars to engage in a "self-conscious effort to adjust the operationalization of concepts, the calibration of measures, and the coding of observations for each case in light of contextual attributes deemed significant by the relevant country or area specialists." Context is not an afterthought in comparative area studies research. Contextual delineation is as important as theorizing causes and specifying causal mechanisms (Sil 2018, 235).

There are a variety of obstacles to undertaking comparative area studies research. They include the costs associated with familiarizing oneself with debates in multiple area studies communities (Köllner et al. 2018, 13–20). From a methodological standpoint, perhaps the biggest complication comes from prevailing advice on case selection. The conventional wisdom prefers tidy case comparisons, which arguably makes it easier to determine the relative influence of different factors on the outcome one is investigating. Cross-regional research designs tend to contravene these strictures because of factors, such as culture or religious traditions, that often vary more inter-regionally than intraregionally. Consequently, comparative area studies may struggle to satisfy standard case selection protocols and the requisites of causal inference.

Fortunately, an alternative exists. Although the dominant approach to social science emphasizes making causal inferences, researchers can also use case studies to craft causal explanations. Explanations are distinct from inferences, as I detail herein. Inferences are made when one uses data to

Ryan Saylor, *Causal Explanation with Ideal Types*. In: *Advancing Comparative Area Studies*. Edited by: Ariel I. Ahram, Patrick Köllner, and Rudra Sil, Oxford University Press. © Oxford University Press (2025). DOI: 10.1093/oso/9780197809365.003.0004

test conformity to an empirical regularity. Explanations focus on individual cases and have different ingredients: they must describe the factors that were present and jointly responsible for generating a particular outcome, provide adequate causal depth, and demonstrate fitness compared to rival accounts. In the spirit of Patrick Köllner, Rudra Sil, and Ariel Ahram's (2018, 13, 4, respectively) declaration that comparative area studies does not "proceed from a uniform epistemic commitment" but rather seeks to "reveal and partially explain convergent or divergent processes unfolding across locales situated in different areas," this chapter details an epistemic approach that can be valuable for researches wanting to undertake comparative area studies but find themselves limited by mainstream methodological guidance.

I highlight how ideal types are useful for producing context-sensitive explanations. Most social scientists are exposed to Weberian ideal types in connection to concept formation. But ideal types can also encapsulate causal claims and be used to craft explanations. I describe what an ideal type is and show why ideal types are poised to fulfill the requisites of a good explanation. I then provide a four-step framework for building and using ideal types. This procedure entails inductive research, hypothesizing a cause-effect sequence, comparing the ideal type to individual cases, and refining the ideal type when necessary. In the chapter's final section, I illustrate the vitality of ideal types through two award-winning books, Peter Evans's *Embedded Autonomy* and Catherine Boone's *Political Topographies of the African State.*

I contend that comparative area studies can best achieve its goal to produce context-sensitive explanations by using ideal types. This approach forces researchers to distill causal claims into ideal-typical statements while also identifying contextual factors that influenced the outcome in a particular case. Using ideal types assists scholars wanting to elevate contextual considerations as fundamental features of cross-regional research. The approach I outline is not a slight deviation from conventional social science. Rather, it breaks with the logic undergirding large-N analyses and the majority of case study comparisons.

I wrote previously that researchers could fruitfully engage in comparative area studies by appealing to contextual circumstances as a case selection justification. I argued that the expectation that certain contextual conditions would give rise to analogous behavior by actors was a strong basis upon which to defend unconventional case comparisons (Saylor 2018). I stand by those claims but note that they are implicitly wedded to a neopositivist approach to social science. The Weberian method I outline in this chapter is consonant with an alternative philosophical tradition, sometimes referred to as analyticism (Jackson 2016). I believe this chapter provides practitioners an equally robust and epistemically distinctive way to engage in comparative area studies.

Case Studies, Causal Inference, and Causal Explanation

This section provides a brief overview of the social science landscape.[1] It sets the groundwork for understanding how ideal types are distinctive and why I believe they offer great promise for comparative area studies. I begin by reviewing the mainstream literature on case studies, which conceives of case studies as representations of a larger population of interest and tests of an empirical regularity. Today, scholars often refer to this goal as making a causal inference. I then contrast a causal inference to a causal explanation. Along the way, I describe why comparative area studies is in tension with the strictures for making a causal inference but is compatible with achieving causal explanation.

Causal Inference and the Mainstream Approach to Case Studies

In his authoritative study, John Gerring (2007, 211) defines a case study as the "intensive study of a single case for the purpose of understanding a larger class of similar units (a *population* of cases)." Alexander George and Andrew Bennett (2005, 17) describe "a case as an instance of a class of events." James Mahoney (2021, 61–64) writes that cases are a "substantive unit of analysis" pertinent to a particular "world," which he defines as "maximal, closed spatiotemporal domains."[2] Case studies exist in relation to broader population of interest.

The conventional wisdom holds that we use case studies to test a general hypothesized relationship within a population. But because case study research designs have a small number of observations, one must be careful when selecting cases. One should examine cases that are representative,

---

[1] This section draws on Saylor 2020.
[2] Worlds are populations, more or less.

avoid selection bias, and increase the N when possible (e.g., Geddes 1990; Gerring 2017, 18–21; King et al. 1994, 213–217). If case selection is done well, the researcher should be able to discern the causal effect of a variable of interest. For example, John Stuart Mill's method of difference pairs cases that are similar in many ways but differ on a key variable. Then the researcher can assess whether variation in that factor yielded different outcomes. The design is akin to estimating experimental treatment effects (Gerring 2012, 219–224; King et al. 1994, 81–82). Crucially, the insights gleaned from case studies are not idiosyncratic: they are usually understood to be representative of an association within a broader population (e.g., Lijphart 1971; Gerring 2007, 86–105, 115–50).

More precisely, case studies test an empirical regularity (e.g., Mahoney 2021, 97–105; Seawright 2016, 19–44). Sometimes scholars get caught up in distinguishing qualitative and quantitative methods based on whether they focus on the "causes of effects" (qualitative) or "effects of causes" (quantitative) (e.g., Mahoney and Goertz 2006, 230–232). Others, such as Gerring (2017, 12–13), Arend Lijphart (1971), and Jason Seawright (2016), stress the affinities between the two approaches. A point of unity among most qualitative and quantitative methods is that their research designs test empirical regularities. This disposition applies not just to classic Millian-style case comparisons, but also to research designs exploring necessary, sufficient, INUS, and SUIN conditions (Mahoney 2021, 97–100).[3] Today, researchers tend to call these endeavors the pursuit of causal inferences—the process of using data to scrutinize a theoretical relationship and evaluate whether it holds generally (Kratochwil 2007, 32; Waldner 2007, 150). The key point is that an empirical regularity provides the basis upon which to substantiate a causal inference (cf. Jackson 2016, 73–82). So when researchers use case studies to analyze a cross-case pattern and see how a case fits within that pattern, they are testing an empirical regularity.

Executing such tests with case studies is difficult because of the "small-N problem"—a situation of having few observations and many potential confounding variables (Campbell 1975; Lijphart 1971). One popular way to mitigate these pitfalls is to focus on causal mechanisms. Most researchers liken a causal mechanism to "the causal pathway, process or intermediate variable by which a causal factor of theoretical interest is thought to affect an

---

[3] These acronyms respectively refer to an insufficient but necessary part of a condition that is itself unnecessary but sufficient for an outcome (INUS) and a sufficient but unnecessary part of a condition that is itself an insufficient but necessary condition for an outcome (SUIN).

outcome" (Gerring 2008, 163). Identifying causal pathways arguably enables one to surmount many of the obstacles associated with the small-N problem by showing how one thing connects to another. Doing so suggests that the cross-case pattern is not a spurious correlation. Causal mechanisms can thereby help one achieve causal inference (Collier et al. 2004).

Another strategy to deal with the small-N problem is to encourage researchers to compare cases from within relatively homogeneous populations, because the greater the heterogeneity in a defined population of cases, the tougher it is "to make a causal inference, [and] the more tenuous that inference is" (Gerring 2007, 52). Studying a relatively homogeneous population is a qualitative analogue to employing control variables in multiple regression. There is a reasonable logic behind this guidance, but it imperils comparative area studies in myriad ways (Köllner et al. 2018, 18–20; von Soest and Stroh 2018, 76–78, 83). Things often differ across world regions, including culture, religion, colonial legacies, geopolitical context, and integration into the world economy. And if one wants to analyze a phenomenon that did not occur contemporaneously, one must grapple with variances in world historical timing, how the diffusion of new ideas might have influenced one's cases, and how actors in later historical eras might have learned from people with similar situations in earlier times. If the small-N problem bedevils conventional case study designs, it may well frustrate comparative area studies.

Finally, according to the conventional wisdom, these imperatives determine whether a research design is scientifically robust. For example, Elman, Gerring, and Mahoney (2016, 377) regard "case studies as tools of causal inference . . . [in contrast to] case studies whose goal is primarily descriptive or where there is no explicit and sustained causal argument." Similarly, George and Bennett (2005, 18–19) write that "'qualitative methods' is sometimes used to encompass both case studies carried out with a relatively positivist view of the philosophy of science and those implemented with a postmodern or interpretive view. We exclude postmodern narratives from our view of case studies . . . [and hew] to the traditional terminology" that excludes such epistemic approaches. These quotations demarcate two realms for case studies: one community where practitioners assess causality via neopositivist causal inference, and another where scholars engage in noncausal analysis. Yet as I describe in the next subsection, this contrast is a false dichotomy.

Causal Explanation Is Distinct from Causal Inference

Although the notions of inference and explanation are often conflated in our discourse, they are distinct. An inference is general, whereas an explanation is particular. An inference marshals data to demonstrate conformity to a hypothesis; it indicates the strength of a theoretical statement via reference to an empirical regularity. Alternatively, a causal explanation describes what happened and what caused that thing to happen in an individual case. It is also a statement about why one thing, and not another, happened (Jackson 2017). To craft an explanation, one must go beyond observed correlations to focus on entities with capacities to bring about change and then describe how those entities exacted change in a specific instance. A key part of an explanation is a statement about manipulability: an understanding of how a purported cause changed something and thereby produced its alleged effect (Jackson 2017; Little 1998, 205–208; Woodward 2003, 9–12).

A good explanation has three ingredients. First, one must describe the factors that were present and jointly responsible for generating a particular outcome (Little 1998, 198–201; Miller 1987, 86–98). This endeavor commonly includes reference to causal mechanisms, which explicate how and why a cause generated its effect (Gerring 2007, 161–164; Hedström and Ylikoski 2010). As I note above, scholars typically conceive of causal mechanisms as the pathway or intervening variable between a cause and effect. Yet there is an alternative definition that lends itself to more easily fulfilling the requisites of a good explanation. David Waldner (2012, 75) defines a causal mechanism as "an agent or entity that has the capacity to alter its environment because it possesses an invariant property that, in specific contexts, transmits either a physical force or information that influences the behavior of other agents or entities." An invariant causal mechanism captures "the fundamental nature of a phenomenon" and remains "unchanged under some transformation" (Waldner 2016, 30, 29). Harnessing the notion of invariance as a core feature of causal mechanisms helps one to construct a compelling explanation. Because the mechanism linking a cause to its effect has an invariant property, it provides an unchanging and therefore persuasive theoretical account of how and why the one thing manipulates and changes the other.

Researchers illuminate these linkages through process tracing. Process tracing invokes a counterfactual notion of explanatory dependence: had X not occurred, then neither would have Y (at least due to X). Or, even if X had occurred, some countervailing force Z may have thwarted the realization of Y (Hedström and Swedberg 1998; Waldner 2007, 2012; see also Woodward 2003, 70–74). When researchers detail the factors jointly responsible for an outcome in a given instance, they are not testing an empirical regularity. They are constructing an explanation of an individual case (Jackson 2016, 162–163).

Second, good explanations must provide adequate causal depth. This imperative requires that one trace causes back to their roots, to avoid wrongfully attributing causality to a factor that is epiphenomenal of another factor (Miller 1987, 98–105). The burgeoning literature on process tracing suggests that good process tracing should not merely describe a sequence of seemingly causally related events. Rather, it should marshal evidence to demonstrate the generative links within a causal chain, in order to show how and why an outcome was bound to occur (e.g., Bennett and Checkel 2015, 6; Waldner 2012, 69; cf. Miller 1987, 98–102).

Third, an adequate explanation also hinges on competition with its rivals. An explanation need not take on a particular logical form. For an explanation to be convincing, one must establish its fitness through a direct comparison to alternative accounts, though such judgments are tentative and subject to change (Miller 1987; see also Hall 2003, 391–395). This comparative assessment centers on a given case-specific explanation, unlike judgments of competing causal inferences, which might be made on the basis of R-squared, predicted marginal effects, or a covariational pattern among cases. Crucially, one can build a compelling explanation without reference to an empirical regularity (Jackson 2017). For instance, I could conceivably explain the onset of the Russian Revolution (consistent with the desiderata I note in this subsection) even if I could not offer a nomothetic statement about the causes of revolution in general. The requirements for achieving causal explanation underscore that an explanation of a case is not simultaneously an inferential test of a cross-case pattern, let alone an "explanation" of such covariation (cf. Jackson 2016, 166–170).

The spirit of comparative area studies aligns well with pursuing causal explanations—more so than causal inferences.[4] For example, the seminal volume on comparative area studies rejects the idea that its practitioners are searching for "nomothetic generalizations" or "lawlike generalizations"

---

[4] Causal explanation and causal inference are not the only conceivable ways to engage in comparative area studies. Another possibility is comparative ethnography (e.g., Simmons and Smith 2019).

(Köllner et al. 2018, 15–16; Sil 2018, 236 n. 3, respectively). In addition, the entreaty to pay close attention to context prods comparative area studies researchers to plumb case study material deeper than they otherwise might. I expect this imperative increases their likelihood of uncovering the factors that were present and together responsible for a particular outcome. So too are comparative area studies practitioners encouraged to engage with area specialists, which expands the viewpoints to which they are subjected and probably assists them in crafting case-specific explanations (Sil 2018, 236). These activities are desirable for producing compelling causal explanations, but they are less central to making a causal inference. Overall, I believe there is an elective affinity between comparative area studies and causal explanation.

Ideal Types and Causal Explanation

This section describes what an ideal type is and how it can be useful for constructing causal explanations. Ideal types receive little explicit attention in methodological texts (Goertz 2006, 83 n. 7). They tend to be discussed with respect to concept formation, even though ideal types can also encapsulate causal claims (Burger 1987, 120, 254 n. 27). After I document the features of an ideal type, I briefly discuss how ideal types are incompatible with making a causal inference but can be harnessed to produce case-specific explanations. I conclude the section by highlighting how the process of employing ideal types has affinities with comparative area studies' desire to pay close attention to context.

What Ideal Types Are

An ideal type is an analytical depiction that reflects a researcher's value commitments and which can be used as a heuristic.[5] As scholars, we have subjective value commitments that inform and orient where we look to find objects of study (Jackson 2016, 156–158). Max Weber writes that "the quality of an event as a 'socio-economic' phenomenon is not something that is 'objectively' inherent in it. Instead, it is determined by the direction of

---

[5] I draw on Burger (1987, 154–155) and Jackson (2016, 156–158), who present similar expositions. I borrow the label "analytical depiction" from Jackson.

our cognitive *interest* resulting from the specific cultural significance that we . . . attach to the event" (Weber 2012, quotation from 108–109; also 116–117, 119; Weber 1949a, 63–64, 76, 80–81).[6] For example, some scholars are motivated to study regime dynamics because they believe democracy to be normatively important. Their choice to study democratization reflects a value commitment. Because subjectivity is an inherent feature of knowledge production, Weber (2012, 119; 1949a, 80) thinks it is "absurd" to believe that researchers can produce an objective set of social laws.

To Weber (2012, 114; 1949a, 72), social scientists pursue "a *science of reality*"—but not one of so-called objective reality. He says we "want to understand *the distinctive character* of the reality . . . in which we are placed and which surrounds us," as well as "the interrelation and the cultural *significance and importance* of its individual elements." The ascertainment of these things necessarily derives from our subjective value commitments. Weber maintains that we can best achieve an understanding of social reality through an ideal type, or analytical depiction. The substance of an ideal type comes from "a one-sided *accentuation* of *one* or a *number of* viewpoints and through the synthesis of a great many diffuse and discrete *individual* phenomena . . . into an internally consistent *mental* image. In its conceptual purity, this mental image cannot be found empirically anywhere in reality. It is a *utopia*" (Weber 2012, 125; 1949a, 90).

This idealized conception is not a straightforward reflection of "objective reality." It is a utopian image that may offer clarity to the researcher when used to scrutinize actual cases (Weber 2012, 128; 1949a, 95). Unfortunately, people sometimes mistakenly interpret the utopian accentuations encased within an ideal type to mean that an ideal type is a concept with few, if any, empirical referents (e.g., Goertz 2006, 83–84; Sartori 2009, 138). This characterization misunderstands how Weber conceives of ideal types. An ideal type deliberately oversimplifies and misrepresents the empirical world such that it could never have a direct referent, or extension, to an actual case (Jackson 2016, 158 n. 35). Instead, an ideal type is an ideational construct that directs our attention in certain ways. It may be useful as a heuristic when applied to individual cases,

---

[6] Weber's most important statement on ideal types is the "Objectivity" essay published in 1904. I quote from the Bruun translation (Weber 2012) but also cite the better-known Shils and Finch version (Weber 1949a) for the reader's convenience. Jackson (2016, 159–160, 160 nn. 38 and 39) and Swedberg (2018, 183, 192 n. 5) find the 1949 translation to be wanting.

The analytical depiction also contains an idealized statement about how humans behave in certain situations. For instance, one might idealize humans as rational actors with complete information and who act deliberately and infallibly—even though such expectations are plain oversimplifications (Swedberg 2018, 187–188; Weber 1978, 20–22). Such behavioral assumptions are analogous to an invariant causal mechanism because they theorize how and why people respond to certain stimuli in specific and foreseeable ways (cf. Waldner 2016). Like the utopian image derived from many individual events, these avowedly "non-factual notions" of human behavior enable one to have "a more tractable account of an object or a process" (Jackson 2016, 155). They can be useful for developing what Weber (1978, 8) referred to as explanatory understanding, whereby a researcher seeks to comprehend an actor's behavior "in an intelligible and more inclusive context of meaning."[7] This emphatic understanding can help one craft an explanation.

Once it is built, a researcher should use the ideal type as a heuristic and juxtapose it to actual cases: "The task of the *historian* then becomes that of establishing, in each *individual case*, how close reality is to, or how distant it is from, that ideal image" (Weber 2012, 125; 1949a, 90). The comparison of the ideal type to a case may result in a case-specific explanation, as the researcher gauges the extent to which the ideal-typical claims, as well as things not encapsulated within the ideal type, influenced the outcome in a particular case (Weber 1949b, 174–177; Aronovitch 2012; Jackson 2016, 156–164). The confrontation between the analytical depiction and an individual case is the main benefit of using an ideal type (Swedberg 2018, 184, 188–189). An ideal type is not an end, but rather a means to better understand the social world (Weber 2012, 126–127, 129; 1949a, 92–93, 97). It is a device for constructing case-specific explanations. Overall, an ideal type emanates from a researcher's value commitments, provides an analytical depiction, and serves a heuristic function.

Using an ideal type to explain an individual case differs fundamentally from how most case study research is conducted. Standard case study research falls under what Patrick Thaddeus Jackson (2016) refers to as neopositivism, whereas Weberian ideal types are part of the "analyticism" tradition. Jackson distills these differences into whether practitioners believe

---

[7] For more on explanatory understanding (*erklärendes Verstehen*) and the context of meaning (*Sinnzusammenhang*), begin with Talcott Parsons's note in Weber 1978, 58 n. 8; Bruun 2016, 44–46; and Ahmed 2022.

in what he calls mind-world dualism or monism. Mind-world dualism presumes that there exists an objective empirical world independent of researchers' minds. Scholars are charged with discovering that world, chiefly by developing theoretical propositions and demonstrating empirical correspondence to them. This assumption is a cornerstone of standard social science (Jackson 2016, 58–82). By contrast, mind-world monism wagers that researchers cannot be extricated from the social world of which they are part. We learn about the social world by studying what we believe to be important, and those underlying value commitments come from our subjective understandings and are inextricable from knowledge production. Weber's (2012, 114; 1949a, 72) quotation earlier about the goal of social science being the pursuit of understanding the world "in which we are placed and which surrounds us" reveals that he was a monist. In sum, standard neopositivist case study research and the Weberian approach I describe emanate from opposed philosophical premises about the nature of social science.

Ideal Types Can Produce Context-Sensitive Explanations

In this subsection, I describe how ideal types are well suited to producing causal explanations but are not compatible with making causal inferences. The pursuit of causal inferences is bound together with advancing nomothetic generalizations and stems from a logic of inquiry entirely different from what Weber envisioned. Weber believed that social scientists wanted to explain individual cases, not develop laws (Weber 2012, 124–129, 131–133; 1949a, 89–97, 101–104; Swedberg 2018, 183; Jackson 2016, 159–167). He did not think that researchers could develop valid laws because the scientific process was bound together with value judgments (Weber 2012, 108–124; 1949a, 63–89). Thus, when one makes an ideal-typical claim, one does not purport to have discovered a nomothetic generalization or even imply that one exists (Aronovitch 2012, 359–360; Jackson 2016, 168). Instead, one proposes how certain factors combine to produce an outcome in some idealized world (Burger 1987, 133–134).[8] Remember: an ideal type "*is not* a *depiction* of reality. . . . It is a *utopia*" (Weber 2012, 125; 1949a, 90). Yet when one

---

[8] Weber (2012, 132; 1949a, 102–103) recognized that it is tricky to make ideal-typical causal claims because one is "almost irresistibly tempted" to present them as law-like statements that cohere to one's empirical knowledge.

makes a causal inference, one implicitly or explicitly references a nomothetic generalization and maintains to have discovered something objectively valid.

Weber likewise objected to the idea that case studies are tests of an empirical regularity. He notes that even if one were to use case studies to test a nomothetic generalization, it does not mean that the general factors that allegedly account for the cross-case pattern were responsible for the outcome in an individual case (Weber 2012, 118; 1949a, 79). To make that determination, one needs to construct an explanation, not merely show inferential consistency with an empirical regularity. Similarly, Weber laments that factors extraneous to a nomothetic generalization are often shunned and treated as "residue" (Weber 2012, 114; 1949a, 72–73). Jackson (2016, 160–161) notes that Weber was reacting to the probabilistic logic championed by Mill and which today underpins regression analysis and causal inference more generally. In rejecting the objective validity of nomothetic generalizations and case studies as tests of them, Weber's approach clashes with the prevailing view of what case studies accomplish.

By contrast, an ideal type is poised to fulfill the requisites of a good explanation. Recall that an explanation has three parts: a description of the factors present and together responsible for generating an outcome; adequate causal depth; and a competition among rival accounts. An ideal type presents a "hypothetical configuration of events." This mental image is like what we commonly refer to as a hypothesis (Burger 1987, 160–161). One might think of an analytical depiction as a general causal claim, which posits a relationship between a cause and an effect, as well as the reasons why the cause should produce its effect (which Jackson 2017 refers to as the manipulability criterion). Such a claim includes expectations for how and why people behave in certain situations. For instance, an ideal-typical statement regarding the economic realm typically presumes that people epitomize homo economicus (Weber 1978, 20). These assumptions can be useful for comparison and to ascertain an actor's subjective motives—and thereby promote explanatory understanding. Such understanding "takes the form of an interpretation establishing causal knowledge" (Burger 1987, 112). In this way, an ideal type can include causal claims about how and why one thing manipulates and changes another.

Ideal-typical claims are also useful for constructing explanations because of the heuristic process Weber envisioned. (I describe this heuristic process more in the following section.) The researcher can apply a general causal claim to a case and assess how well it accounts for the outcome in that case, while simultaneously weighing how case-specific factors extraneous to the ideal type influenced the particular outcome (Jackson 2017, 701–708). For example, Weber knew that homo economicus suffers from what we today call bounded rationality: "The ideal types of social action which for instance are used in economic theory are thus unrealistic or abstract in that they always ask what course of action would take place if it were purely rational and oriented to economic ends alone. This construction can be used to aid in the understanding of action not purely economically determined but which involves deviations arising from" extra-economic factors (Weber 1978, 21; also Swedberg 2018, 187–188). In this example, one can compare the ideal-typical statements about the economic realm to the facts of an individual case. One appraises how the ideal-typical claims combined with extra-economic factors to arrive at a description of the factors present and jointly responsible for the case-specific outcome.[9]

An ideal type directs our attention to certain things while the heuristic process demands that one simultaneously weigh factors that are not accentuated by the ideal type. This procedure coheres with comparative area studies' desire to stress contextual factors when undertaking causal analysis: "What distinguishes (comparative area studies) is the idea that the context conditions across two or more regions—and of countries and locales within those regions—may encompass similarities and differences that affect the operation of more general causal processes and mechanisms" (Köllner et al. 2018, 16). Ideal types force us to analyze context—rather than treating it as a residual—and therefore help us to make contextualized comparisons. There is a plain affinity between using ideal types and achieving the contextually sensitive insights sought by advocates of comparative area studies.

Guidance for Building and Using Ideal Types

This section provides guidance on how to build and use ideal types. These steps come after one's value commitments have oriented them to an object of study. Weber did not provide much guidance on how to construct ideal

---

[9] It is important to underscore that if one uses an ideal type to construct explanations of multiple cases, one has not produced a generalization akin to an empirical regularity. Rather, one has demonstrated that the ideal type is useful as an analytically general claim—which itself is no small feat but which is philosophically distinct from an empirical generalization in the neopositivist sense (Jackson 2016, 168).

88 ADVANCING COMPARATIVE AREA STUDIES

types, which may account for why scholars have typically used them for concept formation, rather than as tools for explanation.[10] I describe four steps for building and using an ideal type: (1) inductively generating a universal statement about the phenomenon under investigation; (2) hypothesizing a cause-effect sequence; (3) heuristically comparing the ideal type to individual cases; and (4) adjusting the ideal type as necessary.

Step 1: Induction

Induction is the first step to form an ideal type. You begin by searching for the characteristics of the phenomenon you wish to better understand (Burger 1987, 124). The researcher gathers a variety of information that may be used later to form the ideal type (Weber 2012, 125; 1949a, 90). This process is grasped most easily when thinking about an ideal-typical concept, such as modern bureaucracy. To determine the features of a modern bureaucracy, Weber studied a variety of administrative forms across time and space. He settled on an ideal-typical definition that included attributes such as meritocratic recruitment, a clear hierarchy, and fixed salaries. This concept could be applied to historical instances that seem relatable to it, such as nineteenth-century Prussia, but not to cases that were obviously dissimilar, such as historical kingdoms in Africa (Weber 1978, 223–226, 969). Weber believed that researchers could inductively generate idealized abstractions, which would direct our attention when examining an individual case and possibly render that case comprehensible (Burger 1987, 139, 160; Weber 2012, 125, 127, 129; 1949a, 90–91, 93, 97).

In addition to constructing ideal types to delineate concepts, Weber (2012, 131; 1949a, 101) noted that they can be used to make causal claims: "*Developments*, too, may be constructed as ideal types." These ideal types are "summary statements about the recurrent occurrence of particular cause-effect sequences" (Burger 1987, 133). They strive to give an account of what "approximately or partly happens in a number of cases" (Burger 1987, 175; also Weber 2012, 132; 1949a, 102). For example, in *The Protestant Ethic and the Spirit of Capitalism*, Weber (1930) makes an ideal-typical declaration about how a Calvinist ethos gave rise to modern capitalism (Swedberg

---

[10] The best guidance on building ideal types that I have found is Burger (1987, 160–167), Jackson (2016, 154–166), and Swedberg (2018).

2018).[11] Just as when one examines many cases to discern the features of a modern bureaucracy, one can inspect cases to inform the creation of an ideal-typical causal claim.

This inductive research should be moderated by pragmatism. At the start of a comparative area studies project, one cannot realistically excavate numerous cases, though one should engage in some case-specific scrutiny. I believe a more practical way to initially develop a causal claim is to couple research on individual cases with a survey of the region-specific conventional wisdoms on one's topic. This recommendation is an obvious starting point. It fits with Weber's entreaty for induction because one is indirectly appraising what others have learned from cases they know well, particularly from area specialists, whose work tends to be more inductive (Sil 2018, 228–231). One can glean much without exhaustively analyzing many cases on their own. Then the orthodox beliefs of scholars working on different regions can be compared for points of convergence and divergence. These comparisons may spark new syntheses and culminate in an idealized "universal statement," which is akin to basic assumptions about the causal process under investigation (Burger 1987, 160–161). For example, one might begin with Dan Slater's (2010, 5, 12, 34, 276) thesis about institutional development in Southeast Asia—that contentious politics and elite collective action determine institutional outcomes—and compare it to studies on state formation in early modern Europe (as he does on 278–282). Such comparisons, coupled with a review of individual cases, can help form the contours of an ideal type.

Step 2: Hypothesize

The second step is to hypothesize, or to form what Jackson (2016, 157) calls the analytical depiction. Based on the information one gathers from examining cases and conventional wisdoms, one can hypothesize a cause-effect sequence. For example: shifting balances of political power cause institutional change (e.g., Knight 1992, 126–139). Such an ideal-typical claim synthesizes and approximates "a number of individual explanatory accounts" known to the scholar, but it does not purport to be a nomothetic

---

[11] Weber's thesis is ideal-typical because he directs our attention to the religious dimensions of the rise of capitalism while acknowledging that he deliberately undervalues relevant material factors (Weber 1930, 27, 183).

90 ADVANCING COMPARATIVE AREA STUDIES

generalization (Burger 1987, 173). Weber (1921, 131) writes, "Those interpretive schemas [i.e., ideal types] . . . are not *only* 'hypotheses' in analogy to the hypothetical 'laws' of natural science. When concrete processes are heuristically interpreted, they can *function* as hypotheses. But in contrast to the hypotheses of the natural sciences the insight that in a concrete instance they do *not* contain a valid interpretation does not affect their usefulness for the establishment of knowledge."[12] Put differently, the cause-effect claim is simply a "*theoretical* accentuation of certain elements of reality" to direct our attention when examining cases (Weber 2012, 124; 1949a, 90; also Jackson 2016, 156).

The second component of a cause-effect sequence is an idealized statement about how people behave in certain situations. The statement conjectures or imputes reasons why people act as they do, so that "the effect of the social action it [the ideal type] describes is clearly linked to the motivation of the actor" (Swedberg 2018, 188; see also Aronovitch 2012, 362; Burger 1987, 161). This postulation offers what we today think of as the microfoundational mechanisms that connect larger-scale developments (Hedström and Swedberg 1998). For instance, the claim that a shifting balance of political power causes institutional change depends on the actors involved seeking to attain distributive political advantage and doing so in instrumentally rational ways. Weber (1978, 20) wanted to achieve "adequacy on the level of meaning" in terms of why people do what they do and how their actions bring about specific results. This notion of "causal adequacy" means that "if the typical actor carries out some action, it should lead to the sought effect in a probable and decisive way" (Swedberg 2018, 188; also Weber 2012, 118, 127; 1949a, 80, 93). These idealized statements articulate why a cause induces people to act in certain ways.

Weber's perspective on causal adequacy indicates the benefits from conceiving of causal mechanisms as having invariant properties. If causal mechanisms possess invariant properties, they theorize unalterable reasons how and why a cause manipulates something and spawns its purported effect. In the example above, political change connects to institutional change by way of actors' quest for distributive political advantage. The desire for distributive advantage is an invariant mechanism; one cannot alter its features without connoting something different (Saylor 2020, 1000). Consequently,

---

[12] Quoted in and translated by Burger (1987, 254 n. 31). Burger (1987, 140) notes that ideal types are sometimes like what we think of as a hypothesis; other times, they help us to find a hypothesis.

the invariance at the core of the mechanism facilitates Weber's goal that ideal types describe "the highest possible degree of logical integration by virtue of their complete adequacy on the level of meaning" (Weber 1978, 20). An unchanging mechanism forms part of a compelling cause-effect sequence. The claim exposits what Weber calls objectively possible causal connections, which can then be used as "an *instrument* of inquiry" (Weber 2012, 118–119; 1949a, 80; also Burger 1987, 139). Note what Weber is saying: He argues that an ideal-typical causal claim—in which actors behave in unfailingly predictable ways—is not a description of a valid scientific law; instead, it is useful as a heuristic.

To me, this formulation is preferable to conceiving of a causal mechanism as a causal pathway or intervening variable. In the mechanism-as-intervening-variable conception, one cannot supply unchanging reasons why a cause generates an effect, because a variable is alterable by definition. Thus the mechanism-as-pathway simply shows that a cause and effect are conditionally independent and connected by the presence of an intervening variable (the "mechanism"). The sequential association nonetheless remains a correlational association (Jackson 2017, 703). This shortcoming makes the associated causal claim less penetrating, especially when one attempts to theorize the "subjective meaning attributed to the hypothetical actor or actors in a given type of action" (Weber 1978, 4). The claim is comparatively opaque and therefore less useful as a heuristic.[13] To fulfill Weber's goal to achieve adequacy on the level of meaning, the idealized statement about human behavior ought to reference an invariant mechanism.

The final part of the analytical depiction is a description of the conditions under which one expects the general causal claim to occur. We often call such outlines boundary (or scope) conditions. But whereas mainstream social science uses boundary conditions to assert unit homogeneity (cf. Mahoney and Goertz 2004, 660–662; Falleti and Lynch 2009), ideal-typical theorizing makes no such declaration. An ideal type "brings together certain relationships . . . to form an internally consistent cosmos of *imagined* interrelations." This theoretical accentuation seeks to highlight causally relevant factors in certain types of cases, even though those factors would be "more present in one place, fewer in another, and occasionally completely absent" when compared to actual cases (Weber 2012, 124–125; 1949a, 90–92). When one

---

[13] Weber (2012, 128; 1949a, 95) mentions clarity as a criterion to determine if an ideal type is useful.

92 ADVANCING COMPARATIVE AREA STUDIES

describes the circumstances in which a cause-effect sequence might prevail, one implies cases that seem pertinent to the ideal type, all the while knowing that the ideal type will, at best, only approximate the empirical facts in any individual case (Burger 1987, 125, 159). Nevertheless, the circumstances pertinent to the ideal type suggest cases that may be relatable to it and thereby offers guidance for case selection.

Step 3: The Heuristic Process

The third step in building and using ideal types is Weber's heuristic process. Unfortunately, Weber provided little guidance for this procedure (Swedberg 2018, 189). The description of the circumstances surrounding an ideal-typical claim offers clues about what cases are relatable to it and appropriate for scrutiny (cf. Burger 1987, 158–159). When selecting cases for in-depth analysis, the researcher makes subjective judgments about their relatability to the ideal type. These judgments are tentative, because the ideal type may turn out not to be useful for explaining a specific case.[14] And these judgments are made without reference to other cases. Unlike standard case selection protocols, a case selected for examination need not share particular characteristics with other cases under investigation nor an empirical regularity with them. Instead, the criterion of seeming relatability is a sufficient basis for case selection. Consequently, researchers are freed from the methodological strictures that often inhibit the sorts of unconventional comparisons that comparative area studies practitioners want to make (Saylor 2020, 1003–1005). Case selection under Weberian auspices can buttress comparative area studies' research designs.

Once a researcher selects a case for analysis, they compare it to the ideal type. The researcher considers whether the factors that are part of the general causal claim (the so-called adequate causes) led to the outcome in the particular case. Weber (2012, 137; 1949a, 110) writes that the "distinctive character of the points of view that are relevant in each case can only be clearly brought out by means of concepts formulated as ideal types, and by *confronting* the empirical material with the ideal type." Weber (2012, 127;

---

[14] Weber argues that we can never know in advance if an ideal type will be useful for explaining an individual case or even if an ideal type will be useful in general: "it is never possible to determine in advance *whether* [such constructive efforts] are mere fantasies or whether they constitute scientifically fruitful concept formation... the only standard is whether [the ideal type] is useful for acquiring knowledge" (Weber 2012, 126; 1949a, 92).

1949a, 93) regarded an ideal type as a "*limiting* concept against which reality is *measured*—with which it is *compared*."

Other factors that are not part of the ideal type may have affected the outcome too. Weber calls these things the coincidental causes (Jackson 2016, 162–163). Thinking through coincidental causes affords one the opportunity to evaluate how context, human subjectivity, and agency caused people to deviate from the idealized expectations described in the ideal type (Aronovitch 2012, 358–359, 365; also Burger 1987, 170–175). For instance, in Weber's discussion of homo economicus, he says that the comparison of an ideal type to a case sensitizes us to context: "by throwing the discrepancy between the actual course of events and the ideal type into relief, the analysis of the non-economic motives actually involved is facilitated" (Weber 1978, 21). By using an ideal type to uncover the adequate causes and then identifying coincidental causes by doing what Charles Tilly and Robert Goodin (2006, 25) refer to as "correcting for context," a researcher can arrive at a singular, case-specific explanation (Jackson 2016, 156–166). Whether that explanation is deemed good ultimately rests upon the judgment of the analyst and their interlocutors in a specific research area (Jackson 2016, 164–165; cf. Miller 1987, 89–98).

This heuristic process places a lot of weight on contextual factors for constructing a robust and compelling explanation. This emphasis is consistent with comparative area studies' sensitivity toward "highly localized contextual attributes" and its desire to get "a better grasp of the challenges involved in interpreting actors' choices and understandings across diverse contexts" (Köllner et al. 2018, 15). This viewpoint clashes, however, with how context is understood in leading methodological texts. Tulia Falleti and Julia Lynch's seminal article defines context "broadly, as the relevant aspects of a setting (analytical, temporal, spatial, or institutional) in which a set of initial conditions leads (probabilistically) to an outcome." Context is akin to "variables that reside 'outside' the theory but nevertheless affect the operation of the causal mechanism" and observed outcomes. Dissimilar contexts are marked by different empirical regularities (Falleti and Lynch 2009, quotations from 1152, 1145, respectively).

Falleti and Lynch's form of contextual delineation essentially distills context into variables, which can then be used to test a nomothetic generalization (cf. Jackson 2016, 119). The approach is not attuned to helping researchers grasp actors' subjective understandings and motivations. By contrast, Weber's method to produce case-specific explanations obviates the

94 ADVANCING COMPARATIVE AREA STUDIES

need to do what Falleti and Lynch propose. He also thought their aim would be impossible to achieve, because ideal types "are theoretical constructions whose relationship to the empirical reality of the immediately given is in each individual case problematical" (Weber 2012, 133; 1949a, 103). Attempts to distill context into a bundle of variables would be fruitless. My basic point is that Weber's heuristic process is not a tired plea for researchers to take context seriously. It is more thoroughgoing and epistemically distinctive.

Step 4: Adjust the Ideal Type, If Necessary

The final step is to potentially adjust your ideal type after confronting it with facts from individual cases. Ideal types are always "provisional" (Aronovitch 2012, 361; also Jackson 2016, 155; Swedberg 2018, 188). Weber (2012, 132; 1949a, 102) maintains that "if the ideal type was *ideally* constructed from a heuristic point of view . . . *then* it will also guide research in a direction that leads to a more precise understanding of what was distinctive and historically important about the elements of" the phenomenon under investigation. "*If* it leads to this result, [the ideal type] has achieved its logical purpose precisely *by demonstrating* its own *un*real character. In that case, it has tested a hypothesis." The revelations from these confrontations may prompt the analyst to refine the ideal type. Such calibration can lead to a clearer—and therefore better and more useful—ideal type (Weber 2012, 128; 1949a, 95). Usefulness is the ultimate criterion for judging an ideal type (Jackson 2016, 159).[15]

Using ideal types could be a boon to comparative area studies. Although Köllner et al. (2018) are undogmatic about the epistemic and methodological form of comparative area studies, I believe the initiative's spirit is best fulfilled through a Weberian approach. Ideal-typical theorizing begins with induction, and comparative area studies places great value on area specialists' inductive knowledge. Ideal types develop general causal claims but

---

[15] This process of adjustment is not unending, however (Swedberg 2018, 184). One might be tempted to think of this iterative procedure as analogous to Lakatos's (1970) idea that scholars protect the hard core of a research program by adding auxiliary hypotheses to it. But it is not. For one thing, Weber (2012, 125–126; 1949a, 90–91) expected that multiple ideal types could be usefully applied to the same phenomenon, unlike the Lakatosian view that a dominant research program with a single hard core would prevail. Jackson (2016, 159 n. 37) discusses how Weber's and Lakatos's approaches are "worlds apart" in terms of their philosophical assumptions.

reject the objective validity of nomothetic generalizations. Similarly, comparative area studies presents itself as an alternative to nomothetic theorizing but nonetheless believes in the possibility of general insights. Ideal types employ a heuristic process to consider how theorized factors (the adequate causes) combine with case-specific factors (the coincidental causes) in order to explain outcomes in individual cases. Likewise, comparative area studies insist on contextual sensitivity as a way to prevent general claims from being stretched inapplicably or running roughshod over important idiosyncratic factors in specific cases. I find a plain affinity between Weberian ideal types and the contours of the comparative area studies project.

Weberian Ideal Types in Action

This section highlights two books that demonstrate the vitality of ideal-typical causal claims: Peter Evans's *Embedded Autonomy* and Catherine Boone's *Political Topographies of the African State*. Both of them are award winners.[16] Evans's work analyzes cases across regions, much as a comparative area studies practitioner might design a research project. Boone examines areas within West African countries, thereby suggesting the feasibility of using ideal types for subnational comparative area studies research (cf. Smith 2018).

Peter Evans's *Embedded Autonomy: States and Industrial Transformation*

Evans's (1995) *Embedded Autonomy* is a landmark study of how states can promote industrial transformation. In brief, he argues that recent developmental successes have exhibited embedded autonomy, a concept that refers to rationalized bureaucracies insulated from political pressure (autonomy) but which retain close ties to social actors intent on economic transformation (embeddedness). Evans rebukes what he calls the neo-utilitarian

---

[16] Evans (1995) won awards from two organized sections of the American Sociological Association. Boone (2003) received the Mattei Dogan Book Award from the Society for Comparative Research.

96   ADVANCING COMPARATIVE AREA STUDIES

approach to bureaucracy, the belief that bureaucrats are prone to rent-seeking. To mitigate rent-seeking and facilitate economic activity, neo-utilitarians advocate that states remain small. Evans challenges this world-view by using a Weberian method and cross-regional research design. His empirical analysis centers on Brazil, India, South Korea, and Zaire (contemporary Democratic Republic of the Congo), with briefer treatment of Austria, Taiwan, and the Indian state of Kerala. The book includes detailed analyses of the information technology industries in Brazil, India, and South Korea as illustration of their developmental trajectories more generally.

To render these cases intelligible, Evans develops a typology of states: from the poles of the deleterious "predatory state" that undermines an economy to the laudable "developmental state" that enables industrial transformation. Evans presents the concepts as ideal types (12, 44–45, 64, 248). A variety of "intermediate states" lie in between. The polar types contribute to a general causal claim: "If the two ideal types consisted only in attaching appropriate labels to divergent outcomes, they would not get us very far. The trick is to establish a connection between developmental impact and the structural characteristics of states—their international organization and relation to society" (12). Evans also hypothesizes about bureaucrats' behavior, which links states to economic outcomes. He doubts that bureaucrats behave as neo-utilitarians expect, because if they did, a state would have trouble accomplishing even rudimentary tasks. Evans suspects that bureaucrats perceive themselves as working together toward collective goals (22–32). Consistent with the Weberian procedure, Evans presents a hypothesis linking a cause to an effect and buttresses his thesis with idealized conjectures about how and why bureaucrats behave as they do.

Evans believes that his comparative institutional approach has "great heuristic promise" (22). But he does not expect correspondence between his polar types and case studies. Individual cases will, at best, approximate the ideal type (12, 64). Evans knows that "analytic generalizations must be grounded in the analysis of specific historical evidence" (42). Evans thinks ideal-typical theorizing is useful because it "focuses attention" so that the comparison of "concrete historical cases offers opportunity for fresh attack on the conceptual issues confronted" in the general causal claim (44). In *Embedded Autonomy*, the heuristic process not only reveals the limits of the ideal-typical claim but also illuminates how state-society relations influenced individual cases: "The concept of embedded autonomy is useful because it concretizes the structural relations that lie behind the efficacy of the ideal typical developmental state. . . . but it also [leads] to a sharper focus on state-society relations" than might have otherwise happened (249; also 42).

Evans's exploration of the Zairian case, for example, reveals the shortcomings of the neo-utilitarian perspective. Whereas neo-utilitarians argue that the growth of states promotes rent-seeking and other pathologies, Evans shows that these things flourish not in a mature, bloated state but in an inchoate one: Zaire "embodies the neo-utilitarian nightmare of a state in which all incumbents are out for themselves" (45; also 47, 248). Zaire lacked both bureaucratic autonomy and any semblance of connectedness to society. At the other end of the continuum, South Korea and Taiwan featured an extraordinarily close relationship between the state and nascent industrialists, something enabled by the countries' unusually comprehensive land reform programs in prior decades. Evans concludes that the embedded autonomy he discovered was a "peculiarly effective amalgam in the developmental states in East Asia." Far from being a common occurrence, Evans notes that it emerged due to "a very unusual set of historical circumstances." Thus South Korea and Taiwan do not fit a broad cross-case pattern— "but this does not detract from the usefulness of the concept of embedded autonomy as an analytical point of reference" (quotations from 59; also 244).

Some people criticize Evans because his work does not fall neatly within standard neopositivist strictures. For instance, Alejandro Portes (1996, 176) maintains that, in addition to South Korea, Evans should have selected cases that had embeddedness or autonomy, but not both. This variation on the independent variables would have enabled a more straightforward test, Portes says. Similarly, William Form (1997, 189) contends that because Evans does not specify the factors that give rise to embeddedness, it makes his claims unfalsifiable and untestable. But as a Weberian, Evans is not trying to formulate or test a falsifiable hypothesis. Instead, he is building an analytical depiction and searching for cases that seem relatable to it, so that he can discern its usefulness.

The virtues of Evans's heuristic process are perhaps best demonstrated in India and Brazil. Evans finds that the "intermediate cases . . . help flesh out the picture of how different blends of autonomy and embeddedness can play themselves out against disparate societal backgrounds" (72; also 12, 64–65). In India, for instance, Evans adjusts for context and realizes that its "ethnic, religious, and regional divisions" compound the challenges to developing effective administration (67). In Brazil, "Reactionary rural elites were never dramatically swept from the stage as in the East Asian cases" (62). Contra Portes, Evans has a case that features embeddedness without autonomy. The Brazilian state is embedded in its society; it just so happens that it is embedded with landed elites who oppose industrial transformation and regard the state as a patronage tool. By confronting Weberian assumptions about bureaucracy with facts from the intermediate cases, Evans discovers that bureaucracies are not self-reinforcing organizations. They depend more on state-society relations, informal networks, and corporate cultures than Weber believed (70–73).

Evans produced a groundbreaking study by taking a thoroughly Weberian approach. Indeed, some of the ostensible criticism of his work indicates its success from a Weberian perspective. Erik Olin Wright (1996) contends that Evans's one-dimensional continuum ranging from predatory to developmental states could be better conceptualized in two-dimensional space (a 2 × 2 matrix). This presentation would allow one to see two other ideal types, which Wright calls the "Bourgeois Clientelist State" and the "Overdeveloped Post-Colonial State." Brazil is largely a bourgeois clientelist state, though India defies easy categorization. Wright's (1996, 178) alteration would enable one "to make subtle diagnoses of the reasons for state failures and partial successes." Wright uses Evans's ideal type as Weber would have hoped: "If the ideal type was '*ideally*' constructed from a heuristic point of view . . . *then* it will also guide research in a direction that leads to a more precise understanding of" the thing being studied (Weber 2012, 132; 1949a, 102).

Catherine Boone's *Political Topographies of the African State: Territorial Authority and Institutional Choice*

Boone's (2003) *Political Topographies of the African State* examines state institutions at the subnational level in the West African countries of Côte d'Ivoire, Ghana, and Senegal. She emphasizes in each locality how the presence or absence of cash-crop production, communal structure (whether a rural social hierarchy exists), and class structure (whether rural elites have economic autonomy) influence the type of institutions that states try to build. The result is a framework of possible institutional outcomes, ranging from situations in which central government agents displace local leaders and impose their own authority ("usurpation") to ones in which states largely disregard localities ("non-incorporation"). Boone presents the institutional configurations and their associated causal claims as ideal types (38, 323, 331).

Boone's epistemic approach is plainly Weberian. She says her book "is a framework and a set of hypotheses for exploring differences in the political trajectories of rural Africa" (3) and that we "need [such] analytic frameworks" (7). Boone's goal is not "to place African trajectories in broader comparative context" (42).[17] She wants to "describe and explain" her cases (38, 40) by focusing on local context (13, 320–321). Boone indicates her Weberian disposition when she criticizes mainstream social science methods that "downplay or ignore" or "stumble over the inconvenient facts of institutional change (path switching) or failure" (12). Her criticism echoes Weber's (2012, 111–112; 1949a, 68–69) frustration with dogmatic thinkers of his time. Boone says her ideal type focuses our attention (324) and hopes it will be useful to explain her cases and for others to use (10).

Boone admits that her framework is a deliberate oversimplification but believes there is a "heuristic advantage of the more parsimonious model" (331). Its value is in the confrontation with case study evidence, to "make it possible to ask whether, and to what extent, social causes produce the expected political and institutional effects in these cases" (38). This heuristic process "places a special premium on a close reading of the internal political dramas of the nationalist era," when central rulers embarked on state building (40). Based on her deep knowledge of West Africa and the attendant scholarly literature, Boone believes "that specificities of local context go far in determining the actual effects of" institution-building efforts (320). Although factors extraneous to her model influence particular outcomes, Boone embraces the need to theorize, in order to "accumulate and amplify insights from research, to think about causality . . . and to make nonarbitrary assessments" (321).

Boone's case studies exemplify the Weberian strategy, especially when she encounters unexpected results. The northern Korhogo (aka Senoufo) region in Côte d'Ivoire featured a rural social hierarchy with an elite dependent on the state, conditions that should produce a "power-sharing" arrangement in which rural elites administer the local level. Early in colonial rule, the

---

[17] Locating Boone's cases within a cross-case pattern would imply that they are tests of a nomothetic generalization. At times Boone refers to her case studies as tests (8, 10, 240) and other times describes aspects of her work in neopositivist terms, but in my estimation these statements are merely semantic inconsistencies amid her overarching Weberian approach.

100   ADVANCING COMPARATIVE AREA STUDIES

French adopted this strategy and ruled indirectly through Senoufo chiefs (252–255). Over time, however, economic changes in the region reduced chieftain power. Meanwhile, the budding nationalist political party, Parti Démocratique de la Côte d'Ivoire (PDCI), was growing stronger. The French responded by pressuring Senoufo chiefs to oppose the PDCI. To counteract the state-chief alliance, the PDCI worked with local merchants to weaken the chiefs by dominating commercial circuits and credit access. As the PDCI solidified power across Côte d'Ivoire, the French changed course, reconciled with the PDCI, and assisted its usurpation strategy in northern Korhogo (255–262). Usurpation persisted after independence but proved unworkable because of its incompatibility with local conditions. By 1970, the PDCI switched paths and reverted to the power-sharing tactic (262–278). According to the ideal type, the usurpation interlude should not have occurred.

Boone's case study of the Senegal River Valley also defies expectations. Like northern Korhogo, the middle and upper parts of the valley featured path-switching (282–285, 301–314). The case of the lower delta portion of the river valley is even more intriguing. Boone's model anticipates "administrative occupation" because the delta lacked a rural social hierarchy; in actuality, Senegalese state officials pursued usurpation. They did so because the state was establishing government-run rice cooperatives in the area. The state-led process of agricultural commercialization forged the local social formation. The transformative delta project exhibited features more often seen in East Africa, such as the Ujamaa villagization program in Tanzania (286, 292, 298–301). Boone states that the delta case "turns out to be a theoretical anomaly" but focuses on the opportunity it creates: "It adds another cause-effect scenario to the original repertoire" (286; also 301, 314, 327, 331 n. 12). Thus when Paul Nugent (2005, 460) wonders how Boone's model would apply to East Africa, she has already provided some clues but recognizes that state-settlement patterns "would have to be incorporated into a more complete theory" of institutional development (Boone 2003, 327; also 314).

These anomalous cases are not tests that Boone's theory fails but instead show the value of considering things extraneous to the ideal type. Boone forthrightly states that "factors that are not fully theorized in this analysis seem to explain the regime's usurpationist drive" in northern Korhogo (244; see 268–269 for the case-specific factors). State officials employed a scheme that "has a trial-and-error dimension that closer inspection would reveal in most of the cases considered" in the book (245). Michael Schatzberg (2004, 547) judges that "like a master artisan, Boone never lets her theoretical tools overwhelm her analysis. She remains in command of her model and indicates when its predictions diverge from reality. . . . Boone has the skill and self-confidence to discuss those cases where aspects of her model fall short." In concluding her case studies, Boone says that government officials sometimes make mistakes or take risks that render their institution-building strategies incompatible with the local social structure (316–317). Like Weber, she highlights how human subjectivity and agency are inextricable from social processes. Boone ends her book by describing her claims as a provisional framework, which other scholars might improve on with an "inductive process of theory refinement or reformulation" (327; also 324). Like Evans, Boone illustrates the fitness of ideal types to help explain social phenomena.

Conclusion

The comparative area studies initiative has features that can secure it as a remarkable approach to social science. Practitioners strive to achieve insights from cases in different world regions while remaining attentive to local context. Yet as I describe, conventional social science pursues causal inferences and tends to distill contextual considerations into variables or something like them, because practitioners are ultimately trying to make nomothetic generalizations about a population of cases. Comparative area studies exist in tension with these strictures. Consequently, I do not think that comparative area studies should chase causal inferences.

The alternative I outline highlights the vitality of ideal types. Ideal types, by their design, demand that researchers articulate precise cause-effect sequences while paying close attention to context when analyzing cases. This epistemic approach moves beyond cross-case patterns and instead focuses on the construction of case-specific causal explanations. Using ideal types to explain individual cases is not a slight departure from standard social science. Rather, it is predicated upon an alternative logic of inquiry and knowledge production. The introductory and concluding chapters to the initial volume on comparative area studies present it as skeptical of nomothetic generalization, attuned to contextual nuance, and seeking explanatory insights. In my estimation, these goals are best met through the embrace of Weberian ideal types.

Bibliography

Ahmed, Amel. 2022. What Can We Learn from History? Competing Approaches to Historical Methodology and the Weberian Alternative of Reflexive Understanding. *Polity* 54 (4): 734–763.

Ahram, Ariel I., Patrick Köllner, and Rudra Sil, eds. 2018. *Comparative Area Studies: Methodological Rationales and Cross-Regional Applications*. New York: Oxford University Press.

Aronovitch, Hilliard. 2012. Interpreting Weber's Ideal-Types. *Philosophy of the Social Sciences* 42 (3): 356–369.

Bennett, Andrew, and Jeffrey Checkel. 2015. Process Tracing: From Philosophical Roots to Best Practices. In Andrew Bennett and Jeffrey Checkel, eds. *Process Tracing: From Metaphor to Analytic Tool*. Cambridge: Cambridge University Press, 3–37.

Boone, Catherine. 2003. *Political Topographies of the African State: Territorial Authority and Institutional Choice*. Cambridge: Cambridge University Press.

Bruun, Hans Henrik. 2016. Weber's Sociology—"verstehend" or "deutend"? *Max Weber Studies* 16 (1): 39–50.

Burger, Thomas. 1987. *Max Weber's Theory of Concept Formation: History, Laws and Ideal Types*. Expanded ed. Durham, NC: Duke University Press.

Campbell, Donald. 1975. Degrees of Freedom and the Case Study. *Comparative Political Studies* 8 (2): 178–193.

Collier, David, Henry Brady, and Jason Seawright. 2004. Critiques, Responses, and Trade-Offs: Drawing Together the Debate. In Henry Brady and David Collier, eds. *Rethinking Social Inquiry: Diverse Tools, Shared Standards*. Lanham, MD: Rowman and Littlefield, 195–227.

Elman, Colin, John Gerring, and James Mahoney. 2016. Case Study Research: Putting the Quant into the Qual. *Sociological Methods & Research* 45 (3): 375–391.

Evans, Peter. 1995. *Embedded Autonomy: States and Industrial Transformation*. Princeton, NJ: Princeton University Press.

Falleti, Tulia, and Julia Lynch. 2009. Context and Causal Mechanisms in Political Analysis. *Comparative Political Studies* 42 (9): 1143–1166.

Form, William. 1997. Review of *Embedded Autonomy: States and Industrial Transformation*, by Peter Evans. *Administrative Science Quarterly* 42 (1): 187–189.

Geddes, Barbara. 1990. How the Cases You Choose Affect the Answers You Get: Selection Bias in Comparative Politics. *Political Analysis* 2: 131–150.

George, Alexander, and Andrew Bennett. 2005. *Case Studies and Theory Development in the Social Sciences*. Cambridge, MA: MIT Press.

Gerring, John. 2007. *Case Study Research: Principles and Practices*. Cambridge: Cambridge University Press.

Gerring, John. 2008. The Mechanismic Worldview: Thinking Inside the Box. *British Journal of Political Science* 38 (1): 161–179.

Gerring, John. 2012. *Social Science Methodology: A Unified Framework*. Cambridge: Cambridge University Press.

Gerring, John. 2017. Qualitative Methods. *Annual Review of Political Science* 20: 15–36.

Goertz, Gary. 2006. *Social Science Concepts: A User's Guide*. Princeton, NJ: Princeton University Press.

Hall, Peter. 2003. Aligning Ontology and Methodology in Comparative Politics. In James Mahoney and Dietrich Rueschemeyer, eds. *Comparative Historical Analysis in the Social Sciences*. Cambridge: Cambridge University Press, 373–404.

Hedström, Peter, and Richard Swedberg. 1998. Social Mechanisms: An Introductory Essay. In Peter Hedström and Richard Swedberg, eds. *Social Mechanisms: An Analytical Approach to Social Theory.* Cambridge: Cambridge University Press, 1–31.

Hedström, Peter, and Petri Ylikoski. 2010. Causal Mechanisms in the Social Sciences. *Annual Review of Sociology* 36: 49–67.

Jackson, Patrick Thaddeus. 2016. *The Conduct of Inquiry in International Relations: Philosophy of Science and Its Implications for the Study of World Politics.* 2nd ed. New York: Routledge.

Jackson, Patrick Thaddeus. 2017. Causal Claims and Causal Explanation in International Studies. *Journal of International Relations and Development* 20 (4): 689–716.

King, Gary, Robert Keohane, and Sidney Verba. 1994. *Designing Social Inquiry: Scientific Inference in Qualitative Research.* Princeton, NJ: Princeton University Press.

Knight, Jack. 1992. *Institutions and Social Conflict.* Cambridge: Cambridge University Press.

Köllner, Patrick, Rudra Sil, and Ariel I. Ahram. 2018. Comparative Area Studies: What It Is, What It Can Do. In Ariel I. Ahram, Patrick Köllner, and Rudra Sil, eds. *Comparative Area Studies: Methodological Rationales and Cross-Regional Applications.* New York: Oxford University Press, 3–26.

Kratochwil, Friedrich. 2007. Evidence, Inference, and Truth as Problems of Theory Building in the Social Sciences. In Ned Lebow and Mark Lichbach, eds. *Theory and Evidence in Comparative Politics and International Relations.* New York: Palgrave Macmillan, 25–57.

Lakatos, Imre. 1970. Falsification and the Methodology of Scientific Research Programmes. In Imre Lakatos and Alan Musgrave, eds. *Criticism and the Growth of Knowledge.* Cambridge: Cambridge University Press, 91–196.

Lijphart, Arend. 1971. Comparative Politics and the Comparative Method. *American Political Science Review* 65 (3): 682–693.

Little, Daniel. 1998. *Microfoundations, Method, and Causation: On the Philosophy of the Social Sciences.* New Brunswick, NJ: Transaction Publishers.

Mahoney, James. 2021. *The Logic of Social Science.* Princeton, NJ: Princeton University Press.

Mahoney, James, and Gary Goertz. 2004. The Possibility Principle: Choosing Negative Cases in Comparative Research. *American Political Science Review* 98 (4): 653–669.

Mahoney, James, and Gary Goertz. 2006. A Tale of Two Cultures: Contrasting Quantitative and Qualitative Research. *Political Analysis* 14 (3): 227–249.

Miller, Richard. 1987. *Fact and Method: Explanation, Confirmation and Reality in the Natural and the Social Sciences.* Princeton, NJ: Princeton University Press.

Nugent, Paul. 2005. Review of *Political Topographies of the African State: Territorial Authority and Institutional Choice,* by Catherine Boone. *Africa: Journal of the International African Institute* 75 (3): 459–461.

Portes, Alejandro. 1996. Review of *Embedded Autonomy: States and Industrial Transformation,* by Peter Evans. *Contemporary Sociology* 25 (2): 175–176.

Sartori, Giovanni. 2009. Guidelines for Concept Analysis. In David Collier and John Gerring, eds. *Concepts and Method in Social Science: The Tradition of Giovanni Sartori.* London: Routledge, 97–150.

Saylor, Ryan. 2018. Gaining by Shedding Case Selection Strictures: Natural Resource Booms and Institution Building in Latin America and Africa. In Ariel I. Ahram, Patrick Köllner, and Rudra Sil, eds. *Comparative Area Studies: Methodological Rationales and Cross-Regional Applications.* New York: Oxford University Press, 185–203.

Saylor, Ryan. 2020. Why Causal Mechanisms and Process Tracing Should Alter Case Selection Guidance. *Sociological Methods & Research* 49 (4): 982–1017.

Schatzberg, Michael. 2004. Review of *Political Topographies of the African State: Territorial Authority and Institutional Choice,* by Catherine Boone. *International Journal of African Historical Studies* 37 (3): 546–548.

Seawright, Jason. 2016. *Multi-Method Social Science: Combining Qualitative and Quantitative Tools.* Cambridge: Cambridge University Press.

Sil, Rudra. 2018. Triangulating Area Studies, Not Just Methods: How Cross-Regional Comparison Aids Qualitative and Mixed-Method Research. In Ariel I. Ahram, Patrick Köllner, and Rudra Sil, eds. *Comparative Area Studies: Methodological Rationales and Cross-Regional Applications*. New York: Oxford University Press, 225–246.

Simmons, Erica, and Nicholas Rush Smith. 2019. The Case for Comparative Ethnography. *Comparative Politics* 51 (3): 341–359.

Slater, Dan. 2010. *Ordering Power: Contentious Politics and Authoritarian Leviathans in Southeast Asia*. Cambridge: Cambridge University Press.

Smith, Benjamin. 2018. Comparing Separatism Across Regions: Rebellious Legacies in Africa, Asia, and the Middle East. In Ariel I. Ahram, Patrick Köllner, and Rudra Sil, eds. *Comparative Area Studies: Methodological Rationales and Cross-Regional Applications*. New York: Oxford University Press, 168–184.

Swedberg, Richard. 2018. How to Use Max Weber's Ideal Type in Sociological Analysis. *Journal of Classical Sociology* 18 (3): 181–196.

Tilly, Charles, and Robert Goodin. 2006. It Depends. In Robert Goodin and Charles Tilly, eds. *The Oxford Handbook of Contextual Political Analysis*. Oxford: Oxford University Press, 3–32.

von Soest, Christian, and Alexander Stroh. 2018. Comparisons Across World Regions: Managing Conceptual, Methodological, and Practical Challenges. In Ariel I. Ahram, Patrick Köllner, and Rudra Sil, eds. *Comparative Area Studies: Methodological Rationales and Cross-Regional Applications*. New York: Oxford University Press, 66–84.

Waldner, David. 2007. Transforming Inferences into Explanations: Lessons from the Study of Mass Extinctions. In Ned Lebow and Mark Lichbach, eds. *Theory and Evidence in Comparative Politics and International Relations*. New York: Palgrave Macmillan, 145–175.

Waldner, David. 2012. Process Tracing and Causal Mechanisms. In Harold Kincaid, ed. *The Oxford Handbook of Philosophy of Social Science*. Oxford: Oxford University Press, 65–84.

Waldner, David. 2016. Invariant Causal Mechanisms. *Qualitative & Multi-Method Research* 14 (1–2): 28–34.

Weber, Max. 1921. *Gesammelte Aufsätze zur Wissenschaftslehre* [Collected Essays in the Logic of Science]. Tübingen: Mohr.

Weber, Max. 1930. *The Protestant Ethic and the Spirit of Capitalism*. London: Routledge.

Weber, Max. 1949a. "Objectivity" in Social Science and Social Policy. In Edward Shils and Henry Finch, eds. *The Methodology of the Social Sciences*. Glencoe, IL: Free Press, 49–112.

Weber, Max. 1949b. Critical Studies in the Logic of the Cultural Sciences. In Edward Shils and Henry Finch, eds. *The Methodology of the Social Sciences*. Glencoe, IL: Free Press, 113–188.

Weber, Max. 1978. *Economy and Society: An Outline of Interpretive Sociology*. Edited by Guenther Roth and Claus Wittich. Translated by Ephraim Fischoff et al. Berkeley: University of California Press.

Weber, Max. 2012. The "Objectivity" of Knowledge in Social Science and Social Policy. In Hans Henrik Bruun and Sam Whimster, eds. *Max Weber: Collected Methodological Writings*. Translated by Hans Henrik Bruun. London: Routledge, 100–138.

Woodward, James. 2003. *Making Things Happen: A Causal Theory of Explanation*. Oxford: Oxford University Press.

Wright, Erik Olin. 1996. Review of *Embedded Autonomy: States and Industrial Transformation*, by Peter Evans. *Contemporary Sociology* 25 (2): 176–179.

5

Advancing Theory Development in Comparative Area Studies

Practical Recommendations for Evaluating the Equifinality of Causal Mechanisms

Marissa Brookes and Jesse Dillon Savage

Introduction

Of the many great strengths of comparative area studies (CAS), perhaps the most remarkable is its ability to provide thick and thorough country-level knowledge in the tradition of classic area studies while also reaching broad conclusions about cause and effect that apply across two or more geographic regions. Examples of CAS range from classics like Dietrich Rueschemeyer, Evelyne Huber, and John Stephens's (1992) analysis of democratization in the advanced industrial countries, Latin America, and the Caribbean to more recent works like Dan Slater and Daniel Ziblatt's (2013) extension of Gregory Luebbert's (1991) Europe-focused *Liberalism, Fascism, or Social Democracy* to cases in Southeast Asia. "The common theme running through these efforts is a desire to uncover portable mechanisms and causal processes, but with due attention to the potential impact of context conditions present in specific historical, socio-cultural, institutional and geographic settings" (Köllner et al. 2018, 14). The case studies conducted by CAS scholars are thus especially valuable for the development of context-sensitive yet generalizable causal theories, given this unique combination of depth and breadth. This chapter argues, however, that CAS scholarship comes closer to reaching its full potential in theory development when it more systematically evaluates causal mechanisms across cases. Causal mechanisms are at the core of theory development, which requires the

Marissa Brookes and Jesse Dillon Savage, *Advancing Theory Development in Comparative Area Studies*. In: *Advancing Comparative Area Studies*. Edited by: Ariel I. Ahram, Patrick Köllner, and Rudra Sil, Oxford University Press. © Oxford University Press (2025). DOI: 10.1093/oso/9780197809365.003.0005

106 ADVANCING COMPARATIVE AREA STUDIES

researcher not only to identify a non-spurious correlation between explanatory variables and the dependent variable of interest but also to explicate *how* and *why* those explanatory variables cause the dependent variable. Although most CAS scholarship either explicitly or implicitly tests whether causal mechanisms are generalizable across cases in different regions, to date there is insufficient methodological guidance on how to interpret the similar or different causal mechanisms found in cross-regional case studies. Our goal therefore is to advance CAS by providing a procedure to guide researchers on how to think about generalizing causal mechanisms in a CAS framework. Doing so, we believe, contributes to understanding what role regions are playing in the causal process.

What does it mean to test for the generalizability of causal mechanisms? The simplest answer is that generalizing causal mechanisms means not only establishing a connection between one or more explanatory variables (X1) and the dependent variable (Y1) but also testing whether a specific set of mechanisms hypothesized to connect X1 to Y1 are in fact those that are actually present in each case featuring the same X1/Y1 relationship.[1] In other words, case studies should not only identify mechanisms that "tell a causal story" linking X1 to Y1; they should also help us understand whether or not those causal mechanisms can be generalized across the larger population of cases. It is generally understood that for this to happen, the researcher must (1) clearly specify in advance the causal mechanisms he or she expects to find linking X1 to Y1, (2) clearly specify alternative causal mechanisms—that is, different sets of processes through which X1 and Y1 were possibly linked instead (one or more competing hypotheses), and (3) use both within- and cross-case methods of qualitative analysis to evaluate these hypotheses about mechanisms in at least two case studies. Beyond these conventional steps, however, the methodology literature offers little in the way of concrete next steps when it comes to interpreting the results of such analyses. The lack of advice is in part due to widespread disagreement over what causal mechanisms are in the first place, as well as a lack of attention to the relationship of causal variables to the outcome of interest in terms of necessity and sufficiency.

John Gerring rightfully questions "whether failure to adequately test causal mechanisms should disqualify a study," and asks, "Is the empirical

---

[1] "X1" is used here as convenient shorthand to represent all relevant explanatory variables hypothesized by the researcher to cause the particular outcome of interest (Y1).

testing of causal mechanisms a necessary condition of causal assessment (as some writers aver)?" (2010, 1505). The answer, of course, is complicated. Causal assessment comes in many forms, and it would make little sense to expect every researcher to always test hypotheses about causal mechanisms in every study, let alone always demonstrate that mechanisms are generalizable across two or more regions. Nevertheless, explanations about processes, unlike those focused only on variables, afford us more external validity—one of the major selling points of CAS. As Slater and Ziblatt point out, "An argument that . . . fails to apprehend causal mechanisms in those cases where it seems to be confirmed, is less externally valid than one that explains dozens of cases or enjoys impressive verisimilitude on causal mechanisms" (2013, 1314). This chapter thus offers some recommendations for how to proceed in evaluating causal mechanisms in CAS. The approach we propose should be especially useful for CAS projects that expand on existing research agendas for which hypotheses about mechanisms have already been proposed.

Case Studies and Causal Mechanisms

Among social scientists there is widespread agreement that a "good social science theory should not merely predict a particular relationship between independent and dependent variables, but it should also explain how and why these factors are related to one another" (Lieberman 2005, 442). In other words, the purpose of a theory is not merely to suggest that there is a causal relationship between some explanatory variable or variables (X1) and the outcome of interest (Y1) but also to explain how and why X1 causes Y1. As Kenneth Waltz admonishes in his classic *Theory of International Politics*, "Associations never contain or conclusively suggest their own explanation" (2010, 4). Fully testing a theory therefore requires the researcher to test hypotheses about *how*, not just *whether*, X is causally related to Y. A good social science theory is thus developed through tests of hypotheses about causal mechanisms.

That said, there remains substantial disagreement over what a causal mechanism actually is, as evidenced by the fact that the methodology literature is teeming with definitions of causal mechanisms that are at odds with one another (Jacobs 2016; Gerring 2010, 1501). Although it became increasingly common in recent years to cite Alexander George and Andrew

108 ADVANCING COMPARATIVE AREA STUDIES

Bennett's definition of causal mechanisms as "ultimately unobservable phys-ical, social, or psychological processes through which agents with causal capacities operate, but only in specific contexts or conditions, to transfer energy, information, or matter to other entities" (2005, 137), even Ben-nett himself continued to grapple with his own definition over the years, updating it to account for James Woodward (2003)'s counterfactual logic and emphasis on invariance. "In this view, mechanisms are structures in the world that, unlike variables, we cannot turn on and off by interven-tions" (Bennett 2016, 35). David Waldner has long maintained that causal mechanisms are invariant, meaning they remain unchanged under some transformation, just as "the area of a surface remains unchanged if the surface is rotated in space (Waldner 2016, 29).

The invariance view lies in contrast to conceptualizations of causal mech-anisms as intervening variables, which hold that "mechanisms lie between X1 and Y in a causal chain . . . [and] variables in this chain can be seen as mechanisms for some research questions or as explanatory vari-ables for other questions" (Weller and Barnes 2014, 12). We argue that this mechanisms-as-variables view renders the term "mechanism" super-fluous and reduces within-case analysis to no more than the identification of different combinations of sequential, causally linked variables. Hence, agreeing with Waldner (2016), Bennett (2016), and Gary Goertz (2017, 40) that "the interpretation of M as an intervening variable is problem-atic," we view mechanisms instead as processes that do not operate apart from the independent variables that produce them and the outcomes that they create.[2] As Ryan Saylor emphasizes (this volume), invariance is a core feature of causal mechanisms. Our view of mechanisms as invariant

---

[2] One way to think about the definition of causal mechanisms used here is to imagine a causal diagram, X1 → Y1, where "X1" represents the explanatory variables, "Y1" represents the depen-dent variable, and the causal mechanism lies within "→" (the arrow). In contrast, those who treat causal mechanisms as intervening variables would represent the mechanism as "M1" in the follow-ing diagram: X1 → M1 → Y1. In the former case, the arrow can be thought of the way one considers combustion to be an invariant process that occurs given a specific interaction of causal variables. Waldner gives the example of combustion in an automobile: "To think of the mechanical parts of an engine as the causal mechanism is to exclude combustion from the causal explanation of how auto-mobiles work. . . . [T]he mechanical parts of an automobile are variables, and as variables, we can intervene to turn each variable to a new value. *Combustion, on the other hand, cannot be turned off; it is an exothermic chemical reaction that occurs under proper conditions.* Each of those conditions—heat, oxygen, and a fuel—can be turned on or off, just as any random variable in a causal graph can be turned on or off. But if heat, oxygen, and a fuel are all present, combustion occurs. One cannot throw a lit match into a pool of gasoline in the presence of oxygen and the absence of any other flame retardant and then somehow intervene to turn off combustion. That makes combustion different from a random variable" (Waldner 2016, 29–30, emphasis added).

processes furthermore maintains that there is no causation without mechanisms, meaning that it is not possible for X1 to "act directly" on Y1 unless X1 is so causally proximate to Y1 as to render any theory of the X1/Y1 relationship practically meaningless. For example, effective military training should increase the effectiveness of the military and sense of corporate identity. The political outcomes might vary depending on the strength and nature of political institutions (Nordlinger 1977; Talmadge 2015) or how this training is transmitted (Böhmelt et al. 2019), among other variables, but the mechanism associated with training is invariant. Absence of effective training should also always result in weaker values of these mechanisms.

While causal mechanisms are themselves unobservable, they have observable implications in the form of causal process observations (CPOs) (Collier 2011). A CPO is "an insight or piece of data that provides information about context, process or mechanism, and that contributes distinctive leverage in causal inference" (Mahoney 2010, 124). CPOs can be uncovered through process tracing, a within-case method of systematically identifying and evaluating evidence of what is linking X1 to Y1, underpinned by an often informal but sometimes explicit Bayesian reasoning (Fairfield and Charman 2017; Collier 2011, 823; Bennett 2008; George and Bennett 2005, 206).

The use of process tracing to identify CPOs is essential for causal inference in case study research (Mahoney 2012, 571). Nevertheless, process tracing is not enough if the researcher aims to assess the generalizability of a causal theory. To do so one must not only identify CPOs that support or refute hypotheses about mechanisms *within* each case but also test whether the same mechanisms are present across multiple cases featuring the same X1/Y1 relationship. While CAS research designs are especially well poised to compare mechanisms across variable-matched cases, it would be a mistake to assume that CAS analyses automatically allow one to assess whether the most important part of one's causal theory (the mechanism) is generalizable.

Although it is often assumed that generalization of causal theories is a hallmark of CAS scholarship, this is only partially true, as the cross-case component of CAS research usually stops short by generalizing claims only about the relationship between independent variables and the dependent variable. Sometimes the same causal mechanism is found across two or more X1/Y1 cases. Other times, different mechanisms appear to connect X1 and Y

110 · ADVANCING COMPARATIVE AREA STUDIES

in different areas, and it is not clear how different CPOs relate to each other across cases. If causal mechanisms are truly invariant, yet appear to differ across X1/Y1 cases in a manner that is not explained ex ante, then one must conduct additional analyses to make sense of these results. Below we offer some guidance for doing so.

Step 1: Additional Case Studies

The foregoing discussion is not meant to imply that case studies do not contribute to theory testing on their own or that there is anything novel or groundbreaking about advocating the analysis of causal mechanisms across cases. Rather, the point is that it is often believed that CAS automatically tests for the generalizability of causal mechanisms, while the reality is that we are usually much more confident about generalizability only at the level of variables (the X1/Y1 relationship), not at the level of mechanisms.

First, assessing the generalizability of causal mechanisms across cases requires the researcher to analyze at least two cases featuring the same X1/Y1 relationship, which most, but not all, CAS research does. Conducting two or more X1/Y1 case studies might appear to be redundant on the surface but is in fact useful for evaluating whether X1 causing Y1 plays out through the same process in the same way across cases in different areas. This repeated case study step assumes that the researcher has already conducted basic congruence-testing across cases. This means that the researcher is fairly confident about his or her causal theory at the level of variables, having found evidence that independent variables and dependent variables align as hypothesized across cases in different regions. This step also assumes that the researcher has at this point conducted within-case analyses to determine that the relationship between X1 and Y1 is not spurious. Only then should the researcher conduct additional, seemingly redundant X1/Y1 case studies to test for the portability of causal mechanisms across regions. One would do so by comparing the CPOs found in one's first X1/Y1 case study ("Case Study A") to the CPOs found in one's second X1/Y1 case study ("Case Study B"), with Case Study B located in a different region from Case Study A. Pragmatically speaking, case selection for this task should involve consulting with other area experts who already have some knowledge of potential additional cases with the aim of identifying a second X1/Y1 case so that Case B is as similar as possible to Case A. This will then provide a test for "areaness"; in other words, it can help validate the CAS approach.[3]

The analysis of seemingly redundant X1/Y1 cases is in line with Slater and Ziblatt's (2013) argument that it is not only possible but also surprisingly common to use controlled comparisons to establish the external validity of a causal theory. Since controlled comparison can do this for variables, this method should also be able to do the same for causal mechanisms—that is, test whether causal mechanisms also operate outside the sample of cases originally analyzed. Slater and Ziblatt's retest of Luebbert's (1991) theory of the rise of right-wing reactionary violence (Y1), in which they demonstrate that the causal mechanism posited by Luebbert to operate in Germany (radical leftists' attempts to organize the rural countryside) is the same general mechanism that operated in Indonesia and Thailand decades later, is a good example of how additional case studies featuring the same X1/Y1 relationship can be used to test for the portability of a causal mechanism. It may be the case that researchers need to consider multiple invariant mechanisms. For example, scholars might assume rational, utility-maximizing actors and have hypotheses regarding the effects of institutions—for example, do they influence information or power? These factors then need to be considered together across the multiple cases. This adds to the complexity. Yet what if one were to find evidence of a completely different mechanism or set of mechanisms in the second case study? It is this second outcome that is of concern (Goertz 2017, 234), and we argue that there are different ways to interpret such results.

Step 2: Reconsider Conceptualization and the Level of Analysis

One way to interpret such a discrepancy is as an error of conceptualization or measurement. When evaluating causal mechanisms across cases, it is important to recall that CPOs (the observable implications of otherwise unobservable causal mechanisms) need not look identical in every case to provide evidence that the same causal mechanism is operating in different cases featuring the same X1/Y1 relationship. Following Richard Locke and Kathleen Thelen (1995), CAS scholars emphasize the importance of using

---

[3] We thank Sara Wallace Goodman for this point.

112 ADVANCING COMPARATIVE AREA STUDIES

different but substitutable indicators for the same causal mechanisms to make sure that those mechanisms travel effectively across countries since indicators for the same mechanisms might be context-specific across countries. Such contextualized comparisons "can reveal and partially explain convergent or divergent processes unfolding across locales situated in different areas" (Köllner et al. 2018, 4). Importantly, the researcher should check to be sure he or she has conceptualized the causal mechanisms in question, as well as any hypothesized alternative mechanisms, in relatively general terms—that is, at a high enough level of abstraction—so that it is clear when seemingly context-specific CPOs are in fact evidence of more general processes.

For example, a researcher might have originally conceptualized the mechanism linking "oil wealth" (X1) to "authoritarian state" (Y1) as "the government using revenue from oil exports to fund *employment programs* to mollify dissatisfied groups that would otherwise fight for democratization" (M1). Having found M1 in Case A, the researcher might then conduct a second X1/Y1 case study and find that the government in Case B used oil revenue to fund *universal health coverage, unemployment insurance, and other de-commodifying benefits* to mollify dissatisfied groups that would otherwise fight for democratization, which appears to be a different mechanism (M2). At another level of analysis, however, M1 and M2 can be thought of as the same mechanism, which would be governments using oil revenue to fund *social welfare programs* to buy off dissent. Reconsidering one's conceptualization of causal mechanisms might thus mean recognizing that what appears to be M2 in Case Study B is actually the same M1 found in Case Study A. One can thus "contextualize" causal mechanisms to compare mechanisms across cases in the same way that one uses contextualized comparisons of independent and dependent variables across cases. Especially valuable is to identify and code CPOs "in light of contextual attributes deemed significant by the relevant country- or area-specialists" (Sil 2018, 233).

A second possibility is that the discovery a new causal mechanism (M2) in the second X1/Y1 case study is that the original finding of M1 in the first X1/Y1 case was due to the case study being conducted at a different level of analysis, and so rather than needing to "zoom out" to a higher level of abstraction, one must instead revisit the first X1/Y1 case and "zoom in" to the micro level to see if M2 is in fact at play in the first case. Assuming one has conceptualized X1 specifically enough to avoid conceptual stretching and ensured that one's case selection has not violated the scope conditions of the theory under examination, the researcher would proceed by revisiting the first X1/Y1 case study with additional data at the new level of analysis to determine whether X1 perhaps produced M2 at the micro level (even as M1 remains valid on the macro level). Level of analysis is especially crucial to take into account because social science researchers rarely assume that abstract social aggregates somehow themselves cause other social aggregates; rather, causal mechanisms likely operate at the level of individual actions and choice.[4]

Step 3: Consider the Necessity or Sufficiency of the Causal Variables

A third possible interpretation of the finding of different causal mechanisms across two cases featuring the same X1/Y1 relationship is that there is true equifinality. That is, while the independent variables and the outcome they cause are the same in both cases, we nonetheless observe variation in the mechanisms connecting X1 to Y1 across the two case studies, which is not due to narrow conceptualization, mismeasurement, or incorrect findings in the first case study. For example, if cross-regional comparative case studies were to reveal a clear relationship between oil wealth and authoritarian regimes at the level of variables, a researcher might then conduct within-case analyses to test the hypothesis that oil wealth (X1) leads to authoritarianism (Y1) through the causal mechanism of governments using the revenue from oil exports to "buy off" the population with various welfare programs (M1). If the researcher finds M1 linking X1 and Y1 in one case study, he or she would then use the repeated case study method to see if M1 is present in a second X1/Y1 case. The researcher might find in this second X1/Y1 case, however, that oil wealth invited more foreign intervention in the country, which propped up a dictatorship, resulting in authoritarianism. This "foreign intervention" mechanism (M2) is conceptually distinct from the original, hypothesized "welfare" mechanism (M1). In the two cases, X1 and Y1 are held constant, but there appears to be equifinality in causal mechanisms.

---

[4] This does not mean that macro causes cannot have macro mechanisms and macro outcomes, but it is likely a less common form of theorizing.

114 ADVANCING COMPARATIVE AREA STUDIES

Such a scenario forces the researcher to consider refining the theory to accommodate the possibility of equifinality. Here it should be especially useful to consider whether X1 (or the package of variables that X1 represents) is *necessary* or *sufficient* for the outcome Y1. If X1 is *necessary* (but not sufficient) for Y1, it is possible that some previously omitted independent variable, X2 or X3, is combining with X1 in each case to produce the new mechanism (M2). In our oil wealth example, this could mean that, in the first case, X1 (oil wealth) combines with strong state capacity (X2) to enable government leaders to direct that wealth into social programs that appease the citizenry, dampening any demands for regime change (M1), thus sustaining authoritarianism (Y1). In the second case, X1 (oil wealth) combines with weak state capacity (X3), which invites intervention from a foreign power with an economic interest in suppressing pro-democracy oppositions that might threaten oil supplies and future profits (M2), thus sustaining authoritarianism. The discovery of X2 in the first case and X3 in the second case thus resolves the equifinality of mechanisms issue since it reveals new variables (the SUIN ["a sufficient but unnecessary part of a condition that is itself an insufficient but necessary condition for an outcome," Ryan Saylor's definition in this volume] causes, X2 and X3) that explain the two separate causal paths. This situation is illustrated in Figure 5.1.

First case: X1 * X2 → M1 → Y1

Second case: X1 * X3 → M2 → Y1

Therefore:

X1 * (X2 + X3) → Y1

(where "*" indicates the logical AND and "+" indicates the logical OR)

Figure 5.1 Equifinality Due to SUIN Causes. This figure illustrates two distinct causal pathways leading to the same outcome (Y1) despite a shared independent variable (X1). In the first case, oil wealth (X1) combines with strong state capacity (X2) to produce a welfare-based mechanism (M1), sustaining authoritarianism (Y1). In the second case, oil wealth (X1) interacts with weak state capacity (X3), leading to foreign intervention (M2) and the same authoritarian outcome (Y1). The equation at the bottom generalizes this pattern, demonstrating how different SUIN causes (X2 and X3) condition the operation of X1, resolving apparent equifinality in causal mechanisms.

Of particular note would be a situation in which cases with M1 tended to cluster in one region, while cases with M2 clustered in a different region. This could lead to a further investigation of contextual factors common within each region that explain why X2 is prominent in one area while X3 tends to exist in the second area. Such an investigation could serve CAS overall by "potentially generating novel analytic frameworks and illuminating theoretically significant connections between scholarly debates unfolding in separate area studies communities" (Sil 2018, 228). Such a finding would also bolster Peter Hall's (2003) assertion that what appears to be equifinality is sometimes just the complex interaction of mechanisms interacting with other mechanisms.

If two different mechanisms are found across two X1/Y1 cases, but X1 (or the package of variables that X1 represents) is instead *sufficient* (but not necessary) for Y1, then this has different and potentially more serious implications. By definition, sufficiency means that X1 (or again, the combination of variables that we take X1 to represent) causes Y1 on its own so that no additional variables beyond X1 are needed to produce Y1. Yet if causal mechanisms are truly invariant, this precludes the possibility of X1 being sufficient for Y1 in different ways across different cases. In other words, with sufficient causation, X1 must cause Y1 through the same causal mechanism for all cases meeting the scope conditions of that causal theory. Finding two different causal mechanisms across X1/Y1 cases when X1 is sufficient for Y1 would therefore call into question the invariant property of causal mechanisms, the equivalent of throwing "a lit match into a pool of gasoline in the presence of oxygen and the absence of any other flame retardant" (Waldner 2016, 30) and a process *other* than combustion occurring.

One possible solution to the problem of equifinality in causal mechanisms in cases of sufficiency causation is to adopt the view that apparent equifinality should always be treated as evidence against the particular causal theory being tested, such that M1 and M2 are competing hypotheses that cannot both be true. A second possible solution, however, is to interpret mechanism equifinality as indicative of a situation where, despite having identified all systematic and jointly sufficient variables for a set of cases, there nonetheless remains some unaccounted for aspect of "context" in the case that features M2. "Context" is a slippery concept that is not often defined even in the increasingly well-developed CAS literature. Here we take "context" to comprise some set of idiosyncratic factors that affect causal relationships within an individual case despite not appearing anywhere else in the relevant

116 ADVANCING COMPARATIVE AREA STUDIES

population of cases. This interpretation of context technically makes such factors variables, but these are unsystematic variables that are not usefully summarized in a causal equation.[5]

Although "context" is often assumed to be an attribute of a whole region or area, this is not always true. One common assumption in CAS scholarship is that a set of features unique to a particular area are doing some of the causal work that explains cross-area differences. This is certainly often the case. Hence, it might seem odd for a researcher to look for consistency in deterministic causal relationships across two or more areas if the whole point of an "area" is that its unique context has unique causal effects. Yet to assume that "context" applies only to whole areas would be a mistake. Not only can one identify causal regularities across areas; one can also evaluate mechanisms on a case-by-case basis rather than simply chalking up any cross-area disjuncture to wholesale "regional differences" when in fact context (i.e., unsystematic factors) might apply more narrowly to one or a few, but not all, cases within a given region. The payoff from considering these factors and how they relate to causal explanation is that it reveals something about the role of region and the extent to which it is in fact influencing outcomes, if at all.

Applying the Approach: Some Examples from the Literature

Below we illustrate how our method can enhance the systematic analysis of causal mechanisms in CAS research. We draw on existing works that are examples of complete research in their own right but whose results could be taken as a starting point for expanding on these various research agendas. In doing so we proceed by following the three steps outlined above.

---

[5] Defining "context" in this way helps reconcile the "completeness" standard proposed by Waldner (2016), who stresses the importance of establishing fully comprehensive accounts of causal mechanisms in process tracing, with Bennett's (2016) contention that it might not be possible to specify all background information about a case necessary to identify a "complete" causal mechanism, especially in the messy and multilevel social world. Bennett notes that Woodward (2003, 29) actually "includes an 'error term' to represent the combined influence of all the other unknown direct causes of Y that are not explicitly represented in the equation" (Bennett 2016, 36). But arguably, that "error term" can be unpacked for one anomalous case at a time to reveal the causal role of unsystematic variables, i.e., the "context," generating an anomalous mechanism. After all, many of the most highly regarded social science theories not only identify empirical regularities but also use anomalous cases to reveal previously unknown causal mechanisms (Rogowski 1995).

More to Explore in the Development of Tax Regimes
(Illustration of Step 1)

In his book on the development of tax regimes, Evan Lieberman (2003) uses a full variance design: The South Africa case features a race-salient national political context (X1) that facilitated intra- and interclass cohesion among whites, who supported the institutions conducive to a cooperative, effective tax state (Y1). In Brazil federalism made *non*racial social cleavages more salient (X2), leading to lower class unity among whites, which resulted in an ineffective tax state (Y2). Confidence about the causal relationship among variables—meaning between X1 and Y1 and between X2 and Y2—is increased by Lieberman's cross-regional comparison of South Africa and Brazil. Confidence about the causal mechanisms—meaning the processes linking X1 to Y1 in South Africa and X2 to Y2 in Brazil—comes instead from Lieberman's within-case analyses.

Yet while within-case process tracing is well suited to test alternative hypotheses about other causal mechanisms that could have plausibly linked X1 to Y1 (or X2 to Y2) that are different from the mechanisms that the researcher initially hypothesized, such within-case analyses do not tell us whether the mechanisms identified and tested for in each case actually "travel" across other cases featuring the same X1/Y1 (or X2/Y2) relationship, especially across regions. The key is to use cross-regional comparisons that test not only for alternative hypotheses about other explanatory *variables* but also for alternative hypotheses about other causal *mechanisms*.

Hence, testing whether Lieberman's causal mechanisms "travel" across other X1/Y1 cases would involve analyzing a new case that, like South Africa, also features a race-salient national political culture that facilitated intra- and interclass cohesion (X1) and an effective tax state (Y1). We would then expect to find in this new case CPOs that suggest evidence of a similar process of calculation among upper groups to cooperate and support institutions conducive to effective taxation. Likewise, an additional X2/Y2 case study should be conducted to compare with Brazil. Of course, these "repeated" cases need not otherwise look like South Africa and Brazil. In fact, it is best if the additional X1/Y1 and X2/Y2 cases analyzed represent as much other variation as possible to ensure representativeness of the population to which one hopes to generalize (Slater and Ziblatt 2013, 1308–1309), which CAS is especially equipped to do.

Revisiting Mechanisms in Studies of Labor and Separatist Power (Illustration of Step 2)

Marissa Brookes's (2019) analysis of transnational labor alliance campaigns in North America, Europe, Australia, and Southeast Asia illustrates the importance contextualizing the comparison of causal mechanisms across cases featuring the same X1/Y1 relationship. According to Brookes, campaigns led by groups of workers from different countries that aim to change the behavior of transnational corporations can succeed (Y1) only when those workers have strong internal coordination, have strong international coordination, and exercise a form of power that threatens the target employer's core material interests (for the sake of simplicity, we can call this package of variables "X1"). In addition to three negative cases (in which labor alliances did not succeed), she analyzes three positive cases that all share the same X1/Y1 relationship.

Upon closer scrutiny of the causal mechanisms revealed in the X1/Y1 cases, however, it appears that at least two different mechanisms are at play in linking workers' exercise of power to employers' changing their behavior. Interview data reveal that the British transnational security services corporation, G4S, conceded to a transnational labor alliance in order to maintain its good relationship with its home union (M1). In contrast, the Cambodian luxury hotel Raffles conceded to the transnational labor alliance in that case to avoid brand damage and reputational costs brought on by bad publicity (M2).

Are desiring to maintain a good relationship with labor at home (M1) and attempting to avoid international brand damage (M2) really two different causal mechanisms? Applying the principles of contextualized comparison to causal mechanisms, according to Step 2 of our method, one can conclude that M1 and M2 are in fact not different mechanisms since both can be conceived of as "actions taken in response to perceptions of a high threat to corporate profits." In other words, the more encompassing concept under which M1 and M2 fall is the "real" mechanism of transnational employers feeling seriously threatened by the tactics of the transnational labor alliance and therefore believing it necessary to make concessions to labor in line with the demands of the transnational campaign.

Another example is useful for illustrating the second part of Step 2 of our method, which suggests that the researcher approach apparent equifinality in causal mechanisms not only by ensuring that mechanisms are conceptualized at an appropriate level of abstraction but also by revisiting the initial X1/Y1 case that uncovered M1 in the first place to determine whether the new casual mechanism M2 was in fact present in that case but simply overlooked. An excellent example of CAS research evaluating causal mechanisms across cases with the same X1/Y1 relationship is Benjamin Smith's (2018) analysis of why some ethnic minority challenges to central governments remain durable over time even in the face of heavy state repression, while other such separatist challenges fail to sustain themselves. Smith's research emphasizes the importance of the nature of early post-independence rebellions and broad historical patterns of resistance for the durability (Y1) or demobilization (Y2) of ethnic minority challenges.

Smith's multilevel analysis examines numerous cases of sustained and unsustained ethnic minority challenges brought by Kurdish minorities in Iran, Iraq, Syria, and Turkey, by Balochistan minorities in Pakistan, Iran, and Afghanistan, by Tuareg minorities in Algeria, Burkina Faso, Libya, Mali, and Niger, and by Aceh minorities in Indonesia.[6] Smith's two main causal variables are whether there was a historically established social hierarchy within the minority separatist ethnicity (X1) and whether that ethnic minority group migrated to a large, minority-dominated urban center (X2), as opposed to a majority-dominated urban center, in response to agricultural reforms imposed by the state (Smith 2018, 173). Mass mobilization of the ethnic minority persists (Y1) only when both X1 and X2 are present. On the macro level, the mechanism (M1) connecting X1 and X2 to Y1 is as follows: Having an established social hierarchy (X1) allowed ethnic elites to mobilize other members of the minority ethnicity either "on the basis of vertical legitimacy and obligation" (179) or by "crafting narratives about the group's current mobilization" in ways that invoked the historical memory of past rebellion (181). Urban migration to minority-dominated cities (X2) radicalized the group and opened up a venue for new organizations and mobilization (174). This macro-level mechanism emerged from an initial analysis of the cases of Kurdish separatism.

Examining cases of Acehnese mobilization, but also moving to the micro level, Smith discovered that rebellious legacies (X1) worked through "a wide array of individual motivations" that explained individuals' decisions to join separatist mobilizations, ranging from emotive attachment to "highly

---

[6] For the sake of brevity, we focus here only on the variables related to the positive cases, that is, cases of durable minority separatist challenges.

120 ADVANCING COMPARATIVE AREA STUDIES

instrumental-rational" motivations (181). These various individual-level decision-making processes can be thought of as a second mechanism, M2, albeit one that plays out on the individual level of analysis. To reconcile the finding of M2 in the Acehnese cases with the finding of M1 in the Kurdish cases, Smith "used the micro-level insights from Aceh to revisit available individual-level data from the Kurdish regions of Turkey and Iraq, again leveraging cross-regional inference but at a second level of analysis" (169). In doing so he found evidence that there were indeed similarities in the calculus of individuals deciding to join the Kurdish separatist mobilizations (183), and so M2 is perfectly compatible with M1.

Considering Necessity or Sufficiency in Paths to (Un)Mediated Rule (Illustration of Step 3)

Ryan Saylor's (2018) excellent analysis of institution building in Argentina, Colombia, and Ghana is useful for illustrating our third step, which is to specify the relationship between variables in terms of necessity or sufficiency in order to interpret the finding of equifinality in causal mechanisms. Saylor's analysis explains why some governments develop mediated rule (Y1), a situation in which autonomous local elites carry out government directives at the local level, while others adopt unmediated rule, in which state agents take over from local elites to administer local-level rule (Y2) (Saylor 2018, 189). He tests the hypothesis that resource booms that benefit coalition outsiders only lead to mediated rule (Y1) when members of the ruling coalition are not exporters (X1) and therefore do not interpret outsiders' newfound economic power as an existential threat. Argentina features the X2/Y2 relationship, while both Colombia and Ghana share the same X1/Y1 relationship, making them great candidates for examining whether, or not, X1 causes Y1 through the same causal mechanism in Latin America as it does in Africa.

At first glance, reading through the explanation of causal mechanisms in each case, it appears as though there are two different mechanisms at play across the two X1/Y1 cases. In Colombia, a resource boom in coffee led the non-exporter ruling coalition (X1) to continue with mediated rule (Y1) because they could use "paper money emissions to shore up coalitional support while reducing the monetary value of coffee wealth via inflation" (198). Additionally, the opposition Liberals "were divided over how to confront the ruling coalition" (198). The causal mechanism in Colombia (M1) thus appears to be a process of maintaining ruling coalition cohesion (while benefiting from division in the opposition). In contrast, in Ghana a cocoa boom led the non-exporter ruling coalition (X1) to continue with mediated rule (Y1) because the ruling coalition "could sideline [opposition] chiefs simply by establishing a single government-run purchasing company" and implementing "various non-institutional measures to thwart the Asante-based NLM" (201–202). The causal mechanism in Ghana (M2) thus appears to be the process of implementing uniquely available noninstitutional measures to thwart the opposition.

Are maintaining coalition cohesion (M1) and implementing obstructive noninstitutional measures (M2) really two different causal mechanisms? For illustrative purposes, let us consider two possibilities. On one hand, applying the principles of contextualized comparison to causal mechanisms, according to Step 2 of our method, one can conclude that M1 and M2 are in fact not different mechanisms since both can be conceived of as "actions taken in response to perceptions of a low threat level." In other words, the more encompassing concept under which M1 and M2 fall is the "real" mechanism of ruling elites feeling only mildly threatened by the resource-empowered opposition and therefore believing it unnecessary to undertake institution building efforts that would lead to unmediated rule. Put another way, the pursuit of distributional competitive advantage and the desire to achieve social mobility are the actual mechanisms revealed by Saylor's various CPOs and the pathways he describes.

On the other hand, let us consider the possibility that M1 and M2 are truly distinct causal mechanisms, and so we are faced with the issue of true equifinality. Applying Step 3 of our approach, one would first consider whether the presence of a non-exporter ruling coalition (X1) is necessary or sufficient for the maintenance of mediated rule (Y1). Although it is not explicitly stated in the text, one can gather that X1 is necessary but not sufficient for Y1, which allows for the possibility that X1 combined with some additional independent variable (X2), such as control over monetary policy, which enabled the ruling coalition in Colombia to keep printing money and use inflation to reduce the value of coffee wealth and therefore reduce the power of the opposition (198), which eliminated the need for unmediated rule, thus allowing for the maintenance of mediated rule (Y1) via the mechanism of maintaining coalition cohesion (M1). Likewise, in Ghana, it is possible that the presence of a non-exporting coalition (X1) combined with some

122   ADVANCING COMPARATIVE AREA STUDIES

additional independent variable (X3), such as the nature of the booming commodity ("Cocoa is a bulky, low-value-added commodity, which deters long-distance smuggling" [201]), which together allowed the ruling elites to establish a single government-run purchasing company so "cocoa producers would have little choice but to sell to the state" (201), which eliminated the necessity of unmediated rule, thus allowing for the maintenance of mediated rule (Y1).

Putting It All Together: Expanding Research on the Origins of Federalism

Ziblatt's *Structuring the State* (2008) opens the door to a research area that has good potential to follow all three steps of our proposed approach. In this work Ziblatt asks why processes of national unification led some states to adopt federalism and others to become unitary states. Specifically, he uses a controlled comparison to examine the causes that led Germany to become a federal state and Italy to become a unitary state upon unification. Since both cases share several factors in common—including the timing of unification, ideological awareness, cultural divisions, power-structural conditions, and the independence and organization of their leading regional states (Prussia and Piedmont) before unification—Ziblatt is able to approximate Mill's method of difference, in which one compares two highly similar cases that nonetheless had different outcomes in order to identify and test for hypothesized causal variables.

The main explanatory variable in Ziblatt's causal hypothesis is whether, or not, the subunits that would later compose each newly unified state had *infrastructural capacity* prior to unification. Infrastructural capacity (X1) refers to whether a given subnational unit had a state apparatus with sufficient rationalization (to regulate), institutionalization (to tax), and embeddedness in society (to maintain order). According to Ziblatt's hypothesis, federal states form when subunits have high infrastructural capacity, whereas subunits lacking infrastructural capacity result in unitary states. He tests this claim about X1 against three alternative explanations and finds evidence that X1, and not other variables, accounts for the difference in outcomes across Germany and Italy.

Crucially, Ziblatt also hypothesizes the causal mechanisms through which each process unfolds: When subunits have high infrastructural capacity

(X1), they are seen as credible negotiation partners with effective governance structures that can deliver benefits to the core; hence, unification occurs through a process of negotiated unification (M1), which in turn results in a federal state. Conversely, when subunits have low infrastructural capacity (X2), they are not seen as credible negotiation partners who can deliver benefits and are therefore instead viewed as impediments to national unification, which then occurs through a process of conquest (M2), leading to a unitary state. Through close and detailed process tracing of these two cases, Ziblatt finds evidence that M1 (negotiation) and M2 (conquest) are indeed the mechanisms that play out in Germany and Italy, respectively.

Structuring the State is an exemplary work in comparative politics, featuring an excellent use of both cross-case and within-case methods of causal inference. How can our approach advance future research on why national unification results in either federal or unitary states? First, Step 1 would be taking Ziblatt's findings as a starting point and performing additional case studies of national unification that resemble the German case but from different regions (and perhaps different historical eras), where subunits have high infrastructural capacity, and the resulting unified state is federal (X1, Y1). Likewise, one could also conduct additional case studies from different regions (and eras) that resemble the Italian case by having subunits that lack infrastructural capacity and have the result of a unitary state (X2, Y2). The initial goal of these additional X1/Y1 and X2/Y2 case studies would be to see if the same causal mechanisms for which Ziblatt found evidence in Germany and Italy also appear in other cases outside of Europe. In other words, using process tracing, one could determine if M1 is generalizable to other X1/Y1 cases in other areas and if M2 is generalizable to other X2/Y2 cases in other areas. In conducting these additional within-case analyses, the researcher should seek evidence not only for the originally hypothesized causal mechanisms but also for one or more rival hypotheses suggesting some different, alternative causal mechanism.

If the researcher conducting these new case studies does in fact find evidence of M1 (negotiated unification) in the new X1/Y1 (infrastructural capacity/federal state) case studies and evidence of M2 (unification by conquest) in the new X2/Y2 (lack of infrastructural capacity/unitary state) case studies, then the researcher has some grounds for believing that M1 and M2 are generalizable to the larger population of X1/Y1 and X2/Y2 cases, respectively. If, however, the researcher finds a different causal mechanism (e.g., M3 in a X1/Y1 case), then Step 2 would be to revisit the conceptualization and level of analysis of the causal mechanisms originally identified (e.g., M1 in Germany) to examine whether or not M3 is really just M1 at a different level of abstraction (applying the principles of contextualized comparison) or whether M3 is part of M1, just at a different (perhaps more micro) level of analysis.

If the researcher follows Step 2 and is then confident that the distinction between M1 and M3 it is not simply the product of different levels of conceptualization or analysis, then the Step 3 would be to consider that there is some genuine equifinality in causal mechanisms, meaning X1 can lead to Y1 through *either* M1 *or* M3. In the example of federal states, that would mean that subunits with high infrastructural capacity led to federalism through the mechanism of negotiated unification in Germany, while subunits with high infrastructural capacity led to federalism through a *different* causal mechanism in states in other regions. To account for the two different mechanisms, however, the researcher should first specify whether X1 was necessary or sufficient for Y1. If X1 is necessary (but not sufficient), then it is appropriate at this stage to return to both the original X1/Y1 case study (Germany) and the new X1/Y1 case study in effort to locate within each case additional explanatory variables with which X1 is combining or interacting to explain the presence of M1 versus M3. In other words, it is possible that Germany emerged as a federal state (Y1) through the process of negotiated unification (M1) because high infrastructural capacity (X1) combined with some additional explanatory variable (X3) to produce M1, as opposed to M3. Likewise, the country examined in the different region, that is, the new X1/Y1 case, might have emerged as a federal state (Y1) through a different process (M3) because X1 combined with a different additional explanatory variable (X4) to produce M3.

To give another example, Paul Staniland (2014) provides an impressive study of rebel groups and their evolution. He does so across groups within countries, across countries, and then, most relevant to this volume, across regions between South Asia and Southeast Asia. Considering departures from his theory in Southeast Asia, Staniland (2014, 213) explicitly considers the necessity or sufficiency of his organizational variables and concludes that, while his variables are necessary, they might not be sufficient, which helps to fully understand the trajectories of groups in some contexts. A more explicit CAS approach would push Staniland to consider how the region shaped these political differences or context.

If, however, X1 is sufficient for Y1, then the researcher would need to either reconsider the fundamental notion of invariance of causal mechanisms or, more realistically, seek out previously unaccounted for "contextual" factors that act as unsystematic, truly idiosyncratic causes that condition the nature of the relationship between X1 and Y1, producing a distinct causal mechanism in the second X1/Y1 case. In other words, is this a product of the region and its characteristics or some contingency inherent to the causal process itself? In either case, by addressing these issues, we will have learned something important about the causal relationships we wish to understand.

Conclusion

CAS research is on the cutting edge of exploring the portability of causal theories across areas and shedding light on variables visible only to those with rich area knowledge. Yet despite CAS scholars' long-standing attention to the crucial importance of causal mechanisms, there has been limited guidance on how to interpret findings about causal mechanisms once we have them. We have therefore suggested an approach to interpreting the results of studies that consider the potential generalizability of causal mechanisms across cases with the same X1/Y1 relationship. This approach relies on three steps: (1) conducting at least one additional X1/Y1 case study, (2) reconsidering the conceptualization of M1 if M2 appears to be present, and (3) evaluating the meaning of M1 and M2 with respect to the necessity or sufficiency of X1 for Y1. As we saw with the examples of Lieberman's (2003) study of taxation systems in Africa and South America, Brookes's (2019) analysis of labor campaigns in Australia, Europe, North America, and Southeast Asia, Smith's (2018) research on the durability of ethnic minority challenges in Africa, Asia, and the Middle East, Saylor's (2018) examination of institution building in Africa and South America, and Ziblatt's (2008) theory of state formation in Europe, our method offers practical tools for evaluating potential equifinality in causal mechanisms. Such evaluations, in turn, will ultimately help us become more confident in our claims about the generalizability of causal theories, which is another step toward CAS reaching its full potential.

Bibliography

Bennett, Andrew. 2008. Process Tracing: A Bayesian Perspective. In Janet M. Box-Steffensmeier, Henry E. Brady, and David Collier, eds. *The Oxford Handbook of Political Methodology*. Oxford: Oxford University Press, 702–721.

Bennett, Andrew. 2016. Do New Accounts of Causal Mechanisms Offer Practical Advice for Process Tracing? *Qualitative and Multi-Method Research* 17–18 (1): 34–39.

Böhmelt, Tobias, Abel Escribà-Folch, and Ulrich Pilster. 2019. Pitfalls of Professionalism? Military Academies and Coup Risk. *Journal of Conflict Resolution* 63 (5): 1111–1139.

Brookes, Marissa. 2019. *The New Politics of Transnational Labor: Why Some Alliances Succeed.* Ithaca, NY: Cornell University Press.

Collier, David. 2011. Understanding Process Tracing. *PS: Political Science and Politics* 44 (4): 823–830.

Fairfield, Tasha, and Andrew E. Charman. 2017. Explicit Bayesian Analysis for Process Tracing: Guidelines, Opportunities, and Caveats. *Political Analysis* 25 (3): 363–80. https://doi.org/10.1017/pan.2017.14.

George, Alexander L., and Andrew Bennett. 2005. *Case Studies and Theory Development in the Social Sciences*. Cambridge, MA: MIT Press.

Gerring, John. 2010. Causal Mechanisms: Yes, but . . . . *Comparative Political Studies* 43 (11): 1499–1526.

Goertz, Gary. 2017. *Multimethod Research, Causal Mechanisms, and Case Studies: An Integrated Approach.* Princeton, NJ: Princeton University Press.

Hall, Peter. 2003. Aligning Ontology and Methodology in Comparative Research. In James Mahoney and Dietrich Rueschemeyer, eds. *Comparative Historical Analysis in the Social Sciences*. Cambridge: Cambridge University Press, 373–401.

Jacobs, Alan. 2016. Introduction: Mechanisms and Process Tracing. *Qualitative and Multi-Method Research* 17–18 (1): 13–15.

Köllner, Patrick, Ariel I. Ahram, and Rudra Sil. 2018. Comparative Area Studies: What It Is, What It Can Do. In Ariel I. Ahram, Patrick Köllner, and Rudra Sil, eds. *Comparative Area Studies: Methodological Rationales and Cross-Regional Applications*. New York: Oxford University Press, 3–26.

Lieberman, Evan S. 2003. *Race and Regionalism in the Politics of Taxation in Brazil and South Africa*. Cambridge: Cambridge University Press.

Lieberman, Evan S. 2005. Nested Analysis as a Mixed-Method Strategy for Comparative Research. *American Political Science Review* 99 (3): 435–452.

Locke, Richard M., and Kathleen Thelen. 1995. Apples and Oranges Revisited: Contextualized Comparisons and the Study of Comparative Labor Politics. *Politics and Society* 23 (3): 337–367.

Luebbert, Gregory. M. 1991. *Liberalism, Fascism, or Social Democracy: Social Classes and the Political Origins of Regimes in Interwar Europe*. New York: Oxford University Press.

Mahoney, James. 2010. After KKV: The New Methodology of Qualitative Research. *World Politics* 62 (1): 120–147.

Mahoney, James. 2012. The Logic of Process Tracing Tests in the Social Sciences. *Sociological Methods and Research* 41 (4): 570–597.

Nordlinger, Eric A. 1977. *Soldiers in Politics: Military Coups and Governments*. Englewood Cliffs, NJ: Prentice Hall.

Rogowski, Ronald. 1995. The Role of Theory and Anomaly in Social-Scientific Inference. *American Political Science Review* 89 (2): 467–470.

Rueschemeyer, Dietrich, Evelyne Huber, and John D. Stephens. 1992. *Capitalist Development and Democracy*. Chicago: University of Chicago Press.

Saylor, Ryan. 2018. Gaining by Shedding Case Selection Strictures: Natural Resource Booms and Institution Building in Latin America and Africa. In Ariel I. Ahram, Patrick Köllner, and

Rudra Sil, eds. *Comparative Area Studies: Methodological Rationales and Cross-Regional Applications.* New York: Oxford University Press, 185–203.

Sil, Rudra. 2018. Triangulating Area Studies, Not Just Methods: How Cross-Regional Comparison Aids Qualitative and Mixed-Method Research. In Ariel I. Ahram, Patrick Köllner, and Rudra Sil, eds. *Comparative Area Studies: Methodological Rationales and Cross-Regional Applications.* New York: Oxford University Press, 225–246.

Slater, Dan, and Daniel Ziblatt. 2013. The Enduring Indispensability of the Controlled Comparison. *Comparative Political Studies* 46 (10): 1301–1327.

Smith, Benjamin. 2018. Comparing Separatism across Regions: Rebellious Legacies in Africa, Asia, and the Middle East. In Ariel I. Ahram, Patrick Köllner, and Rudra Sil, eds. *Comparative Area Studies: Methodological Rationales and Cross-Regional Applications.* New York: Oxford University Press, 168–184.

Staniland, Paul 2014. *Networks of Rebellion: Explaining Insurgent Cohesion and Collapse.* Ithaca, NJ: Cornell University Press.

Talmadge, Caitlin. 2015. *The Dictator's Army: Battlefield Effectiveness in Authoritarian Regimes.* Ithaca, NJ: Cornell University Press.

Waldner, David. 2016. Invariant Causal Mechanisms. *Qualitative and Multi-Method Research* 17–18 (1): 28–34.

Waltz, Kenneth N. (2010). *Theory of International Politics.* Long Grove, IL: Waveland Press.

Weller, Nicholas, and Jeb Barnes. 2014. *Finding Pathways: Mixed-Method Research for Studying Causal Mechanisms.* Cambridge: Cambridge University Press.

Woodward, James. 2003. *Making Things Happen: A Theory of Causal Explanation.* Oxford: Oxford University Press.

Ziblatt, Daniel. 2008. *Structuring the State: The Formation of Italy and Germany and the Puzzle of Federalism.* Princeton, NJ: Princeton University Press.

6

The Best of Two Worlds?

Generalizing and Individualizing through Multi-Method Research in Comparative Area Studies

Matthias Basedau and David Kuehn

Introduction

Different types of comparative area studies (CAS) have been proposed since the debate on CAS started in the mid-2000s (Basedau and Köllner 2007; Ahram 2011; Ahram et al. 2018), including inter-, intra- and cross-regional comparisons. The editors of this volume have suggested a conceptual core that defines CAS as an "approach" combining "deep sensitivity to context in each of the locales being examined with the use of some variant of the comparative method . . . against the backdrop of more general concepts and theoretical debates" (Köllner et al. 2018, 4). In other words, CAS attempts to bridge two different research objectives: *individualization*, which focuses on understanding the particularities of a particular place in time; and *generalization*, which aims at generating more broadly applicable and abstract inferences.

Beyond this general definition, different ontological, epistemological, and methodological aspects and implications of CAS have been discussed in the lively debate that has taken place since the term was first coined. Interestingly, however, while the *ontological* ("What is CAS?") and *epistemological* ("What can CAS as an analytical approach hope to achieve?") perspectives have seen an engaged and increasingly broad debate, up to the publication of this volume the *methodological* discussion has mainly focused on outlining, broadening, and refining the principal method that had already been suggested for CAS early on in most works: small-N research that compares the insights of systematic case studies grounded in in-depth area knowledge within and across world regions. This discussion has suggested

Matthias Basedau and David Kuehn, *The Best of Two Worlds?*. In: *Advancing Comparative Area Studies*. Edited by: Ariel I. Ahram, Patrick Köllner, and Rudra Sil, Oxford University Press. © Oxford University Press (2025).
DOI: 10.1093/oso/9780197809365.003.0006

130 ADVANCING COMPARATIVE AREA STUDIES

a wide range of important solutions to crucial methodological problems specific to the (cross-)regional comparative case study approach, including the conceptual and empirical "meaning" of regions (Pepinsky 2020), the conceptual and practical problems of comparing across regions (von Soest and Stroh 2018), and the challenges of applying historical methods in CAS (Ahmed 2020).

In contrast, the potential contribution and the limits of other methodological approaches within the broader CAS endeavor have hitherto not been systematically mapped beyond some rather basic suggestions (Basedau and Köllner 2007, Table 3). This is also true for multi-method research (MMR), that is, the systematic combination of at least two different methods of empirical inference that operate on different levels of analysis. One of this volume's editors has stressed the important role of cross-regional perspectives for MMR research in the concluding chapter of the 2018 volume on CAS (Sil 2018, 243–244). Drawing on the example of Evan Lieberman's excellent comparative studies of taxation in Brazil and South Africa (2003) and on AIDS policy in Brazil, South Africa, and India (2009), Rudra Sil forcefully argues that the qualitative parts of MMR research benefit from careful selection of contrasting cases across regional boundaries and systematic concern for local context. So, while Sil's observations show how the CAS perspective can strengthen MMR, they do not shed light on how MMR can contribute to the CAS endeavor. In fact, neither the 2018 volume on CAS nor the 2020 symposium on CAS in *Qualitative and Multi-Method Research* (Saylor 2020) has systematically addressed the potential of MMR designs in toto for the CAS endeavor of producing contextually rich but systematic and conceptually and theoretically informed comparative empirical research.

In line with this volume's goal of advancing CAS, this chapter argues that an MMR design that systematically combines a within-case method and a cross-case method can contribute to a CAS study in three ways. First, it provides a methodological framework to reach both *individualizing* and *generalizing* research objectives. Aiming at generalization, we explicitly go beyond the above-mentioned understanding of CAS and argue in favor of including large-N studies, as already suggested in earlier works on CAS (Basedau and Köllner 2007). Second, it requires that the conceptual and theoretical framework be applicable across a broader population while sufficiently context-sensitive to individual cases. Third, it allows the integration of deductive and inductive steps in the research process and their corresponding methodological instruments, which have distinct functions within a research design.

The remainder of this chapter proceeds as follows: We start by systematizing the two main goals of individualization and generalization regarding three dimensions of research design, (a) the basic analytical objectives, (b) the use of concepts and theory, and (c) the resulting methodological orientation and practice; and show how CAS bridges the twin goals. Next, we demonstrate how MMR in the CAS context can be carried out in practice, illustrated by two examples from real-world empirical research, and briefly discuss the potential methodological and practical pitfalls of MMR in CAS. The chapter closes with a brief summary.

Before proceeding, three caveats are in order: First, in our discussions we concentrate on the study of political phenomena. However, most of the reasoning is likely applicable to other social science disciplines as well. Second, we focus on empirical studies, that is, works that intend to explain or understand real-world events or phenomena, thus excluding purely descriptive or theoretical and methodological studies (like this chapter). Finally, given the background of both authors in terms of regional and substantive specialization, examples from Africa and Asia as well as research on political parties, conflict, democratization, and civil-military relations will be overrepresented.

CAS as the Systematic Integration of Individualization and Generalization

The editors of this volume have defined comparative area studies as

> any *self-conscious* effort to do *two* things simultaneously: *(i) balance deep sensitivity to context in each of the locales being examined with the use of some variant of the comparative method to surface causal linkages that are portable across world regions; and (ii) engage ongoing research and scholarly discourse in two or more area studies communities against the backdrop of more general concepts and theoretical debates within a social science discipline.* (Köllner et al. 2018, 3)

Ultimately, then, CAS can be understood as the systematic integration of the goals and analytical tools of traditional *area studies*, with its focus on context-sensitive, deep knowledge on particular locales (Hanson 2009), and *comparative studies*, which aim at abstracting from concrete empirical instances to reach broad inferences that generalize beyond individual cases (Przeworski and Teune 1970). As exemplified throughout the chapters of this volume, this integrative approach is realized in three dimensions of the scientific endeavor: (a) the analytical objectives, (b) the level of conceptual and theoretical abstraction, and (c) the basic methodological orientation and corresponding research designs and instruments.

Objectives: Understanding Places Versus Explaining Classes of Phenomena

On the most basic level, social science research pursues two analytical objectives: to *understand special instances of developments and events in particular places* and to *explain classes of phenomena.*[1] From the perspective of the former, the main interest is *individualization,* that is, to understand places or areas and why certain phenomena happen *within* a particular place (and time). The main object, from this perspective, is therefore ideography or idiosyncrasy and less, if at all, generalization, let alone nomothetic generalization. Generalization, if any, will be confined to a particular and narrowly defined area. This is the typical analytical goal of classical area studies research, which focuses mainly on individual countries. In fact, less than 8 percent of all articles published in 2019 in the three leading academic journals on sub-Saharan Africa focus on the region as a whole or even a subregion like West Africa or southern Africa (Basedau 2020, 196). For Asia, scholars often focus on one country like China or India, or subregions like Southeast Asia. In Latin America, area studies researchers often specialize in subregions like Central America or the Southern Cone.

The second analytical objective of social science research is *explaining classes of phenomena.* This goal focuses on *generalization* and, if possible, nomothetic explanation of the phenomena under investigation rather than the in-depth understanding of specific instances of these classes. Such phenomena can cover a wide range of topics, such as the success of democratization, the onset of civil war, or civilian control over the military, and

---

[1] The juxtaposition of understanding (*Verstehen* à la Max Weber) versus explaining (à la Emile Durkheim) is no coincidence here.

they are typically studied in a large or at least larger number of instances, often across countries and regions.

On the most basic level, the objectives of *individualization* and *generalization* are in opposition to each other (Ahram 2011; Gerring 2012, 61–66). Generalization comes at the cost of individualization and vice versa. However, both principal objectives have their merit and can be combined. Aiming at individualization, one will not know what is special about a case if that case is not compared to general findings or at least contrasting cases. As Sartori (1991, 16) argues, "He who knows only one country only knows none." In turn, generalization, let alone in its nomothetic orientation, needs to consider *all* cases of a given class of phenomena—even if it empirically analyzes only a sample of that population. Especially statistical large-N work is based on probabilistic relationships, although exceptions—often quite many—suggest that variables that might be important at least for some subset of the sample might have been left out. An empirical analysis of selected deviant cases can shed light on the variables that explain the divergence from the general expectations at least in these specific cases (Lieberman 2005; Seawright 2016).

Concepts and Theory: Contextually Sensitive Versus Abstract-Universal

The fundamental difference between the two objectives of social scientific research is reflected in the relative relevance and use of concepts and theory. If the goal is generalization, concepts are typically *abstract* to capture empirical commonalities across many different cases; hence researchers must climb the "ladder of abstraction" (Sartori 1991). Likewise, theories and hypotheses must be abstract and make general assumptions about the relationship between phenomena within the whole class of cases (Gerring 2012, chap. 3). In addition, broadly applicable concepts and theories allow the connection and comparison of multiple different studies. On the other hand, more abstract concepts typically include fewer components and thus contain less information on individual empirical instances: they trade "extension," that is, the applicability across cases, for "intension," that is, conceptual depth (Adcock and Collier 2001).

This makes it easy for more abstract concepts to travel to different contexts, but also runs the risk of lumping together empirical phenomena that share only minimal commonalities under closer inspection. Take the concept of democracy, for instance. A minimal definition of democracy that focuses on regular, free, and fair elections as the sole discriminatory criterion (e.g., Cheibub et al. 2010) provides a clear threshold for dichotomously classifying regime types that is applicable across geographically and temporally different empirical instances. It does, however, treat as conceptually equivalent regimes that often differ quite significantly in terms of the realization of political and civil rights and horizontal checks-and-balances on the executive. These latter aspects of political regimes, however, might be of greater substantive interest than the existence of free and fair elections due to their impact on the political stability, conflict-proneness, or human rights record of a given country.

In contrast, from the perspective of individualization, conceptual "intension" makes concepts more likely to capture regional or country specificities and differences across types (Ahram 2013). Looking closely at cases will sensitize researchers to specific historical, cultural, economic, or other features of the case under investigation. However, the more specific and context-bound a concept, the less likely it will be able to "travel" to other contexts. Consider research on political parties. Developed in a "Western" context, researchers often expect to find the same features of European parties and party systems in an African, Middle Eastern, or Asian context, and their absence is often considered a "deficit." For instance, one hardly finds ideological differences in "left versus right" terms in sub-Saharan Africa. This is hardly surprising when we recall that this difference emerged from the French Revolution and industrialization in the eighteenth and nineteenth centuries. African history is different and created other cleavages (Erdmann 2004).

Yet a strong orientation toward the case limits the relevance of abstract and universal concepts and theory. Highly context-specific concepts and theoretical arguments might do justice to the empirical realities of the case but are often not applicable for a broader range of empirical phenomena. At the same time, the individualization approach does not necessarily exclude the use of universal concepts and theories. Furthermore, in-depth knowledge of a limited empirical phenomenon can generate more broadly applicable concepts and theories. One example for such an empirically grounded yet generalizable concept is neopatrimonialism, which was primarily investigated and developed within the sub-Saharan context but can easily be adapted to other regions (Erdmann and Engel 2007).

Methodology and Research Design: "Deep" Induction Versus "Broad" Deduction

The difference between individualizing and generalizing research objectives implies a different methodological orientation and the use of different research designs, methods, and data: individualization and the understanding of places require context-bound, within-case analyses, while the explanation of classes of phenomena is necessarily based on systematic cross-case comparison. We can compare these different methodological implications according to the following criteria: (a) basic methodological orientation, in particular the juxtaposition of deduction and induction; (b) preferred research designs, especially regarding the number and selection of cases as well as the number and interaction of independent variables (this aspect also includes the orientation of "why versus how"); and (c) preferred research instruments and forms of data and information processing, in particular with regard to primary and secondary sources as well as the use of quantitative versus qualitative processing of information.

The Methodology of Individualization

The typical methodological approach aligned to the individualizing goal of research is the case study. A case study is the in-depth analysis of a well-defined and geographically, temporally, and substantively bounded empirical phenomenon (Rohlfing 2012, 27). Area and geographical boundaries are crucial for individualizing research: a survey of articles published in three leading African studies journals (Basedau 2020) reveals that 85 percent of all research articles are case studies. Individualizing case research usually does not demonstrate a strong need to justify the rules and principles of case selection because the case as such is the primary interest in the first place. Individualizing case research also often starts not from a theoretical problem to be confronted by empirical evidence but from an empirical issue. If concept or theory development is a goal, individualizing research mainly aims at *generating* theory or concepts rather than *testing* them. Therefore, the approach is less, if at all, deductive but rather characterized by induction. Its goal is explorative and open to find new relationships or explanations—*Verstehen* (understanding) in the Weberian sense.

This approach has several advantages. Its first, huge benefit is its smaller dependence on—sometimes questionable—secondary sources. Instead, individualizing research often is based on meticulous archival study and

136 ADVANCING COMPARATIVE AREA STUDIES

can benefit from utilizing sources in multiple languages, including English, French, and Spanish or Portuguese, but also non-European languages.[2] In a seminal study on the repression apparatus in the authoritarian regimes of South Korea and Taiwan, Sheena Greitens (2016) draws upon a wide range of Korean- and Chinese-language archival sources that have never been used systematically by Western scholars. In addition, case studies also make it easier to critically engage with the sources. Fewer cases generally mean that research instruments can be applied that are relatively costly in terms of time and financial resources. Consequently, fieldwork, including interviews and participant observation, plays a substantial role in the individualizing research tradition.

Not surprisingly, individualizing data processing therefore focuses on qualitative techniques. The survey on leading African studies journals shows that less than 9 percent of all articles include quantitative instruments (Basedau 2020, 196). Moreover, and centrally, individualizing analyses do not engage in explicit comparison. Less than 20 percent of articles in the African studies survey engage in explicit comparison. This also affects the goal of causal explanation, which some individualizing research eschews completely. In applied African studies research, for instance, less than 5 percent of articles explicitly address the problem of causality (Basedau 2020), which is also true for individualizing research in other subfields (Morgan 2016). This is not a necessary implication of qualitative research, however, as single case studies are perfectly suitable for tracing historical processes to identify causal mechanisms. Individualizing researchers are, however, interested at least as much in asking "how" questions and uncovering causal mechanisms as in asking "why" questions and the search for causal effects.

The Methodology of Generalization

Generalizing research, in contrast, is based on comparison and thus requires starting from well-defined concepts and hypotheses that are applied systematically to all cases. The basic principle of generalizing research is *deduction*. The number of cases is larger than in the individualizing tradition, and case selection is based on two distinct principles vis-à-vis the universe of cases. Statistical studies try to maximize the number of cases or at least study a representative sample, while small-N controlled comparisons select cases

---

[2] Mastering non-European languages is especially a requirement of students of Asia and the Middle East but not so much for specialists for Latin America and sub-Saharan Africa.

purposefully. In both approaches, the aim is to approximate the experimental logic by allowing the researcher to "control" variation in context variables to identify the causal effect of the core explanatory variable(s) the researcher is interested in. Qualitative Comparative Analysis (QCA) and other set-theoretic methods are based on different assumptions, yet the ultimate goal is still to identify regularities in the relationship between explanans and explanandum through cross-case comparisons (Ragin 2000; Schneider and Wagemann 2012).

The need to include a large(r) number of cases has implications on conceptual "depth" (Sartori 1991) and the type and quality of data used. First, the use of empirical indicators that are sufficiently general to be applied to a broad range of cases leads to a loss in information (Goertz and Mahoney 2012, chap. 10). More complex interactions such as processes or mechanisms are difficult to tease out across large numbers of cases because too many variables are involved and, in some instances, for not all of them is data available. Unfortunately, theoretically more interesting variables are often hard to operationalize in a general or standardized manner, let alone quantify, and it is typically extremely difficult to generate data. Second, and closely related, large-N research often heavily relies on secondary data. Compiling cross-country data sets is costly in terms of time and financial resources, which leads many applied researchers in the generalizing tradition to draw on existing data sets, even though the validity of some of these data sets is dubious. The debate about the utility of the well-known and widely used Polity data set is a case in point (Pemstein et al. 2010). It is not uncommon that specialists on individual countries do not agree on how a particular country is "coded" in a cross-country data set. In the generalizing tradition of small-N controlled comparisons, in contrast, more complex concepts can be accommodated, and historical processes as well as complex interactions can be traced.

In terms of data processing, generalizing research relies on a variety of methods and techniques, which can be either quantitative or qualitative. The former typically makes use of statistical techniques based on standardized data. Qualitative work in the comparative case study tradition can also engage in a more sophisticated way of handling secondary and primary sources, such as archival work and primary sources, as well as fieldwork with interviews and focus groups.

Summing up, individualizing methodology is employed to tease out empirical specifics of a case but cannot generalize across cases, especially

138 ADVANCING COMPARATIVE AREA STUDIES

outside narrowly defined geographical scope conditions. In contrast, the methods employed to fulfill the generalizing research objective maximize the ability to compare across cases, but necessarily fall short of doing justice to individual cases and are typically unable to uncover more complex causal relationships, especially processes and mechanisms. These methods depend on data that is standardized to some degree and often is drawn from sometimes questionable secondary sources.

CAS as an Approach to Bridge Individualization and Generalization

If we return to the definition of CAS reproduced above, CAS can be understood as the attempt to bridge or combine the goals of producing *generalizable* social scientific knowledge without sacrificing the *individualizing* goals of the causal importance of local contexts. Accordingly, the underlying principle of CAS has been described as a "'middle ground' between, on the one hand, context-bound scholarship oriented to idiographic narratives or hermeneutic interpretation and, on the other hand, the analysis of cases according to the dictates of the comparative method in search of nomothetic generalizations intended to cover a larger population of cases" (Köllner et al. 2018, 15–16). This idea of bridging individualization and generalization has implications for all three analytical dimensions discussed in the preceding sections: general objectives, concepts and theory, and methodology and data. Table 6.1 summarizes the different perspectives on these three dimensions in the individualizing and generalizing traditions, and how CAS aims to bridge them.

First, CAS is based on the principle that both generalization and individualization are valuable objectives. In fact, these objectives do not exclude each other but are complementary. We need to understand and explain individual cases *and* make inferences on classes of phenomena. Second and consequently, CAS strives for a careful use of abstract and universal concepts and theory that, however, must be contextually sensitive. The generalizing perspective benefits from the development of concepts and theories or hypotheses from specific cases. In turn, even research focused on an individual case profits from the connection of empirical depth to more abstract and universal theories and concepts. The promise of CAS, then, is the "middle ground" that avoids atheoretical empiricism but also makes theories

THE BEST OF TWO WORLDS? 139

Table 6.1 Goals and Characteristics of Ideal-Typical Area Studies, Comparative Studies, and CAS

Individualization (traditional area studies)	Generalization (classic comparative studies)	Comparative area studies
Idiographic research questions aiming at understanding concrete places	Nomothetic research questions focusing on explaining classes of phenomena	Research questions aiming at nomothetic explanation in classes of phenomena bounded by concrete local contexts
Context-sensitive concepts and theory	Universal, abstract concepts and theory	Both generalization and individualization as valuable objectives
Explorative and open designs that can generate hypotheses and theory	Rigorous research designs with systematic testing of theory	Universal, but context-sensitive concepts and theories
"Deep" knowledge on (causal) mechanisms and processes	"Broad" knowledge on causal effects and sensitivity to causal identification	Iterative inductive and deductive steps to combine deep and broad knowledge

and concepts context sensitive, especially when concepts and theories of a particular regional origin are applied to different regional contexts.

Regarding methodology and method, CAS needs to balance deduction and induction, the basic methodological orientations that follow from the objectives of generalization and individualization. Again, deduction and induction are not mutually exclusive. In fact, they are part of different *steps* in the scientific process—and we can use different designs, sources, and instruments at different stages of a scientific process and for different purposes. This means that single-case studies, small-N, medium-N comparisons, as well as large-N studies each have a place in CAS. When conducting medium- or large-N studies, we will not be able to look deeply into the cases. In-depth analysis comes at the cost of empirical scope and generalizability. When we accept the dual goals of individualization and generalization, CAS should be able to use the full toolbox not just concentrating on a single orthodoxy, however defined.

Yet the methodological discussions on CAS have thus far been focused on maximizing the potential of "cross-regional small-N comparison encompassing cases drawn from different areas while retaining the commitment to context-sensitivity evident in area-bound small-N comparison" (Köllner et al. 2018, 17). Indeed, small-N controlled comparison provides a powerful tool for integrating the individualizing and generalizing research objectives: It is founded on abstract, universal concepts and theory. It aims to make causal inferences by carefully selecting the cases and given the limited number of cases, can look deeply into the empirical specificity of the cases. Moreover, by carefully selecting the cases, small-N controlled comparisons might attain some degree of generalizability based on some assumptions of unit homogeneity (Hertog 2021). Ultimately, however, one cannot escape the trade-off between individualization and generalization. More cases limit the qualitative leverage while generalization remains barely achievable if we do not look at the universe of cases or a representative sample. Even the most advanced selection of cases usually falls short of fully isolating causal relationships. And even if we succeed in doing so, we do not know how effects and mechanisms play out in other cases than the ones studied empirically. Inevitably, other methods and research instruments will be superior in some respects. Following from this, we argue that the methodological discussion on how CAS could best bridge the dual goals of individualization and generalization should not be limited to small-N controlled comparisons across regional boundaries but should be broadened and integrated with the discussion on multi-method research (MMR).

The Application of MMR in CAS

The idea to combine different analytical methods to make use of one method's strengths to counter another method's weaknesses has been explicitly discussed in the social sciences at least since the late 1950s (Campbell and Fiske 1959). Especially since the mid-2000s, the methodological principles and practical application of MMR has received increased attention, following the publication of Gary King, Robert Keohane, and Sidney Verba's 1994 volume *Designing Social Inquiry (DSI)*, which triggered a broad and fruitful debate on the categorical differences, strengths, and weaknesses of different methodological approaches for the purposes of descriptive and causal inference (Brady and Collier 2004; Bennett 2010; Goertz and Mahoney 2012). Much of the literature in the wake of DSI has taken up these discussions in assessing the benefits and limits of combining multiple methods for different analytical purposes (e.g., Ahmed and Sil 2009, 2012). The overwhelming majority of this discussion has focused on the combination of quantitative—typically statistical—and qualitative case-study approaches (Lieberman 2005; Seawright 2016). More recently, the discussion has broadened to include the combination of set-theoretic methods with case studies (Rohlfing and Schneider 2018; Goertz 2017) or with experiments (Basedau 2020). However, as already R. Burke Johnson, Anthony Onwuegbuzie, and Lisa Turner's (2007) non-exhaustive list of nineteen different types of MMR shows, the potential combinations of methods are much more diverse.

We argue that to maximize its contribution to a CAS framework, an MMR approach needs to *systematically combine at least two different methods of empirical inference that operate on different levels of analysis, and which are each supposed to fulfill specific and complementary goals within the research design.* In the following, we will limit our discussion on the combination of two methods; yet our definition of MMR also includes combinations of three or more methods. First, the combination of different methods in MMR is *systematic*, which means on the one hand that their combination is "nested" and aimed at answering a single overarching research question for a well-specified universe of empirical phenomena (Lieberman 2005). At the same time, "systematic" also means that the results of the first method inform the design of the second method, especially in terms of the definition of the sample and the selection of cases. Second, the combination refers to methods of *empirical inference*, either descriptive or causal or both (King et al. 1994). Third, the individual methods are combined such that each method operates on a *different level of analysis*, with one method operating on a cross-case level and the other operating on the within-case level. This ensures that each of the combined methods contributes a specific inferential goal within a CAS study. The cross-case method aims at CAS's goal of identifying cross-case regularities across a well-defined sample or population of empirical instances. The within-case method might fulfill multiple functions through in-depth analyses of individual cases, including the tracing of causal mechanisms, the identification of potentially omitted data, and the evaluation of concept validity and measurement (Seawright 2016).

Objectives and Characteristics of MMR in CAS

Based on this conception of MMR and the discussions of CAS as the systematic integration of generalizing and individualizing research aims above, Table 6.2 summarizes the core contributions of the individual methods that

142 ADVANCING COMPARATIVE AREA STUDIES

Table 6.2 Objectives and Characteristics of Methods Within MMR in CAS

	Cross-case method	Within-case method
Objective	Generalizing	Individualizing
Descriptive inference	Identifying descriptive regularities across cases	Identifying descriptive specificities of individual cases
Causal inference	Identifying causal effects across cases	Identifying causal effects within individual cases
	Identifying regularities concerning causal mechanisms	Identifying causal mechanisms
Integration within MMR design	Case selection for within-case method	(Re)specification of sample/population (scope conditions)
Concepts and theory	Deductive	Inductive or deductive
Concepts	Application of defined concepts and variables	Inductive: generating/modifying concepts
		Deductive: testing applicability of concepts
Theory	Testing of theories on causal effects	Inductive: generating theories on mechanisms
	Testing generalizability of causal mechanisms	Inductive: generating arguments on causal effects, including omitted variables
		Deductive: testing arguments on mechanisms
Methods	Cross-case comparison	Within-case analysis
	Cross-case regression, etc.	Within-case regression, etc.
	QCA and variants, typological theory	Within-case QCA and variants
	Comparative case study	Process-tracing case studies

are combined within a CAS-MMR design in terms of the three dimensions outlined above: objectives, concepts and theories, and methods. In this subsection we discuss each of these dimensions first theoretically, and in the following subsection we illustrate the theoretical discussion based on two examples of applied MMR research within the CAS context.

Before we do so, however, we note three qualifications. First, we are not saying that the summary of the individual methods' contributions to the MMR approach is relevant only for CAS. Many of the differences between the methods and their respective goals are well established in the methods literature and have been discussed outside of the CAS context. We also do not want to imply that these are the only relevant aspects to note in terms in the combination of cross-case and within-case methods. However, we argue that these characteristics are the crucial aspects for the application of MMR in the CAS context. Second, we argue that neither the cross-case nor the within-case part of the MMR design is necessarily wedded to one of the two methods "cultures" (Goertz and Mahoney 2012) or "styles," that is, qualitative or quantitative approaches. In applied MMR, the cross-case method will often be quantitative, and the within-case method will often be qualitative. Yet quantitative approaches such as a regression analysis on standardized panel-survey data can be utilized for individualizing research objectives, and qualitative approaches such as comparative case studies aim for (bounded) generalizations. Third, the application of MMR by necessity is a sequential process, in which one of the methods is done first to generate insights that will be taken up by the other method, which in turn provides insights that are relevant to interpreting the results of the first method. While some authors prefer a predefined sequence of one method, for instance first running a cross-case regression and then conducting case studies (e.g., Lieberman 2005), we are agnostic about the actual order in which the methods are applied. Some functions of one method will only be relevant if that method is applied first in the sequence, others are only sensible if the method comes second, while yet others are relevant either way. From our perspective, the generation of knowledge includes an alternating process of induction and deduction that should not be codified into a single "correct" sequence.

Objectives

Within the MMR design, each of the two methods fulfills different objectives. On the most general level, the cross-case method aims at generalization, while the within-case method aims at individualization. The generalizing and individualizing goals can be further disaggregated into three dimensions: descriptive inference, causal inference, and the integration of the methods within the MMR design.

Descriptive inference refers to the goal of providing some systematic description of the real world by inferring "information about unobserved facts from the facts we have observed" (King et al. 1994, 34). The descriptive goal of the cross-case method is to describe regularities, that is, commonalities and differences, across cases. The scope of these generalized descriptive inferences depends on the overall research goals of the study and can range from a generalizing summary of the descriptive "patterns" in the sample of cases to generalized inferences of the typical characteristics of the phenomenon in question beyond the sample to some well-specified population. The descriptive goal of the within-case method is to identify the specificities of individual cases. This is important for the individualizing objective of understanding places in their own right but also informs the generalizing aspect of the MMR approach by providing the empirical material from which to infer the generalizations.

A second goal of CAS is *causal inference*, that is, the theoretical conclusion that an empirically observed relationship between two phenomena is such that one phenomenon (the cause, X) "produces" the other phenomenon (the outcome, Y) through some kind of mechanism (King et al. 1994, 76–91).[3] Here the cross-case method typically has the function of identifying the causal effect of X on Y. An alternative goal of the cross-case method will be to summarize and generalize findings of individual within-case studies to identify commonalities and differences of cases in terms of causal mechanisms. Again, these insights into causal regularities might be limited to the sample but also could be generalized for a specified population, depending on the research goal, and keeping in mind the high demands out-of-sample generalization puts on the underlying assumptions as well as the quantity and quality of data (Rohlfing 2012). The within-case method can also be used to identify causal effects, for instance by comparing differences in X and Y within the same case at two different times. The most powerful inferential contribution of the within-case method in the MMR design, however, will be the identification of causal mechanisms through which the cause produces the outcome (Weller and Barnes 2014).

Besides these inferential objectives, each of the methods has specific contributions in ensuring the "integration" (Seawright 2016) of the MMR design. The cross-case method can be used to systematize and inform the selection of cases that should be analyzed in-depth in the within-case stage (Lieberman 2005; Gerring 2017). The integrative contribution of the within-case analysis, in turn, is to check whether the population is

---

[3] See also the discussion of causal inference and its relationship to the notion of causal explanation in Saylor's contribution to this volume.

THE BEST OF TWO WORLDS? 145

sufficiently well defined and, if necessary, to redefine the scope conditions that specify the sample or population (Gerring 2012, 64–66).

Concepts and Theory

The different methods within the MMR design also include different approaches to the application and development of concepts and theories. In terms of concepts, the cross-case method requires the existence of pre-defined concepts, definitions, and operationalizations of the main research variables, which are then applied uniformly across each of the cases. As discussed above, while this is necessary for achieving generalizable insights, it runs the risk of applying concepts that are either too "thin" to differentiate important aspects of the phenomenon or are insufficiently context-sensitive. The within-case method, on the other hand, can be used as an inductive tool to generate original or refine existing concepts and measurements based on real-world insights. It also can be used as an empirical pretest to evaluate the "fit" of a given concept within a specific context, before it is applied to the larger sample. In this way, the within-case method ensures and enhances the validity of the conceptual tools applied in both parts of the MMR design and makes sure that the conceptual apparatus is sufficiently context-sensitive to capture the ontologically relevant elements of the phenomenon in question (Goertz and Mahoney 2012, chap. 10).

The same holds for the contribution of the individual methods within an MMR design for theory development. As discussed above, the cross-case method is mainly useful for the deductive testing of theories on causal effects, but sometimes can also be applied for testing the generalizability of causal mechanisms across cases, when the results of multiple within-case analyses are systematically compared. The within-case method can also fulfill a deductive function by testing existing theoretical arguments on the causal mechanisms. In addition, however, it can function as a tool of induction to generate theoretical arguments on causal mechanisms, but also on the causal effect of individual variables. This latter function of within-case analyses has been widely discussed in the existing MMR literature from the perspective of identifying omitted variables to improve the fit of regression models in the combination of statistical and case analyses (Goertz 2017; Seawright 2016).

Methods

Yet, and as noted, statistical and case-study analyses are not the only methods that can be fruitfully combined. In fact, numerous discrete approaches can function as the cross-case method to uncover general patterns, commonalities, and differences across cases. This includes the broad family of regression techniques and other statistical methods; QCA and other set-theoretic approaches, including typological theory (Møller and Skaaning 2017), or case-based, structured-focused comparisons based, for instance, on Mill's methods of agreement and difference (Rohlfing 2012, chap. 4) or the corresponding most-similar-systems design and the most-different-systems design (Sartori 1991). Similarly, the menu of potentially useful methods for within-case analyses includes not merely the well-known qualitative process tracing approach (George and Bennett 2004) but also experimental, statistical, and set-theoretic methods used on within-case data (Flores and Flores-Lagunes 2007).

Two Examples of MMR in CAS

To illustrate the practice and value of MMR within a CAS context, we briefly discuss two book-length examples of published research that fall broadly into the CAS framework and address thematically related research questions yet exemplify the wide range of different research design decisions that are commensurate with the MMR approach in CAS. The first book is *When Soldiers Rebel: Ethnic Armies and Political Instability in Africa* by Kristen Harkness (2018); the second is *Imposing Sanctions on Violent-Non-State Actors to Restore International Peace and Security* by Christopher Huber (2022). The two books center on different phenomena: civil-military relations for democratic development in Harkness's work, and the effectiveness of sanctions in Huber's book. They also differ regarding regions. Harkness focuses on the great variety of countries in sub-Saharan Africa, while Huber has a cross-regional approach that combines global quantitative data and two case studies from the Middle East / North Africa (MENA) and sub-Saharan Africa. Table 6.3 summarizes the commonalities and differences between the two publications along the principles and categories discussed in the previous sections.

Kristen Harkness's book aims to describe the role ethnicity and ethnic inequality play for the explanation of military coups in sub-Saharan Africa. Accordingly, the research question is decidedly region-specific, as sub-Saharan Africa is one of the most coup-prone regions in the world and the only region where military coups are still somewhat frequent. In addition, in sub-Saharan Africa ethnicity and ethnic inequality are relevant issues that have long been thought to affect civil-military relations. Moreover, Harkness

Table 6.3 Two Examples of MMR within a CAS Context

	Harkness 2016	Huber 2022
CAS type and scope		
Type of comparison	Within-region	Cross-region
Region(s)	Sub-Saharan Africa	Global, focus on MENA and Sub-Saharan Africa
Scope of research question	Region-specific	Period-specific
Concept (DV)		
Concept creation	Deductive	Deductive
Concept generality	General	General
Concept complexity	Dichotomous	Dichotomous
Theory		
Theory creation	Deductive, but tailored to region	Deductive and inductive
Independent variables (IVs)	Focus on one variable	Set of variables
Methods		
Sequence of methods	Cross-case method first, within-case method second	Cross-case method first, within-case method second, cross-case method third
Cross-case method	Logistic regression	Logistic regression
Objective of cross-case method	Testing of causal effects; case selection for within-case analysis	Generalizability of causal effects and mechanisms
Within-case method	Process-tracing case study	Process-tracing case study
Objective of within-case method	Testing of causal mechanisms	Inductive identification of causal effects in deviant cases
Generalization claim		
Generalization claim	Bounded: temporal (post-independence; post-democratization) and regional (sub-Saharan Africa)	Bounded: temporal (post-2000)

stresses the region-specific empirical puzzle that, surprisingly, in Africa it is not necessarily the deprived ethnic groups who engage in political violence, but those who benefit from the existing power relationship.

Her dependent variable is one form of such violence, namely military coups, which she defines and conceptualizes deductively based on standard definitions drawn from the existing coup-literature. The dependent variable is dichotomous: either a military coup takes place or it does not. To explain the occurrence of coups in sub-Saharan Africa and the finding that if those coups happen, they are staged surprisingly often by officers belonging to the dominant ethnic groups, Harkness argues that these officers have both the motive and the capability to stage a coup. The motive is to protect existing privileges; the capability results from the fact that they are privileged and thus have access to arms. The single independent variable is, thus, whether an "ethnic army," that is, an army dominated by one ethnic group, exists; the motive and opportunity to stage a coup follow from that and can be considered the mechanism through which the explanatory variable produces the outcome.

Harkness empirically tests this theoretical argument, which is developed deductively but tailored to the specific context of sub-Saharan Africa civil-military relations, in a two-step MMR design, in which the cross-case method is run first and the within-case method is run second. As the cross-case method, Harkness employs logistic, cross-sectional statistical analyses of African countries during two potentially coup-prone moments: during state formation/independence and during democratization periods. The sample includes forty-eight and eighty cases, respectively. The objectives of the cross-case analysis are to test the theorized relationship between the existence of an ethnic army and coup occurrence and to estimate the effect strength of the independent variable when controlling for alternative explanations. Moreover, it also provides the empirical basis for selecting the cases for the within-case part of the empirical analysis. For that, Harkness undertakes a total of seven case studies, in which she traces the civil-military dynamics during four moments of state formation (Cameroon, Sierra Leone, Senegal, Ghana) and three periods of democratization (Benin, Nigeria, Senegal). She selects these cases based on a typical-case logic (cf. Gerring 2017), maximizing variance in the independent variables and outcomes. This approach allows for some generalization within the region as the findings of the cross-case and the within-case analyses provide strong evidence for the theoretical argument in different historical and subregional contexts. Yet Harkness makes sure not to stretch the generalization claim, as she explicitly limits the generalizations to the region under study. The specific value of the MMR design in Harkness's study is the systematic combination of the generalizing inferences on the cross-sample patterns on civil-military relations in sub-Saharan Africa that she draws from the quantitative analyses with the individualizing findings of her case studies. The latter not only allow her to empirically trace the causal mechanisms in the selected countries but also function as a test for the "fit" of her deductively won conceptual and theoretical framework for the local and time-specific contexts in her sample.

While she does not frame it as an explicit exercise of interregional comparison, the study includes two regional comparative perspectives that make it a good example of CAS-MMR. First, the quantitative part includes data on coups and ethnicity from northern African countries such as Algeria, Egypt, Sudan, and Tunisia, which is included in the regression analyses and in passing contrasted to historical patterns of ethnic recruitment of military officers in sub-Saharan Africa. Second, Harkness consciously identifies and systematically contrasts differences within the broader region of sub-Saharan Africa and systematically tests for differences in subregional clusters based on colonial history. In both her quantitative and qualitative analyses, she tests whether and how French and British colonial practices, which are not only distributed along distinct geographical boundaries but constitute two regions based on colonial legacy rather than geography (i.e., anglophone and francophone Africa), affect the recruitment practices of military personnel in the postcolonial regions. Thus, her example shows that even without a dedicated cross-georegional perspective, CAS scholars can leverage empirical variation from within large and highly diverse regions such as sub-Saharan Africa as essentially and functionally equivalent to variations across regions, especially if these are smaller or less diverse.[4]

Huber's study investigates the effectiveness of UN sanctions against violent nonstate actors and, by doing so, addresses a pertinent research gap; the comparative study of the effectiveness of sanctions has primarily dealt with governments and not nonstate targets like rebel or terrorist groups. Methodologically, it combines three steps, starting and ending with a large-N regression. However, two deviant case studies play a crucial role in informing the second round of the large-N regression. Huber starts with compiling a new data set on UN sanctions episodes against nonstate actors across several regions—principally worldwide but especially Africa and the Middle East from 2000 to 2018. Effectiveness of sanctions, the central concept, is measured as the (relative) compliance with the sanctions' goals. In the first, quantitative step, Huber tests several hypotheses deductively drawn from the literature (e.g., simultaneous regional sanctions, economic impact,

---

[4] We thank Rudra Sil for encouraging us to highlight this aspect.

religious ideology). He identifies the absence of religious ideology of the sanctioned groups among others as important determinants of why UN sanctions might have generally (not) worked, in terms of both coercing and constraining the sanctioned target's actions.[5]

He then selects one deviant case from the MENA region and one deviant case from sub-Saharan Africa, the Justice and Equality Movement in Sudan and Al-Shabaab in Somalia, in which sanctions proved to be successful in coercing (Justice and Equality Movement) and constraining (Al-Shabaab) these groups. These cases are deviant as they do not fit the model of the first round of regressions. The case studies engage in (a diminished form of) process tracing by exploring along a timeline what might explain that sanctions actually worked. From this analysis, he generates four more hypotheses, namely that sanctions are effective when (a) the targeted nonstate actors lack internal cohesion and (b) do not receive external financial support and, simultaneously, (c) international mediation takes place and (d) military pressure is used against them. These hypotheses are then put to the test at the cross-country level again, including another round of data collection where necessary, that is, if quantifiable data for the second round of regressions was not readily available. Some of the variables generated through the case studies prove to be significant in the second round of cross-country regression, including after several robustness checks. Coercing is successful when the targeted group is fragmented and when, additionally, mediation efforts are made and military action is taken. Military action also works for coercing: However, except religious ideology, none of the tested determinants seem to affect constraining sanctions.

While the main goal of Huber's study remains generalization, the final results would not have been possible without the individualizing step of exploring two case studies selected according to their deviance vis-à-vis the general findings. The study exemplifies how carefully selected case studies can be critical, if not indispensable, in improving the results of regression analysis. The three-step combination of deductive and inductive inference produces results that would have been largely impossible without mixing methods in this way, in fact, a "positive-sum game" rather than a trade-off (Sil 2018, 225).

---

[5] Coercing sanctions directly punish the sanctioned target's behavior, while constraining sanctions "attempt to prevent the target from continuing one specific action by restricting its access to essential resources needed to engage in this proscribed activity" (Huber 2022, 14).

The two examples outlined above show how the systematic and integrated combination of cross-case and within-case methods of inference informs and helps provide generalizable insights within clearly defined contextual boundaries. In this way it is a natural "fit" to contribute to the core tenets of CAS, which sees both generalization and individualization as valuable objectives; stresses the usefulness of general yet context-sensitive concepts and theories; and relies on research designs that combine deductive and inductive elements (see Table 6.1). The examples also show that there is no fixed template for conducting MMR within a CAS context besides the combination of a cross-case and a within-case method of inference and the explicit concern for the relevance of regional contexts and the boundedness of generalizations. Accordingly, the MMR approach to CAS can include a variety of discrete methods and research techniques, handling a wide range of data for both inductive and deductive purposes. This may also include several forms of experiments (including "natural experiments"), which are now considered some sort of "gold standard" for causal inference.

CAS and the Challenges to MMR

Of course, we do not want to imply that MMR is a panacea for the inferential challenges of social science research in general and CAS in particular, as the combination of different empirical methods cannot hope to solve all problems inherent to individual methods. For instance, the combination of statistical regression analyses with within-case process tracing does nothing to make the assumptions underlying regression analyses on cross-national macrodata less heroic (see Kittel 2006). Nor does it solve the inherent problems of process tracing as a method of causal inference or the still-disputed generalizability of empirical findings on causal mechanisms (Hertog 2021). Moreover, the MMR literature has shown in detail that the combination of different methods might introduce new challenges and problems. These range from fundamental problems such as the potential incommensurability of the respective methods' epistemic and ontological foundations, and the compounding of errors resulting from the application of one method by integrating it with another method, to practical difficulties of publishing the design and results of MMR in articles, and the high demands that high-quality MMR puts on individual researchers who are required to master different methods, research instruments, and tools (Rohlfing 2008; Kuehn and Rohlfing 2010; Ahmed and Sil 2012; Beach 2020).

These concerns are well founded and must be taken seriously. However, over the last years the MMR literature has developed suggestions on how to conduct MMR such that its inferential potential is maximized while the methodological problems are minimized (Weller and Barnes 2014; Seawright 2016; Goertz 2017). Moreover, the basic underlying assumptions of the CAS framework itself ensure that the fundamental potential problem of MMR, the collision of different ontological and epistemological underpinnings, is somewhat mitigated, as the objective of CAS is causal analysis through comparison within and across regions (Köllner et al. 2018, 3). Comparison requires, at least, the "unit homogeneity assumption" (King et al. 1994, 91) that the cases under study are indeed comparable and that the insights from empirical evaluation of the individual cases can be generalized to some well-defined and geographically and temporally bounded population. In consequence, an MMR approach also helps to fulfill CAS's aim of building an intellectual bridge between localized area studies research communities, on the one hand, and, on the other, between area studies and the more general, disciplinary fields of social science (Köllner et al. 2018, 3) by fostering communication between and fruitful integration of the hitherto siloed research of different methodological traditions (Ahmed 2019).

Of course, none of this addresses the problem that MMR puts great technical demands on applied researchers, as they must master the methodological techniques effectively to apply two different methods. Yet, as our empirical examples illustrate, these problems are not insurmountable. First, both Harkness's and Huber's impressive works shows that a single researcher can create an original data set, master the necessary technical knowledge to apply standard regression analyses, and conduct case studies, in the case of Harkness even including fieldwork in franco- and anglophone sub-Saharan Africa within a single project. Second, although both works are single-authored, CAS can be easily done in teams. An example is Aurel Croissant et al. (2013) on civil-military relations in democratizing nations in Asia. This study was organized in a team to do justice to the vast linguistic, cultural, and historical differences between the countries of South, Southeast, and East Asia. In that project, four of the five project contributors became specialists on civil-military relations in one or two countries, while the project's principal investigator took the lead in the comparison. The conceptual and theoretical framework was developed by all project contributors together under the lead of the PI, thus ensuring both the general applicability as well as the context-specificity of the framework. This points to the great potential of teamwork and a "scholarly division of labor" (Sil 2000) to organize MMR in CAS, with each member of the team being responsible for a specific, essential task within an integrated research design.

Conclusion

We started out this chapter by asserting that, ultimately, CAS aims to bridge two different general research objectives: the *individualizing* goal of producing context-sensitive, in-depth knowledge on individual places, and the *generalizing* goal of establishing abstract inferences that generalize beyond the single case. We discussed the implications for applied research of these general objectives along three dimensions: the diverging goals of "understanding places" versus "explaining classes of phenomena"; the different use of concepts and theory; and the corresponding methodological approaches and research instruments. We then argued that a multi-method research design that combines a cross-case and a within-case method in a coherent, systematic, and integrated research design is a helpful approach to bridge the twin goals of individualization and generalization. By combining deductive and inductive aspects as well as cross-case and within-case inference, CAS researchers can ensure both bounded generalization and the necessary context-sensitivity and empirical specificity, which makes the results academically and politically relevant. Of course, we do not argue that MMR is the only way to conduct CAS, even though our definition of MMR is sufficiently general to capture a wide range of methods combinations, and most existing applications of CAS might actually fulfill the criteria of what we define as MMR. Nonetheless, we think it crucial to make the MMR logic underlying these applications explicit, not least to invite applied CAS scholars to draw on insights of the well-developed methodological literature on how to conduct "good" MMR. Indeed, a multitude of opportunities exist to combine methods to advance knowledge both on specific cases and on phenomena in general. Mixing methods can greatly contribute to what Sil points out (2018, 225), namely that "engagement with area studies scholarship and the pursuit of disciplinary knowledge can be a positive-sum game."

Bibliography

Adcock, Robert, and David Collier. 2001. Measurement Validity: A Shared Standard for Qualitative and Quantitative Research. *American Political Science Review* 95 (3): 529–546.

Ahmed, Amel. 2019. Multi-Methodology Research and Democratization Studies: Intellectual Bridges Among Islands of Specialization. *Democratization* 26 (1): 97–139.

Ahmed, Amel. 2020. The Utility of Comparative Area Studies for Historical Analysis. *Qualitative & Multi-Method Research* 17–18 (1): 7–10.

Ahmed, Amel, and Rudra Sil, eds. 2009. Symposium: Cautionary Perspectives on Multi-Method Research. *Qualitative and Multi-Method Research* 7 (2): 2–21.

Ahmed, Amel, and Rudra Sil. 2012. When Multi-Method Research Subverts Methodological Pluralism—or, Why We Still Need Single-Method Research. *Perspectives on Politics* 10 (4): 935–953.

Ahram, Ariel I. 2011. The Theory and Method of Comparative Area Studies. *Qualitative Research* 11 (1): 69–90.

Ahram, Ariel I. 2013. Concepts and Measurement in Multimethod Research. *Political Research Quarterly* 66 (2): 280–291.

Ahram, Ariel I., Patrick Köllner, and Rudra Sil, eds. 2018. *Comparative Area Studies: Methodological Rationales and Cross-Regional Applications*. New York: Oxford University Press.

Basedau, Matthias. 2020. Rethinking African Studies: Four Challenges and the Case for Comparative African Studies. *Africa Spectrum* 55 (2): 194–206.

Basedau, Matthias, and Patrick Köllner. 2007. Area Studies, Comparative Area Studies, and the Study of Politics: Context, Substance, and Methodological Challenges. *Zeitschrift für Vergleichende Politikwissenschaft* 1 (1): 105–124.

Beach, Derek. 2020. Multi-Method Research in the Social Sciences: A Review of Recent Frameworks and a Way Forward. *Government and Opposition* 55 (1): 163–182.

Bennett, Andrew. 2010. Process Tracing and Causal Inference. In Henry E. Brady and David Collier, eds. *Rethinking Social Inquiry: Diverse Tools, Shared Standards*. 2nd ed. Lanham, MD: Rowman & Littlefield, 207–220.

Brady, Henry E., and David Collier, eds. 2004. *Rethinking Social Inquiry: Diverse Tools, Shared Standards*. Lanham, MD: Rowman & Littlefield.

Campbell, Donald T., and Donald W. Fiske. 1959. Convergent and Discriminant Validation by the Multitrait-Multimethod Matrix. *Psychological Bulletin* 56 (2): 81–105.

Cheibub, José Antonio, Jennifer Gandhi, and James Raymond Vreeland. 2010. Democracy and Dictatorship Revisited. *Public Choice* 143 (1–2): 67–101.

Croissant, Aurel, David Kuehn, Philip Lorenz, and Paul W. Chambers. 2013. *Democratization and Civilian Control in Asia*. Basingstoke: Palgrave Macmillan.

Erdmann, Gero. 2004. Party Research: Western European Bias and the "African Labyrinth." *Democratization* 11 (3): 63–87.

Erdmann, Gero, and Ulf Engel. 2007. Neopatrimonialism Reconsidered: Critical Review and Elaboration of an Elusive Concept. *Commonwealth & Comparative Politics* 45 (1): 95–119.

Flores, Carlos A., and Alfonso Flores-Lagunes. 2007. Identification and Estimation of Casual Mechanisms and Net Effects of a Treatment. University of Miami, Department of Economics Working Papers no. 706.

George, Alexander L., and Andrew Bennett. 2004. *Case Studies and Theory Development in the Social Sciences*. Cambridge, MA: MIT Press.

Gerring, John. 2012. *Social Science Methodology: A Critical Framework*. Cambridge: Cambridge University Press.

Gerring, John. 2017. *Case Study Research: Principles and Practices*. 2nd ed. Cambridge: Cambridge University Press.

Goertz, Gary. 2006. *Social Science Concepts: A User's Guide*. Princeton, NJ: Princeton University Press.

Goertz, Gary. 2017. *Multimethod Research, Causal Mechanisms, and Case Studies: An Integrated Approach*. Princeton, NJ: Princeton University Press.

Goertz, Gary, and James Mahoney. 2012. *A Tale of Two Cultures*. Princeton, NJ: Princeton University Press.

Greitens, Sheena Chestnut. 2016. *Dictators and Their Secret Police: Coercive Institutions and State Violence*. Cambridge: Cambridge University Press.

Hanson, Stephen E. 2009. The Contribution of Area Studies. In Todd Landman and Neil Robinson, eds. *The Sage Handbook of Comparative Politics*. London: Sage, 159–174.

Harkness, Kristen A. 2018. *When Soldiers Rebel: Ethnic Armies and Political Instability in Africa*. Cambridge: Cambridge University Press.

Hertog, Steffen. 2021. Taking Causal Heterogeneity Seriously: Implications for Case Choice and Case Study-Based Generalizations. *Sociological Methods & Research*. Published online before print, February 8, 2021. https://doi.org/10.1177/0049124120986206.

Huber, Christopher. 2022. *Imposing Sanctions on Violent Non-State Actors to Restore International Peace and Security. A Systematic Analysis of the Conditions Under Which UN Targeted Sanctions Work*. Berlin: Springer.

Johnson, R. Burke, Anthony J. Onwuegbuzie, and Lisa A. Turner. 2007. Toward a Definition of Mixed Methods Research. *Journal of Mixed Methods Research* 1 (2): 112–133.

King, Gary, Robert O. Keohane, and Sidney Verba. 1994. *Designing Social Inquiry: Scientific Inference in Qualitative Research*. Princeton, NJ: Princeton University Press.

Kittel, Bernhard. 2006. A Crazy Methodology? On the Limits of Macro-Quantitative Social Science Research. *International Sociology* 21 (5): 647–677.

Köllner, Patrick, Rudra Sil, and Ariel I. Ahram. 2018. Comparative Area Studies: What It Is, What It Can Do. In Ariel I. Ahram, Patrick Köllner, and Rudra Sil, eds. *Comparative Area Studies: Methodological Rationales and Cross-Regional Applications*. New York: Oxford University Press, 3–28.

Kuehn, David, and Ingo Rohlfing. 2010. Causal Explanation and Multi-Method Research in the Social Sciences. Committee on Concepts and Methods Working Paper Series no. 26. http://www.concepts-methods.org/WorkingPapers/PDF/1067 (accessed September 8, 2022).

Lieberman, Evan S. 2003. *Race and Regionalism in the Politics of Taxation in Brazil and South Africa*. New York: Cambridge University Press.

Lieberman, Evan S. 2005. Nested Analysis as a Mixed-Method Strategy for Comparative Research. *American Political Science Review* 99 (3): 435–452.

Lieberman, Evan S. 2009. *Boundaries of Contagion: How Ethnic Politics Have Shaped Government Responses to AIDS*. Princeton, NJ: Princeton University Press.

Møller, Jørgen, and Svend-Erik Skaaning. 2017. Explanatory Typologies as a Nested Strategy of Inquiry: Combining Cross-Case and Within-Case Analyses. *Sociological Methods & Research* 46 (4): 1018–1048.

Morgan, Kimberly J. 2016. Process Tracing and the Causal Identification Revolution. *New Political Economy* 21 (5): 489–492.

Pemstein, Daniel, Stephen A. Meserve, and James Melton. 2010. Democratic Compromise: A Latent Variable Analysis of Ten Measures of Regime Type. *Political Analysis* 18 (4): 426–449.

Pepinsky, Thomas B. 2020. What's the "Area" in Comparative Area Studies? *Qualitative and Multi-Method Research* 17–18 (1): 22–26.

Przeworski, Adam, and Henry Teune. 1970. *The Logic of Comparative Social Inquiry*. New York: John Wiley and Sons.

Ragin, Charles C. 2000. *Fuzzy-Set Social Science*. Chicago: University of Chicago Press.

Rohlfing, Ingo. 2008. What You See and What You Get: Pitfalls and Principles of Nested Analysis in Comparative Research. *Comparative Political Studies* 41 (11): 1492–1514.

Rohlfing, Ingo. 2012. *Case Studies and Causal Inference: An Integrative Framework.* Basingstoke: Palgrave Macmillan.

Rohlfing, Ingo, and Carsten Q. Schneider. 2018. A Unifying Framework for Causal Analysis in Set-Theoretic Multimethod Research. *Sociological Methods & Research* 47 (1): 37–63.

Sartori, Giovanni. 1991. Comparing and Miscomparing. *Journal of Theoretical Politics* 3 (3): 243–257.

Saylor, Ryan. 2020. Comparative Area Studies: A Route to New Insights. *Qualitative & Multi-Method Research* 17–18 (1): 1–7.

Schneider, Carsten Q., and Claudius Wagemann. 2012. *Set-Theoretic Methods for the Social Sciences: A Guide to Qualitative Comparative Analysis.* Cambridge: Cambridge University Press.

Seawright, Jason. 2016. *Multi-Method Social Science: Combining Qualitative and Quantitative Tools.* Cambridge: Cambridge University Press.

Sil, Rudra. 2000. The Division of Labor in Social Science Research: Unified Methodology or "Organic Solidarity"? *Polity* 32 (4): 499–531.

Sil, Rudra. 2018. Triangulating Area Studies, Not Just Methods: How Cross-Regional Comparison Aids Qualitative and Mixed Method Research. In Ariel I. Ahram, Patrick Köllner, and Rudra Sil, eds. 2018. *Comparative Area Studies: Methodological Rationales and Cross-Regional Applications.* New York: Oxford University Press, 225–246.

von Soest, Christian, and Alexander Stroh. 2018. Comparison Across World Regions: Managing Conceptual, Methodological, and Practical Challenges. In Ariel I. Ahram, Patrick Köllner, and Rudra Sil, eds. *Comparative Area Studies: Methodological Rationales and Cross-Regional Applications.* New York: Oxford University Press, 66–84.

Weller, Nicholas, and Jeb Barnes. 2014. *Finding Pathways: Mixed-Method Research for Studying Causal Mechanisms.* Strategies for Social Inquiry. Cambridge: Cambridge University Press.

PART III

RETHINKING THE SITES AND SPACES OF COMPARISON

7

Crossing the Boundaries of Comparison

Comparative Area Studies and Comparative Historical Analysis

Amel Ahmed

Introduction

Comparative area studies (CAS) has emerged as a significant contribution to the family of social scientific approaches rooted in contextualized comparison. Its connections to other members of this family, however, have yet to be fully articulated. In their introduction to *Comparative Area Studies: Methodological Rationales and Cross-Regional Applications*, Ariel Ahram, Patrick Köllner, and Rudra Sil offer CAS as a bridge between area studies, which have been primarily concerned with ideographic forms of inquiry, and cross-regional analysis based in disciplinary concerns and oriented toward general theory. While the authors suggest affinities to other approaches that "rely on context sensitive process-tracing and cross-case comparisons" (Köllner et al. 2018, 14), the volume does not explore in great depth its relationship to other modes of comparative analysis. One area that is especially in need of elaboration is the connection between CAS and comparative historical analysis (CHA), which is mentioned only in passing as a complementary mode of analysis. This chapter aims to address this gap. It advances the CAS approach by deepening on our understanding if its connections to CHA and reclaiming a space for "geohistorical sensibilities" in historical analysis.

The relationship between CAS and CHA is an important one to clarify not only because they are fellow travelers but also because, as I will argue here, they share a common intellectual lineage that has been obscured in contemporary social science literature. In particular, both CAS and CHA display

---

Amel Ahmed, *Crossing the Boundaries of Comparison*. In: *Advancing Comparative Area Studies*. Edited by: Ariel I. Ahram, Patrick Köllner, and Rudra Sil, Oxford University Press. © Oxford University Press (2025). DOI: 10.1093/oso/9780197809365.003.0007

160 ADVANCING COMPARATIVE AREA STUDIES

important linkages to a distinctive approach to social scientific analysis inaugurated by the French *Annales* school of historical research. The *Annales* school, so named after its flagship publication, *Annales: Economies, Sociétiés, Civilisations*, took off in the early twentieth century and revolutionized historical methodology by marrying it to social theory while maintaining rich contextualized understanding of particular historical milieus. While the *Annales* school emphasized the need to consider time and space as two co-constituted components of historical analysis, in subsequent developments these two features have been separated, with CHA focused heavily on the temporal elements of comparative analysis and CAS addressing itself to the spatial dimensions.

This has been highly consequential for social science history, as "comparative history" has come to be strongly associated with CHA and its emphasis on understanding the temporal aspects of historical inquiry. It has also come to be associated with a particular understanding of comparison that privileges nomothetic case-based comparisons rather than open-ended historical explanation. What has been lost is the attention to the spatial aspects of historical analysis, which requires one to problematize historical geography, questioning the unit of analysis and often yielding comparisons that may not be easily accommodated within the framework of case-based comparison. Such comparisons may span continents and seaways, slice up regions in unconventional ways, or make connections between far-flung places.

The bifurcation of these two modes of inquiry has its roots in historical intellectual disagreements between different communities of scholars, which revolved around fundamental questions of the validity of social science history. This was a contest between those who wished to have historical analysis follow the laws of scientific inference and those who sought to elucidate historical causation as a distinct logic of inference. This contest featured pioneering figures such as Charles Tilly in the former camp and Fernand Braudel in the latter. In CHA circles Tilly prevailed, moving the field in the direction of case-based, controlled comparisons. While this has been a very fruitful mode of inquiry, moving in this direct inadvertently led scholars to jettison important lessons of the *Annales* tradition that can be reclaimed, I argue here, through engagement with CAS.

CAS, I argue, can help to bring back a much-needed sensibility toward historical geography that has been muted in recent discussions of CHA. At the same time, CAS pushes past some of the self-imposed limitations of the *Annales* school—in particular, a rigid conception of "geohistory" that

CROSSING THE BOUNDARIES OF COMPARISON   161

dictates a particular scope of analysis. Instead, CAS advances what I consider a "geohistorical sensibility", one which maintains some of the most critical insights of the *Annales* school without all of its formal strictures. Accordingly, CAS lends itself to a wide variety of analyses, from case-based comparison to continental and regional histories, bridging one of the central disagreements that led the CAS and CHA communities to part ways. Finally, it can make important contributions to the study of social science history, offering a disciplined way of incorporating a sense of historical space in social scientific inquiry.

I begin below with a discussion of the *Annales* school to illustrate some of its central contributions to the study of social science history. I do so with the goal of understanding some of the intellectual roots of CAS and CHA as well as the intellectual forces that led them to part ways. I focus especially on the contributions of Braudel, who pioneered "geohistory" as a methodology that considers both the spatial and temporal dimensions of historical analysis as critically linked. In Braudel's work we see the connections between historical time and historical space articulated most explicitly. Within his framework of geohistory, structure rather than events delineates historical time, and geography is taken to be the deepest of structuring elements, revealing continuities that may not appear from the perspective of episodic history. The rejection of geohistory in some circles of the social sciences led to the marginalization of the spatial aspects of historical analysis. This can be seen in the CHA tradition, at first as an explicit intellectual commitment and later as a practice or norm that few now question. In the final section, I return to a discussion of CHA and CAS to examine how the two can complement and reinforce each other, offering a more robust approach to contextualized historical comparison.

The *Annales* School: The Quest for Total History

The *Annales* school of historical research represents one of the most important developments in social science methodology of the twentieth century.[1] Yet its influence within the social sciences is surprisingly underappreciated.

---

[1] While there have been divergent views of the nature and homogeneity of the *Annales* school, historians have uniformly identified it as one of the most important influences on twentieth-century scholarship, solidifying the position of social history and historical analysis within the social sciences (Stoianovich 1976; Clark 1985; Burke 1990; Iggers 2005).

Though the contextualist methodology that distinguishes the *Annales* school from other approaches is a guiding principle of both CHA and CAS, for example, one rarely finds references to the works of Marc Bloch, the founding figure who first articulated this approach within the social sciences (Ahmed 2022). And while common conceptual categories such as the *longue durée* are often deployed in comparative analysis, mentions of Fernand Braudel, the *Annales* historian who introduced this approach, are also rare. In discussions of both CHA ad CAS, it is common to find references to Karl Marx, Émile Durkheim, and Max Weber as the classical founders, but *Annales* scholars are usually absent from the accounting of influences.

Before discussing its relevance for CHA and CAS, in this section I seek to elucidate the approach of the *Annales* school and the features that distinguish it from others. Pioneered by Bloch and Lucien Febvre in the 1920s, the *Annales* school has been closely associated with a contextualist approach to historical methodology. This approach challenged prevalent realist methodologies found in both traditional historical accounts and the ascendent approach of Marxian historical materialism (Ahmed 2022; see also Harsgrove 1978). The contextualist approach of *Annales* scholars sought an empathetic understanding of historical subjectivities through a reconstruction of the context in which they operated.

Annales scholars shared with Marxian analysis a rejection of traditional historical methods in which history was essentially a history of great men and monumentalized events. These traditional historical accounts typically treated such phenomena as the succession of kings and dynasties. And historical knowledge was understood to be the accumulation of historical facts through the examination of political, diplomatic, and other formal documentary evidence. This approach was typically accompanied by an unreflexive methodological realism, which took historical subjects as given and their meaning unchanging. The turn to "the social" in historical inquiry, for both Marx and *Annales* scholars, was part of a project to undermine these traditional accounts and the forms of authority which relied on them.

However, *Annales* scholars also defined themselves against the tradition of Marxian analysis that had come to dominate the study of social history. Of particular concern were Marx's claims that, through a process of abstraction, one can derive concepts and categories that transcend particular contexts to offer a universal logic of history. In contrast, *Annales* scholars saw as the key to historical analysis a mode of inquiry that could tap into actors' subjective understandings of their situation. While historical subjectivities

CROSSING THE BOUNDARIES OF COMPARISON   163

were of course central to Marx's analysis as well, they were treated as obstacles to historical understanding, reflecting the particularity of the material conditions in which they were embedded. This can be seen for example in Marxian claims about consciousness and especially the idea of "false consciousness", which suggests that subjects could be deceived by their material conditions and downgrades the epistemic status of such subjectivities.[2] For *Annales* scholars, however, far from an impediment, these subjectivities were the key to understanding. The ability to view the world as it was experienced by historical subjects was essential for an authentic reading of history.

This kind of understanding required a reconstruction of and immersion in the relevant historical context. To this end, *Annales* scholars advanced a mode of inquiry that they referred to as "total history," which sought deep contextualized understandings for specific historical periods, rather than sweeping accounts across epochs. The name "total history" is somewhat deceptive, as it conjures images of universal history. However, the intent was quite the opposite—*Annales* scholars insisted on the need to bound historical investigation spatially and temporally, establishing what today we might refer to as "scope conditions" for generalization. The "total" in total history refers to the substantive purview of historical investigations that was meant to expand the definition of the "the social." Against the heavy reliance on economic determinants in Marx's work, *Annales* scholars maintained the need to incorporate all aspects of social life within historical analysis (Lyon 1987, 200). It was through this combination of narrowing the spatial and temporal focus and expanding the substantive orientation of social inquiry that one could gain confidence in historical inferences.

Grounded empathetic understanding of historical subjectivities was a central commitment of *Annales* scholars. They approached history with something akin to an "ethnographic sensibility" (Schatz 2009), drawing insights from various dimensions of social life and utilizing a wide array of nondocumentary sources such as maps, coins, topographical details, climate patterns, and architectural styles. These unconventional sources became the hallmark of *Annales* scholarship and extended to the generation of new source material. Bloch, for example, was known to create replicas of

---

[2] Though Marx never used the term "false consciousness" much of his historical materialism rested on an ideological determinism which held that subjects' consciousness could be erroneous, that is, in conflict with reality. Subsequently, Marxian scholars have developed this claim further (Eyerman 1981; Mills 1989).

164   ADVANCING COMPARATIVE AREA STUDIES

agricultural tools to better understand the materialities of labor in feudal society (Chirot 1984, 30). Such practices were criticized by traditional historians who saw history as static and our knowledge of it as transmitted through found artifacts. For Bloch, however, such artifacts could only offer fragments of understanding. He sought to construct historical context in its multidimensional totality. Only then could one understand the subjectivity of those they studied—their beliefs, fears, values and priorities—a *histoire des mentalités*, as he described it. In one of his central works, *Feudal Society*, Bloch used such methods to develop a sensibility toward his subjects that considered "modes of feeling and thought," "folk memory," and "intellectual milieus" ([1939] 1961). In doing so, Bloch painted a complex picture that challenged the primacy of the material over the spiritual in accounts of economic development (Chirot 1984, 26).

It is for this reason that *Annales* scholars placed such emphasis on comparative history, which they contrasted with universal history (Sewell 1967; Hill and Hill 1980). In contrast to Marx's historical methodology, which aimed to ascertain a universal logic to history, for *Annales* scholars there could be many logics. Through comparative history, one could discern *mechanisms* that would operate similarly given similar conditions, but it would not require the historian to attribute them to a single universal cause. Moreover, *Annales* scholars resisted the sweeping claims of ontological regulatory found in universal history, leaving as the subject of empirical investigation the question of whether social processes can be applied to multiple contexts. Whether or not concepts traveled and how far was a question that had to be answered through contextualized comparisons, not assertions to be posited a priori.

In his work *Royal Touch*, for example, Bloch centered the experiences of England and France, the only European cases that engaged in the practice, but also drew on comparisons with Polynesia, where the practice emerged under very different circumstances (Bloch [1924] 1973, 46–48). The boundaries of comparison in this instance were driven by the logic of the study, rather than a priori determinations. The result would be a far more fragmented and contingent reading of history than the proponents of universal history would accept, but it was for *Annales* scholars a necessary condition for historical explanation.

The emphasis on comparison in historical inquiry was not unique to *Annales* scholars. In fact, it had much deeper roots in the French academy, going back to Durkheim's inaugural address at the University of Bordeaux,

CROSSING THE BOUNDARIES OF COMPARISON   165

in which he called for a more scientific approach to historical methodology, placing emphasis on comparison as a central feature of that approach ([1887] 1974). But while the comparative method for Durkheim was a means of disciplining historical inquiry, for *Annales* scholars it was also meant to enrich social scientific inquiry and introduce much-needed complexity to social science explanations.

The Space of History: The *Annales* School and Historical Geography

Many of the features of the *Annales* approach described above will be familiar to students of comparative historical analysis, particularly given the emphasis on understanding events in context with attention to historical subjectivities and the temporalities of historical processes. However, an aspect of the *Annales* approach that has been much less appreciated is its emphasis on historical geography and the need for a grounded understanding of space. Indeed, a central component of comparative history in the *Annales* tradition was a critical approach to geography (Chirot 1984, 32). *Annales* scholars sought to acquire an understanding of historical geography through open-ended inquiry and grounded exploration, which challenged conventional understandings of the relevant geographic references points for historical inquiry.

A concern with geography was evident in some of the earliest works of the *Annales* school. Bloch's interdisciplinary approach regularly problematized geographic boundaries, going so far as to question the idea of a "region." Such delineations, he maintained, depended on the question one was asking: "Why should one expect the jurist who is interested in feudalism, the economist who is studying the evolution of property in the countryside in modern times, and the philologist who is working on popular dialects, all to stop at precisely identical frontiers?" (Bloch [1913] 1971, 122). In a similar vein, Febvre argued that the boundaries of investigation must be defined by the object of study. In his work on the Reformation, he assailed scholars who attempted a comparison between the "French Reformation" and the "German Reformation," insisting that in view of the beliefs, attitudes, and appetites of the historical subjects, the Reformation was a European phenomenon, transcending the particularities of national structures (Febvre 1929; Clark 1999, viii).

166 ADVANCING COMPARATIVE AREA STUDIES

Annales scholars differed on the extent to which the material environment determined social action. Febvre, for example, offered a humanist understanding of historical geography, suggesting that the significance of geographic structures could be altered by actors' subjective understanding of them. In *A Geographic Introduction to History*, he contends that "a forest, which was a boundary and a defense in one epoch, may be a bond and a bridge at another." (Febvre [1924] 1966, 306). In this view, the material environment became one of possibility rather necessity, the consequences of which could only be appreciated through consideration of prevalent social structures and ideas. Later scholars, following Braudel who will be discussed in greater detail below, saw geography much more as a constraint structuring human interactions. Regardless of their commitments to material determinism, however, all maintained that acquiring the appropriate orientation to historical geography is necessary for historical explanation. And all promoted an open-ended view of geography that would problematize the geographic scope of historical investigation.

Fernand Braudel and Geohistory

If these early pioneers paved the way for a distinctive *Annales* approach to historical geography, this direction was firmly solidified by Braudel, who after Bloch and Febvre is seen as the most influential of *Annales* scholars (Trevor-Roper 1972; Clark 1985). Braudel is widely viewed as the main force behind the second wave of *Annales* scholarship, launched in the 1960s and 1970s. During this period, the engagement with historical geography became a signature feature of the *Annales* school. Under Braudel's editorship of the journal, in fact, it became standard practice to offer a geographical introduction of the subject matter for all articles.

Braudel's own work became the standard for the kind of geographic engagement expected. His central work, *The Mediterranean and the Mediterranean World* (Braudel [1972] 1995), stands out for its treatment of historical geography and helped to shape in important ways the development of social science history in the twentieth century. In this groundbreaking work, Braudel examines the history of the Mediterranean through a three-tiered view of historical time: (1) geographic time or geohistory, which is structured by the physical environment and moves at an almost imperceptibly slow pace referred to as the "long term" (*longue durée*); (2) social time or

CROSSING THE BOUNDARIES OF COMPARISON 167

social history, animated by the interactions of social grouping and representing the "medium term" (*moyenne durée*); and (3) individual time or episodic history, which focuses on events and actions that constitute the "short term" of historical time. The proper consideration of historical time was a central concern of the work, as each category suggests a different kind of periodization and different understandings of what constitutes a historical explanation. Though he treated each category separately, Braudel maintained that all three were necessary for historical understanding: "One must consult many snapshots of the past, each with its own exposure time, then fuse times and images together, rather as the colours of the solar spectrum, focused together, combine at last into pure white light" (Braudel 1993, xl).

The first category of geographic time represents one of his most novel contributions to social science history. It is on this category that I will focus attention, as it also elucidates a critical link between time and space that was the hallmark of Braudel's work and can potentially provide the link between CHA and CAS that has been lost due to the nature of disciplinary development. *Geographic time*, or "geohistory," represents the slowest-moving frame of historical time, the snapshot with the longest exposure, to use his metaphor. Within geographic time, human interactions are understood to be structured by the physical environment, the relative permanence of which establishes what he refers to as the long term (*longue durée*)[3] of human history, "whose passage is almost imperceptible, that of man in relation to the environment, a history in which all change is slow, a history of constant repetition, everlasting cycles" (Braudel [1972] 1995, 20). In his conception of the *longue durée*, time and space are not only two factors to consider, they are co-constituted. Geographic structures, he maintained, represent "a reality which can distort the effect of time, changing its scope and speed" (Braudel [1972] 1995, 18).

It should be stressed that this is not a relativist view of time. In other words, it is not the subjective understanding of actors that defines the *longue durée* but the stubborn reality of the physical environment that serves to

---

[3] In some instances, this is referred to as the very long term (*très longue durée*) and in others just as the long term (*longue durée*). Braudel himself is not consistent, and in his later methodological writings he refers to both geographic history and social history as the *longue durée* as his goal is to distinguish these structural approaches from episodic history, which at the time dominated political history. This ambiguity contributed to the developments discussed below where the role of geographic history is gradually diminished in works of comparative history and CHA.

168 ADVANCING COMPARATIVE AREA STUDIES

constrain human interactions, for example by defining trade routes and maritime hubs that cannot be changed without risking major social dislocation. Geographic structures, of course, do change, but at a pace that spans lifetimes and generations. Within this span, he writes, "Man is a prisoner for long centuries of climates, of vegetations, of animal populations, of types of crops, of slowly constructed equilibria, which he cannot transform without the risk of endangering everything. Take the role of transhumance in mountain life, or the persistence of certain sectors of maritime life, rooted in privileged shoreline locales. Look at the endurance of roads and trade routes, and the surprising unchangeability of the geographic boundaries of civilization" (Braudel 2009, 179).

In his methodological writings Braudel often combined the first two categories of geohistory and social history into his conception of the *longue durée* since both emphasize the importance of structure for historical understanding. These structural explanations he contrasted with episodic history, which, he lamented, had come to occupy an outsized place in the social sciences. Such histories focused on sequences of events within short time frames, attributing greater causal influence to the actions of individuals within these episodes. Neglecting the structural determinants found at the level of geographic history or social history, however, led to a distorted view that placed undue significance on proximate factors. As he explained it, "An event is an explosion, something that has the 'sound of newness' (*nouvelle sonnante*) as they said in the sixteenth century. Amid its deceptive smoke, it fills the conscious domain of today's people, but it doesn't last long, disappearing almost as soon as one sees its flame" (Braudel 2009, 174). This is not to say that episodic time has no value, but rather that what it offers by way of historical explanation is superseded by social and geographic history, which reveals the structural factors underlying the events and actions highlighted in the former.

Another way to think of these conceptions of time is to view them as different kinds of periodization. Within each, there will be a different understanding of historical explanation. What qualifies as an explanation from the perspective of episodic history may appear epiphenomenal from the perspective of the *longue durée*. Take the classical example of the fall of the Weimar Republic, which has occupied the attention of students of democratization and comparative historical analysis for nearly a century. A history of events might look at the death of Gustav Stresemann, the formation of the von Papen government, and the election of the National Socialist German

CROSSING THE BOUNDARIES OF COMPARISON   169

Workers' Party as critical factors in the fall of the Republic. All three events offer explanations that rely on the actions of individuals as decisive. If not strictly agentic, they deal primarily with proximate factors.

The history of the *longue durée*, on the other hand, might look at structural factors determined at the time of national and state formation to understand the economic systems that led to the weakness of the bourgeoise and the dominance of landed *Junker* interests. Some may look farther back to understand the emergence of these economic systems in the historical space of Europe, the geographic factors that led to late unification, or the impact of imperial conquests on political and economic development. In this view, the actions of individuals, while important and relevant to the explanation, are heavily determined by the overarching structural factors. Certainly, structural explanation cannot predict the fall of the Republic or the rise of a genocidal fascist, but it does tell us that the structural foundations would push various actors into decisions that would undermine the possibility of democratic government and open the door for such a figure to emerge.

Parting Ways: Competing Conceptions of Comparison and History

The temporal dimensions of the *longue durée* have been readily embraced by historically minded social scientist. This is clear in the classical tradition of macro-historical analysis (Gerschenkron 1962; Moore 1966). It is also true of more recent formulations along the lines of comparative historical analysis (Mahoney and Rueschemeyer 2003) as well as the related field of historical institutionalism (Thelen 1999; Mahoney and Thelen 2010). As it has been deployed in the social sciences, however, the *longue durée* has often been stripped of its spatial dimensions, which Braudel saw as critical to historical explanation. As discussed above, the *longue durée* is in fact defined in terms of the physical geography that structures human interactions. Yet today scholars working in the various traditions of social science history tend to neglect historical geography (Šubrt and Titarenko 2020), often taking areas as fixed or given, and even more problematically, sometimes reading contemporary geographic delineations backward onto historical periods in which they may not be relevant (Ahmed 2018).

This development is, at least in part, due to a division that emerged within the social sciences over one of Braudel's central claims regarding geographic history—that its scope is global. We live in one single world, he maintained, and from the perspective of the *longue durée*, that world constitutes a complete historical system. In this view, political borders do not block human interaction; rather, they establish different chains of interaction, and taking these connections into account is necessary for a historical explanation.

This is not to say that the historian must account for all of world history to offer an account of a given phenomenon, but that the history of any particular place must begin with an examination of the whole system. Such an examination would problematize the connections and categories that delimit the scope of investigation. Indeed, the tradition of total history requires that one delineate the geographic scope of the inquiry, and *Annales* scholars typically did focus on a specific region. But the global perspective was necessary to determine the appropriate geographic scope within a given time period. Without this, one could not even discern the significance of a place as a unit of analysis—whether that be a country, a continent, or a sea. At a fundamental level, our understanding of a "place" contains within it an understanding of its global placement in relation to others. This is what Braudel did with his history of the Mediterranean, and this is what he invites us to do as we explore other historical contexts, problematizing not only the periodization but also the geographic boundaries of the *longue durée*.

This view was most readily embraced by world systems theory and was exemplified by the work of Immanuel Wallerstein, who became one of Braudel's most influential interlocutors (Wieviorka 2005).[4] However, it received a much cooler reception within the various traditions of comparative historical analysis, where attention increasingly turned to case-based comparison (Lee 2018). With respect to its geographic reach, Charles Tilly would quip that Braudel's analysis had an N of 1. In a review of *The Mediterranean*, he referred to this classical work as a "rambling survey" that lacked theoretical precision (Tilly 1980). To be sure, the logic of analysis within Braudel's geohistory was not conducive to the kind of causal inferences Tilly had in mind but rather followed the logic of *historical causation* in which historical understanding could only be achieve through a multidimensional analysis of the totality of a historical context.

---

[4] Wallerstein held the inaugural directorship of the Braudel Center from 1976 to 1999, establishing it as an intellectual hub for Braudelian history and world systems theory.

In rejecting this mode of analysis as untheoretical, however, Tilly and others within the comparative historical tradition inadvertently pushed out of historical analysis some of the most important insights of Braudel's geohistory—the need for a grounded understanding of historical geography. In doing so, they have thrown out the proverbial geohistorical baby with bathwater, losing important insights that, I will argue below, a comparative area studies framework can help restore.

Just as the temporal elements of the *longue durée* might reveal deeper structural dynamics, so too do the spatial dimensions help us to understand connections that would not appear if we accept a priori what the geographic historical unit should be. In his treatise *On History*, Braudel illustrates this with the example of an economic crisis in Florence between 1580 and 1585, which had been attributed to individual failings because historians had not considered the impact of distant economic forces. Braudel's geohistorical analysis, in contrast, revealed the significant role of trade with the Far East. Failing to take a global view in this instance led to a limited understanding of the crisis. Much as episodic history may appear epiphenomenal from the perspective of the *longue durée*, the development of specific locales may not be understandable without placing them in a larger geographic context. It is this that led Braudel to look for insight into the history of the Mediterranean in Antwerp and Genoa. And in the example of the economic crisis in Florence, the answers to questions about Europe are not be found in Europe but rather in the Far East, a connection that could not be gleaned without understanding Europe in a global context with far-flung economic ties.

What we get from Braudel's method is a grounded approach to understanding historical geography and determining what the relevant spatial scope should be. Whether or not one wishes to offer a world systems explanation on the scale of Braudelian history, this geographic orientation is important for comparative analysis and especially for comparative history. The spirit of open-ended investigation helps to orient us to the appropriate geographic units and connections of a given period, opening the door to comparisons that may not seem viable within more limited views of geography. This starts from the simple premise that if we are to identify specific regions to focus on for our studies, we need to first understand them in context and ascertain inductively what are the appropriate spatial parameters, setting aside our assumptions and expectation about the relevant geographic units.

172 ADVANCING COMPARATIVE AREA STUDIES

The Uneven Inheritances of the *Annales* School

While the influence of the *Annales* school within the social sciences has been profound, it has also been unevenly distributed, especially among different approaches to comparative analysis. Within the preceding discussion, there will surely be many features that are familiar to scholars of comparative historical analysis. In their introduction to *Comparative Historical Analysis*, James Mahoney and Dietrich Rueschemeyer (2003, 6) state that such an approach is "defined by a concern with causal analysis, an emphasis on processes over time, and the use of systematic contextualized comparison." In articulating the principles of this approach, they place great emphasis on both the temporal and spatial dimensions of such inquiry. As they state, "These fundamental processes could not—and cannot—be analyzed without recognizing the importance of temporal sequences and the unfolding of events over time." Further, they maintain that "such big processes were— and still are—most appropriately studied through explicit comparisons that transcend national or regional boundaries" (Mahoney and Rueschemeyer 2003, 7).

However, while CHA has arguably always recognized the importance of attending to the complexities of comparison across both time and space, the temporal aspects of CHA have received much more attention, the complexities of comparing across regions much less. This oversight is surprising, especially given the increased emphasis on the need to understand historical processes from actors' points of view, taking into account actors' subjective understandings of their situations and the context in which they are fighting their fights. However, even this attention to subjectivity has had a temporal dimension, as historically minded social scientists have stressed the need to understand politics "in time" and "read history forward" (Pierson 2004; Kreuzer 2010; Capoccia and Ziblatt, 2010; Ahmed 2010). This emphasis has come with important methodological innovations in accounting for sequencing, critical junctures, and also actors' perception of the tempo of events (Pierson 2000; Cappocia and Keleman 2007; Grzymala-Busse 2011). However, it has left the spatial dimensions of historical inquiry largely untouched. Thus, while CHA readily accepts the need to move away from the nation-state to explore the relevant geographic region, it does not offer a disciplined way of historicizing such regions.

If this grounded approach to historical analysis, appreciating the subjectivity of actors, is important for understanding time and temporality, so too

CROSSING THE BOUNDARIES OF COMPARISON   173

is it necessary to shed light on space and historical geography. And this is precisely where CAS can help us reclaim a lost dimension of the *Annales* school's teachings that is crucially important for historical analysis.[5] In theorizing and making explicit approaches to conducting research across areas, the CAS framework pushes us to be more rigorous in our understanding of what constitutes a relevant "area" or world "region" for the purposes of comparison. And the basic intuition of CAS, much like that of *Annales* scholars in an earlier period, is that this determination depends on the purposes of the investigation and a contextualized understanding of geographic demarcations. Physical geography is surely one element of this, but, just as surely, geography is not determinative of what constitutes an area or region.

CAS scholars have illustrated that the very idea of an "area" or "world region" is not self-evident. Rather, the relevant boundaries may shift depending on the subject of analysis and the specific context. In their introduction to the CAS volume, Köllner, Sil, and Ahram (2018, 7) write that "no standard physical, biological, historical, political, economic, or sociocultural criteria suffice to demarcate world regions—or even continents—in a coherent and consistent manner." Quoting Amitav Acharya, they note that such constructs are "born out of imagination, discourse, and socialization" (Köllner et al. 2018, 7). As Lawrence Whitehead points out in that volume, even with seemingly clear boundaries, "What counts as Latin America is a matter of social construction, not a physical given. The Malvinas belong, but not the Falkland Islands. And what of French Guyana?" (Whitehead 2018, 49). There is not a great distance from here to Febvre's or Braudel's understanding of geography as emanating from psychological factors and social practices.

But it should be stressed that in many ways CAS pushes past Braudelian notions of geohistory, which rarely accommodated actor's subjective understanding of time and space. By drawing our attention to the constructed nature of geographic units, CAS scholars invite us to examine geographies

---

[5] While CAS scholarship may not typically understand itself as "historical," it is important to note that for many comparative historical approaches including CHA, history is a methodological, and specifically ontological, commitment, rather than a reference to the subject of inquiry. Against the universalist ontologies of many rationalist approaches that assume that the causal forces act in a constant manner (e.g., via individual utility maximizing calculations), a historical approach holds that the most interesting causes are neither constant nor proximate. In other words what causes something to happen may have existed long before the outcome it caused. Moreover, causes may act differently in different contexts. In this way history becomes a key to the kind of causal explanation and open-ended inquiry which is at the heart of both CHA and CAS. And for both, the focus tends to be on historical mechanisms rather than general causes.

from the perspective of the social actors who inhabit them. In this way, CAS can be seen as promoting a "geohistorical sensibility," advancing some of the central goals of the *Annales* school without accepting the formal strictures of global history.

This geohistorical sensibility builds on the interdisciplinary work of political geographers, anthropologists, and historians who have questioned not only the construction of areas and regions as political entities (Fawn 2009; Holbig 2017), but also the physical geography on which these constructions are based (Lewis and Wigen 1997; Schulten 2001). As Marshall Hodgson (1993, 4) has put it, "Why is Europe a continent but India is not? Not because of any geographic features, nor even because of any marked cultural breach at the limits we have chosen." The historically contingent nature of geographic demarcations can clearly be seen in contemporary fights over what constitutes an area and the criteria for membership within it, fights that revolve as much around physical geography as they do around an array of sociopolitical and historical associations.

It is for this reason, for instance, that Haiti can be imagined as part of Africa, while Turkey remains beyond the boundaries of Europe: In 2016, the African Union (AU) considered and voted on the inclusion of Haiti. And while the bid was ultimately unsuccessful, it exemplifies the ways in which the geographical imagination need not correspond to accepted political boundaries. Rather, these boundaries produce new sites of human interaction. On this occasion the relevant geographical unit was understood in terms of historical economic connection related to the slave trade and led to several initiatives to deepen ties between the AU and the African Diaspora, defined as "the communities throughout the world that are descended from the historic movement of peoples from Africa" (quoted in Amao 2018, 50). In contrast, negotiations for Turkey to join the European Union, which began in 2005, continued for a decade and ultimately stalled out for failure to meet the political requirements for membership (Ugur 2010).

With these considerations in mind, CAS embraces a spirit of open-ended inquiry toward geography, problematizing standard approaches toward case selection. It is precisely because CAS cuts against the grain of within-area comparisons and cross-regional studies that scholars have had to question the underlying assumptions that limit in-depth investigation to specific regions and transgress these boundaries only for the purposes of large-N comparisons. According to Christian von Soest and Alexander Stroh, standard assumptions of context similarity that are at the heart of studies that confine their investigations to specific regions are not always borne out by case attributes. For cross-regional studies, the assumption of similarity is typically relaxed because the logic of inference does not require special sensitivity to context, but at the same time these studies miss opportunities for in-depth comparison. In staking out an in-between space, von Soest and Stroh argue that "the full potential of cross-regional CAS become clear only when one transcends the regional horizons of knowledge communities" (2018, 77). Similarly, Ariel Ahram argues that using regions as de facto controls can lead to "arbitrary and ambiguously construed scope conditions" (2018, 156) and Ryan Saylor (2018) argues that the use of detailed process tracing across regions is preferable to the reliance on regions within a Millian framework of comparison.

In various ways, CAS scholars have helped to problematize both our assumptions about areas and world regions and our approach to comparison across different geographic units. To be sure, CAS scholars vary in the extent to which they seek to tap into the subjectivity of actors, but the drive toward contextualized comparisons means that they must necessarily attend to the particularity of place in a way that other comparative approaches might not.

The Illusion of "Familiarity" in Historical Geography

If this critical approach toward geography is important for comparison across regions in contemporary contexts, it is all the more pressing for historical analysis, where the scholar typically has no firsthand experience of the subject matter. This is because both our conventional understandings of areas and our disciplinary conventions around area studies are situated in specific cultural and historical contexts that may not translate to the period under investigation.

The challenge of developing a grounded conceptualization of regions is compounded in historical research because we often bring contemporary understandings of what constitutes a theoretically significant "area" to our research about historical phenomena. We are often deceived by what Quentin Skinner referred to as a sense of "familiarity" when reading historical texts. On this he wrote:

> It is the very impression of familiarity, however, which constitutes the added barrier to understanding. The historians of our past still tend, perhaps in consequence, to be much less aware than the social anthropologists

176 ADVANCING COMPARATIVE AREA STUDIES

have become about the danger that an application of familiar concepts and conventions may actually be self-defeating if the project is the understanding of the past. (Skinner 1970, 136)

Maintaining our "distance" from the past, according to Skinner, is in fact the only way we can learn from it. This distance consists in an acknowledgment that we do not share the subjectivity of those we study, that the categories of analysis we bring to bear on our investigations may not be the most appropriate for the context, and that we need to disrupt our sense of the familiar in order to achieve historical understanding. Without such distance we fill historical concepts with our present, and our relationship to the past becomes a circular one—we get out what we put in, though we take it to be evidence of something external to our own perceptions.

Though Skinner is part of a different contextualist tradition, concerned with intellectual rather than social or political history,[6] he similarly recognized that historical understanding requires that we problematize our conceptual frameworks to recognize what is different about the historical contexts we wish to study. It is telling that Skinner compared the task of a historian to that of an anthropologist. Both need to develop modes of "seeing" that are different from those used to navigate familiar contexts. However, ethnography affords opportunities for immersion in which researchers can gain firsthand knowledge of the context and in which there are frequent reminders that they are in a "foreign land": the gaze of local residents, the ridiculing smiles of vendors at a word mispronounced, unfamiliar surroundings, food, currency, and various other materialities of life that serve as a revealing barrier between scholars and their subjects.

Such reminders that we are strangers in a "foreign land" are not readily available to historical researchers, making it much easier to mistakenly assume familiarity. This is especially true where physical and political boundaries remain constant. For example, for comparative analysis of nineteenth-century Europe, this slippage is quite easy because the political geography remains more or less unchanged. Therefore, it may be possible

---

[6] While there are strong affinities between the Cambridge school to which Skinner belonged and the *Annales* school, Skinner criticized *Annales* scholars for an overreliance on the material aspects of social life, replacing Marx's emphasis on economic determinism, with an emphasis on a wider array of material factors but practicing a kind of material determinism nonetheless. These ontological differences notwithstanding, Skinner does help to elucidate an important epistemological dimension of contextualism that is highly complementary to the approach of the *Annales* school.

to imagine that the idea of Germany today is what it was then, or that the physical geographical boundaries of Europe constituted the relevant political demarcations of space. These projections of the familiar onto the past would be very problematic given that German unification did not happen until 1871 and would remain contested for decades after. In addition, Europe of the nineteenth century was understood by many to extend to colonial spaces, especially with regard to the settler colonies.

It follows that our understanding of the relevant area for comparison needs not only to emanate from the questions we ask but to make sense for the period in question. Moreover, we do not even know if we are engaged in intraregional or cross-regional investigation without ascertaining what the proper geographic delineations are for a given period. As has been shown in the context of nineteenth-century democracies, for example, the distinction between American and European political development can do more harm than good, as these cases are so closely linked on matters of institutional development that they may be considered to constitute one area for the purposes of comparative analysis Ahmed (2018).

Disrupting our familiar conceptions of space can be daunting given that specific notions of geographic areas are built into our discipline. Even with the ebb and flow of area studies as separate fields, entrenched ideas about where a given politics begins and ends are embedded in the organization of the academy. Organization such as the Latin American Studies Association, the Council for European Studies, the Middle East Studies Association, and so on provide opportunities to continually question the construction of regions but also maintain the prevalent practices of regional delineation. This is often reinforced by disciplinary conventions and training that starts very early on and can silo off important avenues for exploration.

Approaching questions with a sensitivity to actors' subjectivity requires that we reassess contemporary understandings of political geography and investigate what, for the actors in question, is the relevant sense of political space. The CAS framework moves us helpfully in this direction. With such an approach, researchers can leverage deep contextual understandings of particular locales to creatively configure research strategies that stretch beyond specific area specialties. To be sure, CAS also requires notions of areas, and those too will be constructions. This is inescapable. But in breaking out of the typical regional delineations, it invites greater reflexivity with regard to the way in which areas are deployed in our research.

Conclusion

This chapter has sought to grapple with the relationship between CAS and CHA. Tracing the intellectual lineage of both to the French *Annales* school, I identify a lost legacy of the *Annales* tradition that has led to the neglect of historical geography within the study of comparative history. CAS, I argue, helps to restore this critical element to historical analysis and brings back a sensibility toward historical geography that has been muted in recent discussions of social science history. At the same time, CAS is not simply derivative of the *Annales* school, but pushes back against some of the self-imposed limitation of "geohistory" as articled in Braudelian methodology. In this way, it offers a "geohistorical sensibility," carrying forward some of the central lessons of the *Annales* school to a new generation of scholars while releasing historical geography from the formal requirement of global history. This geohistorical sensibility can be incorporated in a wide range of comparative analysis, from the nomothetically oriented case-based comparisons to the sweeping regional histories of the Braudelian tradition. Closer ties between CAS and CHA can help remedy the bifurcation of the spatial and temporal dimensions of historical analysis and offer powerful tools for the grounded and open-ended study of history.

Bibliography

Ahmed, Amel. 2010. Reading History Forward: The Origins of Electoral Systems in Advanced Democracies. *Comparative Political Studies* 43 (8–9): 1059–1088.

Ahmed, Amel. 2018. American Political Development in the Mirror of Europe. In Ariel I. Ahram, Patrick Köllner, and Rudra Sil, eds. *Comparative Area Studies: Methodological Rationales and Cross-Regional Applications.* Oxford: Oxford University Press, 103–118.

Ahmed, Amel. 2022. What Can We Learn from History? Competing Approaches to Historical Methodology and the Weberian Alternative of Reflexive Understanding. *Polity* 54 (4): 734–763.

Ahram, Ariel I. 2018. Comparative Area Studies and the Analytic Challenge of Diffusion: Explaining Outcomes in the Arab Spring and Beyond. In Ariel I. Ahram, Patrick Köllner, and Rudra Sil, eds. *Comparative Area Studies: Methodological Rationales and Cross-Regional Applications.* Oxford: Oxford University Press, 152–167.

Amao, Olufemi. 2018. *African Union Law: The Emergence of a Sui Generis Legal Order.* London: Routledge.

Bloch, Marc. [1913] 1971. *The Ile-de-France: The Country Around Paris.* London: Routledge.

Bloch, Marc. [1924] 1973. *The Royal Touch.* London: Routledge.

Bloch, Marc. [1939] 1961. *Feudal Society.* London: Routledge & Kegan Paul.

Braudel, Fernand. 1993. *A History of Civilizations.* New York: Penguin Books.

Braudel, Fernand. [1972] 1995. *The Mediterranean and the Mediterranean World in the Age of Phillip II.* New York: Harper & Row.

CROSSING THE BOUNDARIES OF COMPARISON 179

Braudel, Fernand. 2009. History and the Social Sciences: The Longue Durée. *Review* (Fernand Braudel Center) 32 (2): 171–203.

Burke, Peter. 1990. *The French Historical Revolution*. Cambridge: Polity Press.

Capoccia, Giovanni, and R. Daniel Kelemen. 2007. The Study of Critical Junctures. *World Politics* 59 (3): 341–369.

Capoccia, Giovanni, and Daniel Ziblatt. 2010. The Historic Turn in Democratization Studies. *Comparative Political Studies* 43 (8–9): 931–968.

Chirot, Daniel. 1984. The Social and Historical Landscape of Marc Bloch. In Theda Skocpol, ed. *Vision and Method in Historical Sociology*. Cambridge: Cambridge University Press, 22–46.

Clark, Stuart. 1985. The Annales Historian. In Quentin Skinner, ed. *The Return of Grand Theory in the Human Sciences*. Cambridge: Cambridge University Press, 177–198.

Clark, Stuart. 1999. *The Annales School: Critical Assessments*. Vol. 4, *Febvre, Bloch, and Other Annales Historians*. London: Routledge.

Durkheim, Émile. [1887] 1974. Emile Durkheim's Inaugural Lecture at Bordeaux. Translated by Neville Layne. *Social Inquiry* 44 (3): 189–193.

Eyerman, Ron. 1981. False Consciousness and Ideology in Marxist Theory. *Acta Sociologica* 24 (1–2): 43–56.

Fawn, Rick. 2009. "Regions" and Their Study: Where From, What for and Whereto? *Review of International Studies* 35 (1): 5–34.

Febvre, Lucien. [1924] 1966. *A Geographical Introduction to History*. London: Routledge.

Febvre, Lucien. 1929. Une question mal posée: Les origins de la réforme française et la problème des causes de la réforme. *Revue Historique* 161 (1): 1–73.

Gerschenkron, Alexander. 1962. *Economic Backwardness in Historical Perspective: A Book of Essays*. Cambridge, MA: Belknap Press of Harvard University Press.

Grzymala-Busse, Anna. 2011. Time Will Tell? Temporality and the Analysis of Causal Mechanisms and Processes. *Comparative Political Studies* 44 (9): 1267–1297.

Hargrove, Michael. 1978. Total History: The Annales School. *Journal of Contemporary History* 13 (1): 1–13.

Hill, Alette Olin, and Boyd H. Hill Jr. 1980. Marc Bloch and Comparative History. *American Historical Review* 85 (4): 828–846.

Hodgson, Marshall G. 1993. *Rethinking World History: Essays on Europe, Islam and World History*. Cambridge: Cambridge University Press.

Holbig, Heike. 2017. Reflecting on the Moving Target of Asia. In Katja Mielke and Anna-Katharina Hornidge, eds. *Area Studies at the Crossroads: Knowledge Production After the Mobility Turn*. New York: Palgrave Macmillan, 309–326.

Iggers, George. 2005. *Historiography in the 20th Century*. Middletown, CT: Wesleyan University Press.

Knight, Melvin M. 1950. The Geohistory of Fernand Braudel [Review of *La Méditerranée et le monde méditerranéen à l'époque de Philippe II*, by F. Braudel]. *Journal of Economic History* 10 (2): 212–216.

Köllner, Patrick, Rudra Sil, and Ariel I. Ahram. 2018. Comparative Area Studies: What It Is, What It Can Do. In Ariel I. Ahram, Patrick Köllner, and Rudra Sil, eds. *Comparative Area Studies: Methodological Rationales and Cross-Regional Applications*. New York: Oxford University Press, 3–26.

Kreuzer, Marcus. 2010. Historical Knowledge and Quantitative Analysis: The Case of the Origins of Proportional Representation. *American Political Science Review* 104 (2): 369–392.

Lee, Richard E. 2018. Lessons of the Longue Durée: The Legacy of Fernand Braudel. *Historia Crítica*, No. 69: 69–77.

Lewis, Martin W., and Kären Wigen. 1997. *The Myth of Continents: A Critique of Metageography*. Berkeley: University of California Press.

Lyon, Bryce. 1987. Marc Bloch: Historian. *French Historical Studies* 15 (2): 195–207.

Mahoney, James, and Dietrich Rueschemeyer, eds. 2003. *Comparative Historical Analysis in the Social Sciences.* Cambridge: Cambridge University Press.

Mahoney, James, and Dietrich Rueschemeyer. 2013. Comparative Historical Analysis: Achievements and Agendas. In James Mahoney and Dietrich Rueschemeyer, eds. *Comparative Historical Analysis in the Social Sciences.* Cambridge: Cambridge University Press, 3–40.

Mahoney, James, and Kathleen Thelen. 2010. *Explaining Institutional Change: Ambiguity, Agency, and Power.* Cambridge: Cambridge University Press.

Mills, Charles. 1989. Determination and Consciousness in Marx. *Canadian Journal of Philosophy* 19 (3): 421–445.

Moore, Barrington. 1966. *Social Origins of Dictatorship and Democracy: Lord and Peasant in the Making of the Modern World.* Boston: Beacon Press.

Pierson, Paul. 2000. Increasing Returns, Path Dependence, and the Study of Politics. *American Political Science Review* 94 (2): 251–267.

Pierson, Paul. 2004. *Politics in Time: History, Institutions, and Social Analysis.* Princeton, NJ: Princeton University Press.

Saylor, Ryan. 2018. Gaining by Shedding Case Selection Strictures: Natural Resource Booms and Institution Building in Latin American and Africa. In Ariel I. Ahram, Patrick Köllner, and Rudra Sil, eds. *Comparative Area Studies: Methodological Rationales and Cross-Regional Applications.* Oxford: Oxford University Press, 185–203.

Schatz, Edward. 2009. Political Ethnography: What Immersion Contributes to the Study of Power. Chicago: University of Chicago Press.

Schulten, Susan. 2001. *The Geographical Imagination in America, 1880–1950.* Chicago: University of Chicago Press.

Sewell, William. 1967. Marc Bloch and the Logic of Comparative History. *History and Theory* 6 (2): 208–218.

Skinner, Quentin. 1970. Conventions and the Understanding of Speech Acts. *Philosophical Quarterly* 20 (79): 118–138.

Stoianovich, Traian. 1976. *French Historical Method.* Ithaca, NY: Cornell University Press.

Šubrt, J., and L.G. Titarenko. 2020. Dimensions of Time and Space in Sociology. *RUDN Journal of Sociology* 20 (4): 752–762.

Thelen, Kathleen. 1999. Historical Institutionalism in Comparative Politics. *Annual Review of Political Science* 2: 369–404.

Tilly, Charles. 1980. Broad, Broader ... Braudel. CRSO Working Paper no. 219, University of Michigan.

Trevor-Roper, Hugh R. 1972. Fernand Braudel, the Annales, and the Mediterranean. *Journal of Modern History* 44 (4): 468–479.

Ugur, Mehmet. 2010. Open-Ended Membership Prospect and Commitment Credibility: Explaining the Deadlock in EU-Turkey Accession Negotiation. *Journal of Common Market Studies* 48 (4): 967–991.

von Soest, Christian, and Alexander Stroh. 2018. Comparisons Across World Regions: Managing Conceptual, Methodological, and Practical Challenges. In Ariel I. Ahram, Patrick Köllner, and Rudra Sil, eds. *Comparative Area Studies: Methodological Rationales and Cross-Regional Applications.* New York: Oxford University Press, 66–84.

Whitehead, Laurence. 2018. Depth Perception: Improving Analytic Focus Through Cross- and Interregional Comparisons. In Ariel I. Ahram, Patrick Köllner, and Rudra Sil, eds. *Comparative Area Studies: Methodological Rationales and Cross-Regional Applications.* Oxford: Oxford University Press, 45–65.

Wieviorka, Michel. 2005. From Marx to Braudel to Wallerstein. *Contemporary Sociology* 34 (1): 1–7.

8

Comparison as Ontology, Region as Concept

On the Synergies of Comparative Area Studies

Erik Martinez Kuhonta

Introduction

Comparative area studies (CAS) is premised on an emphasis on both comparison and area studies knowledge.[1] Its specific value added is its focus on comparisons across regions. Although scholars have long been comparing countries across regions, no other large-scale initiative has made this call in terms as systematic as the CAS initiative. At the same time, the CAS project makes clear that it seeks to build upon rather than displace conventional area studies work. The editors (Köllner et al. 2018, 13) write in the introductory chapter of their agenda-setting volume, "Importantly, this work is *building* on—not ignoring or undercutting—qualitative research focused on given areas." Later on, they state in clear terms what is at stake:

It is at least as important to reaffirm that CAS is not intended to subsume or substitute for research produced by area specialists. Rather, it is a vehicle for (a) bringing more of this research to light for members of other area studies communities as well as generalists in social science disciplines, and (b) directly leveraging the research produced by different area studies communities in questioning preexisting assumptions, finessing commonly used concepts, and generating fresh, grounded insights into important research problems. Area studies (particularly in the United

---

[1] I am grateful to the editors for their incredible enthusiasm and encouragement; to all authors for such stimulating discussions; and to Nora Fisher Onar and Erica Simmons for very helpful comments.

Erik Martinez Kuhonta, *Comparison as Ontology, Region as Concept*. In: *Advancing Comparative Area Studies*. Edited by: Ariel I. Ahram, Patrick Köllner, and Rudra Sil, Oxford University Press. © Oxford University Press (2025). DOI: 10.1093/oso/9780197809365.003.0008

States) toils under threat. . . . Without continued investment in area studies, social science risks losing the unique kinds of knowledge about a wide range of locales that area studies scholars bring to the table. (Köllner et al. 2018, 26)

What CAS aims for, then, as one central goal is the reinvigoration and "continued investment" in area studies. Comparison is key to this reinvigoration. In particular, CAS emphasizes comparisons across regions, as system-wide regional comparisons or comparisons across regions. While this is important in taking one's claims to a wider community beyond the confines of one's regional home, the larger point is that area studies can thrive and gain a more secure footing when it engages proactively in the analytical exercise of comparison.

In light of the comments quoted above, and on the basis of a broad assessment of the kind of work being advanced within the CAS canopy, I argue that the deeper element and most important contribution of CAS is *not* comparison across regions but *comparisons in and of themselves*. Furthermore, I posit that it is the analytic method and metatheory of comparison that is central to the social sciences, to theory building, and to productive engagement with area studies.

Comparison is the bedrock of any theoretical proposition because it inherently goes beyond particularity to interrogate similarities and differences rooted in the "why" question. Even when comparison is not sought out by a researcher, a comparative element cannot be avoided.[2] Any question that asks why something is the way it is must have as an a priori question, whether consciously or unconsciously articulated: why has that something not occurred in another way or at another place or another time? In other words, any question implies a comparative reference point. What distinguishes research is not whether a comparative reference is pertinent and inherent in a study, but whether it is conceptualized as such and exploited methodologically and theoretically.

Tweaking Laurence Whitehead's (2018) point, in his chapter in *Comparative Area Studies*, that comparisons across regions provide "depth of perception," I would argue that it is really comparison as an ontological prior that is most important for this perceptual depth. By "comparison as

---

[2] There is a tendency in some area studies work, or at least earlier area studies research, to smuggle in comparative and theoretical references without being explicit about these larger points. Thus, an opportunity is often missed to extend one's broader ideas.

an ontological prior," I mean that researchers take it as fundamental that comparison is at the root of how they visualize, analyze, and give meaning to social facts. By emphasizing comparison as an ontological prior, we move comparison to its rightful place at the core of social science. But the idea of comparison as an ontological prior rests firmly within the context of area-based knowledge rather than in the service of universal propositions. In other words, comparison must be embedded in context.

By anchoring comparison within context, especially regional context, the enterprise of comparison being advocated here is centered theoretically at the middle range (Merton 1968; Sartori 1970). This means that comparison is intended to explore and uncover theoretical arguments that are rooted in grounded empirics and in the historical developments of a specific region. Comparison as an ontological prior then refers here to two very specific things: (1) comparison of cases for the purpose of theoretical development or concept formation; and (2) anchoring of the comparison through deep knowledge of the empirics of the cases. These two cardinal points— comparison for the purposes of theory and concept, as well as deep empirical knowledge—bring together some of the core contributions of the CAS enterprise. They prioritize some degree of generalizability, and they give value to region and context.

It should be noted that these points also emphasize the social construction of knowledge. Comparison is a social act that requires creativity and construction. There is nothing given about "thinking comparatively." What propels a comparative ontology is a researcher's mindset attuned to the contrasts of the social world and the need to identify those contrasts within strong contextual fields. We will furthermore see in this chapter that the idea of what constitutes a region and how that matters for concept formation is very much a process of social construction driven both by broad structural forces and by the researcher's response to those forces. Keeping to social science at the middle range means remaining cognizant of the element of creativity and construction that is furthered in the process of comparison, region making, and theory building.

My aim in this chapter is to show how dialogue between regional knowledge, comparison, and concept provides synergy for knowledge accumulation. I will argue that comparison lies at the core of the CAS project and that comparison is centered in area studies knowledge and regional analysis. I further argue that the construction of regions that underlines contrasts and

184 ADVANCING COMPARATIVE AREA STUDIES

similarities inside that geographical area provides a rich landscape for concept formation and theory building. Immersion in a region provides vital grounds for conceptualizing and theorizing.

I start the chapter by contrasting other ontological positions in the social sciences with the comparative perspective to clarify at the outset what is distinct about the position emphasized here. I then shift the analysis to look at the nature of regions—how they are constructed in the social realm and how they become cemented in discourse and practice. Through a close analysis of the construction of the region of Southeast Asia, I show that grappling with this region as a category that shares common properties but also exhibits deep contrasts lends itself to comparative analytics—both within and beyond the region. This exercise of comparison, built upon awareness of differences within the region, can in turn spur concept formation and theory building precisely because the act of comparison generates larger abstract questions. I specifically make this point by examining the comparative-historical work of the Southeast Asianist Victor Lieberman, as well as that of the Middle East specialist Nikki Keddie.

The last part of the chapter focuses on how concepts are generated from deep area knowledge. Here I look at the concept of the plural society, developed by British colonial civil servant J. S. Furnivall, and then explain how this concept is rooted in depth of knowledge of Southeast Asia and in comparisons within Southeast Asia. I then show that the concept of the plural society has had a deep impact beyond Southeast Asia, and in that sense has fit the cross-regional ideals of CAS. The chapter concludes by emphasizing the synergistic relations between regional knowledge, comparison, and concept formation, as well as theory building.

Comparison Versus Noncomparison

It is important at the outset to emphasize what is distinct about comparison as an ontological prior. By addressing other ontological perspectives in the social sciences that are very different from the position advocated here we can get a better sense of what is unique about comparison as an ontological prior. These other perspectives include rational choice, globalization studies, interpretivism, and what I call "area studies sui generis" arguments.[3]

---

[3] The discussion below emphasizes these ontological perspectives as "ideal types." I acknowledge that there may be some works within these perspectives that take comparison as ontology more fully

COMPARISON AS ONTOLOGY, REGION AS CONCEPT   185

Rational choice theory differs from a comparative ontology to the extent that the focus of rational choice, as ontology, is on a universal postulate of human behavior. Comparison does play a role in rational choice scholarship but is often employed to lay out general patterns rather than contrasts among cases or mid-level theories or concepts (Bates et al. 1989; Geddes 1996). In that sense, comparison when part of rational choice theory is especially about a method that can help increase confidence in a theoretical model, rather than about an ontology of social behavior.[4] This is different from comparison as ontology, wherein comparison is fundamentally anchored in a view of the world that sees the need to differentiate institutional, behavioral, and historical contrasts at the outset in the interest of concept and mid-level theory formation.

Globalization studies emphasize the porosity of borders and the eclipse of the nation-state as the central process shaping people's lives.[5] Economic, political, social, cultural, and technological change is presumed to be inexorable and universal. What matters more than traditional state units is the movement of transnational forces—ideas, actors, and physical things. Books with catchy titles like *The World Is Flat* underscore the lack of difference between countries, leading to the view that studies of distinct nations are becoming less pertinent.[6] In this framework, comparison is not a central, analytical prism because social processes are universal.

The process of globalization does not, however, eviscerate the importance of comparison. Studies that emphasize different local or subnational responses to globalization, such as in the political economy literature, may also frame their work comparatively.[7] Other studies focused on globalization do take nations and regional identity seriously, but the variables they emphasize may still be wider processes of *systemic* change. Arjun Appadurai's work, for example, gives a nod to area studies but under very different parameters. Here, "fluidity" is granted analytical priority (Appadurai 2001, 7–8):

than depicted here. But on average, each perspective offers an ontological position fundamentally different from that of comparison as advanced here.

[4] Levi's 1997 chapter on rational choice as ontology and its relationship with comparative-historical analysis captures this point well: "A Model, a Method, and a Map."

[5] A useful volume on theories of globalization is Held and McGrew (2007).

[6] The increasing thrust of globalization in the 1990s was crucial to the decisions of granting agencies to move away from support of area studies that remain rooted in national differences. This was the case for the Social Science Research Council and the Ford Foundation. See Prewitt 1996 and Ford Foundation 1999.

[7] See, for example, the contribution of Hsueh to this volume.

We need an architecture for area studies that is based on process geographies and sees significant areas of human organization as precipitates of various kinds of action, interaction, and motion—trade, travel, pilgrimage, warfare, proselytization, colonization, exile, and the like. These geographies are necessarily large scale and shifting. . . . Regions are best viewed as initial contexts for themes that generate variable geographies, rather than as fixed geographies marked by pregiven themes.

A third ontological perspective is interpretivist and ethnographic. Here the emphasis is on questions of meaning, through close attention to actors' discourse, behavior, and ideas. Comparison can play a role here, but it may not be central to the analysis. Rather, what matters most is providing deep insight, especially understanding, of the characteristics of the local unit being described. However, it would be a mistake to assume that interpretivism does not engage in conceptual enterprises like those of small-N comparative analysis. James Scott's ethnographic and interpretivist research (1985) has given us powerful concepts like "weapons of the weak" and the "hidden transcript" that aim for theoretical abstraction. More recently, the work of Diana Kim (2020), centered in the importance of meaning and in a distinct form of comparison, has also generated theoretical ideas about the role of low-level bureaucrats in colonial regimes.

Anthropologist Clifford Geertz, perhaps the most preeminent interpretivist-ethnographer, is often assumed to be antithetical to theoretical generalization, but this is incorrect. It is true that in pursuing an interpretivist agenda, Geertz eventually turned against the big theoretical abstractions advocated by his mentor, Talcott Parsons. Yet his programmatic statement for an interpretivist agenda, "Thick Description: Toward an Interpretive Theory of Culture," was not, as is often believed, just about "thick description" in the sense of being a form of atheoretical description. In fact, in that essay, Geertz articulates the need for ethnography to engage with concepts and to generalize. This kind of generalization and concept engagement is, for sure, different from a positivist search for identifiable, causal patterns, but it is still in dialogue with mid-level concepts and theories. Above all, it is anchored in context. As Geertz (1973, 28) writes:

A repertoire of very general, made-in-the-academy concepts and systems of concepts—"integration," "rationalization," "symbol," "ideology," "ethos," "revolution," "identity," "metaphor," "structure," "ritual," "world view," "actor," "function," "sacred," and, of course, "culture" itself—is woven into the body of thick description ethnography in the hope of rendering mere occurrences scientifically eloquent. The aim is to draw large conclusions from small, but very densely textured facts.

Finally, what I term "area studies sui generis" arguments are claims based on area studies knowledge that a country's experience is unique and therefore, for the most part, not comparable. Although authors of such works do not explicitly state that their studies are "not comparable," their general premise is that studying one unit in and of itself is more valuable than comparison, or that comparison will not yield much insight because the political dynamics in that specific country are so distinct. Normative elements can also come into play when articulating sui generis arguments. For example, case studies of genocide, because they are morally fraught, may limit possibilities for comparison through claims of distinctiveness.[8]

Another version of the "area studies sui generis" position is the view that a nation can only be compared with other nations that have undergone very similar experiences. For example, scholars of Malaysia have historically been averse to direct comparisons between Malaysia and other countries unless those other countries have similar ethnic divisions. Often underlying this position is the view that social structure, as opposed to, say, institutional arrangements, "naturally" explains political outcomes.[9] Yet these kinds of studies, by delineating so tightly the scope of permissible comparison, limit the possibilities for new interpretations and insights.

Thus, if one were to array the perspectives discussed above in a spectrum, with the right side representing theories aiming for a total or universal framework (rational choice and globalization studies), those on the left side emphasizing the particular (interpretivism and "area studies sui generis"), comparison as ontology would sit squarely in the middle. In contrast to rational choice and globalization studies, comparison as ontology gives greater importance to contextual factors, while compared to interpretivism and "area studies sui generis" it has stronger interest in some degree of abstraction. In that sense, the comparative ontological perspective speaks to an audience that takes seriously, and gives equal importance to, empirical

---

[8] Thanks to Nora Fisher Onar for this insight. On the fraught and problematic nature of scholarship on one particular genocide, the Armenian genocide, see some of the writings and reviews of the Middle East historian Jeremy Salt.

[9] See, for example, Kuhonta (2011, 21–23 and the appendix).

detail and broad insight. It is worth emphasizing, however, that, as suggested above, a comparative ontology sits closest to the interpretivist position, at least in the form pursued by scholars like Scott and Geertz, because of common interests in concept formation and some degree of concern with mid-range generalization.

From Regional Knowledge to Comparative Analysis

So far I have focused on the importance of comparison as an ontological prior. I now want to shift the discussion to one of the key elements that make up comparison as ontology, that is, the role of context, and specifically region. In turning to the formation of regions, one should emphasize from the outset that no world region or area study is a "natural thing." Although superficially it may appear as if certain regions share a common cultural identity—ethnic, religious, linguistic—when one scratches the surface and looks at the historical process and intellectual discourse through which regions have become categorized as "area studies," it becomes apparent that no region of the world fits in a natural sense. A region like Europe, which might plausibly make a claim for being one of the most naturally coherent in terms of its Latin and Christian roots, is not a slam-dunk case of cultural commonality.[10] Nor is Latin America, although "on the area studies map . . . [it] is one of the most clear-cut and conceptually cohesive regions of all. . . . Closer inspection, however, reveals it, too, to be deeply problematic" (Lewis and Wigen 1997, 181).

The idea of world regions emerged out of a historical process in which Western cartographers sought to break down continental land masses into more manageable parts. By the eighteenth century, maps of Asia were notable for breaking down the massive Asian continent into distinct groups. However, these divisions lacked a consistent logic in the way that they were structured. Political, cultural, and physiographic dimensions were all employed without concern for analytical coherence (Lewis and Wigen 1997, 159).

World War II was the catalyst for the shaping of the world regions we know today. In response to the urgent need to comprehend a fluid global situation,

[10] Throughout much of European history, the continent was characterized by remarkable diversity. It is only when looking at regions from the vantage point of our postwar contemporary stance that Europe may look to some like a coherent entity. See Dawson 1956, 240.

four organizations in the United States—the National Research Council, the American Council of Learned Societies, the Social Science Research Council, and the Smithsonian Institution—came together to form the Ethnogeographic Board with the purpose of getting a handle on geographical regions (Lewis and Wigen 1997, 163). This board, heavily influenced by anthropologists, was responsible for the shaping of area studies into the form we know today. Although the delineations that the board used continued to evolve, this initiative set the basis for conceptualizing regions as distinct areas separate from continental land masses.

The process begun by the Ethnogeographic Board during the 1940s was indicative of the importance of regions for geopolitical interests. Indeed, war proved to be the ultimate driving force for the categorization and shaping of world regions. As Martin Lewis and Kären Wigen (1997, 163) note: "Simply put, the old continental architecture, anchored by the vast category of Asia, proved useless for strategic planning." Southeast Asia provides an especially good example of how war has helped shape regional construction, as laid out by Donald Emmerson (1984) and Amitav Acharya (1999, 2014), and discussed in the next section.

Constructing the Idea of Southeast Asia

Although the idea of Southeast Asia was already established in the minds of travelers to the area, known by the Chinese as *Nanyang* and by the Japanese as *Nampo*, it was World War II that brought the region into greater focus. Japan's lightning ability to take over Southeast Asia prompted the Allies to respond with the creation of a Southeast Asia Command (SEAC), whose ultimate goal was to reclaim the whole region. The SEAC, led by Lord Louis Mountbatten, was headquartered in Kandy, Sri Lanka, which today does not form part of Southeast Asia, and it did not include the Philippines under its ambit. But in other respects, Mountbatten's SEAC created the template for the perimeters of contemporary Southeast Asia.

In the aftermath of World War II, Southeast Asia began to take shape largely through the formation of regional organizations. These included the Southeast Asia Treaty Organization (SEATO), the Association of Southeast Asia (ASA), and Maphilindo. But all these associations were partial to the extent that they did not include most of the countries in the region. SEATO

190   ADVANCING COMPARATIVE AREA STUDIES

was an early attempt to create a mutual defense association, but its membership was anything but Southeast Asian, including only Thailand and the Philippines from the region, and then stretching to the United States, United Kingdom, France, New Zealand, Australia, and Pakistan. ASA included only Thailand, Malaysia, and the Philippines. Maphilindo, on the other hand, included the "Malay" nations—Malaysia, Philippines, and Indonesia. But it quickly fell apart with the war of *konfrontasi* (confrontation) between Indonesia and Malaysia.

The formation of the Association of Southeast Asian Nations (ASEAN) in 1967 in Bangkok was pivotal in moving from Mountbatten's SEAC to the imperatives of the Cold War. With the sidelining of Sukarno and of the conflict between Indonesia and its Malay neighbors, ASEAN grouped together the five capitalist, staunchly anticommunist countries—Indonesia, Malaysia, the Philippines, Singapore, and Thailand—and paved the way for imagining a region as sharing common bonds. This was an association marked by illiberal regimes that all hoped to defeat internal enemies, whether communist, ethnic, or religious insurgencies. Although ostensibly geared toward economic and social interests, in point of fact ASEAN was committed to ensuring that illiberal elites would be able to hold onto power in an unstable environment. ASEAN thus provided the bulwark for common goals of eradicating internal opponents.

Some thirty years after its founding, ASEAN comprised all ten countries in the region, adding Brunei in the mid-1980s, and then by the mid-1990s, the socialist regimes of Vietnam, Laos, Myanmar, and Cambodia.[11] The sense of regional identity has thus taken on a very strong political, and especially geopolitical, dynamic. Building upon the foundations of SEAC but taking it initially toward an anticommunist direction, ASEAN has come to embody the sense that the region is a coherent whole or at the very least holds together based on common identities and values. This is, of course, an exaggeration that masks the interest of the leaders in the region. Yet, despite the political interests that drive the goals of ASEAN, the association has also gained a life of its own. What distinguishes ASEAN is not just the political commonalities and interests of elites, but the social, cultural, and nongovernmental exchanges and discourses that surround and move beyond the elites.

---

[11] Only Timor Leste remains currently out of the association.

In contrast to an argument emphasizing war or geopolitics is a position espoused primarily by historians that Southeast Asia shares commonalities that help define it as a coherent region. Although this is not a claim that there is something natural to a geographical area, it is an argument that an area "fits together" because there are inherent shared properties. The French historian George Coedès (1948) was one of the first scholars to argue that common attributes, such as wet-rice cultivation, the role of women in society, and mythologies, as well as the use of waterways, made Southeast Asia a distinct geographical body.

The concept of the mandala, or "circle of kings," most fully developed by Cornell historian Oliver Wolters (1999) and later by Harvard anthropologist Stanley Tambiah, also provided an extremely valuable conceptual scaffolding to link together the region. The concept of the mandala posits that certain kingdoms established hegemony over other lesser kingdoms and vassal states through a tributary system. These mandalas were found across Southeast Asia—Ayudhya, Sriwijaya (the Malayan peninsula and Sumatra), the Philippines, Majapahit (Java), and Angkor—and therefore gave some basis for conceiving of the region as having common foundations.[12]

It is, however, the New Zealand historian Anthony Reid (1988) who makes the strongest and most ambitious effort to stake out a vision of Southeast Asia as a region with a deep historical and cultural basis. Inspired by Fernand Braudel's vision of the Mediterranean Sea structuring a region through maritime intercourse (see Ahmed's chapter in this volume), Reid argues that the waterways in Southeast Asia were central in the long sixteenth century in forging linkages and commonalities that established a common bond for the region. Reid charts numerous practices that were common across the region: the Austronesian language, adaptations to a common ecological system, widespread commercial exchange, the relatively high status of women, the way in which debt structures social relations, and so forth. Despite Reid's emphasis on the maritime nations of Southeast Asia—the Malay nations of Indonesia, Malaysia, and the Philippines—he stretches his argument conceptually to encompass the region as a whole, including mainland Southeast Asia.

---

[12] Wolters himself was deeply skeptical whether the fact that many ancient kingdoms in the region were structured as mandala polities really meant that Southeast Asia should be seen as a unitary whole: "The mandala seems to provide a convenient framework for subregional histories, but they do not take us very far in identifying a shape to the history of the region as a whole" (1999, 38).

The claim that there are cultural or social patterns and relations that have historically linked the peoples of Southeast Asia comes closest to the idea that there is something inherent to the region of Southeast Asia. This kind of claim stands in contrast to a more contemporary view, espoused by political scientists Emmerson and Acharya, that Southeast Asia gained its geographical perimeters and its sense of self from recent wars and geopolitical processes. Juxtaposing these two positions, we have in essence a more "cultural-historical" position (Reid) and a more "processual-political" position (Emmerson, Acharya). These positions articulate very different ways of understanding the emergence and the nature of a region. They are both useful in setting out the terms by which to visualize Southeast Asia as a region.

I would argue, however, that Southeast Asia has merit as a region in analytical terms not just because we can identify some social and cultural commonalities rooted in history, or because of political processes linked to elites, but also because the region provides a cartographical structure—indeed, an imaginative but circumscribed canvas—through which to compare and contrast both within the region and with other regions.[13] By virtue of its vast diversity, Southeast Asia helps push the comparative logic of identifying similarities and contrasts to its fullest, and in the process strengthens the idea of region as concept. In this sense, Southeast Asia qua region provides an excellent example of what I argue is the essence of CAS: the comparative ontology.[14]

This argument should not be misunderstood to mean that Southeast Asia has value only from the intellectual's interest in comparative analytics. But it is to argue that the value of a region, and therefore of area studies, must be understood not just in terms of whether the region coheres as a whole—for which we have identified strong arguments rooted in history and political science. Rather, the value of a region should also be understood in terms of its *capacity to generate theoretical and conceptual constructs* emanating from comparison from within and beyond the region. These comparisons

[13] Here I want to contrast my argument to that of a strong defender of area studies, Stephen Hanson. Hanson (2009) has forcefully defended the legitimacy of area studies on the basis of three key themes: shared historical legacies, diffusion and interaction within the region, and common linguistic and cultural elements. While I agree with these points, I want to put the emphasis not on commonalities within a region but on analytical comparisons and contrasts within a region that generate broader abstractions.

[14] For a related review, analyzing comparative-historical analysis and Southeast Asian studies in the fields of political science, history, and anthropology, see Kuhonta (2014).

"work" because there is an idea of a region in which both commonalities and contrasts have been articulated effectively by a community of scholars. This community of scholars operates in a structure and perimeter (geographic as well as analytic) in which concepts and theories can be generated. It bears emphasizing that it is not just that regional embeddedness helps generate theory, but that it generates theory and concepts *through comparison.* Comparison thus flows from the idea of a region and of differences within the region.

What this suggests, then, is that regions are very much constructs of scholarship—efforts to find meaning within regions, often for the purpose of drawing out larger comparative themes. Regions should therefore be understood as conceptual formations to the extent that they are abstractions of empirical material. Given the role that scholars play in articulating the significance of regions, it is important to stress that creativity and social construction must be seen as central in this process of comparison. Ultimately this implies a strong urge from within the academy to grant order to raw, empirical facts by identifying themes that enable regional comparisons and contrasts. Southeast Asia fundamentally showcases this creative, constructive thrust through the valuable comparisons and contrasts that it yields, as well as the social science concepts that it generates.[15]

Comparisons and Contrasts from Within Southeast Asia and the Middle East

It may be helpful to immediately illustrate the larger claim being made here—that comparison and concept formation are rooted in the idea of a region, and crucially, of contrasts within a region—through two examples, lest the abstract discussion engaged in so far obfuscate the main point. First, I will highlight the work of a Southeast Asia comparative historian, Victor Lieberman (2009), whose massive books have sought to compare and contrast state and nation consolidation in Southeast Asia with other countries in Eurasia. Second, I will draw on Nikki Keddie's influential article "Is There a Middle East?" (1973) to show how contrasts within a region help define a geographical area as well as draw out its analytical value.

---

[15] The essays in Kuhonta et al. (2008) flesh out this argument: that qualitative methods and area studies have helped generate theories and concepts at the core of political science.

Lieberman has put forth one of the most sophisticated arguments regarding the idea of Southeast Asia. Critical of Reid's effort to draw out some coherence from Southeast Asia, he moves instead toward laying out contrasts within the region, as well as similarities between some parts of Southeast Asia and other world regions. What he sees are similar patterns and waves of state and nation consolidation within mainland Southeast Asia (particularly Burma, Siam, and Vietnam), as well as with France, Russia, and Japan. Hence, the title of his book, *Strange Parallels*. By contrast, Lieberman claims that maritime Southeast Asian nations have taken a very different path toward state formation and are more similar to states in South Asia and China. In these states, consolidation was less successful.

Identifying waves of political, territorial, and national consolidation from 800 to the early nineteenth century, Lieberman argues that the countries of mainland Southeast Asia, as well as France, Russia, and Japan, were shaped by structural, ecological forces that led to ebbs and flows of state consolidation. Demographic and economic conditions were especially important in explaining the consolidation of states. The maritime nations of Southeast Asia, on the other hand, were undermined by foreign interventions and unfavorable geography and communications.

Lieberman visualizes Southeast Asia as a region, but not one that is internally coherent. Instead, his vision of Southeast Asia is one of contrasts. These contrasts allow him to draw parallels with countries outside of Southeast Asia. This vision of contrasts and comparisons puts Lieberman's work starkly at odds with Reid's idea of an interlinked and coherent Southeast Asia. What is striking here is that comparisons and contrasts play a central role in thinking of Southeast Asia as a region. It is not necessary that a region be understood as having such clearly defined and identified commonalities. While a region's rough geographical parameters are taken seriously, more important is that they are used not to define boundedness or assert complete likeness but to draw out contrasts within and without.

Another powerful example of internal contrasts within a region—this time, the Middle East—also works within what are commonly accepted as the parameters of the region, but challenges one to think harder about those parameters. In asking whether there is such a thing as the Middle East, Keddie sets out to debunk the easy assumptions that countries usually lumped in the Middle East share much in common. In particular, Keddie argues that simply because Islam is a common religion throughout the region cannot serve as the basis for assuming regional coherence. The thrust for making this point is to draw out a sharp contrast between political development in the Ottoman Empire and in Iran.

Prior to the nineteenth century, the Ottoman and Safavid Empires had very different religious, economic, and political organizations. When both came under modernization pressures, these differences became even more stark, as the Ottomans embarked on extensive centralizing reforms of the military, bureaucracy, and elite structure, while the Iranians remained in a more traditional and fragmented political system, with the shah ruling over largely tribal groups. In the long run, the Ottoman Empire—and therefore the countries that emerged in its wake—and Iran had very different paths of political development.

While Keddie effectively shows that a country, Iran, often included in the Middle East has had a distinct pattern of political development compared to the agglomeration of the Ottoman Empire, which controlled much of today's Middle East, her point is not to argue that the idea of the Middle East should be discarded, as much as to caution against reifying it. But the larger implications that one can draw from Keddie's exercise in comparative-historical analysis is that the construction of the Middle East can serve as a useful terrain for theoretical engagement. As she puts it: "The purpose here is . . . to propose that we not reify concepts so as to distort our ability to look at history and reality afresh. . . . *We must look within the Middle East for contrasts and outside the Middle East for comparisons*" (Keddie 1973, 269; emphasis added).

Despite having drawn out clear contrasts between two of the most important political units in the region, Keddie concludes that the Middle East "continues to have valid meaning." Lieberman takes seriously the idea of Southeast Asia and grapples with it as a concept but takes a sharp turn toward laying out contrasts of political structures that end up illuminating similarities with other world regions. These analytical exercises suggest that the regional areas that geopolitics, profession, convention, and indeed imagination have given us should continue to be worked with and continue to have meaning. But world regions should not be taken for granted as natural or fixed. This kind of static, or even passive, view of a region pulls one away from the kind of interrogations that generate deep comparative analysis as seen in the works of Keddie and Lieberman. Precisely by working with a region and yet also breaking it apart, comparisons and contrasts can unfold

196   ADVANCING COMPARATIVE AREA STUDIES

and generate, in the words of Keddie, new ways of looking at history and, I would argue, theoretical and conceptual constructs that deepen knowledge of a region and beyond.

Building Concepts from Regional Knowledge and Comparative Analysis

The study of regions matters at a broad level because it has given the academy powerful concepts and theories—including the conceptual idea of a region itself. But equally important is that these concepts and theories have traveled beyond the regions in which they were first developed. Their capacity to travel is rooted in the way that regions and concepts or theories dialogue with each other. This dialogue is about comparing facts and patterns within a particular landscape and thinking about how they reach beyond the initial area from which they were derived.

Area studies scholarship has been especially prolific in terms of developing original concepts that have traveled far beyond their shores of origin and had a powerful impact on social science theory. East Asia has produced the "developmental state" and "embedded autonomy"; Latin America is well known for "bureaucratic authoritarianism" and "dependent development"; the Middle East has advanced the concept of the "rentier state"; Africa has furthered the originally Weberian concept of "neo-patrimonialism"; Europe has been the source for a rich literature on "consociationalism," "social capital," and "varieties of capitalism"; and sociologically oriented scholars of the United States have developed "polyarchy," "civil religion," "civil society," and even a term that is both concept and ethnic identifier, "WASP."[16]

These concepts are distinct terms in the sense that they are, for the most part, created by scholars to capture particular developments in a region or country. This creativity is significant because it indicates that scholars are constantly going back and forth between abstraction and particularity.[17] Any attempt to craft a concept is an effort to generalize, but the fact that a specific conceptual term is being created or remolded is also an effort to keep the idea moored in its regional setting. The concept, if compelling, will travel in subsequent intellectual forays. But in its initial formulation,

---

[16] This last term comes from the University of Pennsylvania sociologist E. Digby Baltzell.
[17] See also Saylor's chapter in this volume, particularly his discussion of the way Peter Evans and Catherine Boone developed Weberian ideal types in their award-winning books.

COMPARISON AS ONTOLOGY, REGION AS CONCEPT   197

a scholar by devising a specific term—for example, "developmental state" or "consociationalism"—is trying to give significance to the particular historical context that is central to that concept. Concepts are therefore human constructs, reflecting efforts to give a clearer order and shape to empirical patterns. This enterprise is ultimately not very different from the endeavor to give meaning to regions and to construct and institutionalize regional identity.

Among area studies, Southeast Asian studies has a rich lineage of work that is conceptual as well as comparative. Concepts such as "agricultural involution," "clientelism," "weapons of the weak," "moral economy," "bureaucratic polity," and "imagined community" have either originated or been deepened intensively through empirical work on Southeast Asia. These concepts have also pushed comparative analysis, either within the region or between Southeast Asia and other regions. In this section, I will look at one key concept—the plural society—that has come out of scholarship in Southeast Asian studies and that has extended much beyond the region. I focus on the concept of the plural society because it is widely debated and heavily cited across many disciplines and many regions.

The Plural Society

J. S. Furnivall's concept of the plural society (1939, 1948) is one of the best-known concepts in the social sciences, engaged extensively by political scientists, sociologists, historians, and anthropologists. A civil servant in colonial Burma who later became an academic at Cambridge University and subsequently an adviser to the Burmese government, Furnivall developed the concept of the plural society based on his analysis of the politics and social structure of Java and Burma. Critical of colonial policy in the "tropics," Furnivall wrote as a scholar with a deep concern for reform. The concept of the plural society is thus both an analytical construct and a normative critique of colonial policy.

Furnivall argues that a plural society is one in which several ethnic groups come together, meet, and share public space—yet have nothing in common. The only thing that links ethnic groups together are the material interests of the market. In Java, Burma, and other parts of Southeast Asia, Furnivall saw native peoples (Burmans, Javanese, or Malays), Chinese, Indians, and Europeans interacting but without any common purpose. These different ethnic groups engage in market transactions, but apart from this, they have no common bond, resulting in a society characterized by the absence of a social will. This ultimately leads to social atomization. In Furnivall's eloquent words (1948, 304), the plural society is a "medley, for its people mix but do not combine"—"it is a crowd and not a community."

The plural society could be thought of as referring in its most rudimentary terms to any society that has pluralistic elements. Yet Furnivall is quite clear about the scope of his concept. He states that the plural society results from colonial dominance in the tropics and that it is distinct from precolonial life or Western "homogeneous" societies, both of which may have elements of pluralism. What is distinct is the fact that in the plural society there is no common will or a common cultural heritage. Thus, we have a concept that is distinctively rooted in developing countries and that has colonial dominance as its overarching canopy.

The comparative element of this concept is noteworthy, first, because it was employed in relation to two countries that Furnivall studied closely: Burma and Indonesia (especially Java). In fact, Furnivall initially drew upon materials on Indonesia to develop the idea of the plural society, although he was much more knowledgeable about Burma. Given their comparable ethnic divisions, both countries are represented in the social matrix that defines the plural society. Although Furnivall does not go into much depth as to why he chose both cases to represent the plural society, he clearly chose well in terms of commonalities. Burma and Indonesia are two of the most ethnically diverse countries in Southeast Asia.

It is also worth underscoring that the plural society has another comparative dimension, which is that of Western "homogeneous" societies. Implicitly, Furnivall takes European society as the comparative reference point for the "tropics," observing that in Europe there is some basis for society and markets to hold together. This background contrast, perhaps analogous to the way France haunts the pages of Tocqueville's *Democracy in America*, helps put in sharp relief what is distinct about social structure in Burma and Indonesia.[18]

Second, the emphasis on the pluralism of ethnic groups grants the concept a wide comparative ambit given the ethnic diversity that characterizes many countries. But it is not the pluralism alone that matters here, as much as the fact that this pluralism is atomistic and ultimately detrimental to

---

[18] This background contrast with "homogeneous" societies is picked up by Smith (1965).

social progress. Furnivall's concept points to instability, and possibly conflict, as a consequence of pluralism, since this pluralism is not anchored in a common will.

Finally, the plural society sets a historical boundedness to the concept by referring to colonialism as the ultimate political authority under which such conditions emerge. Colonialism, and its emphasis on the free market, creates the conditions for this kind of unmoored social structure. At the same time, colonialism also keeps such a society from completely falling apart. While colonialism forms the historical context in which to understand the origins and development of the plural society, the consequences of such a society extend to a postwar world in which colonial structures no longer sustain these social divisions.

The contrasts and similarities across Southeast Asia help make the concept of the plural society comparative and analytically tractable. The colonial impact in the region decisively shaped the political development of all countries in Southeast Asia. This overarching experience enables Furnivall to claim that the plural society is found in both Indonesia and Burma. Yet differing colonial regimes were also present in both countries, with the Dutch in Indonesia and the British in Burma. We therefore need to ask whether the structures and policies put in place by colonial authorities were completely equivalent. Furthermore, were the underlying social structures in Indonesia and Burma so completely similar in their atomistic qualities?[19] These kinds of comparative questions naturally lend themselves to such a concept, in part due to the analytical versatility of a scholar like Furnivall, but in part also due to engagement with a region as dynamic, and full of contrasts, as Southeast Asia.

The concept of the plural society has been deeply influential and has traveled in most world regions. It has gained traction in the Caribbean (Smith 1965), Africa (Morris 1956; Kuper and Smith 1969), the Middle East (Longva 2019), and South Asia (Jannuzi 1989). Within Southeast Asia, the plural society has especially been applied to the politics of Malaysia (Ratnam 1961; Vasil 1971). Some work on the plural society has renamed it as the "segmented society" (Hoetnik 1967). At the same time, the traveling exploits

---

[19] One important critique, focusing only on Netherlands Indies, is that Javanese society was much more mixed than Furnivall allowed. Wertheim (1968) and, with greater elaboration, Coppel (1997) have both advanced the idea that urban Java in the 1930s was a "mestizo society." But note the qualifications of its urban setting.

of the plural society have not come without criticism. Much of this criticism has been motivated by an effort to deepen the concept in more abstract terms (Rex 1959; Smith 1965; Morris 1967).

Thus, the concept of the plural society has grown from field observations, comparative analysis within a region (as well as with a "background" region of Europe), and abstract thinking. This, in turn, has allowed it to resonate with other research communities and engage with the historical experience of other nation-states. In that sense, the concept of the plural society fulfills the ideals of CAS because of the synergies at play between area knowledge, comparison, and theory.

Conclusion: The Synergies of Comparative Area Studies

"If doubt is the chief enemy of the Southeast Asia specialist, desire is the best ally" (Acharya 2014, 467). So wrote Acharya in analyzing the status of Southeast Asia as an area study vis-à-vis the disciplines. I would argue that Acharya's statement, while eloquent, can actually be inverted. Instead of seeing doubt as the chief enemy of the Southeast Asianist, it can play a useful role. A different way of thinking about this (and of conceiving of "doubt") is to see the interrogation of common assumptions as of great utility to the scholar who cares about area studies and theory.

Taking this point further, it is precisely by opening up the idea of a region while still granting it meaning that area studies specialists can make inroads in the academy. Area studies most decisively needs to be rejuvenated to remain viable. This rejuvenation can come through thinking of a region not as a coherent system—or at least not as necessitating coherence—but rather as a theoretically fertile landscape in which to identify, visualize, and theorize contrasts and similarities that are regionally embedded. This, it bears emphasizing, is a willful act of a researcher: creatively thinking through and visualizing something broad out of myriad elements that allow for comparison.

A central point in this chapter is, then, that analytic comparisons are vital to how we should think of regions. The work of Lieberman and Keddie illustrates that contrasts within regions are fodder for original theoretical work. The work of Furnivall is centered on comparisons within Southeast Asia. And if one were to take a brief detour away from the social sciences, one could also gain insights about comparison as ontology from evolutionary biology, where the work of Alfred Russell Wallace has powerfully demonstrated how comparison centered in a region (Southeast Asia), but with background knowledge of other regions (South America), can further revolutionary, scientific discoveries (the Wallace Line, dividing the flora and fauna of Asia from Oceania).[20] It is this process of conceptual comparison within and across regions that provides the real-world basis for sustaining and revitalizing area studies knowledge.

It is finally worth observing that concepts associated with regions often have a definite article preceding them. Although this chapter has only focused on the plural society, other important concepts coming out of area studies knowledge that were briefly mentioned, such as the developmental state, the neo-patrimonial state, and the rentier state, all are thought of in terms of the definite article, "the." This distinction is not trivial. It matters because use of a definite article indicates that the concept was developed and rooted with reference to a specific place and context. That the concept traveled afterward is testament to the depth of its analytical scaffolding but does not take away from the fact that its origins have a specific and precise mooring. In essence then, the synergy between region and concept is one in which not only definite articles but also proper nouns matter. Dialogue between area studies and concepts provides one of the most robust answers to the false dichotomy laid out decades ago, and still perpetuated today, that the specificities of countries and the anchoring of knowledge tightly with countries are of minimal value to theoretical and disciplinary goals.[21]

Thus, dialogue about the formation of regions and between area studies and concepts has deep value for theoretical growth and for knowledge accumulation. Self-doubt about a region does not have to be a basis for paralysis, but rather can be an engine for pushing harder on new and distinct questions. Understanding how regions have been constructed and debated is important not just in itself, but because it provides a basis for thinking of the region as an abstraction, a concept, an idea. If regions are pursued in this manner, it is not hard to see how they can also be a fertile ground for comparisons, concept formation, and theory building—and, in the process, the generation of valuable analytic synergy.

---

[20] For a review of the validity of the Wallace Line, see Mayr (1944).

[21] The classic piece positing the case against proper nouns is Przeworski and Teune (1970). In its contemporary incarnation, see King (1996).

Bibliography

Acharya, Amitav. 1999. Imagined Proximities: The Making and Unmaking of Southeast Asia as a Region. *Southeast Asian Journal of Social Science* 27 (1): 55–76.

Acharya, Amitav. 2014. Remaking Southeast Asian Studies: Doubt, Desire and the Promise of Comparisons. *Pacific Affairs* 87 (3): 463–483.

Appadurai, Arjun. 2001. Grassroots Globalization and the Research Imagination. In Arjun Appadurai, ed. *Globalization*. Durham, NC: Duke University Press, 1–21.

Bates, Robert H., Avner Greif, Margaret Levi, Jean-Laurent Rosenthal, and Barry R. Weingast. 1989. *Analytic Narratives*. Princeton, NJ: Princeton University Press.

Coedès, Georges. 1948. *Les états hindouisés d'Indochine et d'Indonésie*. Paris: E. de Boccard.

Coppel, Charles. 1997. Revisiting Furnivall's "Plural Society": Colonial Java as a Mestizo Society? *Ethnic and Racial Studies* 20 (3): 562–579.

Dawson, Christopher. 1956. *The Making of Europe*. New York: Meridian.

Emmerson, Donald K. 1984. Southeast Asia: What's in a Name? *Journal of Southeast Asian Studies* 15 (1): 1–21.

Ford Foundation. 1999. *Crossing Borders: Revitalizing Area Studies*. New York: Ford Foundation.

Furnivall, J. S. 1939. *Netherlands India: A Study of Plural Economy*. Cambridge: Cambridge University Press.

Furnivall, J. S. 1948. *Colonial Policy and Practice: A Comparative Study of Burma and Netherlands India*. Cambridge: Cambridge University Press.

Geddes, Barbara 1996. *Politician's Dilemma: Building State Capacity in Latin America*. Berkeley: University of California Press.

Geertz, Clifford. 1973. *The Interpretation of Cultures*. New York: Basic Books.

Hanson, Stephen E. 2009. The Contribution of Area Studies. In Todd Landman and Neil Robinson, eds. *The Sage Handbook of Comparative Politics*. London: Sage, 159–174.

Held, David, and Anthony McGrew. 2007. *Globalization Theory*. London: Polity Press.

Hoetnik, Harry. 1967. *The Two Variants in Caribbean Race Relations: A Contribution to the Sociology of Segmented Societies*. Oxford: Oxford University Press.

Jannuzi, F. Tomasson. 1989. *India in Transition: Issues of Political Economy in a Plural Society*. Boulder, CO: Westview Press.

Keddie, Nikki. 1973. Is There a Middle East? *International Journal of Middle East Studies* 4 (3): 255–271.

Kim, Diana. 2020. *Empires of Vice: The Rise of Opium Prohibition Across Southeast Asia*. Princeton, NJ: Princeton University Press.

King, Gary. 1996. Why Context Should Not Count. *Political Geography* 15 (2): 159–164.

Köllner, Patrick, Rudra Sil, and Ariel I. Ahram. 2018. Comparative Area Studies: What It Is, What It Can Do. In Ariel Ahram, Patrick Köllner, and Rudra Sil, eds., *Comparative Area Studies: Methodological Rationales and Cross-Regional Applications*. Oxford: Oxford University Press, 3–26.

Kuhonta, Erik Martinez. 2011. *The Institutional Imperative: The Politics of Equitable Development in Southeast Asia*. Stanford, CA: Stanford University Press.

Kuhonta, Erik Martinez. 2014. Southeast Asia and Comparative-Historical Analysis: Region, Theory, and Ontology on a Wide Canvas. *Pacific Affairs* 87 (3): 485–507.

Kuhonta, Erik Martinez, Dan Slater, and Tuong Vu, eds. 2008. *Southeast Asia in Political Science: Theory, Region, and Qualitative Analysis*. Stanford, CA: Stanford University Press.

Kuper, Leo, and Michael G. Smith, eds. 1969. *Pluralism in Africa*. Berkeley: University of California Press.

Levi, Margaret, 1997. A Model, a Method, and a Map: Rational Choice in Comparative Historical Analysis. In Mark Lichbach and Alan Zuckerman, eds. *Comparative Politics: Rationality, Culture, and Structure*. Cambridge: Cambridge University Press, 19–41.

Lewis, Martin W., and Kären E. Wigen. 1997. *The Myth of Continents: A Critique of Metageography*. Berkeley: University of California Press.

Lieberman, Victor. 2009. *Strange Parallels: Southeast Asia in Global Context, c. 800–1830*. Cambridge: Cambridge University Press.

Longva, Anh Nga. 2019. *Walls Built on Sand: Migration, Exclusion, and Society in Kuwait*. New York: Routledge.

Mayr, Ernst. 1944. Wallace's Line in the Light of Recent Zoogeographic Studies. *Quarterly Review of Biology* 19 (1): 1–14.

Merton, Robert. 1968. *Social Theory and Social Structure*. New York: Free Press.

Morris, H. S. 1956. Indians in East Africa: A Study in a Plural Society. *British Journal of Sociology* 7 (3): 194–211.

Morris, H. S. 1967. Some Aspects of the Concept Plural Society. *Man* 2 (2): 169–184.

Prewitt, Kenneth. 1996. Presidential Items. *Items* 50 (1): 15–18.

Przeworski, Adam, and Henry Teune. 1970. *The Logic of Comparative Social Inquiry*. New York: Wiley.

Ratnam, K. J. 1961. Constitutional Government and the "Plural Society." *Journal of Southeast Asian History* 2 (3): 1–10.

Reid, Anthony. 1988. *Southeast Asia in the Age of Commerce, 1450–1680*. New Haven: Yale University Press.

Rex, John. 1959. The Plural Society in Sociological Theory. *British Journal of Sociology* 10 (2): 114–124.

Sartori, Giovanni. 1970. Concept Misformation in Comparative Politics. *American Political Science Review* 64 (4): 1033–1053.

Scott, James C. 1985. *Weapons of the Weak: Everyday Forms of Peasant Resistance*. New Haven: Yale University Press.

Smith, Michael G. 1965. *The Plural Society in the British West Indies*. Berkeley: University of California Press.

Vasil, R. K. 1971. *Politics in a Plural Society: A Study of Non-Communal Political Parties in West Malaysia*. Kuala Lumpur: Oxford University Press.

Wertheim, Wim. 1968. Asian Society: Southeast Asia. In David Sils, ed. *International Encyclopedia of the Social Sciences*. Vol. 1. New York: Free Press, 423–438.

Whitehead, Laurence. 2018. Depth Perception: Improving Analytic Focus Through Cross- and Interregional Comparisons. In Ariel I. Ahram, Patrick Köllner, and Rudra Sil, eds. *Comparative Area Studies: Methodological Rationales and Cross-Regional Applications*. Oxford: Oxford University Press, 45–65.

Wolters, Oliver. 1999. *History, Culture, and Religion in Southeast Asian Perspectives*. Singapore: Institute of Southeast Asian Studies.

9

The Contextualized Comparative Sector Approach

Comparative Area Studies at the Sectoral Level of Analysis

Roselyn Hsueh

Introduction

We are in an age of post-neoliberal globalization, whereby complex interdependence has integrated many economies and industries within them, and in parallel led to the rise of varied national and subnational political and economic responses. These forces have witnessed the rise of a new political economy that requires new methodologies and new approaches. Building on the broader comparative area studies (CAS) enterprise's readiness to conduct comparisons that account for context across time and space, this chapter introduces the contextualized comparative sector approach (CCSA).

The CCSA showcases the empirical and analytical value of contextualized comparisons at the sectoral level of analysis. It transcends the limits of traditional area studies' assumptions of similarities and differences between cases, identifies new sites of inquiry at the sector level for theory development and testing, and adjudicates competing explanations. New and extant studies on states and markets, employing qualitative and quantitative methods, in the Global South in the political economy of development (PED) demonstrate the analytical leverage for theoretical clarity and generalizability of CCSA. CCSA makes possible the controlled comparisons and midrange theorizing of vast complex political and economic interdependencies, whether they are government and business actors in the domestic economy or global market, or economic relations in and between countries.

Roselyn Hsueh, *The Contextualized Comparative Sector Approach*. In: *Advancing Comparative Area Studies*. Edited by: Ariel I. Ahram, Patrick Köllner, and Rudra Sil, Oxford University Press. © Oxford University Press (2025). DOI: 10.1093/oso/9780197809365.003.0009

206 ADVANCING COMPARATIVE AREA STUDIES

The CCSA accounts for the function of context-specific, value-laden, and institutional arrangements at the sectoral level of analysis undertheorized by studies in mainstream political economy and behavioral economics focused on universal laws and individual-level behavior, respectively. The multilevel contextualized sectoral comparisons made possible by CCSA broaden and deepen analysis of contextual specificities at the regional and/or country levels of analysis and identify the multidimensional impacts of industrial sectors, including social and political constructions of sectors, structural sectoral attributes, and context-specific sectoral institutions. The rest of this introduction discusses how CCSA dovetails with and promotes the CAS research agenda to conduct investigations at different levels of analysis unencumbered by traditional area studies, at the same time paying attention to context-specific sectoral characteristics.

The second section of the chapter advances the focused analysis of sectoral structures and organization of institutions and the social and political construction of sectors in a single country and in multiple-country comparisons. It shows how single- and multiple-sector studies in one country or in multiple countries uncover the ways in which country-level and sectoral characteristics interact and shape the role of state and economic actors in industrial and political development in the context of globalization. The second section also discusses how CCSA adjudicates dominant PED debates.

The third section of the chapter illustrates the added value for developing theories and testing generalizability by comparing sectors within and across countries with a step-by-step demonstration of the power of CCSA. The final section of the chapter reiterates the empirical and analytical leverage gained by bridging cross-regional and cross-national comparisons that transcend traditional assumptions of similarities and differences and contextualized sectoral analysis. Uncovered are new inquiries and prevailed are new explanations unexploited by mainstream political economy and behavioral economics.

Transcending Traditional Assumptions of Similarities and Differences

The CAS agenda has promoted contextualized cross-regional comparisons as the dynamic engagement of and departure from existing area studies scholarship. CAS as a method, if thoughtfully situated in existing debates and when scope conditions are clearly delineated and claims are unambiguously defined, can theoretically and substantively further our understanding of individual and collective cases. Extant comparative studies on the development and globalization of China, India, and Russia show that archetypical expectations may no longer hold (due to changing circumstances or timing or both) or were based on outmoded stereotypes that burden rather than enlighten (Ahram et al. 2018).

Russia is often compared with countries in post-Soviet Eurasia. Cheng Chen persuasively argues for comparing the "two largest post-Communist giants" (Chen 2018, 134) in new inquiries, such as the ways in which the authoritarian party-state controls economic corruption, where the combination of capitalism and political authoritarianism serve as a control in the research design. All the same, it may not always make sense to compare China and Russia, such as when research questions "assume scope conditions found primarily in one geographic area" (Chen 2018, 134), including studies on postcommunist party systems, electoral institutions, and European integration.

CAS thus agrees with Tulia Falleti and Julia Lynch that "if causal mechanisms are portable but context-dependent, then to develop causal theories, we must be able to identify analytically equivalent contexts as well as specify where one context ends and another begins" (2009, 1154). By carefully delineating commonalities and similarities across cases, CAS contributes to the endeavor of generalizability in theory building. The precise combination of capitalism and postcommunist authoritarianism in China and its impacts might be overlooked by situating China only in Asia. Likewise, understanding Japan only as an Asian country might overlook how its coordinated market economy functions in patterns not unlike those found in Germany and France (Vogel 1996).

Indeed, systematic comparisons of countries that seriously consider contextual factors assumed to be similar have shown profound differences leading to different outcomes. Shedding light on differences between China and newly industrialized countries (NICs) of East Asia, my first book, *China's Regulatory State: A New Strategy for Globalization* (Hsueh 2011), questions traditional assumptions of similarities due to ethnocentric expectations and historical associations. The book engages dominant perspectives about modes of global economic integration and relationship to state control. China has historical and cultural ties to neighboring East Asian countries;

however, the country's post-1978 global economic integration in the context of neoliberalism and post–Cold War global politics, and Japanese colonialism and the Cold War during the NICs' similar stage of development, are important contextual factors that have profoundly shaped variation in China and the NICs' globalization trajectories.

More nuanced comparative analysis grounded in deeper substantive understanding of regions and countries empowers the analyst to uncover the actual causal mechanisms at work. Pranab Bardhan's (2010) comparative study of China and India shows that political institutions matter for development; however, it is not regime type per se but rather accountability institutions at different levels that shape development outcomes. Without them, authoritarianism can distort development while severe accountability failures mar democratic governance. Likewise, the comparative studies brought together by Martin Dimitrov (2013) showcase the work of respected scholars of China and Russia, including Kellee Tsai and Thomas Remington, on understanding why in the post-1991 Soviet collapse, communism endured in five countries but fell away in five others. They show that differences in institutional adaptations shape the extent and scope of communist resilience.

Cross-regional contextualized comparisons as advocated by CAS synergize with the analytical leverage identified by Richard Locke and Kathleen Thelen (1995) in the comparison of similar political developments in very different institutional contexts to understand their differences in extent and scope. Dan Slater and Daniel Ziblatt (2013, 3) more recently underscore the indispensability of controlled case comparisons in generating internal and external validity despite political science's "multi-method turn." Slater's study with Richard F. Doner and Bryan K. Ritchie, which challenges conventional wisdom about state autonomy in the developmental state, is developed with East Asian cases and tested with their deep knowledge of cases from Southeast Asia (Doner et al. 2005).

Indeed, in the study of PED, Atul Kohli's (2004) systematic comparison of colonialism and the origins of patterns of state construction and intervention in Brazil, India, Nigeria, and South Korea exemplifies the best of controlled comparisons and portable causal mechanisms and regularities. In addition to Kohli, an expert on India, China scholar Dorothy Solinger (2009) shows how countries from different regions (China, France, and Mexico) recalibrated their revolution-inspired political compacts between labor and the state to join supranational economic organizations with the aim of alleviating crises of capital shortage. In *World Politics*, Mary Gallagher (2002) compares China to eastern Europe (Hungary) and East Asia (South Korea and Taiwan) to problematize the relationship between economic and political reforms. Yu-Shan Wu's book, which systematically compares China, the Soviet Union, Hungary, and Taiwan, is an earlier endeavor of area studies meeting generalizable inquiries (Wu 1995). So is Chalmers Johnson's book (1962) contrasting the communist mobilizations of China and the Soviet Union.

More recent contextualized cross-regional research includes Mark W. Frazier's (2019) comparative historical analysis on the impacts of urban land commodification on variation in patterns of contentious politics in Shanghai and Mumbai and Selina Ho's (2019) comparison of public goods provision in India and China across municipalities. Taking controlled comparisons to China, India, and Russia and comparing labor-intensive and capital-intensive sectors, my second book, *Micro-Institutional Foundations of Capitalism: Sectoral Pathways to Globalization in India, China, and Russia* (Hsueh 2022), illuminated in further detail below, shows how internal and external pressures and state elite responses to them and sectoral structures and institutions shape dominant sectoral patterns of market governance in the era of post–Cold War neoliberalism.

Transcending the traditional boundaries of area studies, these recent book-length treatments join the growing number of systematic comparisons of China to other globalizing countries of comparable circumstances and demographics.[1] These studies, employing cross-regional contextualized comparisons with China, India, and Russia as major cases, amplify arguments that scholarship on China contributes to building theory in comparative political economy and political behavior of development (K. Tsai 2013; L. Tsai 2017; Frazier 2018). Whether emphasizing structural endowments, domestic and global actors and institutions, or the enduring salience of ideas, these works adopt the comparative method to examine national, subnational, and sectoral variations. Cross-national analysis and controlled subnational disaggregation enable systematic investigations that otherwise would not be possible with a focus only on macro- or micro-level factors that make these countries seemingly difficult to track together.

---

[1] Relevant studies include Bardhan 2010; Kennedy 2011; Dimitrov 2013; Chen 2016; Bartley 2018; Ho 2019; Hurst 2018; and Ye 2014.

Bridging Comparative Area Studies and Sectoral Analysis

Eschewing traditional assumptions of similarities and differences between countries and regions and taking CAS seriously, integrating sectoral analysis with cross-regional and cross-country comparisons recognizes that today's global economy is marked by complex interdependence and rapid technological change. In the context of neoliberal ascendance and open-economy politics, it is at the industrial sector that countries and regions today are exposed to the global economy. Extant and new scholarship in the study of states and markets in the PED literature show how understanding economic internationalization today necessitates the integrated investigation of national and sectoral units of analysis together, enabling the development and refinement of theory in addition to delineating scope conditions.[2]

Importantly, studying the multidimensional impacts of sectors requires the contextualization missing in conventional political economy accounts that eschew the function of context-specific sectoral arrangements between the state and economic actors. Taking the study to the industrial sector thus allows for and uncovers inquiries at the intersections of macro-national and micro-sectoral level structural and context-specific changes and continuities experienced by countries around the world, especially in the Global South. Doing so crisscrosses traditional boundaries of area studies and uncovers new sites of inquiry at the intersection of regions, countries, and sectors.

Focused comparative analysis of sectoral structures and institutional setups and relationship to macro-national developments provides added value for developing generalizable theories. As I show in detail in the next section of the chapter, single-industry studies in one country (such as Wengle 2015) and multiple countries (including Doner et al. 2021) illustrate how contextualized sectoral analysis uncovers the ways in which global and country-level characteristics interact with sectoral characteristics to shape political economic development.

The third section demonstrates how CCSA advances the concept of the perceived strategic value of sectors and theorizes interactions with sectoral structures and organization of institutions in China (Hsueh 2011 and 2022). The addition of India and Russia, countries in other regions,

---

[2] Levi-Faur (2006) contends that combining two or more comparative approaches (at the national, sectoral, and/or temporal levels of analysis) serves to identify patterns of similarities and differences in regulatory capitalism.

and sectors at varying levels of technological and labor intensity within them in the multilevel comparative case research design in Hsueh (2022) further develops and tests the theoretical framework. In the concluding section of this chapter, I focus on the utility of CCSA in maximizing the benefits of combining comparative area studies and sectoral analysis.

Comparative Area Studies at the Sectoral Level of Analysis

Bringing CAS to the sectoral level uncovers sectoral structures and organization of institutions and the values, identities, and norms associated with sectors as important political contexts worthy of empirical investigation. Whether single-sector studies or multisector comparisons across regions, the focused comparison of the multidimensional effects of sectors in the contextualized comparative sector approach maximizes analytical and theoretical leverage. In the political economy of development, the CCSA revolutionizes our understanding of comparative and international political economy, alternatives to the neoliberal paradigm, and the new complex interdependence. Understanding the global economic integration of Global South countries during and after neoliberal ascendence necessitates investigating how internal political economic developments are shaped by the multidimensional impacts of sectors. A focus on contextualizing sectors, missing in conventional political economy approaches, uncovers the ideational, structural, and institutional dimensions and relationships in the extent and scope of the role of the state in development and globalization.

Contextualizing the multidimensional impacts of sectoral characteristics, detailed below, within and across countries discovers and uncovers heretofore unexplored politics. Doing so avoids the "apolitical and ahistorical" reification of the market as a neutral and natural institution warned against by Kiren Chaudhry (1993, 246). Additionally, the CCSA sheds light on the relative impacts of the competing explanations of open-economy politics, global markets and institutions, subnational geography, and regime type. Studies highlighted in this section investigate and compare manufacturing to services, labor-intensive sectors to capital-intensive, emerging technologies, and extractive sectors to renewable energy. Within-country, across-country, and transregional comparisons include developed and developing

212 ADVANCING COMPARATIVE AREA STUDIES

countries and democracies and autocracies in Africa, East Asia, Eurasia, Latin America, Southeast Asia, and South Asia. A stepwise discussion of the adoption of CCSA Hsueh (2022) demonstrates the merits of CCSA underscored in this section.

Sectoral Structural Attributes

Integrating sectoral analysis into comparative area studies predicates the examination of *sectoral structural attributes* as measured by technological properties of sectors, forms of industrial organization, and the global division of labor and global value chains. The nature of technological properties and core competencies of sectors influence the choice and efficiency of governance structures and innovation strategies, which, once established, are predisposed to solve certain types of technologically complex problems (Kitschelt 1991; Shafer 1994). The type of commodity chain dominant in a sector in the expanding scope of global production networks, which incorporates capital intensity, asset specificity, and global learning, also shapes how market governance structures vary.[3] Complex versus linear technology, low versus high asset specificity, labor versus capital intensity, tangible versus intangible assets, and the nature of commodity chains are salient sources of change in sectoral analysis.

Context-Specific Sectoral Organization of Institutions

Importantly, sectoral analysis also incorporates the relative political weight of preexisting sectoral bureaucratic and corporate stakeholders comprising the *sectoral organization of institutions*, which are context-specific. Scholarship shows that the preexisting sectoral level organization of political economic relationships creates political interests, embodies complex motivations and interdependencies, and engages in qualitatively different types of transactions.[4] Specifically, existing sectoral institutions and attendant political struggles for strategic control and power within economic exchange

---

[3] Gereffi 2001 and Gereffi et al. 2005. See also Yeung (2016) on global production networks.
[4] Atkinson and Coleman 1989; Campbell and Lindberg 1990; and Hollingsworth et al. 1994. See Kurth 1979 on a sector's position in the product cycle and international market and timing of industrialization as the "political tendency of industry."

(and not necessarily the search for efficiency) affect the political choices of state elites that manipulate property rights and ratify or select particular market governance structures.

Variation in state capacity and in societal mobilization reflected in bureaucratic arrangements and relationships with key societal actors at the sector level (whether within country or across countries) uncovers the degree and scope of the state's ability and intention to intervene in the economy and in the implementation of industrial policy. This organizational conception of sectoral structural and institutional attributes captures land, labor, and capital endowments and implications for sectoral governance and development.[5] It also captures variation in forms of capitalist organization, from craft manufacturing and mass production to high-tech services and manufacturing (Crouch et al. 2009). Furthermore, the arena of actors and the transmission mechanisms that power global value chains are the state, firms, and nongovernmental stakeholders and their standards, norms, and conventions at the sector level (Dallas et al. 2019).

Social and Political Construction of Sectors

The contextualization of sectors further calls for recognizing the social and political construction of sectors by state and other economic actors. Historically rooted circumstances situate how such objective conditions – sectoral structural and institutional attributes, macroeconomic tools, and economic crises – are perceived intersubjectively by state and market actors and affect the content and the enforcement of economic policies whether intentionally and purposefully constructed by the state (Hsueh 2011 and 2022). An intersubjective understanding of the role of sectoral structural attributes and organization of institutions becomes salient when comprehending what may appear to be idiosyncratic decisions to intervene based on economic or political criteria. Variation in intersubjective assessments of "objective" values are confirmed and complemented by investigations are the sectoral level of analysis.

---

[5] See Gregg (2015) on factor endowments and Gaddy (1996) on spatial dynamics.

Contextualized Sectors and the Value of Comparisons

The growing literature at the contextualized sector level of analysis contributes to scholarship on the role of the state in market governance and regulation; sector coalitions and policy networks; state choices and industrial development, environmental transitions, and industrial upgrading and technology transfers; and natural resources and political economic impacts. Examining sectoral structural attributes and existing organization of institutions at the sector and subsector led to questions and discoveries about how the Chinese government was able to increase state capacity and achieve industrial development even while liberalizing foreign direct investment, contrary to dominant perspectives on open-economy politics and state-led development (Hsueh 2011, 2016). These questions were particularly salient given that China became a member of the World Trade Organization in 2001, committing to liberalized markets across the macroeconomy.

Exploring these questions and explicating the seeming conundrum, Hsueh's (2011) focused comparisons of technologically and institutionally disparate sectors and subsectors, including those in telecommunications, underscore the analytical leverage of investigation at the sectoral level. In paying close attention to the interplay between state goals and sectoral contexts, the study unravels the causal mechanisms linking economic liberalization and authoritarianism in China—when conventional wisdom suggested that global economic integration in China might lead to a transition to democracy. Instead, the Chinese state has maximized the national technology base, enhanced the competitiveness of the domestic economy, and maintained authoritarian rule.

Take, for example, telecommunications services, which facilitate communication and disseminate information to users. The systematic comparison of subsectors of telecommunications services uncovers China's "liberalization two-step," defined as macro-level liberalization and sectoral-level reregulation. Telecommunications services are differentiated between, on the one hand, basic service providers that operate backbone infrastructure with high asset specificity and, on the other hand, value-added service providers with lower asset specificity, operating on top of wireline or wireless network infrastructure connected by cell phone towers.

Examining state goals, government-business relations, and state methods in the context of the structural and organizational attributes of telecommunications services reveals that the Chinese government has retained state ownership of telecommunications infrastructure but liberalized the market entry and ownership of the value-added services operating on top of the infrastructure. The introduction of competition has enhanced knowledge and technology transfers, but the state is able to control information dissemination and manage telecommunications infrastructure through rules and regulations that calibrate market entry, level of investment, ownership arrangement, and business scope of nonstate business and FDI across subsectors. Sarah Eaton's (2015) comparison of Chinese state-owned enterprises in telecommunications and aviation industries also shows protracted state intervention based on their political and economic significance.

Not only in China are the impacts of global and domestic interests refracted by domestic ideas and institutions at the sectoral level. Going against the grain of conventional wisdom on weak state capacity in the wake of the Soviet Union's collapse, Susanne Wengle (2015) shows the centralizing role of the state in the liberalization and privatization of Russia's electricity sector. Examining policymaking in the electricity and telecommunications sectors in transitioning democracies in Latin America, Maria Victoria Murillo (2009) shows how electoral competition and the partisan orientation of reformers mediated the impacts of open-economy politics. To better understand Big Bang liberalization in India, Rahul Mukherji (2014) traces telecommunications policymaking from decades prior to identify the "tipping point" where ideas and interests converge. Controlling for sector across regime types, Rudra Sil and Allison Evans (2020) show how extraction at fixed sites, volatile prices, and shareholder pressures led to similar labor militancy in platinum mines in Kazakhstan and South Africa.

National Versus Sectoral Patterns

Incorporating sectoral analysis in single-country and cross-regional studies serves the function of controlled comparisons in different ways. To begin with, scholars in analytically equivalent sector studies have controlled for sectoral attributes to understand national patterns of political development. Investigating the role of the state vis-à-vis business, comparing textiles trade in Morocco and Tunisia, Melani Cammett (2007) shows the balance of power between them before economic opening and the preexisting business class structure shape national variation in industrial upgrading. Examining national variation in responses to resource booms, Ryan Saylor (2014) highlights the importance of export-oriented coalitions in the development of commodity sectors in Africa and Latin America. Ken Shadlen (2017) characterizes national variation in coalitional dynamics between transnational firms, domestic industry, and the state in intellectual property rights policymaking in pharmaceuticals across Latin America.

Whereas comparing single or analytically equivalent sectors across countries can tease out the effects of national differences, it may not be able to clearly show what are functions of sectoral structural attributes and what are functions of national institutional characteristics. Combining controlled comparisons at the national and sectoral levels provide analytical traction. Steven K. Vogel's (1996) cross-country and within-country sectoral comparisons of Japan and the United Kingdom test whether theorized national regulatory patterns hold across sectors. Comparing new energy sectors in Brazil and South Africa, Kathryn Hochstetler (2020) identifies the causal primacy of sectoral differences and the consequential effects on and of state choices. She shows empirically how the adoption of solar versus wind power in these countries has threatened existing interests in other forms of renewable energy, ultimately shaping national responses to energy transitions. Building on their extant work, Richard Doner, Gregory Noble, and John Ravenhill (2021) investigate national variation in automotive value chain development across Asia by focusing analysis on the match between national institutional capacities and technological requirements. Constrained resource endowments, external threats, and domestic political pressures shape differences in national institutional strength and thereby position in the automotive value chain.

Comparing sectors can also identify and adjudicate national versus subnational differences in political and economic development. Employing comparative sectoral analysis in one national context, Eric Thun and Adam Segal (2001) explain the different development of the automobile industry and information technology in China by examining the role of subnational governments and the ways in which these sectors are organized. Hsueh (2011) exposes the match between industrial sectors and subnational or national-level regulation based on how labor- and capital-intensive sectors contribute to Chinese state imperatives based on a strategic value logic. John Minnich (2023) demonstrates variation in technology transfers by comparing strategic and non-strategic sectors, whereby the level and scope of state intervention have varied.

It is not so much that subnational geography factors do not have effects; rather, systematic comparative sectoral analysis uncovers their relative importance in understanding sociopolitical and economic outcomes. John Yasuda (2017) attributes the dynamics of multilevel governance to geographical scale in his investigation of the foodstuffs sectors in China. Scholars such as Doug Fuller (2016) examining semiconductors, Jonas Nahm (2021) on renewable energy, and Xiao Ma (2022) on high-speed rail find that variations in the growth and development of industries are shaped by intergovernmental relations and economic coalitions. Jean Hong and Wenhui Yang (2024) test the effects of oil, natural gas, and coal production on local corruption levels, finding sectoral variation based on local regulatory environment and labor intensity.

Investigating the interacting effects of sectoral structural and institutional attributes and the political salience of industrial sectors, Hsueh's (2022) cross-regional and cross-sectoral analysis of the role of the state in market governance in China, India, and Russia during neoliberal ascendence shows how national patterns reflect within-country sectoral differences. The different controls at the national and sectoral levels in the research design serve different purposes. They uncover generalizable dynamics in the multidimensional effects of sectors in addition to case-specific findings. In the study, systematically examining the same sectors across different regime types controls for the technological properties of sectors.

This revealed, for example, higher levels of central state intervention in infrastructural sectors as a function of the higher investment and coordination requirements regardless of regime type. In contrast, when holding the national constant and comparing sectors within countries, the study shows how national level differences in perceived strategic value orientation shape sectoral variation in state control. The process tracing of sectoral trajectories further reveals how national differences affect the ways in which historically rooted values and institutions replicate, reinforce, and transform over time.

The Contextualized Comparative Sector Approach

This section shows how comparative sectoral analysis in any given geographical context offers opportunities for developing grounded explanations. When combined with controlled comparisons across regions, it can also establish generalizability and boundary/scope conditions. The step-by-step demonstration of the empirical and analytical utility of the contextualized comparative sector approach in this section reflects on the theory building and theory development and testing in Hsueh (2022). The multi-level comparisons within and across medium-N national and sectoral cases allow concepts developed in one set of cases to be tested for generalizability and to generate context-specific knowledge. The different levels of analysis involve cross-regional country comparison, within-country comparative sectoral analysis, and process tracing across time from industrial origins.

Rudra Sil (2018) proffers that theories based on within-case analysis (whether intracountry or intraregion) can be tested in another area, triangulating as different types of data would. The merits of qualitative research and controlled comparisons are beyond the "close-up process-tracing analysis of a well-fitted case that usually confirms or illuminates a general proposition derived statistically or deductively" (Sil 2018, 227). The adoption of different qualitative methods achieves generalization and individualization, generates universal and context-sensitive theories and concepts, and involves inductive and deductive processes, pointing to the power of multi-method research in comparative area studies, as extolled by Matthias Basedau and David Kuehn in their contribution to this volume. In Hsueh (2022), historical process-tracing from sectoral origins shows the evolution of perceived strategic value as state elites respond to internal and external pressures. Cross-regional and within-country comparative sector case studies show how variation in the details of market governance are based on sectoral structures and organization of institutions.

Empirical and Theoretical Puzzles

The employment in Hsueh (2022) of the contextualized comparative sector approach began with the self-conscious engagement of existing debates on the relationship between development and globalization in political science and respective area studies. What is the relationship between internal development and integration in the global economy in developing countries? How and why do state-market relations differ? And do these differences matter in the post–Cold War era of global conflict and cooperation? Existing models of development shed some light on the impacts of globalization: Global South countries today have departed from the developmental states of East Asia, which strictly regulated foreign direct investment. They have also eschewed the historical experience of Latin American countries in a similar stage of development. There, liberalization facilitated coalitions of foreign investors, the state, and local businesses exploiting physical and natural resources.

Moreover, recent studies debate state capacity and policies to upgrade human capital and innovation, coalitional dynamics, and resource endowments. They have done so in the context of the adoption of neoliberal policies advocated by the Washington Consensus, the influence of economic groups vis-à-vis the state during the rapid disintegration of the Soviet Union and related dismantling of the communist state, and relatively high growth rates in China and India. These dominant perspectives, however, pay less attention to the constellation of path-dependent values and institutions negotiated by political economic elites during significant moments in developing countries' attempts at national consolidation. They are also less informative in explicating the extent and scope of market governance (and attendant socioeconomic development).

Theoretical Framework and Hypotheses

To tackle the empirical and theoretical puzzles and building on and extending Hsueh (2011 and 2016), the China-sector cases develop the Strategic Value Framework. The explanatory model shows the how, why, and with what of sectoral patterns of market governance, process-tracing how state elites respond to internal and external pressures and the responses' effects on market governance. The inductive function is comparative sectoral analysis in China, and the deductive function, further refining the theoretical framework, is performed through cross-regional country and within-country cross-sector analysis. Comparing industrial trajectories in the same country from the origins of mechanized sectoral development to the introduction of market competition uncovers how the strategic value logic, as a function of internal and external pressures at critical junctures, is reflected and refracted by sectoral structures and the existing organization of institutions. Case-specific findings for each country demonstrate the empirical leverage of the Strategic Value Framework. They also support the analytical discovery of *national configurations of sectoral models*, which mediate the relationship between globalization and development.

220 ADVANCING COMPARATIVE AREA STUDIES

The Strategic Value Framework contends that state elite decision-makers, having been socialized over time with values and identities born of significant phases of institutionalization, respond to internal domestic and external pressures to globalize, making use of fundamentally divergent *market governance structures* that vary by country and sectors within countries. Geopolitical insecurity and resource constraints, their perception by state elites, and sectoral structures and context-specific institutions motivate the mobilization of limited state capacity as well as the state goals and state methods in the dominant patterns of market governance. The *perceived strategic value of sectors* and *sectoral structures and organization of institutions* are the key independent variables that interact to shape dominant patterns of market governance.

Market governance structures comprise two related but separate dimensions of the actual and various imperfect coordination mechanisms as they occur in practice: level and scope of the state in market coordination and the dominant distribution of property rights. This conceptualization, first operationalized in Hsueh (2016) across labor-intensive textiles and capital-intensive telecommunications, develops a taxonomy of market governance, which recognizes the various state and market authorities in coordination mechanisms and broadens measures of institutional quality beyond de jure private property rights and credible commitment.

The Strategic Value Framework first identifies the economic and political pressures confronted by state elites in the context of global economic integration. On the one hand, considerations of pressures associated with external and internal security are important political challenges to state elites. On the other hand, the relative advancement of the national technology base and the competitiveness of domestic industry are economic pressures and threats. Importantly, *intersubjectivity* shapes how state elites define, make claims upon, and contest contemporary political and economic pressures associated with industrial development. In this understanding, institutions are born of intersubjective processes and the sedimentation of the knowledge of the day and not just from objective material circumstances.

The following expectations operationalize the impacts of *perceived strategic value* on how the state formulates goals and methods, who controls industrial policy, and what kinds of measures are employed: The higher the perceived strategic value of a sector, the more likely state elites will employ purposive and deliberate action to regulate market entry, business scope, and ownership to achieve state goals. The state will enhance state control and bring to bear resources and state capacity to coordinate market activities. The property rights arrangements that dominate involve the state's holding controlling rights and interests in ownership and public-private partnerships, and in participating in corporate governance.

In contrast, the lower the perceived strategic value of a sector, the more likely the state will relinquish its control to decentralized and nonstate actors and employ incidental control to coordinate markets and regulate market entry and business scope. Private ownership, private-private joint ventures, and public-private partnerships are typical property rights arrangements. Lower degrees of perceived strategic value can translate into the decentralization of bureaucratic coordination and deregulation of market entry and business scope in decentralized governance. It can also lead to the private regulation by private owners of private governance.

Importantly, the Strategic Value Framework further contends that sectoral technological attributes and existing organization of sectoral institutions influence market governance details. Sectoral structural attributes and nation-specific organization of institutions of sectors are expected to have the following impacts on how government goals associated with perceived strategic value are implemented and on what kinds of measures are employed: The state is more likely to impart deliberate market coordination and enhance its regulatory authority when a service or product entails complex technology because of the high investment required in learning by trial and error of technology with highly uncertain causal structures.

When the drivers of producer-driven commodity chains are industrial capital, when research and development (R&D) and production are core competencies, and when main network links are investment based, the state is more likely to mobilize investment and coordination of industrial activities to maximize domestic exposure to R&D. These measures and their implementation are observed in centralized governance or regulated governance. Conversely, incidental coordination by the state is more likely for products or services comprising linear technology because of the lower investment required in the incremental and programmed learning of less ambiguous technological structures. Likewise, when the drivers of buyer-driven commodity chains are commercial capital, core competencies are design and marketing, and main network links are trade-based, the state is less likely to mobilize investment and coordinate industrial activities.

Multilevel Comparative Case Research Design:
Regions/Countries and Sectors

To show how interacting strategic value and sectoral logics shape dominant patterns of market governance across countries and sectors, Hsueh (2022) adopts a structured, longitudinal case comparison of the development trajectories of labor- and capital-intensive industries (textiles and telecommunications and their subsectors) in China, India, and Russia. The multilevel research design, based on the deliberate selection of cases, controlled for the similar timing of market reform, existing industrial bases, country size and federal structure, and geopolitical significance historically and in the neoliberal era.

Showing that the *perceived strategic value* of state elites operates across countries at the national level as well as within country at the sectoral level maximizes the utility of analytical comparisons that Theda Skocpol and Margaret Somers (1980, 175) identify as "parallel demonstration of theory" and "the contrast of contexts." It also aligns with the CAS endeavor to identify and characterize generalizable political processes with regional and national variations. As noted in the first CAS volume, "A well-matched and context-sensitive comparison could reveal significant divergence in the elite politics and institutional capacities of these regimes that would otherwise likely be obscured by single-case studies or studies restricted to one single geographical area" (Chen 2018, 134–135).

Though Russia is most often compared with countries in post-Soviet Eurasia, incorporating both China and India in the research design controls for the combination of capitalism and political authoritarianism, in addition to regime type. And, as Hsueh (2012) points out, comparing India with China (and Russia), and controlling for similarities such as timing in market reform, allows for determining the causal relevance of regime type. It also enables the examination of the actual impacts of the hypothesized strategic value and sectoral logics and other competing explanations, such as open-economy politics and international markets, organizations, and norms.

Hsueh (2012) first advanced the contextualized comparative sector approach to uncover market governance as an important mechanism for understanding the relationship between globalization and development—despite differences between China and India in regime type and historical cultural connections. In their integration into the global economy, China and India have departed from neoliberalism and the developmental state. Both countries have taken a "liberalization two-step," which follows macro-liberalization with micro-level sectoral reregulation. Yet China and India have reregulated with political logics historically rooted in very different perceptions of strategic value and country-specific sectoral organization of institutions.

The telecommunications and textile sectors of China, India, and Russia are ideal country and sector cases to test the hypotheses of the Strategic Value Framework on how countries have governed markets in the context of economic internationalization. As rising powers and the world's largest and fastest-growing developing countries, the three countries introduced market competition and administrative and corporate restructuring, beginning in the late 1980s and into the 1990s. Macro-liberalization coincided with the height of the global neoliberal movement, the end of the Cold War, and the transformation of socialist economic policies. A systematic cross-national comparison of telecommunications and textiles, industries with different institutional legacies and structural attributes—the former a technologically advanced sector with new political stakeholders and the latter a labor-intensive and politically and developmentally established industry—provides leverage in examining market governance.

Comparing the same industries across countries controls for sectoral characteristics, and comparing different industries within a country checks country-specific characteristics. Variation in market governance structures for the same industry across countries reflects differences, including ideological, political, and institutional, in how markets are governed. Likewise, sectoral variation within the same country reflects the importance of sectoral attributes.

The CCSA at different levels of analysis identifies the theorized objective and intersubjective dimensions of state elite decision-making. It has uncovered how the perceived strategic value of sectors is rooted in state elite responses to successive national episodes of internal and external pressures. Longitudinal process-tracing from sectoral origins (historically and from 1980 to 2020), highlighting key episodes of global economic integration (including historically and, more recently, the Multifiber Agreement, General Agreement on Tariffs and Trade, and World Trade Organization) and political and economic reverberations (such as debt and economic crises, and the emergency in India, Tiananmen Square incident in China,

224   ADVANCING COMPARATIVE AREA STUDIES

and collapse of the Soviet Union), facilitates the periodization of significant internal and external pressures.

Importantly, the cross-time analysis identifies the *intersubjective* nature of interacting strategic value and sectoral institutional logics. Objective measures of strategic value are important; and equally significant are how state elites perceive the strategic importance of sectors during episodes of national consolidation. Starting national-level analysis at sectoral origins allows history to make assignments on the independent variable of perceived strategic value of a sector, creating "as if" randomization of the within-country sector and subsector cases and increasing the validity of the strategic value logic. Examining sectoral trajectories identifies impacts of boom-bust cycles and financial crises, in addition to uncovering other causes when comparing from sectoral origins, which can reveal "dose effects" of theorized causes.[6]

The CCSA thus discloses how industrial sectors are governed differently within the same country as well as how the same sectors are governed differently across countries as a function of variation in perceived strategic value of sectors operating at the national level. On the one hand, interacting strategic value and sectoral logics in Russia have given rise to *resource security nationalism*, whereby non-defense textiles became deregulated and privatized during perestroika reforms the decade before the Soviet collapse. In contrast, the Russian Federation never privatized the telecommunications backbone infrastructure shared by civilian and defense sectors of the military industrial complex. What is more, beginning in 1998 and beyond, during Vladimir Putin's ascendence, oblast-level telecommunications operators became centralized in one corporatized carrier under the telecommunications ministry.

On the other hand, the strategic value orientation of *techno-security developmentalism* shaped how, a decade before China's joining the WTO in 2001, the Chinese government deregulated and privatized textiles, not perceived as critical for national security imperatives or the national technology base. In contrast, despite Big Bang liberalization, the Ministry of Textiles of India has governed the liberalization of textiles production and trade with fiscal policies that protect artisan handlooms and permit highly polluting power looms grounded in the strategic value orientation of *neoliberal self-reliance*. Characterized by labor-intensive, small-scale, and low value-added

---

[6] See Barnes and Weller (2017) on how combining process-tracing and comparative case studies maximizes their analytical utility.

producers and retailers since prior to independence, the fate of the textile industry has rested on its contribution to local employment and its role in the nationalist imagination promoted by Gandhi's vision of *swadeshi*.

Conclusion

This chapter introduces and showcases the contextualized comparative sector approach as embedded in and extending the research agenda of comparative area studies. The CCSA dovetails with the contextualized comparisons and the readiness to do comparisons in CAS, with specific and special focus on the sectoral level of analysis. The preceding sections disclose how empirical and analytical leverage can be gained and midlevel theorizing made possible based on cross-regional and cross-country comparisons at the sectoral level of analysis. The integrated midrange approach transcends the limits of traditional area studies' assumptions of similarities and differences between cases based on national models and outmoded cultural approaches.

The adoption of CCSA has uncovered new sites of inquiry at the sectoral level of analysis. In doing so, in the political economy of development literature, this approach has adjudicated states and markets debates on open-economy politics, global norms and institutions, regime type, and subnational geography. New and extant scholarship on developing economies and regional powers of the Global South provides concrete examples of the analytical power and theoretical value of bringing sectoral analysis to contextualized regional and country comparisons. Paying attention to context-specific, value-laden, and institutional arrangements missing in the conventional political economy approach of studying industrial sectors provides critical insights to key outcomes, such as market governance and industrial development, that involve state and economic actors affected and organized by sectoral structures and institutions and the ideas, norms, and values associated with industrial sectors.

The state-by-step account of the research design and theory development and testing in Hsueh (2022) shows how the contextualized comparative sector approach exposes the ways in which macro-national and micro-sectoral contexts matter. Recognizing differences between China, India, and Russia and their counterparts in traditional area studies in terms of level of development, timing of global economic integration, and regime type, the comparative case research design exploits the empirical and analytical leverage gained from cross-regional comparative investigations at the national and sectoral levels of analysis. Uncovering the ideational, institutional, and structural effects of sectors, multilevel comparative case studies, which include process tracing from sectoral origins, develop and test the Strategic Value Framework. Hsueh (2022) thus demonstrates how the contextualized comparative sector approach can be used to investigate heretofore unexplored inquiries, facilitate empirically grounded analysis, and support theory development and theory testing—all without the unreasonable requirement to master deep knowledge of multiple countries from multiple regions.

Bibliography

Ahram, Ariel, Patrick Köllner, and Rudra Sil, eds. 2018. *Comparative Area Studies: Methodological Rationales and Cross-Regional Applications.* New York: Oxford University Press.

Atkinson, Michael M., and William D. Coleman. 1989. Strong States and Weak States: Sectoral Policy Networks in Advanced Capitalist Economies. *British Journal of Political Science* 19 (1): 47–67.

Bardhan, Pranab K. 2010. *Awakening Giants, Feet of Clay: Assessing the Economic Rise of China and India.* Princeton, NJ: Princeton University Press.

Barnes, Jeb, and Nicholas Weller. 2017. Case Studies and Analytic Transparency in Causal-Oriented Mixed-Methods Research. *PS: Political Science & Politics* 50 (4): 1019–1022.

Bartley, Tim. 2018. *Rules Without Rights: Land, Labor, and Private Authority in the Global Economy.* New York: Oxford University Press.

Cammett, Melani. 2007. *Globalization and Business Politics in Arab North Africa: A Comparative Perspective.* Cambridge: Cambridge University Press.

Campbell, John L., and Leon N. Lindberg. 1990. Property Rights and the Organization of Economic Activity by the State. *American Sociological Review* 55 (5): 634–647.

Chaudhry, Kiren. 1993. The Myths of the Market and the Common History of Late Developers. *Politics & Society* 21 (3): 245–274.

Chen, Cheng. 2016. *The Return of Ideology: The Search for Regime Identities in Postcommunist Russia and China.* Ann Arbor: University of Michigan Press.

Chen, Cheng. 2018. Comparing Post-Communist Authoritarianism in Russia and China: The Case of Anti-Corruption Campaigns. In Ariel I. Ahram, Patrick Köllner, and Rudra Sil, eds. *Comparative Area Studies: Methodological Rationales and Cross-Regional Applications.* New York: Oxford University Press, 133–151.

Crouch, Colin, Martin Schroeder, and Helmut Voelzkow. 2009. Regional and Sectoral Varieties of Capitalism. *Economy and Society* 38 (4): 654–678.

Dallas, Mark, Stefano Ponte, and Timothy J. Sturgeon. 2019. Power in Global Value Chains. *Review in International Political Economy* 26 (4): 666–694.

Dimitrov, Martin, ed. 2013. *Why Communism Did Not Collapse: Understanding Authoritarian Regime Resilience in Asia and Europe.* Cambridge: Cambridge University Press.

Doner, Richard, Gregory Noble, and John Ravenhill. 2021. *The Political Economy of Automobile Industrialization in East Asia.* Oxford: Oxford University Press.

Doner, Richard, Bryan Ritchie, and Dan Slater. 2005. Systemic Vulnerability and the Origins of Developmental States: Northeast and Southeast Asia in Comparative Perspective. *International Organization* 59 (2): 327–361.

Eaton, Sarah. 2015. *The Advance of the State in Contemporary China: State-Market Relations in the Reform Era*. Cambridge: Cambridge University Press.

Evans, Allison, and Rudra Sil. 2020. The Dynamics of Labor Militancy in the Extractive Sector: Kazakhstan's Oilfields and South Africa's Platinum Mines in Comparative Perspective. *Comparative Political Studies* 53 (6): 992–1024.

Falleti, Tulia G., and Julia F. Lynch. 2009. Context and Causal Mechanisms in Political Analysis. *Comparative Political Studies* 42 (9): 1143–1166.

Fuller, Douglas. 2016. *Paper Tigers, Hidden Dragons: Firms and the Political Economy*. Oxford: Oxford University Press.

Frazier, Mark W. 2018. China and the Challenges of Comparison. In Weiping Wu and Mark Frazier, eds. *The Sage Handbook of Contemporary China*. Vol. 2. London: Sage, 1227–1244.

Frazier, Mark W. 2019. *The Power of Place: Contentious Politics in Twentieth-Century Shanghai and Bombay*. Cambridge: Cambridge University Press.

Gaddy, Clifford. 1996. *The Price of the Past: Russia's Struggle with the Legacy of a Militarized Economy*. Washington, DC: Brookings Institution.

Gallagher, Mary. R. 2002. 'Reform and openness': Why China's economic reforms have delayed democracy. *World Politics* 54 (3): 338–372.

Gereffi, Gary. 2001. Shifting Governance Structures in Global Commodity Chains. *American Behavioral Scientist* 44 (10): 1616–1636.

Gereffi, Gary, John Humphrey, and Timothy J. Sturgeon. 2005. The Governance of Global Value Chains. *Review of International Political Economy* 12 (1): 78–104.

Gregg, Amanda Grace. 2015. Factory Productivity, Firm Organization, and Corporation Reform in the Russian Empire, 1894–1908. PhD dissertation, Yale University.

Ho, Selina. 2019. *Thirsty Cities: Social Contracts and Public Goods Provision in China and India*. Cambridge: Cambridge University Press.

Hochstetler, Kathryn. 2020. *Political Economies of Energy Transition: Wind and Solar Power in Brazil and South Africa*. Cambridge: Cambridge University Press.

Hollingsworth, J. Rogers, Philippe C. Schmitter, and Wolfgang Streeck. 1994. *Governing Capitalist Economies: Performance and Control of Economic Sectors*. New York: Oxford University Press.

Hong, Ji Yeon, and Wenhui Yang. 2024. How Natural Resources Affect Corruption in China. *World Development* 175. https://www.sciencedirect.com/science/article/abs/pii/S0305750X23002899.

Hsueh, Roselyn. 2011. *China's Regulatory State: A New Strategy for Globalization*. Ithaca, NY: Cornell University Press.

Hsueh, Roselyn. 2012. China and India in the Age of Globalization: Sectoral Variation in Post-Liberalization Reregulation. *Comparative Political Studies* 45 (1): 32–61.

Hsueh, Roselyn. 2016. State Capitalism, Chinese-Style: Strategic Value of Sectors, Sectoral Characteristics, and Globalization. *Governance* 29 (1): 85–102.

Hsueh, Roselyn. 2022. *Micro-Institutional Foundations of Capitalism: Sectoral Pathways to Globalization in China, India, and Russia*. Cambridge: Cambridge University Press.

Hurst, William. 2018. *Ruling Before the Law: The Politics of Legal Regimes in China and Indonesia* Cambridge: Cambridge University Press.

Johnson, Chalmers. 1962. *Peasant Nationalism and Communist Power: The Emergence of Revolutionary China, 1937–1945*. Stanford, CA: Stanford University Press.

Kennedy, Scott, ed. 2011. *Beyond the Middle Kingdom: Comparative Perspectives on China's Capitalist Transformation*. Stanford, CA: Stanford University Press.

Kitschelt, Herbert. 1991. Industrial Governance Structures, Innovation Strategies, and the Case of Japan: Sectoral or Cross-National Comparative Analysis? *International Organization* 45 (4): 453–493.

Kohli, Atul. 2004. *State-Directed Development: Political Power and Industrialization in the Global Periphery*. Cambridge: Cambridge University Press.

228 ADVANCING COMPARATIVE AREA STUDIES

Kurth, James. 1979. The Political Consequences of the Product Cycle. *International Organization* 33 (1): 1–34.

Levi-Faur, David. 2006. Varieties of Regulatory Capitalism: Getting the Most of the Comparative Method. *Governance* 19 (3): 367–382.

Locke, Richard, and Kathleen Thelen. 1995. Apples and Oranges: Contextualized Comparisons and the Study of Comparative Labor Politics. *Politics & Society* 23 (3): 337–367.

Ma, Xiao. 2022. *Localized Bargaining: The Political Economy of China's High-Speed Railway Program*. Oxford: Oxford University Press.

Minnich, John D. 2023. Re-Innovation Nation: The Strategic and Political Logic of Technology Transfer Policy in Rising China. PhD dissertation, Massachusetts Institute of Technology.

Mukherji, Rahul. 2014. *Globalization and Deregulation: Ideas, Interests, and Institutional Change in India*. New York: Oxford University Press.

Murillo, Maria Victoria. 2009. *Political Competition, Partisanship, and Policymaking in the Reform of Latin American Public Utilities*. New York: Cambridge University Press.

Nahm, Jonas. 2021. *Collaborative Advantage: Forging Green Industries in the New Global Economy*. New York: Oxford University Press.

Saylor, Ryan. 2014. *State Building in Boom Times: Commodities and Coalitions in Latin America and Africa*. New York: Oxford University Press.

Segal, Adam, and Eric Thun. 2001. Thinking Globally, Acting Locally: Local Governments, Industrial Sectors, and Development in China. *Politics and Society* 29 (4): 557–588.

Shadlen, Kenneth. 2017. *Coalitions and Compliance: The Political Economy of Pharmaceutical Patents in Latin America*. Oxford: Oxford University Press.

Shafer, Michael. 1994. *Winners and Losers: How Sectors Shape the Developmental Prospects of States*. Ithaca, NY: Cornell University Press.

Sil, Rudra. 2018. Triangulating Area Studies, Not Just Methods. In Ariel I. Ahram, Patrick Köllner, and Rudra Sil, eds. *Comparative Area Studies: Methodological Rationales and Cross-Regional Applications*. New York: Oxford University Press, 225–246.

Sinha, Aseema. 2016. *Globalizing India: How Global Rules and Markets Are Shaping India's Rise to Power*. New York: Cambridge University Press.

Skocpol, Theda, and Margaret Somers. 1980. The Uses of Comparative History in Macrosocial History. *Comparative Studies in Society and History* 22 (2): 174–197.

Slater, Dan, and Daniel Ziblatt. 2013. The Enduring Indispensability of the Controlled Comparison. *Comparative Political Studies* 46 (10): 1301–1327.

Solinger, Dorothy. 2009. *States' Gains, Labor's Losses: China, France and Mexico Choose Global Liaisons, 1980–2000*. Ithaca: Cornell University Press.

Tsai, Kellee. 2013. China's Political Economy and Political Science. *Perspectives in Politics* 11 (3): 860–871.

Tsai, Lily. 2017. Bringing In China: Insights for Building Comparative Political Theory. *Comparative Political Studies* 50 (3): 295–328.

Vogel, Steven K. 1996. *Free Markets, More Rules: Regulatory Reform in Advanced Industrialized Countries*. Ithaca, NY: Cornell University Press.

Wengle, Susanne. 2015. *Post-Soviet Power: State-Led Development and Russia's Marketization*. Cambridge: Cambridge University Press.

Wu, Yu-Shan. 1995. *Comparative Economic Transformations: Mainland China, Hungary, the Soviet Union, and Taiwan*. Stanford, CA: Stanford University Press.

Yasuda, John. 2017. *On Feeding the Masses: An Anatomy of Regulatory Failure in China*. Cambridge: Cambridge University Press.

Ye, Min. 2014. *Diasporas and Foreign Direct Investment in China and India*. Cambridge: Cambridge University Press.

Yeung, Henry Wai-Chung. 2016. *Strategic Coupling: East Asian Industrial Transformation in the New Global Economy*. Ithaca, NY: Cornell University Press.

PART IV
COMPARATIVE AREA STUDIES AND THE PROMISE OF GLOBAL IR

10

The Promise of Comparative Area Studies for the Study of Human Rights

Eileen Doherty-Sil

Introduction

International relations scholars have long noted the absence of non-Western theories in "mainstream" IR scholarship (Puchala 1997, 1998; Tickner and Blaney 2012; Acharya and Buzan 2017, 2019) and the disproportionate influence of European history in informing concepts and theories thought to be universally useful (Chakrabarty 2008; Tickner and Wæver 2009; Hobson 2012). In an effort to move beyond starkly dichotomizing debates, Amitav Acharya's 2014 presidential address to the International Studies Association (ISA) called for a "global IR" research agenda—that is, a positive and inclusive research agenda that embraces a multiplicity of "voices, experiences, knowledge claims and contributions" not only from the West, but from states as well as societies throughout the world (Acharya 2014, 647). Since then, global IR has made important progress, particularly in surfacing and highlighting cases where understandings and lived experiences of international relations do not match the assumptions reflected in mainstream IR. But it has done less to move beyond what Cynthia Enloe (2021) refers to as the "confusing, complex, dynamic, gritty, nuanced realities of the little picture" in ways that produce insights applying to more than one locale or region.

In this regard, CAS may serve as a powerful ally in taking the next step to go beyond merely saying the world is diverse and complex. With its commitment to posing substantive questions that involve an open-ended search to identify and explain similarities and differences across regions, CAS offers an opportunity to generate novel insights that are at least partially portable across regions or within a given population of cases. To be sure, this is not the first call for more collaboration between IR and area studies (e.g., Modelski 1961; Onar and Nicolaïdis 2013). But the emphasis here is on the utility of

Eileen Doherty-Sil, *The Promise of Comparative Area Studies for the Study of Human Rights*. In: *Advancing Comparative Area Studies*. Edited by: Ariel I. Ahram, Patrick Köllner, and Rudra Sil, Oxford University Press. © Oxford University Press (2025). DOI: 10.1093/oso/9780197809365.003.0010

comparative area studies—that is, something that combines an area specialist's sensitivity to context conditions with the desire to explore comparisons across and within regions, in order to mediate between IR and multiple area studies communities (see also D'Amato et al. 2022).

This question of Western hegemony is particularly evident in human rights scholarship and practice, where debates about the universality/relativism of rights, as well as the contribution of non-Western actors to the global human rights regime, continue unabated in academic as well as policy circles. This chapter explores the specific potential of CAS research for scholarship on human rights, with the aim of moving past stale dichotomies about universality and relativism. To do so, I turn to CAS to identify a small sample of empirical puzzles about commonalities and differences in regional interests or actions vis-à-vis the international human rights regime, cross-regional variation relating to human rights strategies and outcomes, as well as intraregional variation and outlying cases. The goal here is not only to generate richer insights into regional experiences with regard to specific human rights issue areas, but also to make mid-level generalizations across regions, especially in the Global South.

Specifically, the chapter considers three questions concerning cross-regional variations relating to human rights strategies and outcomes, while also identifying cases that are outliers within their regions. First, what explains the stark cross-regional variation in International Criminal Court (ICC) membership, as well as outlier cases within geographic regions? Second, why are treaty-based regional human rights courts more prevalent in some regions (e.g., Europe and Latin America) than in others (e.g., Asia and the Middle East)? Third, what explains the positioning of non-Western global or regional powers (e.g., India, Brazil, South Africa) vis-à-vis the Human Rights Council? These represent a small sample of puzzles that can benefit from cross-regional contextualized comparison and lend themselves to modest middle-range theoretical propositions that can simultaneously advance the agenda of global IR and enrich human rights scholarship writ large.

Global IR's "Pluralistic Universalism"

Long before the emergence of the global IR research tradition, critical and postcolonial scholars countered the hegemony of Western IR scholarship, though as Felix Anderl and Antonia Witt (2020) note, those efforts have come under a variety of labels (e.g., "non-Western," "post-Western," "world-ing," "decolonization"). And famously, the predominance of US scholars and scholarship in the field led to Stanley Hoffman's designation of IR as an "American social science" (Hoffman 1977; Walt 2011). In this regard, Acharya's 2014 ISA speech built on a rich body of existing scholarship that marked the field as contested terrain (Biersteker 1999). What was new was Acharya's research agenda, which he stressed should not be "global IR the-ory" but a commitment to inclusivity and diversity in IR scholarship. His call for "pluralistic universalism" emphasized the need to take seriously non-Western ideas, institutions, and experiences on their own terms rather than as case studies that "reinforce the image of area studies as little more than provider of raw data to Western theory" (Acharya 2014, 650). In this regard, global IR gives center stage to regions, regionalisms, and area studies, with regions being understood not as fixed geographic or cultural units, nor essentially state-centric, but as complex, dynamic, and overlapping socially constructed spaces.[1]

Key to Acharya's vision is the rejection of cultural exceptionalism, regard-less of whether such claims come from hegemonic actors such as the United States or from non-Western actors who emphasize their differences with dominant actors. This is because the emergence of culture-specific schools of IR would only further fragment knowledge and undermine dialogical possibilities. For example, Matteo Dian argues that efforts to build a "Chi-nese School of IR" (Qin 2011, 2016; Zhang 2012; Zhang and Chang 2016) may create a "positive orientalism" that overemphasizes the uniqueness of certain concepts or practices in order to legitimize existing regimes (Dian 2022, 264). In the same vein, Acharya (2018, 7) argues against an "Indian school of IR," stressing instead the way that India's nonaligned posture as an exportable practice was founded on a "syncretic or pluralistic universalism" rather than an outright rejection of global liberalism. And with respect to Africa, Luca Raineri and Edoardo Baldero (2022, 247) stress the need for a dialectical approach to regional and area studies and explore the way that studying African experiences can shed light on other regions of the world (including the West). While there is by no means a consensus on how best

---

[1] Two strands of global IR scholarship have emerged, each with different implications questions of portability and knowledge cumulation. One strand calls for a fundamental deconstruction and reconceptualization of the ontological bases in dominant IR theory (e.g., Shahi 2018; Fierke and Jabri 2019). The second (e.g., Acharya and Buzan 2017; Foulon and Meibauer 2020) emphasizes incorporating or engaging dominant theory. It is this second strand that engages most comfortably with CAS.

234 ADVANCING COMPARATIVE AREA STUDIES

to ensure dialogue across geographies or theories (Hutchings 2011), these arguments stress the importance of strategies and methodologies that illuminate marginalized perspectives without lapsing into "narcissistic turf wars" (Eun 2018; 2019).

In short, global IR has made great strides in exposing mainstream IR's disproportionate emphasis on Western experience but has been less successful in identifying patterns across non-Western regions to identify which experiences are truly distinctive and which are simply at variance with the experience of the West. What is needed is an empirical basis for the construction of alternative theories, as well as strategies to interrogate and reassess broad categories that are assumed to be universal and natural, including state, sovereignty, anarchy, market, and international order (Dian 2022, 253). I turn now to the specific challenges in global human rights scholarship before considering the role that CAS can play in overcoming some of these challenges.

The Contested Terrain of Human Rights in IR Scholarship

"Pluralistic Universalism" in Human Rights

The question of Western hegemony, specifically the universality/relativism of rights, has plagued the human rights project since the 1948 adoption of the Universal Declaration of Human Rights (UDHR). On the one hand, the UDHR is written in undeniably Western philosophical language and was adopted in a world of only fifty-six voting states, with most of today's non-Western states still under colonial rule. On the other hand, every country in the world has ratified at least one of the nine core international human rights treaties (with 80 percent ratifying four or more); furthermore, the UDHR also holds the record for being the most translated document in the world (United Nations, n.d.a). And although the UDHR was adopted unanimously[2] in 1948, the thin nature of that consensus was illustrated by United Nations Educational, Scientific and Cultural Organization member Jacques Barrington's comment that agreement was possible "as long as we did not ask why" (Witte 2009). Similarly, at the 1993 Vienna World Conference on Human Rights, the declaration adopted by consensus was hailed as

---

[2] There were eight abstentions: South Africa, Saudi Arabia, USSR, Czechoslovakia, Poland, Byelorussian SSR, Ukrainian SSR, Yugoslavia.

a post–Cold War affirmation that human rights are "indivisible, interdependent and interrelated," but this too was not without controversy. Despite the surface appearance of consensus, the negotiations coexisted with proclamations about cultural diversity, relativism, and the role of economic rights in the broader human rights regime (Tan 2016; Burke 2020).

In the decade following the Vienna conference, Singaporean Prime Minister Lee Kuan Yew and Malaysian President Mahathir Mohamad emerged as advocates for an "Asian values" argument, which embraced a communitarian rather than individual-based vision of rights (Zakaria 1994; Barr 2000). While critics maintained that this was a political maneuver to counter charges of authoritarianism and political repression, the Asian values argument opened debates not just about communitarianism versus individualism, but also about the extent to which "Asian values" had contributed to regional economic growth and development. Perhaps because the argument was linked so clearly to economic growth, it largely faded after the 1997 Asian economic crisis—but not before it came to symbolize the broader universalism/relativism debate and to launch a wave of empirical research (e.g., Dalton and Ong 2005; Kim 2010; Welzel 2011).

Similarly, "African values" arguments begin with the premise that the human rights project is essentially Western. Similar to the Asian values narrative, these arguments stress the communal rather than individualistic foundations of African society, including implications for differences in issues like private versus communal landownership (Cobbah 1987; see also Pollis and Schwab 1979). Furthermore, arguments exist about "Islamic values," though these arguments range from nuanced comparisons (Mazrui 1997) to starker predictions about the inevitability of civilizational clash between Islam and the West (Huntington 1993).

More recently, the universalism/relativism debate has reemerged in full force, this time led by China.[3] What China has called its "people-centered philosophy" (Chinese Ministry of Foreign Affairs 2022) focuses on national sovereignty and civilizational diversity, with particular emphasis on a development-focused "right to subsistence" (Chinese Ministry of Foreign Affairs 2021; see also Sun 2016; Zhang and Buzan 2020). Within the UN Human Rights Council (HRC), China has pushed an alternative human rights model privileging socioeconomic rights and national sovereignty

---

[3] Russia has been another vocal critic of universalism, for example, in its advocacy for "universal traditional values" in debates at the UNHRC regarding sexual orientation and gender identity (Symons and Altman 2015; Stoeckl and Medvedeva 2018).

(Piccone 2018; Foot 2022), a move that some argue has affected HRC member voting behavior (Pauselli et al. 2022).[4] Beijing has even gone so far as to establish an alternative human rights forum, the South-South Human Rights Forum, which emphasizes the "diversity of civilization," the "unity and particularity of human rights," and the role of China itself as a model for the development of human rights (China Daily 2017).

Concepts like the "right to subsistence" are of course not new; recall Senegal President Léopold Senghor's famous assertion that "human rights start with breakfast." Nor is there a shortage of scholars who emphasize the normative force of development-focused rights discourse. For example, Makau Mutua (2017) warns of the legitimacy dangers of putting liberal democracy as the "northern lights" of the global human rights regime, which he argues obscures more compelling issues of economic justice for much of the world. The normative force of the development discourse only increases the importance of avoiding simplistic dichotomies such as universalism/relativism in thinking about the coexistence of civilizational diversity and universal rights. In this regard, Amartya Sen's "Human Rights and Asian Values," which is perhaps the most prominent rejection of cultural relativism (specifically the Asian values debate), is explicit about the need to embrace cultural diversity, not only between cultures but also within them:

> The recognition of diversity within different cultures is extremely important in the contemporary world, since we are constantly bombarded by oversimple generalizations about "Western civilization," "Asian values," "African cultures," and so on. These unfounded readings of history and civilization are not only intellectually shallow, they also add to the divisiveness of the world in which we live. (Sen 1997, 31)

Sen's emphasis on cultural diversity has been echoed by others, including Jack Donnelly's (2007) work on the "relative universality of human rights," discussions of "universality, diversity and cultural rights" (Bennoune and Soyinka 2018), and cross-cultural approaches to universalism (An-Na'im 1992, 2021).

---

[4] A particularly visible example was the HRC's October 2022 vote rejecting a draft decision to open a debate on human rights violations in China's Xinjiang region (Amnesty International 2022).

Contestation in Decentering Human Rights

Global IR's call to decenter international relations underscores two key areas of controversy in "mainstream" human rights scholarship. First, how do we understand the agency of non-Western actors vis-à-vis international human rights? Second, how does this understanding change when we move away from the international level of analysis and toward regionally or locally rooted strategies? On the first question about non-Western agency vis-à-vis the international human rights regime, there is extensive scholarship highlighting the role of non-Western actors in the development of international human rights law. For example, Kathryn Sikkink has documented the influence of Latin American and other small countries before and during the drafting of the UDHR (Sikkink 2014, 2017).[5] Glenda Sluga (2013) notes that the Haitian delegation proposed that the word "universal" be added to the declaration of human rights, and Manu Belur Bhaganan (2013) has explored the central role of India in launching a transnational campaign against South African apartheid. Others have emphasized the contributions of specific individuals, including Kuomintang Chinese delegate P. C. Chang's incorporation of Confucian ideas into rights discussions (Roth 2018), Jawaharlal Nehru's strong support of the international human rights regime (Acharya 2018), and Hansa Mehta's role in ensuring gender-neutral language in the UDHR (Glendon 2001).

Moving to the postcolonial era, Roland Burke (2010) documents the importance of newly independent states in the passage of the first binding human rights treaties, as well the central role they played in institutionalizing the norm of national self-determination as the first and foundational article in both the International Covenant on Civil and Political Rights and the International Covenant on Economic Social and Cultural Rights. Similarly, Steven Jensen (2016) traces the leadership of Jamaica, Liberia, Ghana, the Philippines, and other postcolonial countries during the 1960s in pushing for human rights instruments on race and religion and, in the process, reinvigorating what had become a stalled UN human rights process. And Acharya (2016, 350) examines the Bandung Conference as a forum where

---

[5] Sikkink draws on extensive scholarship to do this (e.g., Burgers 1992; Morsink 2000; Waltz 2001; Carozza 2003; Obregon 2005; Glendon 2003; Grandin 2012, 2007). Nonetheless, some global IR scholars argue that this work "inadvertently recreates the ethnocentrism of IR and flattens multiplicity as variation on Western/Northern norms" (Blaney and Tickner 2017, 295).

newly independent states challenged Western dominance but simultaneously affirmed global norms of universalism and human rights. While not all these scholars identify as part of the global IR tradition, each explicitly engages the issue of multiple agencies and the need to rethink scholarship with regard to universalism/relativism.

The above studies locate their focus at the level of international law and institutions. While important, that lens misses a second and perhaps more fundamental aspect of decentering: the need for "center stage" to be given to regions, regionalisms, and area studies rather than a Western epicenter of what we imagine to be "international relations." In this regard, Stephen Hopgood (2013) emphasizes the tensions between what he calls *Human Rights* (the largely professional, globalized superstructure of Western-based norms, institutions, and organizations) and *human rights* (culturally and community-rooted actions to reduce suffering, which are often rooted in religious, nationalist, ethnic, or family structures rather than global liberal norms). This latter category, he argues, is too often neglected in mainstream human rights scholarship.

Consistent with Hopgood's distinction between Human Rights and human rights, Abdullahi Ahmed An-Na'im calls for a reinterpretation and reconstruction of universal standards both in the context of specific cultures and across cultures (An-Na'im 1991, 1992, 2003; An-Na'im and Deng 1990). His most recent work, *Decolonizing Human Rights* (An-Na'im 2021), takes an even stronger position in its rejection of external coercive enforcement of rights under international law and instead embraces what he calls "self-determined universality" that relies on people-centered practice of human rights norms through cultural transformation and political mobilization. This, he argues, would "reclaim the glorious rationale and vision" of the UDHR.

The bottom line is that human rights scholarship has not made much progress in specifying what Acharya's "pluralistic universality" means in specific cases, nor in the broader decentering project. Global IR scholarship takes a critical first step by highlighting experiences and local particularities that do not fit with prevailing theories and revealing some of the assumptions of those theories to be Western-centric. But global IR does little to cumulate insights across regions and, in fact, tends to be skeptical of advancing generalizable propositions, preferring instead to embrace "the transgressive power of diversity and difference" (Tickner and Smith 2020, 4).

Here CAS provides obvious space for collaboration. Drawing on the insights of global IR research as well as comparative areas studies scholars, CAS can interrogate the reasons for regional differences by taking a problem-centered approach, with an eye toward teasing out commonalities and differences in regional interests or actions vis-à-vis the international human rights regime, cross-regional variation relating to human rights strategies and outcomes, as well as intraregional variation and outlying cases. The goal is to generate richer insights into regional experiences with regard to specific human rights issue areas, and to make mid-level generalizations across regions. The next section examines empirical questions in the field of human rights, with the aim of highlighting progress that has already been made and identifying unexplored puzzles, to demonstrate the potential of CAS to move past what have become stale dichotomous debates about universalism/relativism.

Enter CAS: The Promise for Human Rights Scholarship

Below I examine three sets of human rights puzzles. First, IR scholars and practitioners are acutely aware of the stark cross-regional variation in ICC membership. What explains this variation? And why are there outlier cases within geographic regions? What do the answers to these questions suggest about the meaning of human rights in specific regional and national contexts? Second, why do treaty-based regional human rights systems exist in Europe, Latin America, and Africa, but not in Asia or the Middle East? What accounts for this difference, or for the differences in which the treaty-based systems have proven effective in protecting the rights of vulnerable groups? Third, how should we understand self-proclaimed "like-minded" states with regard to global human rights? For example, just how similar are the members of the India-Brazil–South Africa Dialogue Forum in their actions at the HRC? As will be discussed below, answers to such problems all gain from efforts to leverage regional expertise to understand the dynamics in particular cases while also relying on cross-regional, contextualized comparison to aggregate insights and construct middle-range theoretical arguments about patterns of human rights practices and experiences situated between the universal and the particular.

240   ADVANCING COMPARATIVE AREA STUDIES

The International Criminal Court

The 1998 adoption of the Rome Statute created the ICC as the first truly international mechanism to hold perpetrators of mass atrocity accountable for genocide, war crimes, crimes against humanity, and crimes of aggression (Bosco 2014). The vote to adopt the Rome Statute was 120 in favor, 7 against,[6] with 21 abstentions. That some countries opposed the ICC is not surprising. What is more surprising is the stark regional variation in membership, with state parties coming overwhelmingly from Europe, Latin America, and Africa. Much work has been done on the decisions of the United States (e.g., Scharf 1999; Mayerfeld 2003) and China (e.g., Tao 2015; Zhu 2018) not to join the court, as well as the increasing opposition from countries on the African continent (Jalloh and Bantekas 2017; Clark 2018; Clarke 2019). Less has been done on broader geographic variation; in short, what explains the outlier cases between and within world regions?

Some analyses of the Middle East's relationship with the court emphasize a long-standing regional distrust of the organization, especially the perception among Arab states about entrenched double standards that effectively exempt Western powers (including Israel) from ICC scrutiny (Bruno 2011). This would suggest that the reasons for Middle East nonmembership are primarily geopolitical in nature. Yet there may be a more complex story to tell about the relationship between Arab states and the ICC, especially as it relates to the broad relationship of Islamic law and international human rights law, and in particular, the failure to have experts in Islamic law participate in the drafting of the UDHR and subsequent human rights treaties (Khan 2018, 170).

Consistent with global IR's emphasis on pluralistic universalism, the scholarship written from the perspective of Islamic jurisprudence tends not to claim fundamental incompatibility between the two traditions, but rather the potential for mutual accommodation of Islamic jurisprudence and the ICC (Roach 2005; Malekian 2009; Badar 2011), including a greater reliance of the ICC in drawing on Islamic law in its rulings (Fraser 2020). As Siraj Khan (2018, 148) contends,

---

[6] United States, China, Libya, Iraq, Israel, Qatar, and Yemen.

A more measured and methodological approach to Islamic law and its application would be beneficial and would have the potential to indigenise international law to the Islamic legal context. Such culturally sensitive approaches have the potential to achieve greater buy-in from Muslim-majority states in which the Sharī'ah features strongly in the legal system.

Similarly, Shaheen Sadar Ali and Satwant Kaur Heer (2018) examine actual Muslim state practice by using official deliberation records of the Rome Conference in the drafting of the Rome Statute, in order to challenge the argument that the relatively few ratifications of the statute reflect some fundamental incompatibility between Islamic and "international" law. Their close reading of the negotiations reveals a more complex picture than Muslim/non-Muslim or Western/non-Western, as evidenced by differences among Islamic state delegations as well as the alliances based on factors other than religion. The authors conclude that

> arguments linking non-ratification of the Rome Statute by Muslim states to Islamic law and Sharī'ah implies uncritical evaluation of Muslim state practice in international law as well as within their countries. To be taken seriously by Muslim states in particular, and the international community more generally, scholarship on the ICC, the Rome Statute and international criminal law must be informed by credible and deep knowledge of Muslim state practice, how Muslims actually live Islam. Most importantly, there is no single monolithic Islam; neither is there one single homogenous body of Sharī'ah or Islamic law. Dropping everything vaguely "Islamic" into one basket is probably the most serious correction the world community will have to reflect upon to arrive upon universality of norms. That respectful inclusivity of diversity will be the measure of universality. (Ali and Heer 2018, 199)

Another fruitful inquiry may be to examine reasons for systematic differences in membership of the ICC *within* world regions. Strikingly, Jordan is the only state party from the Middle East to have joined the ICC and was in fact was a founding member. Tunisia is the only North African member, having joined in 2011 in the midst of the Arab Spring. Within South Asia, Bangladesh stands as the only party to the ICC, having signed the treaty in 1999 along with founding members, though not ratifying until

2010. Perhaps the reasons for these outlier cases would be immediately apparent to regional experts, and therefore not puzzling at all. But that is exactly the point: the reasons are *not* immediately apparent for human rights IR scholars. There are important stories in each of these data points, and not just for our understanding of the domestic and foreign policy environments of the countries themselves. These outliers stand to push us past the simplistic generalizations about participation of "Middle Eastern," "Asian," or "Islamic" countries in the ICC—and to tease out the specific contexts in which countries that follow under those categories do indeed accede to the court. In short, these regional variations and the country-specific outliers are puzzles for our understanding of international human rights.

Regional Human Rights Systems

Regional human rights systems exist in the Americas, Europe, and Africa to monitor, protect and promote human rights within member states. All three systems were established by treaty within larger regional integration systems (Organization of American States; Council of Europe; African Union), and all three include human rights mechanisms (notably, human rights commissions and courts) to implement the human rights and adjudicate complaints. By contrast, no treaty-based system exists in different parts of Asia or in the Middle East.

Much of the existing comparative literature on regional human rights systems tends to focus on articulating the institutional/procedural differences of the three existing systems (Heyns et al. 2006; see also Weston et al. 1987). An exception is Alexandra Huneeus and Mikael Rask Madsen's (2018) comparative institutional history:

> Our comparative regional approach moreover allows us to push back on the tendency to view human rights institutions and international courts as creations of the West that are transplanted, copied, or otherwise vernacularized by the South embedded in and responsive to a region with distinct cultural, political, and social contexts. . . . [I]nternational human rights have provided a global "script" which has been enacted in radically different settings in Europe, Latin America, and Africa and has resulted in a relative diversity of institutions and practices. (2018, 137, 138, see also Merry 2006; Meyer et al. 1997)

Similarly, Başak Çalı, Mikael Rask Madsen, and Frans Viljoen lay out a research agenda that is not simply descriptive in nature, but begins with regional human rights regimes themselves as units of comparative analysis:

> We theorize regional human rights regimes as manifestations of a global phenomenon: international human rights law. We also hold that these regimes have semi-autonomous properties that make them neither a mere extension of a global human rights regime nor an amalgamation of regional constitutional cultures. The very rationale for regional regimes (in addition to, or alongside the UN system and constitutional systems) lies in their ability to articulate and institutionalize human rights in ways that are more responsive to and legitimate in a certain region and its particular cultural, legal, and political contexts. The making of regional human rights is a dynamic process, which defines the central characteristics of a "region" along the way. The three established human rights regimes—the European, Inter-American, and African—therefore, are "imagined communities" delineated by dynamics of (human rights) law. Regions are both geographical and law-made yet can reconstruct symbolic spaces as hardened social structures changing public perception of what constitutes regional identity and where its boundaries lie. (2018, 130; see also Anderson 2016)

It is worth noting that much of the explicitly comparative work on regional human rights systems appears in law journals rather than international relations or comparative politics journals. A notable exception is Leiry Cornejo Chavez and Andreas Føllesdal's (2013) special issue of the *Nordic Journal of Human Rights*, which compares the European Court of Human Rights and the Inter-American Court of Human rights to investigate scope conditions and intervening mechanisms by which regional courts create positive outcomes for democracy.

In short, comparative area studies scholarship is emerging in the field of regional human rights systems, but it is still quite rare. Furthermore, the comparative studies that do exist tend to focus on existing treaty-based systems. This begs the question of why treaty-based systems exist in some regions of the world, but not others. For example, in Asia, there is no treaty-based human rights system, but rather a ten-member subregional body: the ASEAN Intergovernmental Commission on Human Rights. Most studies of Asia appear not to be in conversation with the studies discussed

244 ADVANCING COMPARATIVE AREA STUDIES

above, but rather are stand-alone studies of such issues as the prospects for a regional human rights mechanism (e.g., Hashimoto 2004; Aydin 2016; Nandyatama et al. 2019). Regarding the Middle East, there are promising studies of the Organization of Islamic Cooperation (OIC) Independent Permanent Human Rights Commission, created in 2011 as the first explicitly Islamic human rights framework (Kayaoglu 2019; Petersen and Kayaoglu 2019; see also Petersen 2012; Gunn and Lagresa 2016). Of particular interest to both global IR and CAS scholars is the fact that the OIC initiative is defined by religion rather than geography, which creates new challenges for our understanding of "regional" (or in this case cross-regional) human rights systems.

The HRC, the BRICS, and IBSA

Another promising area of CAS for human rights scholarship involves understanding country-specific differences vis-à-vis the global human rights regime. Here the BRICS grouping is instructive, particularly its explicit positioning as a counter to Western-dominated global institutions. More recently, the group appears to be in the midst of an identity crisis, as evidenced by tensions around such issues as the implications of China-Russia cooperation for the group, the existence of China-India geopolitical tensions, and the implications of membership expansion (Tharoor 2022). Yet on the issue of human rights, at least until recently, the five-country bloc was viewed as more alike than different. For example, Ramesh Thakur wrote that "BRICS are far from homogeneous in their domestic political systems on democracy, human rights, and the rule of law. But they are surprisingly similar in their resistance to democracy promotion and human rights monitoring and enforcement by external state, intergovernmental, and nongovernmental actors" (2014, 1797).

The role of the BRICS received much attention in relation to the 2011 Libya intervention and the Responsibility to Protect norm, but attention vis-à-vis human rights has waned in recent years. This is especially true with regard to the HRC, where the overwhelming focus is on the individual countries of Russia and China, especially Russia's suspension in 2022 and China's concerted challenges to the normative foundation of the Council. The roles of Brazil, India, and South Africa within HRC receives less attention, despite the existence of an India-Brazil-South Africa Dialogue Forum (IBSA) that was launched in 2003 as an alliance of like-minded democracies of the south to advocate for a more equitable international economic system vis-à-vis the Global North (Chevallier et al. 2008; Stuenkel 2014). Although the foundations of IBSA are rooted in trade and development issues (as opposed to human rights per se), the three states have explicitly affirmed their common understanding and vision vis-à-vis human rights. Specifically, after the first IBSA summit in 2006, the countries stated that the HRC "will benefit from the coordinated contributions" from the IBSA states, and that they had "a common understanding regarding the Council's agenda and structure" as well as "common visions regarding the promotion and protection of human rights" (Jordaan 2015, 463; see also Flemes 2009).

An obvious question is just how "like-minded" these three countries are with regard to specific issue areas. On this question, there is some promising comparative research. For example, Jörg Husar (2016) compares the three countries' foreign policy discourse to assess the "alleged like-mindedness" reflected in IBSA declarations on three key dimensions: their claims about their status as both global and regional actors, their shared democratic values, and their positions with regard to development cooperation. Regarding human rights specifically, Eduard Jordaan (2015) compares the voting records and statements of IBSA Forum members on seven controversial country-specific cases and four thematic issues[7] at the HRC. He concludes that although the countries tended to concur on economic and antiracism initiatives (Jordaan 2015, 477), they are otherwise not generally aligned, with Brazil being the most supportive of universal human rights initiatives at the HRC. Joel Voss's (2019) broader examination of norm contestation in the HRC provides additional context on differences among the countries, although its core focus is on highlighting the use of amendments as norm contestation rather than on surfacing the motivating reasons underlying individual state behavior.

On all three of the puzzles discussed above, there is IR scholarship that surfaces controversies within international human rights institutions as well as broad patterns of state behavior vis-à-vis those institutions. Global IR sheds further light on these studies by interrogating the underlying reasons, experiences, and meanings of individual countries and regions (in the case of IBSA, see, e.g., Moore 2015; Acharya 2018; Stuenkel 2020; Kristensen

---

[7] Economic rights, racism, freedom of expression, sexual orientation.

2021; Milani 2021). But IR scholars typically do not have the area expertise to theorize the reasons underlying country-specific behavior, and global IR scholars frequently focus on specific regional or national particularities. CAS can fill this chasm by recognizing the value of area-specific sensitivity to context conditions alongside cross- and intraregional comparison. Within the context of human rights, CAS can mediate between ardent proponents of universalist and particularistic visions of human rights interpretations by systematically triangulating expert knowledge from different non-Western regions and, in so doing, go beyond critiques and correctives to illuminate new research agendas in the study of human rights.

Conclusion: CAS and the Evolution of Global IR

This chapter has argued that global IR has done much to correct for the disproportionate attention to Western history in the building of bedrock concepts and theoretical frameworks within international relations. By illuminating the experiences of "human rights" and "international relations" across different national and regional contexts, global IR creates space for new voices and sheds greater light on experiences across the Global South, while sparking creative interventions and illuminating the limitations of dominant analysis.

But as currently configured, it can take us only so far. As Michael Barnett has noted, we must consider whether particular, often highly local, insights not only suffice to upend existing scholarship but also shed light on more than one locale or region. Without a strategy to aggregate insights in theoretically meaningful ways, global IR risks becoming little more than an assortment of oppositional moves, bound more by a normative commitment to counter dominant IR theories than by a sustained effort to developing alternative substantive theories (Barnett 2021).

The bottom line is that global IR's recognition of diversity and inclusivity need not come at the expense of cumulating insights from across the Global South and providing alternative conceptual schemes that can anchor new research agendas. Here, CAS stands as a natural ally. With its commitment to posing substantive questions that surface and explain similarities and differences across regions, CAS offers new opportunities for IR scholars to formulate novel middle-range arguments that are both portable and capable of moving beyond the stalemate of dichotomies such as "West/non-West" and "universalism/relativism" in IR theory. Furthermore, CAS–global IR collaborations that focus on south-south cross-regional comparisons increase the potential to move beyond the prevalence of "hub and spoke" patterns of IR theory, whereby emerging nodes of scholarship from the Global South have tended to engage more with dominant theory than with scholarship in other non-Western regions (Sil and Ahram 2020).

In short, despite their different starting points, global IR and CAS share significant affinities that can fill in some of the analytical gaps of human rights scholarship specifically and mainstream IR theory more generally. Both global IR and CAS are predicated on appreciating the significance of local context in interpreting social phenomena and individual action. Both embrace a pluralistic ethos and seek to preserve space for a wide range of research agendas and methodologies. And, for those proponents of global IR (e.g., Fisher-Onar, this volume) pursuing research questions that transcend local contexts but cover a limited number of weighty cases, CAS's epistemic commitments to "middle range" approaches and contextualized comparison offer a pragmatic foundation that is recognizable yet flexible, as evident in several of the previous chapters in this volume as well as its predecessor (Ahram et al. 2018). CAS–global IR collaborations are therefore likely to open channels of communication across various boundaries—those between area studies communities, between subfields of political science, and between social science disciplines—that have fragmented the production of knowledge in or about non-Western regions.

Bibliography

Acharya, Amitav. 2014. Global International Relations (IR) and Regional Worlds: A New Agenda for International Studies. *International Studies Quarterly* 58 (4): 647–659.

Acharya, Amitav. 2016. Studying the Bandung Conference from a Global IR Perspective. *Australian Journal of International Affairs* 70 (4): 342–357.

Acharya, Amitav. 2018. Imagining a Global IR OUT of India. ORF Issue Brief no. 224. https://www.orfonline.org/wp-content/uploads/2018/01/ORF_Issue_Brief_224_GlobalIR_.pdf.

Acharya, Amitav, and Barry Buzan. 2017. Why Is There No Non-Western International Relations Theory? Ten Years On. *International Relations of the Asia-Pacific* 17 (3): 341–370.

Acharya, Amitav, and Barry Buzan. 2019. *The Making of Global International Relations: Origins and Evolution of IR at Its Centenary.* Cambridge: Cambridge University Press.

Ahram, Ariel I., Patrick Köllner, and Rudra Sil, eds. 2018. *Comparative Area Studies: Methodological Rationales and Cross-Regional Applications.* New York: Oxford University Press.

Ali, Shaheen Sardar, and Satwant Kaur Heer. 2018. What Is the Measure of "Universality"? Critical Reflections on "Islamic" Criminal Law and Muslim State Practice Vis-à-Vis the Rome Statute and the International Criminal Court. In Tallyn Gray, ed. *Islam and*

International Criminal Law and Justice. Brussels: Torkel Opsahl Academic EPublisher, 175–200.

Amnesty International. 2022. China: Xinjiang Vote Failure Betrays Core Mission of UN Human Rights Council. https://www.amnesty.org/en/latest/news/2022/10/china-xinjiang-vote-failure-betrays-core-mission-of-un-human-rights-council/.

Anderl, Felix, and Antonia Witt. 2020. Problematising the Global in Global IR. *Millennium* 49 (1): 32–57.

Anderson, Benedict R. O'G. 2016. *Imagined Communities: Reflections on the Origin and Spread of Nationalism.* Rev. ed. New York: Verso.

An-Na'im, Abdullahi Ahmed. 1991. Islam, Islamic Law and the Dilemma of Cultural Legitimacy for Universal Human Rights. In Claude E. Welch Jr. and Virginia A. Leary, eds. *Asian Perspectives on Human Rights.* London: Routledge, 31–54.

An-Na'im, Abdullahi Ahmed, ed. 1992. *Human Rights in Cross-Cultural Perspectives: A Quest for Consensus.* Philadelphia: University of Pennsylvania Press.

An-Na'im, Abdullahi Ahmed. 2003. *Human Rights Under African Constitutions: Realizing the Promise for Ourselves.* Philadelphia: University of Pennsylvania Press.

An-Na'im, Abdullahi Ahmed. 2021. *Decolonizing Human Rights.* Cambridge: Cambridge University Press.

An-Na'im, Abdullahi Ahmed, and Francis M. Deng, eds. 1990. *Human Rights in Africa: Cross-Cultural Perspectives.* Washington, DC: Brookings Institution Press.

Aydin, Mücahit. 2016. The Potential Role of Turkey Toward a Regional Human Rights Arrangement in Asia. *Uluslararası Politik Araştırmalar Dergisi* 2 (3): 23–30.

Badar, Mohamed Elewa. 2011. Islamic Law (Shari'a) and the Jurisdiction of the International Criminal Court. *Leiden Journal of International Law* 24 (2): 411–433.

Barnett, Michael. 2021. SIS Global IR Dialogues, Session 1. American University School of International Service. https://www.youtube.com/watch?v=F5v0PbJFjGE&list=PLnS6BuPUSqzRAIKrjzcHvqw932yLpXzcs&index=3.

Barr, Michael D. 2000. Lee Kuan Yew and the "Asian Values" Debate. *Asian Studies Review* 24 (3): 309–334.

Bennoune, Karima, and Wole Soyinka. 2018. Universality, Diversity and Cultural Rights. https://www.youtube.com/watch?v=ipJwdnF-zxE.

Bhagavan, Manu Belur. 2013. *India and the Quest for One World: The Peacemakers.* Houndmills: Palgrave Macmillan.

Biersteker, Thomas J. 1999. Eroding Boundaries, Contested Terrain. *International Studies Review* 1 (1): 3–9.

Blaney, David L., and Arlene B. Tickner. 2017. Worlding, Ontological Politics and the Possibility of a Decolonial IR. *Millennium* 45 (3): 293–311.

Bosco, David L. 2014. *Rough Justice: The International Criminal Court in a World of Power Politics.* New York: Oxford University Press.

Bruno, Greg. 2011. A Decade of Reasons Why Arab Countries Distrust the ICC. The National. June 5, 2011. https://www.thenationalnews.com/uae/a-decade-of-reasons-why-arab-countries-distrust-the-icc-1.413167.

Burgers, Jan Herman. 1992. The Road to San Francisco: The Revival of the Human Rights Idea in the Twentieth Century. *Human Rights Quarterly* 14 (4): 447–477.

Burke, Roland. 2010. *Decolonization and the Evolution of International Human Rights.* Philadelphia: University of Pennsylvania Press.

Burke, Roland. 2020. The 1993 World Conference on Human Rights and the Retreat of a Redistributive Rights Vision. *London Review of International Law* 8 (2): 233–260.

Çalı, Başak, Mikael Rask Madsen, and Frans Viljoen. 2018. Comparative Regional Human Rights Regimes: Defining a Research Agenda. *International Journal of Constitutional Law* 16 (1): 128–135.

Carozza, Paolo G. 2003. From Conquest to Constitutions: Retrieving a Latin American Tradition of the Idea of Human Rights. *Human Rights Quarterly* 25 (2): 281–313.

Chakrabarty, Dipesh. 2008. *Provincializing Europe: Postcolonial Thought and Historical Difference*. Princeton, NJ: Princeton University Press.

Chavez, Leiry Cornejo, and Andreas Follesdal. 2013. Fragile Democracies, Strong Human Rights Courts: Comparing European and Inter-American Cases Special Section: Fragile Democracies. *Nordic Journal of Human Rights* 31 (4): 471–495.

Chevallier, Romy, Christian von Drachenfels, and Andreas Stamm. 2008. India-Brazil-South Africa (IBSA)—a New Geography of Trade and Technology Cooperation? *Zeitschrift für Wirtschaftsgeographie* 52 (1): 35–49.

China Daily. 2017. Full Text of Beijing Declaration Adopted by the First South-South Human Rights Forum. December 8, 2017. https://www.chinadaily.com.cn/a/201712/08/WS5a2aaa68a310eefe3e99ef85.html.

Chinese Ministry of Foreign Affairs. 2021. Position Paper on China's Cooperation with the United Nations. https://www.fmprc.gov.cn/mfa_eng/wjdt_665385/wjzcs/202110/t20211022_9609380.html.

Chinese Ministry of Foreign Affairs. 2022. Remarks on the Value Adherence of the Contemporary Chinese Perspective of Human Rights. September 29, 2022. http://gb.china-embassy.gov.cn/eng/PressandMedia/Spokepersons/202209/t20220930_10775989.htm.

Clark, Philip. 2018. *Distant Justice: The Impact of the International Criminal Court on African Politics*. New York: Cambridge University Press.

Clarke, Kamari Maxine. 2019. *Affective Justice: The International Criminal Court and the Pan-Africanist Pushback*. Durham, NC: Duke University Press.

Cobbah, Josiah A.M. 1987. African Values and the Human Rights Debate: An African Perspective. *Human Rights Quarterly* 9 (3): 309–331.

Dalton, Russell J., and Nhu-Ngoc T. Ong. 2005. Authority Orientations and Democratic Attitudes: A Test of the "Asian Values" Hypothesis. *Japanese Journal of Political Science* 6 (2): 211–231.

D'Amato, Silvia, Matteo Dian, and Alessandra Russo. 2022. Reaching for Allies? The Dialectics and Overlaps Between International Relations and Area Studies in the Study of Politics, Security and Conflicts. *Italian Political Science Review / Rivista Italiana di Scienza Politica* 52 (2): 153–171.

Dian, Matteo. 2022. The Rise of China Between Global IR and Area Studies: An Agenda for Cooperation. *Italian Political Science Review / Rivista Italiana di Scienza Politica* 52 (2): 252–267.

Donnelly, Jack. 2007. The Relative Universality of Human Rights. *Human Rights Quarterly* 29 (2): 281–306.

Enloe, Cynthia. 2021. SIS Global IR Dialogues, Session 1. American University School of International Service. https://www.youtube.com/watch?v=F5v0PbJFjGE&list=PLnS6BuPUSqzRAIKrjzcHvqw932yLpXzcs&index=4.

Eun, Yong-Soo. 2018. Beyond "the West/Non-West Divide" in IR: How to Ensure Dialogue as Mutual Learning. *Chinese Journal of International Politics* 11 (4): 435–449.

Eun, Yong-Soo. 2019. Opening Up the Debate over "Non-Western" International Relations. *Politics* 39 (1): 4–17.

Fierke, Karin M., and Vivienne Jabri. 2019. Global Conversations: Relationality, Embodiment and Power in the Move Towards a Global IR. *Global Constitutionalism* 8 (3): 506–535.

Flemes, Daniel. 2009. India-Brazil-South Africa (IBSA) in the New Global Order: Interests, Strategies and Values of the Emerging Coalition. *International Studies* 46 (4): 401–421.

Foot, Rosemary. 2022. Positioning Human Rights in China-US Relations. In Christopher Sabatini, ed. *Reclaiming Human Rights in a Changing World Order*. Washington, DC: Brookings Institution Press, 31–49.

Foulon, Michiel, and Gustav Meibauer. 2020. Realist Avenues to Global International Relations. *European Journal of International Relations* 26 (4): 1203–1229.

Fraser, Julie. 2020. Exploring Legal Compatibilities and Pursuing Cultural Legitimacy: Islamic Law and the International Criminal Court. SSRN Scholarly Paper. Rochester, NY.

Glendon, Mary Ann. 2001. *A World Made New: Eleanor Roosevelt and the Universal Declaration of Human Rights.* New York: Random House.

Glendon, Mary Ann. 2003. The Forgotten Crucible: The Latin American Influence on the Universal Human Rights Idea. *Harvard Human Rights Journal* 16: 27–40.

Grandin, Greg. 2007. Human Rights and Empire's Embrace. In Jeffrey N. Wasserstrom, ed. *Human Rights and Revolutions.* 2nd ed. Lanham, MD: Rowman & Littlefield, 191–212.

Grandin, Greg. 2012. The Liberal Traditions in the Americas: Rights, Sovereignty, and the Origins of Liberal Multilateralism. *American Historical Review* 117 (1): 68–91.

Gunn, T. Jeremy, and Alvaro Lagresa. 2016. The Organisation of Islamic Cooperation: Universal Human Rights, Islamic Values, or Raisons d'Etat. *Human Rights & International Legal Discourse* 10 (2): 248–274.

Hashimoto, Hidetoshi. 2004. *The Prospects for a Regional Human Rights Mechanism in East Asia.* New York: Routledge.

Heyns, Christof, David Padilla, and Leo Zwaak. 2006. A Schematic Comparison of Regional Human Rights Systems: An Update. *Sur: International Journal on Human Rights* 3 (4): 163–171.

Hobson, John M. 2012. *The Eurocentric Conception of World Politics: Western International Theory, 1760–2010.* New York: Cambridge University Press.

Hoffman, Stanley. 1977. An American Social Science: International Relations. *Daedalus* 106: 41–60.

Hopgood, Stephen. 2013. *The Endtimes of Human Rights.* Ithaca, NY: Cornell University Press.

Huneeus, Alexandra, and Mikael Rask Madsen. 2018. Between Universalism and Regional Law and Politics: A Comparative History of the American, European, and African Human Rights Systems. *International Journal of Constitutional Law* 16 (1): 136–160.

Huntington, Samuel P. 1993. The Clash of Civilizations? *Foreign Affairs* 72 (3): 22–49.

Husar, Jörg. 2016. *Framing Foreign Policy in India, Brazil and South Africa: On the Like-Mindedness of the IBSA States.* New York: Springer.

Hutchings, Kimberly. 2011. Dialogue Between Whom? The Role of the West/Non-West Distinction in Promoting Global Dialogue in IR. *Millennium* 39 (3): 639–647.

Jalloh, Charles, and Ilias Bantekas, eds. 2017. *The International Criminal Court and Africa.* Oxford: Oxford University Press.

Jensen, Steven L. B. 2016. *The Making of International Human Rights: The 1960s, Decolonization, and the Reconstruction of Global Values.* New York: Cambridge University Press.

Jordaan, Eduard. 2015. Rising Powers and Human Rights: The India-Brazil–South Africa Dialogue Forum at the UN Human Rights Council. *Journal of Human Rights* 14 (4): 463–485.

Kayaoglu, Turan. 2019. The OIC's Human Rights Regime. In Marie Juul Petersen and Turan Kayaoglu, eds. *The Organization of Islamic Cooperation and Human Rights.* Philadelphia: University of Pennsylvania Press, 65–88.

Khan, Siraj. 2018. Arab and Islamic States' Practice: The Shari'ah Clause and Its Effects on the Implementation of the Rome Statute of the International Criminal Court. In Tallyn Gray, ed. *Islam and International Criminal Law and Justice.* Brussels: Torkel Opsahl Academic EPublisher, 145–173.

Kim, So Young. 2010. Do Asian Values Exist? Empirical Tests of the Four Dimensions of Asian Values. *Journal of East Asian Studies* 10 (2): 315–344.

Kristensen, Peter Marcus. 2021. The South in "Global IR": Worlding Beyond the "Non-West" in the Case of Brazil. *International Studies Perspectives* 22 (2): 218–239.

Malekian, Farhad. 2009. The Homogeneity of International Criminal Court with Islamic Jurisprudence. *International Criminal Law Review* 9 (4): 595–621.

Mayerfeld, Jamie. 2003. Who Shall Be Judge? The United States, the International Criminal Court, and the Global Enforcement of Human Rights. *Human Rights Quarterly* 25 (1): 93–129.

Mazrui, Ali. 1997. Islamic and Western Values. *Foreign Affairs* 76 (5): 118–132.

Mearsheimer, John J. 2016. A Global Discipline of IR? Benign Hegemony. *International Studies Review* 18 (1): 147–149.

Merry, Sally Engle. 2006. *Human Rights and Gender Violence: Translating International Law into Local Justice.* Chicago: University of Chicago Press.

Meyer, John W., John Boli, George M. Thomas, and Francisco O. Ramirez. 1997. World Society and the Nation-State. *American Journal of Sociology* 103 (1): 144–181.

Milani, Carlos R. S. 2021. The Foundation and Development of International Relations in Brazil. *Review of International Studies* 47 (5): 601–617.

Modelski, George. 1961. International Relations and Area Studies: The Case of South-East Asia. *International Relations* 2 (3): 143–155.

Moore, Candice. 2015. Disciplining the Developing World? Perspectives from a South African IR. In Paul-Henri Bischoff, Kwesi Aning, and Amitav Acharya, eds. *Africa in Global International Relations: Emerging Approaches to Theory and Practice.* London: Routledge, 64–84.

Morsink, Johannes. 2000. *The Universal Declaration of Human Rights: Origins, Drafting and Intent.* Philadelphia: University of Pennsylvania Press.

Mutua, Makau. 2017. HLS in the World | How Does International Human Rights Make a Difference in the World? November 7. https://www.youtube.com/watch?v=F-R9DKU9nGk.

Nandyatama, Randy Wirasta, Dio Herdiawan Tobing, and Shah Suraj Bharat, eds. 2019. *The Evolution of the ASEAN Human Rights Mechanism: Institutional and Thematic Issues Within.* Yogyakarta, Indonesia: ASEAN Studies Center, Faculty of Social and Political Sciences Universitas Gadjah.

Nassar, Ahmad E. 2003. The International Criminal Court and the Applicability of International Jurisdiction Under Islamic Law. *Chicago Journal of International Law* 4 (2): 587–596.

Obregon, Liliana. 2005. The Colluding Worlds of the Lawyer, the Scholar and the Policy Maker: A View of International Law from Latin America. *Wisconsin International Law Journal* 23 (1): 145–172.

Onar, Nora Fisher, and Kalypso Nicolaïdis. 2013. The Decentring Agenda: Europe as a Post-Colonial Power. *Cooperation and Conflict* 48 (2): 283–303.

Pauselli, Gino, Federico Merke, and Francisco Urdinez. 2022. Shaping the Regime from the Inside: Chinese Influence in the UN Human Rights Council. Unpublished manuscript.

Petersen, Marie Juul. 2012. *Islamic or Universal Human Rights? The OIC's Independent Permanent Human Rights Commission.* Copenhagen: Danish Institute for International Studies.

Petersen, Marie Juul, and Turan Kayaoglu, eds. 2019. *The Organization of Islamic Cooperation and Human Rights.* Philadelphia: University of Pennsylvania Press.

Piccone, Ted. 2018. China's Long Game on Human Rights at the United Nations. Brookings Institution Report. September. https://www.brookings.edu/wp-content/uploads/2018/09/FP_20181009_china_human_rights.pdf.

Pollis, Adamantia, and Peter Schwab, eds. 1979. *Human Rights: Cultural and Ideological Perspectives.* New York: Praeger.

Puchala, Donald J. 1997. Some Non-Western Perspectives on International Relations. *Journal of Peace Research* 34 (2): 129–134.

Puchala, Donald J. 1998. Third World Thinking and Contemporary International Relations. In Stephanie G. Neuman, ed. *International Relations Theory and the Third World*. New York: St. Martin's Press, 133–157.

Qin, Yaqing. 2011. Development of International Relations Theory in China: Progress Through Debates. *International Relations of the Asia-Pacific* 11 (2): 231–257.

Qin, Yaqing. 2016. A Relational Theory of World Politics. *International Studies Review* 18 (1): 33–47.

Raineri, Luca, and Edoardo Baldaro. 2022. The Place of Africa in International Relations: The Centrality of the Margins in Global IR. *Italian Political Science Review / Rivista Italiana Di Scienza Politica* 52 (2): 236–251.

Roach, Steven C. 2005. Arab States and the Role of Islam in the International Criminal Court. *Political Studies* 53 (1): 143–161.

Roth, Hans Ingvar. 2018. *P.C. Chang and the Universal Declaration of Human Rights*. Philadelphia: University of Pennsylvania Press.

Scharf, Michael P. 1999. The Politics Behind the U.S. Opposition to the International Criminal Court Remarks. *New England International and Comparative Law Annual* 5: 1–10.

Sen, Amartya. 1997. *Human Rights and Asian Values: 16th Morgenthau Memorial Lecture on Ethics and Foreign Policy*. New York: Carnegie Council on Ethics and International Affairs.

Shahi, Deepshikha. 2018. *Advaita as a Global International Relations Theory*. London: Routledge.

Shahi, Deepshikha. 2021. SIS Global IR Dialogues, Session 3. American University School of International Service. https://www.youtube.com/watch?v=oqoiKf_9PFY&list=PLnS6BuPUSqzRAIKrjzcHvqw932yLpXzcs&index=1.

Sikkink, Kathryn. 2014. Latin American Countries as Norm Protagonists of the Idea of International Human Rights Special Section: Principles from the Periphery. The Neglected Southern Sources of Global Norms. *Global Governance* 20 (3): 389–404.

Sikkink, Kathryn. 2017. *Evidence for Hope: Making Human Rights Work in the 21st Century*. Princeton, NJ: Princeton University Press.

Sil, Rudra, and Ariel Ahram. 2020. Comparative Area Studies and the Study of the Global South, *Vestnik RUDN: International Relations* 20 (2): 279–287.

Sluga, Glenda. 2013. *Internationalism in the Age of Nationalism*. Philadelphia: University of Pennsylvania Press.

Stoeckl, Kristina, and Kseniya Medvedeva. 2018. Double Bind at the UN: Western Actors, Russia, and the Traditionalist Agenda. *Global Constitutionalism* 7 (3): 383–421.

Stuenkel, Oliver. 2014. *India-Brazil-South Africa Dialogue Forum*. New York: Routledge.

Stuenkel, Oliver. 2020. Toward a Global IR? A View from Brazil. In Yaqing Qin, ed. *Globalizing IR Theory: Critical Engagement*. London: Routledge, 124–138.

Sun, Pinghua. 2016. Chinese Discourse on Human Rights in Global Governance. *Chinese Journal of Global Governance* 1 (2): 192–213.

Symons, Jonathan, and Dennis Altman. 2015. International Norm Polarization: Sexuality as a Subject of Human Rights Protection. *International Theory* 7 (1): 61–95.

Tan, See Seng. 2016. The "Singapore School" of Asian Values: Down but Not Out? January 26. https://www.carnegiecouncil.org/media/series/gen/the-singapore-school-of-asian-values-down-but-not-out.

Tao, Jing. 2015. China's Socialization in the International Human Rights Regime: Why Did China Reject the Rome Statute of the International Criminal Court? *Journal of Contemporary China* 24 (96): 1092–1110.

Thakur, Ramesh. 2014. How Representative Are BRICS? *Third World Quarterly* 35 (10): 1791–1808.

Tharoor, Shashi. 2022. Are the BRICS Breaking Up? Project Syndicate. July 7. https://www.project-syndicate.org/commentary/brics-strategic-direction-enlargement-indian-unease-by-shashi-tharoor-2022-07.

Tickner, Arlene B., and David L. Blaney, eds. 2012. *Thinking International Relations Differently*. New York: Routledge.

Tickner, Arlene B., and Karen Smith, eds. 2020. *International Relations from the Global South: Worlds of Difference*. New York: Routledge.

Tickner, Arlene B., and Ole Wæver, eds. 2009. *International Relations Scholarship Around the World*. New York: Routledge.

United Nations. N.d.a. The Foundations of International Human Rights Law. https://www.un.org/en/about-us/udhr/foundation-of-international-human-rights-law.

United Nations. N.d.b. Universal Declaration of Human Rights. OHCHR. https://www.ohchr.org/en/universal-declaration-of-human-rights.

Voss, M. Joel. 2019. The Use (or Misuse) of Amendments to Contest Human Rights Norms at the UN Human Rights Council. *Human Rights Review* 20 (4): 397–422.

Walt, Stephen M. 2011. Is IR Still "an American Social Science?" *Foreign Policy* (blog). June 6. https://foreignpolicy.com/2011/06/06/is-ir-still-an-american-social-science/.

Waltz, Susan. 2001. Universalizing Human Rights: The Role of Small States in the Construction of the Universal Declaration of Human Rights. *Human Rights Quarterly* 23 (1): 44–72.

Welzel, Christian. 2011. The Asian Values Thesis Revisited: Evidence from the World Values Surveys. *Japanese Journal of Political Science* 12 (1): 1–31.

Weston, Burns H., Robin Ann Lukes, and Kelly M. Hnatt. 1987. Regional Human Rights Regimes: A Comparison and Appraisal. *Vanderbilt Journal of Transnational Law* 20 (4): 585–638.

Witte, John, Jr. 2009. *Human Rights Language in Today's Globalized World*. https://www.youtube.com/watch?v=IRyHKJDYif8.

Zakaria, Fareed. 1994. A Culture Is Destiny: A Conversation with Lee Kuan Yew. *Foreign Affairs* 73 (2): 109–127.

Zhang, Feng. 2012. The Tsinghua Approach and the Inception of Chinese Theories of International Relations. *Chinese Journal of International Politics* 5 (1): 73–102.

Zhang, Yongjin, and Barry Buzan. 2020. China and the Global Reach of Human Rights. *China Quarterly* 241 (March): 169–190.

Zhang, Yongjin, and Teng-Chi Chang. 2016. *Constructing a Chinese School of International Relations*. London: Routledge.

Zhu, Dan. 2018. *China and the International Criminal Court*. New York: Springer.

11

Revisionist (Eurasian) Powers and the West

A Comparative Area Studies Bridge Between International Relations Theory and Area Expertise

Nora Fisher-Onar

Introduction: A Singular Battlespace?

Prominent pundit Robert D. Kaplan's 2019 book entitled *The Return of Marco Polo's World: War, Strategy and American Interests in the Twenty-First Century*, begins with the following declaration:

> AS EUROPE DISAPPEARS, EURASIA COHERES
> The supercontinent is becoming one fluid, comprehensible unit of trade and conflict, as the Westphalian system of states weakens and older, imperial legacies—Russian, Chinese, Iranian, Turkish—become paramount. Every crisis from Central Europe to the ethnic-Han Chinese heartland is now interlinked. There is one singular battle space. (Kaplan 2019, 2)

Kaplan's striking prose evokes a preoccupation with Eurasia among Western geo-strategists that has deep roots, dating back to at least the "long nineteenth century."[1] At that time, great power rivalry revolved around what Western analysts called the "Eastern question": Who would control the

---

[1] Eric Hobsbawm seminally periodized the "long nineteenth century" as starting with the French Revolution and ending with World War I (1789–1914). During this period, the "Eastern Question"—which Ottoman analysts, for their part, described as the "Western question"—drove much geopolitical debate. That said, intensive preoccupation with threats and opportunities emanating from greater Eurasia arguably goes back to at least the Ottoman penetration of European spaces in the early modern era, and further back still to collective memories of "marauding" hordes" such as the Mongols and Huns, whose incursions inscribed onto the collective imaginary of Christendom a sense that the "scourge of God" would arise in Eurasia to punish a civilization that had lost its way (Malcolm 2019).

Nora Fisher-Onar, *Revisionist (Eurasian) Powers and the West*. In: *Advancing Comparative Area Studies*. Edited by: Ariel I. Ahram, Patrick Köllner, and Rudra Sil, Oxford University Press. © Oxford University Press (2025). DOI: 10.1093/oso/9780197809365.003.0011

vast territories and peoples up for grabs as the Ottoman as well as Persian and Chinese empires went into decline? The answers developed by Anglo-American thinkers like Halford Mackinder and Alfred Thayer Mahan informed a "great game" for control of the world's Eurasian "heartland" on political chessboards from Afghanistan to the eastern Mediterranean (Frankopan 2015). Iterations of this game have shaped Western perceptions of greater Eurasia ever since, including during the Cold War and even more clearly in the post-9/11 "hot wars" in the Middle East.

However, the costs of maintaining troops and allies from the Mediterranean to the Pacific became unsustainable after the 2008/2009 economic crisis. At this time, emerging economies'—and especially China's—relative position was elevated within the global pecking order. Transatlantic anxieties were amplified when Beijing launched its own grand strategy for multiregional influence via instruments like the Asian Infrastructure Investment Bank, the Shanghai Cooperation Organization, and, more recently, the Belt and Road Initiative (BRI). The vision underlying these measures effectively reimagines the world map such that the western hemisphere recedes to the sidelines while a Sino-centric, Afro-Eurasia rises (Mayer 2018; Fisher-Onar and Kavalski 2022). Other factors contributing to Kaplan's concern that Eurasian momentum may absorb Europe—and sideline the United States—include Iran's nuclear trajectory, roller-coaster relations with NATO ally Turkey, and, especially since 2022, Russia's invasion of Ukraine. For many observers with liberal inclinations, these developments suggest that despite the increase in our era of economic, infrastructural, and security projects connecting multiple state and nonstate actors, the defining new cleavage in global politics is between the democratic and the authoritarian capitalists driving such projects. Realism takes this logic further in its vision of post–Cold War liberalism in general as giving way to renewed great power rivalry (Kroenig 2020; Mead 2014).

While the jury is still out regarding the magnitude and implications of these complex, intersecting challenges for US interests and Western primacy, the question remains: How to make sense of dynamics across greater Eurasia as it becomes an increasingly significant arena for both emerging socioeconomic linkages and geopolitical rivalries? What types of conflict, alliance-making (and breaking), and/or cooperation may emerge from these dynamics? And what are the implications for how we think about world order? To answer these questions, we must recognize that while popular pundits like Kaplan are often good at raising questions, they rarely immerse themselves in the spaces that they survey. This task falls to the academy and, in particular, to those willing to pursue both in-depth knowledge and contextualized comparison.

In this chapter, I propose a strategy to overcome the problems stemming from the hub-and-spokes structure of our analytical apparatus. In short, because this structure privileges a Western standpoint and sequesters expertise on non-Western world regions, our ability to engage in open-ended, cross-regional analysis is obstructed. Area studies, I suggest, offers a partial solution, but is no panacea due to the exceptionalism that can sometimes characterize area expertise, preventing it from interfacing with disciplinary IR. A flourishing body of global IR scholarship also grapples with this limitation. The tendency, however, is to critique existing theories and focus more on conceptual rather than empirical phenomena. This feature can inform mainstream IR resistance to alternative ways of reading world order, not least because skeptical reviewers and funding bodies can shut down critical, decentering, and decolonial work on methodological as much as substantive grounds.

Enter comparative area studies (CAS), which can help to reinforce the methodological foundations of direct "spoke-to-spoke" comparisons across non-Western regions while supporting fresh theoretical conversations. Toward this end, I propose a "family resemblances" approach to comparing former empires that are revisionist powers (FERPs). The notion of FERPs cuts across the regions within which scholars often silo large states carved out of former empires, such as China in East Asia; Russia in Eurasia; and Turkey and Iran in the Middle East (Fisher-Onar 2013, 2018, 2020, 2022). Identifying a set of *structural, agential, and processual* family resemblances across these FERPs, I provide a baseline for systematic, cross-case and cross-regional analysis. The purpose: to capture, via CAS, similarities but also differences, conflicts but also cooperation across Eurasia without a priori reducing the complex dynamics of this vast "supercontinent" to a Kaplanian "battlespace."

IR Theory's Hub-and-Spokes Problem

In this post–Cold War era, China, Russia, Iran, and Turkey are some of the most restive players on the international chessboard. In pursuit of their respective ends, they communicate, coordinate, and compete with

258   ADVANCING COMPARATIVE AREA STUDIES

each other, and with interlocutors in what we conventionally call the "West"[2] and the "Global South." National-level dynamics jostle, moreover, against local and transnational social, economic, and security concerns—and opportunities—that may impel these states in directions other than those envisaged in their own corridors of power. These complex patterns animate Chinese, Russian, Iranian, and Turkish trajectories in ways that bear comparison. Dynamics that are ripe for investigation include similarities (e.g., the deployment of imperial nostalgia in statecraft; increasingly authoritarian leadership; assertive agendas vis-à-vis regional and global order), and differences (e.g., their relative magnitude or the differentiated intensity of their revisionist agendas).

Dominant approaches in international relations (IR) scholarship, however, have difficulty in grappling with Chinese-Russian-Iranian-Turkish—among other non-Western—comparisons due to the "hub-and-spokes" structure of our analytical apparatus. This refers to the wheel-like structure of IR knowledge production in which the transatlantic, especially the US, hub commands the vast majority of institutional resources and legitimacy (Biersteker 2009). Meanwhile, knowledge production about non-Western world regions like East Asia, Eurasia, or the Middle East forms the spokes of the wheel. Sources of the hub's primacy include the number and endowments of its research institutions (Ahram and Stovall, this volume), and the organic relationship between these institutions and national (e.g., the US, UK, and EU member states) as well as supranational (e.g., the European Union) and intergovernmental strategic planning bodies and budgets.

This forcefield emanates from a long history of knowledge production about non-Western places for the purposes of (neo)colonial administration (Said 1978). The process arguably began with the foundation of entities like the School of Oriental and African Studies at the peak of British imperialism, and comparable "Oriental Institutes" across European states likewise scrambling to build empires during this period. It was followed up by the institutionalization of today's area subfields in sync with the early Cold War calculus. That expertise on non-Western regions has long been commissioned by the West for the West is captured by the reflections of a renowned

---

[2] I employ widely used geocultural referents like "West," "East," and "South" even as I recognize that these are socially constructed categories the content of which shifts according to user and context.

expert on Eurasia who trained at an Ivy League institution at the height of the Cold War. In his words: "At the end of the day, Foggy Bottom paid for my PhD."[3]

This hub-and-spokes structure is evident in IR's very foundation story as taught in intro-level classrooms across the transatlantic space (Tickner 2011; Thakur and Smith 2021). Rooted—like the Westphalian international system itself—in Western diplomatic history, the field took a theoretical turn when British- and German-born scholars sought to grapple with the relative weight of material and ideational forces in World War I and World War II (conflicts that originated in European great power rivalry).[4] IR's subsequent "great debates" between American behavioralist and eclectic English traditions, or between North American metatheories (e.g., neorealism vs. neoliberal institutionalism), have by and large ignored non-Western perspectives, claiming universality for Western approaches. Constructivist and critical alternatives likewise tend to emanate from European linguistic, poststructural, and Marxist philosophies that entail their own mechanisms of dismissal of non-Western histories, agencies, and preferences (Hobson 2012; Fisher-Onar and Nicolaïdis 2013, 2021).

The result is a system in which analysts who are not trained in the language (above all, English) or methods (above all, positivist and increasingly quantitative) of the Anglo-American and European academies, nor embedded in these epistemic communities' disciplinary and funding networks, face hard and soft barriers.[5] This dynamic can inhibit scholars from the periphery from contributing significantly to the cumulation of the most valued—though not necessarily the most accurate—forms of knowledge. Access to the center from the spokes is further limited by the formidable resources necessary to attend scholarly conventions in expensive, Global North destinations (where hiring often happens and to which visa access alone is far from guaranteed). Another challenge is the peer review processes that is primed to reject intellectual products that do not conform to criteria that are transparent only to those trained in the hub. When penetration is possible, moreover, in the form of, say, PhD scholarships, students are often incentivized to develop projects that translate insights on their

---

[3] Off-the-record webinar.

[4] Or, in the case of Japan, in a European-inspired race for empire.

[5] These patterns are probed and substantiated in a growing number of studies on the Global South and North alike. See, for example, Tickner and Waever 2009; Sil and Ahram 2020; Risse et al. 2022; and Aydınlı and Erpul 2022.

spoke origins to the Western hub, rather than probe spoke-spoke dynamics. Similarly, established area scholars in non-Western settings are typically invited to the hub to debrief on current events (e.g., refugees, terrorism, the latest diplomatic crisis) regarding their country or region, while the task of generalizing is reserved for hub-based analysts. The upshot of all these dynamics is that theorists at the hub may not draw on nuanced knowledge about the spokes, nor is there significant communication between analysts at the spokes with each other about inter-spoke or trans-spoke, as it were, dynamics.

The consequences of this omission are evident in two bodies of IR theory that arguably have engaged most concertedly with Eurasia's revisionist powers: neorealism one hand, and neoliberal institutionalism on the other. The former manages the lack of "thick" knowledge of non-Western cases and regions by bracketing culture altogether—attributing causal force to patterns of material power (re)distribution in the international system (e.g., Schweller 1994; Tammen 2008).[6] Thus, even when social forces like the pursuit of status by revisionist states are brokered in this literature, the process is read with reference to systemic categories as conceptualized in Western theory (e.g., pursuit of "great" or pivotal "medium" power status). An approach that instead examines what status (and indeed "power" itself) mean in emic perspective might come to different conclusions about the drivers of FERP behavior (Anno 2018). In the case of China, Iran, and Turkey, for instance, historical transitions from universal empires in their own right to second-class, nation-states in the Western-dominated system were accompanied by traumatic experiences at the internal/external nexus with significant reverberations in debates over national projects and foreign policy to this day (Fisher-Onar 2020, 2022).

Neoliberal institutionalism, for its part, does not take into adequate account the specific conditions of later developing, postcolonial, and post-Soviet states. The Bretton Woods institutions, for example, are read by neoliberal institutionalists as serving "global" good governance and prosperity (Keohane 2005; Ikenberry 2016). Yet there is ample empirical evidence that the preferences and mechanisms thus embedded in international financial institutions (IFIs) disproportionately serve Western/northern interests

---

[6] What I elsewhere call "geo-cultural realism" (Fisher-Onar 2022) along the lines of Huntington's (1993) civilizational reasoning has arguably been debunked in the IR academy for its grossly inaccurate generalizations about cultural blocs' behavior on the basis of essentialized religious categories. That being said, residual notions of civilizational clash continue to inform policy rhetoric in great powers that claim geocultural gravitas like China, Russia, and the United States.

(Parmar 2018). Thus, IFIs are perceived in many Global South contexts as buttressing a hierarchical system that reproduces elements of colonialism from resource extractivism to the erasure of non-Western agencies. As a result, while liberals may read attempts to create alternative architectures like the BRICS[7] initiative or China's Asian Infrastructure Investment Bank as signs of a fragmenting world order, these initiatives are arguably seen by their Global South champions and intended users as ways to decolonize global economic governance (Fisher-Onar and Kavalski 2022). Nor, for instance, is the fact that emerging powers like China may weaponize economic (inter)dependence or engage in, say, "debt diplomacy" particularly shocking to highly indebted countries across the formerly colonized world (Rutazibwa 2019; Bhambra 2020). Politically too, the increasing view among liberals that the world is coalescing into "democratic" versus "authoritarian" camps is perceived by many positioned in the Global South as inconsistent with Western cherry-picking when it comes to which principles of the "rules-based order" are adopted and which are ignored in fields from migration and security to climate governance.

How then to do justice to cross-regional comparisons that can help us make sense of Kaplan's "supercontinent" without erasing the specificities of the countries and regions under scrutiny and privileging Western perceptions over views from the ground? In other words, how to overcome the ways in which the hub-and-spokes structure of IR knowledge production inhibits our ability to address timely questions at the dawn of a post-Western world?

Toward a Solution: Global IR and (Comparative) Area Studies

Interdisciplinary area studies offer a partial solution, supplying a wealth of insights into the intricacies of a case or region by brokering "sustained engagement with a multidisciplinary research community united by shared concerns about a particular region despite cross-disciplinary differences in epistemic norms, methodological styles and evaluative standards" (Sil 2018, 226). The "thickness" of area studies knowledge (Geertz 2008) draws on engagement of the languages, histories, cultures, societies, economies, politics, and foreign policies of a given country or region. The approach not only

---

[7] Brazil, Russia, India, China, South Africa.

supports ethnographic sensitivity but is useful for policy planning. This is because insights derived from deep knowledge are likely to be both more accurate and—since the real world is complex—more *qualified* than generalist accounts deduced from an IR theory itself abstracted from Western historical experiences (Kang 2003; Fisher-Onar and Nicolaïdis 2013). For example, experts from or with immersive knowledge of China / East Asia, Russia/Eurasia, and the Middle East command expertise on key issues like local, regional, and transnational security dilemmas; economic patterns; domestic and foreign policy processes, refugee and migration patterns; social movements; and ethnic, religious, and sectarian, among other, identity commitments, to name just a few substantive questions that animate Western anxieties and Eurasian dynamics.

Yet area studies are no silver bullet for several reasons. First, the production of "thick" knowledge requires intensive investment of energy and resources. This is often obtained over years of field immersion and interpretive methods like archival research, among a wide variety of time-consuming research tools. This fine-grained approach engenders respect for specificity that, in turn, can lead to a perception of incommensurability across cases and especially regions. The upshot is that a major strength of area studies—its richness—also silos area expertise, leading to its subordination to IR. For example, the very depth (and politics) associated with area expertise can inform resistance to importing concepts from other regions, much less to exploring contingent generalizations across regional phenomena. As Christian von Soest and Alexander Stroh (2018) experienced when seeking to broker Latin American–African comparisons, perceived status hierarchies between area studies communities spurred resistance to comparison. Similarly, habits of epistemological primacy may impel some Europeanists, for instance, to resist being situated on an "area studies" rather than disciplinary plane altogether (Fisher-Onar and Kavalski 2022).

Exceptionalist emphasis on case and regional particularism is also incentivized by national academies that encourage scholars to produce actionable information regarding local, national, and regional concerns. As a result, IR studies in spoke settings tend to be quite descriptive and policy oriented.[8] That said, lack of interest in (grand) theory or cross-regional comparisons can be overcome when there is a concrete impetus.

---

[8] This feature—along with the various structural obstacles that spoke scholars face when seeking to access the hub—is noted in contributions across almost all the country and regional case studies featured in Tickner and Waever's 2009 book on IR around the world.

The incentives and challenges introduced by China's multi-billion-dollar BRI, for example, are stimulating national academies across Afro-Eurasia to embark upon fledgling East-South and South-South conversations (Benabdallah 2022).

A further practical dilemma is the challenge faced by area studies communities in, say, US universities, where neoliberal budgetary prerogatives on one hand and steep competition for declining numbers of students on the other impact programming. Confronted with apparent student (or parental) preferences for majors that offer clear paths to remunerative early careers, university administrators are defunding area studies even at a number of elite research universities. Such decisions are exacerbated by federal budget cuts and the explicit hostility to area studies articulated by populist politicians (who rail against the field's allegedly esoteric intellectualism) (King 2016.). That such trends are counterproductive to area studies, IR, and foreign policy practice alike is attested to by decisions like the 2013 move to defund Title VIII support for in-depth study of eastern Europe—a program that cost only US$3.3 million. Only a few months later, the Ukraine's Maidan protests kicked off dynamics that culminated in the annexation of Crimea in the short term and Russian invasion of Ukraine within the decade. Underpinning this real-world lack of care for global and area dynamics, moreover, are the very philosophical foundations of neoliberalism, which, at its core, "implies freedom from responsibility to any kind of alterity, in favor of responsibility only to one's self" (Looser 2012, 99). Such an ethos is hardly a healthy basis for more equitable hub-spoke interactions or exploratory spoke-spoke conversations.

To overcome the above challenges to area and international studies alike, we need to build bridges—from the spokes to the periphery, but also across spokes. The flourishing subfield of global IR offers one such pathway. In a programmatic call for work in this vein, Amitav Acharya specified six principles with relevance to bridging area studies and disciplinary expertise: pluralistic universalism as ontological foundation (i.e., recognition of our common humanity but cultural difference); grounding in global and not only Western histories; complementarity with existing IR frameworks; the study of regions, regionalisms, and area studies; the eschewing of exceptionalism; and the recognition of multiple forms of agency. Work that is aligned in analytical and normative thrust with this call includes a wide range of historical, sociological, critical, postcolonial, and intersectional gender approaches that challenge (mis)perceptions within mainstream IR regarding non-Western subjects[9]. And while much such work has concentrated on critique,[10] a growing number of studies draw on emic concepts and empirical patterns to theorize IR in non-Western perspective. Thus, IR theoretical categories can be inductively generated from, say, "non-Western" or syncretic national or regional experiences (Fisher-Onar 2025), or by drawing on Sikh, Hindu, Confucian, Daoist, Rastafari, indigenous and other "cosmologies" (e.g., Shani 2008; Shahi 2018; Ling 2013; Shilliam 2010; Kavalski 2017; Trownsell et al. 2021) toward pluralizing IR theory. In other words, just as second-generation constructivist scholars moved beyond the first wave's critique of positivism to produce a rich array of applied analyses, so too, are global IR analysts increasingly generating work that leverages the theoretical critique to addressing outstanding, real-world problems. It is to this second-generation knowledge production to which my pairing here of global IR and CAS speaks.

That said, the field faces several challenges when it comes to a bridging role. First, it arguably remains stronger on spoke-hub communication than spoke-spoke communication. This may be because many global IR scholars are products of the same knowledge apparatus that they critique (Alejandro 2018). Hence, they often come to global IR from regional specializations that are shaped by the same siloed structures as area studies proper. These epistemic structures mean that relatively few resources are channeled toward bridging non-Western regional expertise (although a growing body of collaborative work in special issues and textbook production is changing this pattern; see, e.g., Tickner and Smith 2020; Thakur and Smith 2021; Fisher-Onar and Kavalski 2022).

A second challenge is associated with the critical thrust of global IR, which, while appropriate to the bid to dismantle Eurocentrism, can pique diffuse forms of resistance—active and structural alike—among mainstream analysts. Further research is required to pinpoint the sources, mechanisms, modalities, and implications of this dynamic, but, in broad strokes, resistance, in some cases, appears to entail a visceral element—an expression of

---

[9] That said, not all scholars across these camps identify with the label "global IR," and some explicitly object for a variety of reasons (for a more thorough discussion of contests over how to label this flourishing space of knowledge production, see Fisher-Onar 2023). Given the wider audience at which this edited volume is aimed, in this chapter I use the term with a lower case *g* to signal a baseline analytical and ethical orientation that is critical of "Euromodernity" (Hutchings 2019).

[10] See, for example, Michael Barnett's commentary in the first session of three sets of talks/debates entitled "Global IR Dialogues." Global IR Sessions 1, School of International Studies (SIS), at American University. Available at https://www.youtube.com/watch?v=F5v0PbJFjGE&list=PLnS6BuPUSqzRAIKrjzcHvqw932yLpXzcs&index=4:.

the broader "culture wars" over structural racism and persistent patriarchy that inform our broader zeitgeist. Similarly, but evocative of broader contestations on the political and academic left (where much global IR scholarship is situated), there are internal divisions between globally oriented scholars who are more reformist and those who are more radical in their take on the mainstream.

A third challenge—which is related to both the hub-and-spokes problem and the tensions associated with global IR's normative thrust—is that the critical and interpretive methodologies adopted by many global IR scholars tend to use methods that are rarely rewarded in the top-ranked universities and journals of the Global North,[11] impeding access to wider audiences and resources (see Doherty-Sil, this volume). The danger is that mainstream conversations about urgent, cross-case, and cross-regional problems continue to occlude perspectives from the cases and regions themselves.

Recognizing these challenges, both area studies and global IR arguably can benefit from engagement with CAS, which Ariel Ahram, Patrick Köllner and Rudra Sil (2018, 3) characterize as any "self-conscious effort to . . . (i) balance deep sensitivity to context in each of the locales being examined with the use of some variant of the comparative method to surface causal linkages that are portable across world regions; and (ii) engage ongoing research . . . in two or more area studies communities against the backdrop of more general concepts" and debates. Offering a sort of middle way, as Eileen Doherty-Sil argues in this volume, CAS's intensive attention to methodological questions in relation to varied regional patterns can help to communicate area studies insights across hub and spokes alike. At the same time, CAS supports those global IR analysts who—out of conviction, practicality, or a combination thereof—wish to persuade the mainstream by selectively using, rather than wholly deconstructing, the mainstream's tools. In other words, CAS can serve as a bridge-builder, not just for spoke-to-spoke conversations but also for conversations between critical/interpretive perspectives and more mainstream, (neo)positivist ones.

A key contribution of CAS at this intersection of cross-regional comparison, disciplinary concerns, and global IR critique is that it enables a problem-driven approach to area studies categories. Thus, we can move

---

[11] Some established IR journals that are relatively open to critical / global IR insights include *Millennium, International Studies Quarterly, Review of International Studies*, and, increasingly, the *Journal of Common Market Studies*.

beyond the Anglo-American inheritance and its geographically defined categories (Ahram 2011; Pepinsky 2020) that may appear intuitive to the Western gaze (e.g., the "Middle" vs. "Far East") but occlude other "relevant similarities" (Basedau and Köllner 2007) unrelated to geographic adjacency (Brookes 2020). A case in point is the "family resemblances" (Fisher-Onar 2020) that I canvas below between the imperial inheritances of China, Iran, Russia, and Turkey, and how these legacies condition behavior in distinctive ways.

To think outside of mainstream categories in a controlled, comparative fashion requires, however, CAS research to be highly explicit (Whitehead 2018) due to the "incommensurability" challenge (Fisher-Onar 2013): namely, how to compare the proverbial "apples and oranges" when it comes to cases that, despite family resemblances, may display significant differences. In the case of revisionist former empires, for example, cross-regional variation encompasses but is hardly limited to different, dominant "religions, geopolitical context, integration into the global economy, and the world historical timing of . . . independence" (Saylor 2018, 184). Broad methodological answers to the challenge might include comparative ethnography (Simmons and Smith 2019) and other interpretive approaches (see Fünfgeld, this volume). A further approach could be to triangulate idiographic work with quantitative and/or experimental methods (Peisakhin 2015; Sil 2018) for multi-method strategies involving explicit epistemic protocols and cross-checking procedures (Whitehead 2018; Ahmed 2019). That being said, the sweet spot of CAS in terms of balancing thick expertise and cross-regional ambition is arguably controlled, small-N, macrohistorical comparisons (Sil 2009; Saylor 2018). Scaling research at this level is also conducive to collaboration between experts on different world regions, united in their commitment to rigorous, contextualized comparison (Hsueh 2020). The goal: cross-regional studies that "absorb prevailing understandings" of the cases in the respective area studies communities (Saylor 2018, 18) and communicate these insights to the discipline.

A key, in turn, to executing small-N, macrohistorical comparisons (whether the analyst is working with traditional geographic regions or with "conceptual" articulations of "regions as analytical categories" [Ahram 2011, 71])—is to establish "boundary conditions" that specify "the precise scope of the 'region'" and why one boundary has been selected over others (Whitehead 2018, 50). In other words, findings need to clock in "at the same level of abstraction and empirical depth" to avoid concept stretching (von Soest and Stroh 2018, 72). When these conditions are met, "Unconventional comparison can challenge received wisdom" in productive ways (Saylor 2018, 187, 188).[12]

A CAS Approach to Eurasia's Revisionist Former Empires

Channeling the small-N, macrohistorical comparison strengths of CAS, it is my contention that Eurasia's four imperial successor states, while geographically proximate in ways that inform their national trajectories and international relationships, can be comparatively studied less on the basis of this physical proximity (which is complicated by many intervening variables) than by attending to overlap in their responses to a common, overarching *problematique*: the world-historical challenge posed by Western hegemony since the long nineteenth century. The experience for imperial states that were long accustomed to primacy in their own right, I argue, was qualitatively different than for smaller entities that were formally colonized. This major, overlapping feature that distinguishes these four states from most other actors in and beyond their regions begs comparison. As Ryan Saylor (2018, 186) puts it, "When one finds actors responding similarly to analogous stimuli, one has a powerful justification to compare such cases." The impetus to cross-regional comparison is especially salient when the common stimulus to action has had a meaningful impact over the *longue durée* and continues to inform dynamics within and across the cases under scrutiny (Hanson 2009). My goal, then, in categorizing the otherwise very different FERPs under a common heading is not to claim equivalence (which would be absurd with cases as disparate in magnitude and thick cultural attributes as China, Russia, Iran, and Turkey). Instead, as von Soest and Stroh (2018, 71–72) suggest, I aim to offer a "conscious cross-area research design" that "actually generate[s] the more complete picture by (a) identifying commonalities and differences among cases of a particular world region and (b) establishing" more general "mechanisms (which hold beyond particular world regions), thereby allowing us to transcend the notion of regional uniqueness."

The common *problematique*—namely, how non-Western empires should respond to the rise of Western great powers—engendered multiple family

---

[12] See also Skocpol 1979 on revolutions; Barkey and von Hagen 1997 on imperial legacies; Solingen and Wan 2016 on security institutions; Tudor and Slater 2021 on postcolonial nationalisms.

resemblances. "Family resemblances" offer a legitimate basis for comparison of this set of cases since China, Russia, Iran, and Turkey differ in their "thick" characteristics yet also display "intuitively understandable" overlapping features as revisionist former empires (Goertz 1994, 25). As Ludwig Wittgenstein (1958, 17) put it in his *Blue Book* via the notion of "games," we have a

> tendency to look for something in common to all the entities which we commonly subsume under a general term. We are inclined to think that there must be something in common to all games, say, and that this common property is the justification for applying the general term "game" to the various games; whereas games form a *family*, the members of which have family likenesses. Some of them have the same nose, others have the same eyebrows, and others again the same way of walking; and these likenesses overlap, but need not be identical to warrant comparison.

This view of categorization is widely recognized in the natural sciences, where it is a pillar of biological reasoning. It is based on the logic of "polythetic," or multiple overlapping, features as opposed to insistence on phenomena sharing a "monothetic," or single common, feature. My contention is that "family resemblances" likewise offer an apt tool of social scientific inquiry into complex phenomenon like revisionist former empires, especially when the small-N scale of macrohistorical, comparative inquiry allows for rigorous contextualization (Fisher-Onar 2020; 2022). Accordingly, in the following section, I identify a set of family resemblances found across China, Russia, Iran, and Turkey. I organize these features under three headings—structural resemblances, agential resemblances, and processual resemblances—the interplay between which drives comparable, if by no means identical, patterns and outcomes.

Structural Family Resemblances

First, as noted, China, Russia, Iran, and Turkey are successor states of the imperial cores of the Chinese, czarist, Persian, and Ottoman empires. These entities dominated multiregional environs through their own hub-and-spokes forms of governance for centuries. Accordingly, ruling elites and social groups accustomed to primacy experienced the incremental—but, ultimately, existential—challenge presented by ascendent Western military power, norms, and capitalism in a differentiated way than societies that did not have indigenous imperial institutions. In other words, the political cultures of China, Russia, Iran, and Turkey arguably have as many "post-imperial" (Nicolaïdis and Fisher-Onar 2015) features as they share characteristics with properly "postcolonial" states.

Second, despite these imperial habits, China, Russia, Iran, and Turkey were all subject to pressures from an expansive West (and a Japan that was successfully adopting the Western model of Weberian state modernization, industrialization, and imperial capitalism) (Buzan and Lawson 2013). These pressures played out in a variety of ways—including pitting the FERPs against each other. But all four cases entailed the experience of humiliating battlefield losses and treaty settlements (and, sometimes, the reversal of battlefield victories when Western great powers intervened on behalf of their various protégés).

Another overlapping if not identical forcefield faced by the FERPs was what Turan Kayaoğlu (2010) calls European "legal imperialism" through mechanisms like "capitulations." Particularly acute in the Chinese, Persian, and Ottoman cases, capitulations included major trade and legal concessions like extraterritoriality for the subjects and protégés of Western/Japanese colonial powers (see also Özsu 2016). Achieved via gunboat and other forms of coercive diplomacy, capitulatory regimes overlaid the acute experience of battlefield humiliations.[13]

Taken together, this overlapping experience of penetration—but, crucially, not full-fledged colonization—was associated with "semi-civilized" status in nineteenth-century international law. According to this hierarchical framework, states were codified as "civilized" (i.e., warranting sovereign recognition), "semi-civilized" (i.e., warranting capitulatory regimes), or "barbaric" or "savage" (i.e., warranting colonization and civilizing missions) (Keene 2002; Nicolaïdis et al. 2014). And while in the case of Russia, the stigma of being "semi-civilized" within Western-dominated international society was somewhat mitigated by the salience of Christianity (albeit the "wrong" type), and the white-presenting features of many within the Russian elite, the fact remains that Russia, like the Chinese, Persians, and Ottomans, has long served as a constitutive "Other" of the European geocultural

---

[13] For extensive theorization of this experience and its legacies—which I call the "capitulations syndrome" in conversation with the psychosocial IR literature on "ontological insecurity"—see Fisher-Onar 2022.

270 ADVANCING COMPARATIVE AREA STUDIES

imagination (Zarakol 2010; Morozov and Rumelili 2012)—an overlapping structural condition.

Agential Family Resemblances

How did China, Russia, Persia, and the Ottoman Empire respond to their "semi-civilized" status? Answers to this question reveal a further set of overlapping features. First, a range of programs along a spectrum of engagement to resistance were articulated by rival imperial factions (Fisher-Onar and Evin 2010; Sil 2002).[14] Factions included *neo-traditionalists* who sought inspiration in principles and practices from perceived golden ages within each state's imperial tradition.[15] Others were *selectivists*, seeking to cherry-pick or explicitly syncretize native and Western practices. The strategy here was to cultivate the perceived components of Western success through military, economic, or political reform, while seeking to revitalize elements of Chinese, Russian, Persian, or Ottoman ethics and culture (whose Confucian, Orthodox and Islamic inheritances were envisaged as morally superior to a West that was seen as polluted by instrumental reason). A third camp whose activities can be compared across all three cases were the *Westernists*, who mobilized around programs of defensive modernization that critiqued many aspects of indigenous governance and society. The significant differences in these strategies and the tools for which they called notwithstanding, there was a key, cross-cutting thread: a paradoxical will to defensive modernization that incorporated elements of Western-dominated modernity for the paradoxical purpose of securing autonomy from the West.

These modernizing strategies—and their anguished relationship with Western power, capitalism, and norms—would prove foundational to each state's project as the painful transition from empire to nation-state unfolded. At one level that, again, distinguishes the FERPs from nonimperial polities that were fully colonized by the West, this reinvention of agency entailed attempts to compete in the broader nineteenth-century race for empire among (would-be) great powers. Russia was the most successful of the

[14] Sil's comparison of the Russian and Japanese modernizing projects employs an aligned typology of "modernist," "revolutionary," "syncretist," and "traditional" strategies on the part of actors negotiating the encounter an ascendent West.

[15] Such projects were not necessarily "fundamentalist" in the sense of rejecting modernity, but rather invoked ideals and instruments of eclipsed eras of perceived greatness to give meaning and legitimacy to contemporary projects.

four cases, expanding aggressively through tools like its own capitulatory demands vis-à-vis the Ottomans, Persians, and Chinese. It was therefore well positioned to reinvent the Russian empire on the ashes of the czarist enterprise. But even the "sick man of Europe," a term for the Ottomans coined by Nicholas I, whose Romanov dynasty would in fact pre-decease his Ottoman counterparts by several years, engaged in its own civilizing missions. These included what Minawi (2016) calls the "Ottoman scramble for Africa," as well as pan-Turkish attempts to conjure antidotes to European— and Russian—imperialism (consequential chapters in nineteenth-century multipolarity that are often overlooked in Eurocentric accounts of empire) (Fisher-Onar 2015, 2022).

Despite the mixed, at best, successes of attempts to reconfigure empire, defensive modernization ultimately generated an overlapping ability in Russia and Turkey, Iran and China, to resist relatively short-lived, Western/Japanese incursions/occupations (at least compared to the more intensive domination experienced by fully colonized states).[16] The upshot was that it was internal, not external agents, who deposed or reconfigured monarchies to embark upon authoritarian, state-building projects that sought to recalibrate governance and economic institutions along Western lines, capitalist and communist alike. Yet, neo-traditionalist and selectivist strategies also continued to animate FERP agencies (authorizing, for instance, Maoism in China or, in the case of Iran, a religious-leftist revolutionary coalition that eventually overturned the Westernist shah, enabling the savvy Ayatollah Khomenei's neo-traditionalists to capture the state).

Processual Family Resemblances

The overlapping structural features and strategies of response that have animated Chinese, Russian, Iranian, and Turkish management underwrote the transformative process from empire to nation-state described above. In the nation-state period, a further family resemblance has been the process via which historical memory has been enshrined in collective repertoires— not least the mechanisms via which memories are channeled to specific policy outcomes to this day. In this regard, FERPs' post-imperial national

---

[16] The occupation of significant swaths of China's by Japan as well as the forcible repression of several major rebellions by a coalition of powers that enjoyed capitulatory privileges was arguably the most extensive experience of semi-colonization among the three states.

272 ADVANCING COMPARATIVE AREA STUDIES

projects were all pursued via the tools of identity inculcation identified by modernist scholars of nationalism (e.g., Anderson's (2006) mass media; Gellner's (2008) national education; and Hobsbawm and Ranger's (2012) "invention of tradition" through commemorative practices). Tropes, frames, and narratives thus generated offer productive site for empirical comparison across the FERPs. Analysis could be pursued via data on official statements, national curricula, media output, the scripts of national holidays and memorials, and state- and well as market-generated cultural production.

Comparisons could probe Chinese, Russian, Iranian, and Turkish narratives during a given period, that is, synchronously (such as in the buildup to and aftermaths of critical junctures like each state's early twentieth-century constitutional revolutions), or in response to external shocks (like the end of the Cold War or the 2008–2009 global economic crisis). Dynamics of overlap and divergence in state narratives also can be probed over time, that is, diachronically. Interesting patterns emerge, for example, when one compares earlier periods of state building with more recent processes. Twentieth-century state narratives, for their part, often sought to negate the recent—and traumatic—imperial heritage. These amnesiac projects in the cases of China, Russia, and Turkey authorized full-fledged cultural revolutions (while in Iran the shah's modernist posture was radical enough to engender intensive, neo-traditionalist resistance). More recently, however, the glory days of Chinese, czarist/Soviet, Perso-Islamic, and Turco-Islamic imperium have been celebrated. Accordingly, today, there are palpable family resemblances in the rousing tales of imperial eclipse and national rebirth that are narrated across all four cases.

These ideational repertoires—and the strong emotions that they generate among wide segments of the population—not only inform political culture but furnish a policymaking mechanism. In other words, the FERPs' foundational paradox—namely, their resentment of second-class status combined with the will to achieve first-class status within the very Western-dominated system by which they have been "stigmatized" (Zarakol 2010)—exerts causal force in policymaking. Cases in point include the ways that leaders across all three states invoke tropes akin to the Chinese state's injunction to "never forget national humiliation"[17] in order to shore up political coalitions, confront domestic scandals, or navigate diplomatic crises.

---

[17] Comparable frames are the notion of "Westoxification" in Iran and the "Sevres syndrome" in Turkey (which refers to the post–World War I treaty that would have dismembered the remnants of the Ottoman Empire but whose terms were rendered moot by nationalist resistance and the foundation of the Republic of Turkey).

Likewise on the foreign policy front, FERPs' overlapping repertoires inform a comparable style: the pursuit of "anti-imperialist" foreign policy agendas in which imperialism is equated with Europe historically and the United States today. This attribution of imperialism to the West alone enables Beijing, Moscow, Tehran, and Ankara to characterize their own increasingly assertive policies at the regional scale as benign. In other words, there is a common thread of dissonance between FERP calls for greater pluralism in global governance even as they pursue expansive policies in former, imperial hinterlands. This dissonance can lead to regional tensions. Cases in point include China vis-à-vis Taiwan, among others in the South China Sea; Russia vis-à-vis Ukraine, among others in eastern Europe, Iran vis-à-vis Saudi Arabia, among others in the Middle East; and Turkey vis-à-vis Cyprus and Greece, among others in the eastern Mediterranean.

In sum, the set of structural, agential, and processual "family resemblances" identified in this chapter render FERPs a distinct type of revisionist power. One notable implication of the affinities between the FERPs and postcolonial critiques of Western neo-imperialism is that wider audiences in the Global South—namely, those not directly affected by FERPs' revisionist regional behavior—may sympathize with and/or pragmatically engage China, Russia, Iran, and Turkey at sites of global governance like the UN.

Conclusion

In this chapter, I have argued that problem-driven comparisons across non-Western world regions—and, specifically, across (Eurasia's) former empires/revisionist powers (FERPs)—can help us to bypass or overcome the hub-and-spokes problem of Western IR theory. The epistemological structures informing Western IR theory prevent or obscures fresh insights that can be generated through cross-case and cross-regional analysis across fields, such as Chinese/East Asian, Russian/Eurasian, and Turkish/Iranian/Middle Eastern studies. This can help correct for a persistent tendency among IR realists to ignore (or reify) the role of cultural factors in shaping greater Eurasian resurgence. At the same time, it can help to explore sources for thinking about cooperation and engagement that are not predicated on Western historical experience and liberal expectations as the "normal" framework for theory and practice. Probing possible solutions, I show how area studies and the flourishing field of "global IR" can come together to develop more historically and sociologically nuanced frameworks. This is precisely where CAS holds much promise, providing a bridge when it comes to channeling these nuances across area studies communities on one hand and linking them to the disciplinary mainstream on the other.

I illustrated these advantages by showing how CAS's strengths can be leveraged to reveal important and consequential "family resemblances" across Eurasian FERPs, most notably the cases of China, Russia, Iran, and Turkey. A family resemblance approach also acknowledges that not every structural, agential, and processual feature will necessarily be equally significant in each of these states. Nevertheless, taken together, these resemblances inform a foundational paradox—a visceral anti-Westernism yet the paradoxical will to (re)claim status as imperial successor states—that animates a distinctly FERP style of policymaking. Drawing out the overlapping features of FERP revisionism vis-à-vis the projects of bona fide postcolonial actors in the states, I further identified a range of sites and data that could be compared across cases.

Future studies could consider a wider subset of cases that share some but not all of the family resemblances identified here (e.g., India, Brazil, South Africa), infusing debates about, say, BRICS revisionism with insights into the emic logics at play (for work in this vein see, e.g., Roberts et al. 2018). My effort to employ CAS to bridge interdisciplinary, non-Western area studies and disciplinary debates could also be extended to—and benefit from—further engagement with the literature on regionalism in IR (e.g., Katzenstein 1996; Sbragia 2008). This corpus likewise mediates between particular non-Western experiences and midrange theorizing, between deductive and inductive theorizing, and between nomothetic and idiographic styles of analysis. Thus, there may be significant scope for a cross-fertilizing conversation in which CAS helps to infuse scholarship on regions and regionalism in IR with out-of-the-box insights generated by bottom-up, spoke-to-spoke comparisons that incorporate historical and anthropological nuance (Kuhonta 2014).

In short, CAS is primed to deliver a rich array of insights by connecting the theoretical correctives offered by global IR to an empirically and methodologically mindful exploration of a wide range of family resemblances across actors from different regions—with due attention to the implications for cooperation and conflict.

Bibliography

Ahmed, Amel. 2019. Multi-Methodology Research and Democratization Studies: Intellectual Bridges Among Islands of Specialization. *Democratization* 26 (1): 97–139.

Ahram, Ariel I. 2011. The Theory and Method of Comparative Area Studies. *Qualitative Research* 11(1): 69–90.

Ahram, Ariel I., Patrick Köllner, and Rudra Sil, eds. 2018. *Comparative Area Studies: Methodological Rationales and Cross-Regional Applications*. New York: Oxford University Press.

Alejandro, Audrey. 2018. *Western Dominance in International Relations? The Internationalisation of IR in Brazil and India*. New York: Routledge.

Anderson, Benedict. 2006. *Imagined Communities: Reflections on the Origin and Spread of Nationalism*. London: Verso.

Anno, Tadashi, 2018. *National Identity and Great-Power Status in Russia and Japan*. London: Routledge.

Aydinli, Ersel, and Onur Erpul. 2022. The False Promise of Global IR: Exposing the Paradox of Dependent Development. *International Theory* 14 (3): 419–459.

Barkey, Karen, and Mark von Hagen, eds. 1997. *After Empire: Multiethnic Societies and Nation-Building*. Boulder, CO: Westview.

Basedau, Matthias, and Patrick Köllner. 2007. Area Studies, Comparative Area Studies, and the Study of Politics: Context, Substance, and Methodological Challenges. *Zeitschrift für vergleichende Politikwissenschaft* 1 (1): 105–124.

Benabdallah, Lina. 2022. A Relational Approach to Gift-Giving: China's Aid Exchanges in the Global South. *Global Studies Quarterly* 2 (4). https://doi.org/10.1093/isagsq/ksac071.

International Relations Scholarship Around the World. London: Routledge, 322–341.

Bhambra, Gurminder. 2020. Colonial Global Economy: Towards a Theoretical Reorientation of Political Economy. *Review of International Political Economy* 28 (2): 307–322.

Biersteker, T. J. 2009. The Parochialism of Hegemony: Challenges for "American" International Relations. In Arlene B. Tickner and Ole Waever, eds., *International Relations Scholarship around the World*. London: Routledge, 322–341.

Brookes, Marissa. 2020. The Sweet Spot in Comparative Area Studies: Embracing Causal Complexity Through the Identification of Both Systematic and Unsystematic Variables and Mechanism. *Qualitative and Multi-Method Research* 17 (1): 20–22.

Buzan, Barry, and George Lawson. 2013. The Global Transformation: The Nineteenth Century and the Making of Modern International Relations. *International Studies Quarterly* 57 (3): 620–634.

Fisher-Onar, Nora. 2013. Historical Legacies in Rising Powers: Toward a (Eur)Asian Approach. *Critical Asian Studies* 45 (3): 411–430.

Fisher-Onar, Nora. 2015. Between Memory, History, and Historiography: Contesting Ottoman Legacies in Turkey 1923–2012. In Kalypso Nicolaidis, Berny Sebe, and Gabrielle Maas, eds. *Echoes of Empire: Memory, Identity, and Colonial Legacies*. London: I.B. Tauris, 141–155.

Fisher-Onar, Nora. 2018. Former Empires, Rising Powers: Turkey's Neo-Ottomanism and China's New Silk Road. In Maximillian Mayer, ed. *Rethinking the Silk Road*. Singapore: Palgrave Macmillan, 177–190.

Fisher-Onar, Nora. 2020. Making Sense of Multipolarity: Eurasia's Former Empires, Family Resemblances, and Comparative Area Studies. *Qualitative and Multi-Method Research* 17–18 (1): 15–19.

Fisher-Onar, Nora. 2022. The Capitulations Syndrome: Why Revisionist Powers Leverage Post-Colonial Sensibilities to Post-Imperial Projects. *Global Studies Quarterly* 2 (4). https://doi.org/10.1093/isagsq/ksac077.

Fisher-Onar, Nora. 2023. From Realist Billiard Balls and Liberal Concentric Circles to Global IR's Venn Diagram? Rethinking International Relations via Turkey's Centennial. *Uluslararası İlişkiler Dergisi* 20, no. 78: 97–118.

Fisher-Onar, Nora. 2025. *Contesting Pluralism(s): Islamism, Liberalism and Nationalism in Turkey and Beyond*. Cambridge: Cambridge University Press.

Fisher-Onar, Nora, and Ahmet Evin. 2010. Convergence and Resistance: The European Dilemma of Turkish Intellectuals. In Justine Lacroix and Kalypso Nicolaïdis, eds. *European Stories: Intellectual Debates on Europe in National Contexts*. Oxford: Oxford University Press, 294–314.

Fisher-Onar, Nora, and Emilian Kavalski, 2022. From Trans-Atlantic Order to Afro-Eur-Asian Worlds? Revisioning IR as Interlocking Regional Worlds. *Global Studies Quarterly* 2 (4). https://doi.org/10.1093/isagsq/ksac080.

Fisher-Onar, Nora and Kalypso Nicolaïdis. 2013. The Decentring Agenda: Europe as a Post-Colonial Power. *Cooperation and Conflict* 48 (2): 283–303.

Fisher-Onar, Nora and Kalypso Nicolaïdis. 2021. The Decentering Agenda. A Post-Colonial Appraoch to EU External Action. In Sieglinde Gstöhl and Simon Schunz, eds. The External Action of the European Union: Concepts, Approaches, Theories,. London: Macmillan Education, 288-304.

Frankopan, Peter. 2015. *The Silk Roads: A New History of the World*. London: Bloomsbury.

Geertz, Clifford. 2008. *Thick Description: Toward an Interpretive Theory of Culture*. New York: Routledge.

Gellner, Ernest. 2008. *Nations and Nationalism*. Ithaca, NY: Cornell University Press.

Goertz, Gary, 1994. *Contexts of International Politics*. Cambridge: Cambridge University Press.

Hobsbawm, Eric, and Terence Ranger, eds. 2012. *The Invention of Tradition*. Cambridge: Cambridge University Press.

Hobson, John M. 2012. *The Eurocentric Conception of World Politics: Western International Theory, 1760–2010*. Cambridge: Cambridge University Press.

Hsueh, Roselyn. 2020. Synergies of CAS: New Inquires, Theory Development, and Community. *Qualitative and Multi-Method Research* 17–18: 10–14.

The External Constitution of European Identity: Russia and Turkey as Europe-makers. *Cooperation and Conflict* 47 (1): 28–48.

Huntington, Samuel P. 1993. The Clash of Civilizations? *Foreign Affairs* 72 (3): 22–49.

Hutchings, Kimberly. 2019. Decolonizing Global Ethics: Thinking with the Pluriverse. *Ethics & International Affairs* 33 (2): 115–125.

Ikenberry, John. 2016. The Rise, Character and Evolution of International Order. In Orfeo Fioretos, Tulia G. Falleti, and Adam Sheingate, eds. *The Oxford Handbook of Historical Institutionalism*. Oxford: Oxford University Press, 538–553.

Kang, David C. 2003. Getting Asia Wrong: The Need for New Analytical Frameworks. *International Security* 27 (4): 57–85.

Kaplan, Robert. 2019. *The Return of Marco Polo's World: War, Strategy, and American Interests in the Twenty-First Century*. New York: Random House.

Katzenstein, Peter. 1996. Regionalism in Comparative Perspective. *Cooperation and Conflict* 31 (2): 123–159.

Kavalski, Emilian. 2017. *The Guanxi of Relational International Theory*. London: Routledge.

Kayaoğlu, Turan. 2010. *Legal Imperialism: Sovereignty and Extraterritoriality in Japan, the Ottoman Empire, and China*. Cambridge: Cambridge University Press.

Keene, Edward. 2002. *Beyond the Anarchical Society: Grotius, Colonialism and Order in World Politics*. Cambridge: Cambridge University Press.

Keohane, Robert. 2005. *After Hegemony: Cooperation and Discord in the World Political Economy*. Princeton, NJ: Princeton University Press.

King, Charles. 2016. The Decline of International Studies: Why Flying Blind Is Dangerous. *Foreign Affairs.* July–August. https://www.foreignaffairs.com/articles/united-states/decline-international-studies.

Kuhonta, Erik Martinez. 2014. Southeast Asia and Comparative-Historical Analysis: Region, Theory and Ontology on a Wide Canvas. *Pacific Affairs* 87 (3): 485–507.

Kroenig, Matthew. 2020. *The Return of Great Power Rivalry: Democracy Versus Autocracy from the Ancient World to the U.S. and China.* Oxford: Oxford University Press.

Laruelle, Marlène. 2008. *Russian Eurasianism: An Ideology of Empire.* Washington, DC: Woodrow Wilson Center Press and Baltimore: John Hopkins University Press.

Ling, L. H. M., 2013. *The Dao of World Politics: Towards a Post-Westphalian, Worldist International Relations.* New York: Routledge.

Looser, Tom. 2012. The Global University, Area Studies, and the World Citizen: Neoliberal Geography's Redistribution of the "World." *Cultural Anthropology* 27 (1): 97–117.

Malcolm, Noel. 2019. *Useful Enemies: Islam and the Ottoman Empire in Western Political Thought, 1450–1750.* New York: Oxford University Press.

Mayer, Maximilian. 2018. China's Historical Statecraft and the Return of History. *International Affairs* 94 (6): 1217–1235.

McDaniel, Tim. 1991. *Autocracy, Modernization and Revolution in Russia and Iran.* Princeton, NJ: Princeton University Press.

Minawi, Mostafa. 2016. *The Ottoman Scramble for Africa: Empire and Diplomacy in the Sahara and the Hijaz.* Stanford, CA: Stanford University Press.

Morozov, Viatcheslav, and Bahar Rumelili. 2012. The External Constitution of European Identity: Russia and Turkey as Europe-makers. *Cooperation and Conflict* 47 (1): 28–48.

Mead, William R. 2014. The Return of Geopolitics: The Revenge of the Revisionist Powers. *Foreign Affairs* 93 (3): 69–79.

Nicolaïdis, Kalypso, and Nora Fisher-Onar. 2015. Europe's Post-Imperial Condition. In Hartmut Behr and Yannis Stivachtis, eds. *Revisiting the European Union as Empire.* London: Routledge, 115–133.

Nicolaïdis, Kalypso, Claire Vergerio, Nora Fisher-Onar, and Juri Viehoff. 2014. From Metropolis to Microcosmos: The EU's New Standards of Civilisation. *Millennium* 42 (3): 718–745.

Özsu, Umut, 2016. The Ottoman Empire, the Origins of Extraterritoriality, and International Legal Theory. In, Anne Orford, Florian Hoffmann, and Martin Clark, eds. *The Oxford Handbook of the Theory of International Law.* New York: Oxford University Press, 123–137.

Parmar, Inderjeet. 2018. The US-Led Liberal Order: Imperialism by Another Name? *International Affairs* 94 (1): 151–172.

Peisakhin, Leonid. 2015. Cultural Legacies: Persistence and Transmission. In Norman Schofield and Gonzalo Caballero, eds. *The Political Economy of Governance.* Cham, Switzerland: Springer, 21–39.

Pepinsky, Thomas. 2020. What's the "Area" in Comparative Area Studies? *Qualitative and Mixed-Methods Research* 17–18: 22–26.

Risse, Thomas, Wiebke Wemheuer-Vogelaar, and Frank Havemann. 2022. IR Theory and the Core-Periphery Structure of Global IR: Lessons from Citation Analysis. *International Studies Review* 24 (3). https://doi.org/10.1093/isr/viac029.

Roberts, Leslie Armijo, and Saori Katada. 2018. *The BRICS and Financial Statecraft.* Oxford: Oxford University Press.

Rutazibwa, Olivia. 2019. What's There to Mourn? Decolonial Reflections on (the End of) Liberal Humanitarianism. *Journal of Humanitarian Affairs* 1 (1): 65–67.

Said, Edward. 1978. *Orientalism.* New York: Penguin.

Saylor, Ryan. 2018. Gaining by Shedding Case Selection Strictness: Natural Resource Booms and Institution Building in Latin America and Africa. In Ariel I. Ahram, Patrick Köllner, and Rudra Sil, eds. *Comparative Area Studies: Methodological Rationales and Cross-Regional Applications.* New York: Oxford University Press, 185–203.

278 ADVANCING COMPARATIVE AREA STUDIES

Sbragia, Alberta. 2008. Comparative Regionalism: What Might It Be. *Journal of Common Market Studies* 46 (s1): 29–49.

Schweller, Randy, L. 1994. Bandwagoning for Profit: Bringing the Revisionist State Back. *International Security* 19 (1): 72–107.

Shahi, Deepshikha. 2018. *Advaita as a Global International Relations Theory.* London: Routledge.

Shani, Giorgio. 2008. Toward a Post-Western IR: The Umma, Khalsa Panth, and Critical International Relations Theory. *International Studies Review* 10 (4): 722–734.

Shilliam, Robbie, ed. 2010. *International Relations and Non-Western Thought: Imperialism, Colonialism and Investigations of Global Modernity.* London: Routledge.

Sil, Rudra. 2002. *Managing "Modernity": Work, Community, and Authority in Late-Industrializing Japan and Russia.* Ann Arbor: University of Michigan Press.

Sil, Rudra. 2009. Area Studies, Comparative Politics, and the Utility of Cross-Regional Small-N Comparison. *Qualitative & Mixed-Method Research* 7 (2): 26–32.

Sil, Rudra. 2018. Triangulating Area Studies, Not Just Methods: How Cross-Regional Comparison Aids Qualitative and Mixed-Method Research. In Ariel I. Ahram, Patrick Köllner, and Rudra Sil, eds. *Comparative Area Studies: Methodological Rationales and Cross-Regional Applications.* New York: Oxford University Press, 225–246.

Sil, Rudra, and Ariel Ahram. 2020. Comparative Area Studies and the Global South. *Vestnik RUDN: International Relations* 20 (2): 279–287.

Simmons, Erica S., and Nicholas Rush Smith. 2019. The Case for Comparative Ethnography. *Comparative Politics* 51 (3): 341–359.

Skocpol, Theda. 1979. *States and Social Revolutions: A Comparative Analysis of France, Russia and China.* Cambridge: Cambridge University Press.

Solingen, Etel, and Wilfred Wan. 2016. Critical Junctures, Developmental Pathways, and Incremental Change in Security Institutions. In Orfeo Fioretos, Tulia G. Falleti, and Adam Sheingate, eds. *The Oxford Handbook of Historical Institutionalism.* Oxford: Oxford University Press, 553–571.

Tammen, Ron. 2008. The Organski Legacy: A Fifty-Year Research Program. *International Interactions* 34 (4): 314–332.

Thakur, Vineet, and Karen Smith. 2021. The Multiple Births of International Relations. *Review of International Studies* 47 (5): 571–579.

Tickner, Arlene B., and Karen Smith, eds. 2020. *International Relations from the Global South.* London: Routledge.

Tickner, Arlene B., and Ole Wæver, eds. 2009. *International Relations Scholarship Around the World.* London: Routledge.

Tickner, J. Anne, 2011. Retelling IR's Foundational Stories: Some Feminist and Postcolonial Perspectives. *Global Change, Peace & Security* 23 (1): 5–13.

Trownsell, Tamara A., Arlenee B. Tickner, Amaya Querejazu, Jarred Reddekop, Giorgio Shani, Kosuke Shimizu, Navinta C. Behera, and Anahita Arian. 2021. Differing About Difference: Relational IR from Around the World. *International Studies Perspectives* 22 (1): 25–64.

Tudor, Maya, and Dan Slater. 2021. Nationalism, Authoritarianism, and Democracy: Historical Lessons from South and Southeast Asia. *Perspectives on Politics* 19 (3): 706–722.

von Soest, Christian, and Alexander Stroh. 2018. Comparisons Across World Regions: Managing Conceptual, Methodological, and Practical Challenges. In Ariel I. Ahram, Patrick Köllner, and Rudra Sil, eds. *Comparative Area Studies: Methodological Rationales and Cross-Regional Applications.* New York: Oxford University Press, 66–84.

Whitehead, Laurence. 2018. Depth Perception: Improving Analytic Focus Through Cross- and Interregional Comparisons. In Ariel I. Ahram, Patrick Köllner, and Rudra Sil, eds. *Comparative Area Studies: Methodological Rationales and Cross-Regional Applications.* New York: Oxford University Press, 45–65.

Wittgenstein, Ludwig. 1958. *The Blue and Brown Books.* Oxford: Blackwell.

Zarakol, Ayşe. 2010. *After Defeat: How the East Learned to Live with the West.* Cambridge: Cambridge University Press.

PART V

ORGANIZATIONAL CHALLENGES AND INSTITUTIONAL FRAMEWORKS FOR COMPARATIVE AREA STUDIES

12

Comparative Area Studies

Programs, Departments, Constraints, Opportunities

Sara Wallace Goodman and Thomas B. Pepinsky

Introduction

Comparative area studies (CAS) is a powerful approach to comparative politics that combines deep engagement with area studies and a theoretical and empirical scope that spans world regions. The recent methodological literature on CAS has shown its promise in allowing qualitative, historical, and contextually focused research to contribute explicitly to theory building, concept formation, and theory testing in research that strives to make transregional or global contributions.

In this chapter, we draw on our expertise as scholars of two world regions (Europe and Southeast Asia) and our experiences working with institutions that are defined by their regional coverage to reflect critically on how research communities can facilitate or inhibit the scholarly practices that are necessary to produce CAS. Pitched most generally, we ask, what organizational and institutional structures facilitate or inhibit the enterprise of CAS? At a more practical level, we ask whether European studies and Southeast Asian studies as currently practiced are suited to producing area studies knowledge that is amenable to cross-regional comparative research.

We will argue that the institutional structures that encourage deep area knowledge (a prerequisite for CAS) are different from the institutional structures that encourage cross-regional comparative work that is the essence of CAS. That is, area studies programs as traditionally constituted tend to encourage area knowledge that focuses on the particularities of world regions rather than on cross-regional insights. This is by design: area studies organize academic knowledge production around world regions for practical, ideological, and political reasons. Other ways to organize comparative research—into disciplines, or via research themes—are better suited to

Sara Wallace Goodman and Thomas B. Pepinsky, *Comparative Area Studies*. In: *Advancing Comparative Area Studies*. Edited by: Ariel I. Ahram, Patrick Köllner, and Rudra Sil, Oxford University Press. © Oxford University Press (2025). DOI: 10.1093/oso/9780197809365.003.0012

encouraging cross-regional comparative work, but at the cost of discouraging the types of deep area-focused research that transcends country studies to contribute to area studies. The result is that the two most common models of producing comparative research in the social sciences work at cross purposes, to the detriment of the CAS enterprise. And our concerns lie deeper: the decades-long crisis of area studies (Chua et al. 2019; Jackson 2003; Karp 1997; Lewis and Wigen 1999; Mielke and Hornidge 2017; Szanton 2002)—which dates at least to the early 1990s—means that the very foundations of area studies as a paradigm for inquiry have been subject to withering internal critique. We will argue that although individual scholars will continue to produce excellent CAS scholarship, institutionalizing CAS as a research enterprise will require new models for organizing area studies across world regions.

Our central focus in this chapter is accordingly on how academic and other research institutions support area studies, and the implications of those structures for CAS. We believe that area studies is worth defending on its own, but CAS creates new tensions and cross-pressures by highlighting comparisons across regions but still requiring a solid area studies basis for those comparisons. We must recognize these tensions and appreciate the constraints facing area-focused scholars if we are to identify how best to adapt research-focused institutions to meet the intellectual goals of CAS.

Before proceeding, it is important that we delimit our scope of inquiry. We are interested in CAS as understood either in the sense of applying the comparative method to world regions (e.g., Solingen 2007 rather than Huntington 1993) or in the sense of employing the comparative method for cross-case comparisons while drawing intentionally and explicitly on area studies knowledge (Ahram et al. 2018). CAS, in this understanding, is not isomorphic with comparative politics that includes comparisons across more than one world region (see the discussion in Pepinsky 2020). We naturally believe that such qualitative comparisons that include countries from multiple world regions—for instance, including France as a case study in the developmental state literature (Loriaux 1999), or including Japan and the United States as paradigmatic cases in the varieties of capitalism literature (Estévez-Abe 2005)—are essential parts of comparative social inquiry. But we shall have little to say about such contributions because they do not theorize world regions, nor do they invoke area studies knowledge in order to build their arguments. Likewise, we view foundational works of cross-regional qualitative comparative politics such as Skocpol 1979 as making theoretical and empirical contributions that are divorced from the concerns of European and Asian area studies. We focus on scholarship that engages with area studies in a substantive way that encompasses knowledge about world regions, not just individual countries that happen to be in different world regions. But because it is exactly this engagement with area studies that makes CAS a distinct form of comparative social inquiry, we think that this is the approach that best engages with CAS on its own terms. CAS is not simply comparative politics with cases from multiple regions: CAS is a distinct way of engaging substantively with area studies in an explicitly comparative framework.

In the next section, we examine the forms of substantive knowledge needed for CAS to be successful before reviewing different institutional models for producing area studies knowledge. In the subsequent section we outline the tensions inherent in area-based knowledge production as an input for CAS. We illustrate these arguments using examples—both public and personal—of how European and Southeast Asian studies communities understand their intellectual work.[1] We conclude our discussion and reflection by outlining what we believe are the institutional structures and organizational practices that will make CAS most viable in the coming years, in the face of both scarce resources for area studies and the ongoing crisis of area studies itself.

What Makes Area Studies?

CAS faces a fundamental tension. Area studies are foundational for CAS; note, from above, that our conceptualization of CAS requires engagement with area studies. But CAS must also transcend area studies if it is to be *comparative*: scholars working in CAS must engage with multiple forms of area knowledge across world regions, looking for points of comparison or contrast based on commonalities or differences across those regions. CAS thus normally proceeds in a bottom-up fashion, where the area knowledge or insights must exist prior to the point of comparison. It is possible to imagine a top-down model—cross-regional comparative exercises producing the very area knowledge that subsequently becomes foundational within the area studies community—but the general approach is that scholarly and

---

[1] This chapter is itself an example of CAS in action.

284 ADVANCING COMPARATIVE AREA STUDIES

intellectual communities first produce the stock of area knowledge that is subsequently used for comparative social research beyond regions.

Where, then, does area knowledge come from? We can identify four general institutional structures that produce area studies knowledge as such: programs, departments, institutes, and communities.

The area studies *program* is the dominant institutional form for area studies knowledge production in the United States and in many European countries.[2] Area studies program are characterized by their relationship with disciplinary departments within the higher education setting, as faculty in area studies programs normally hold tenured appointments in disciplinary departments (political science, history, anthropology, performance studies, art history, literature, and others) rather than in an academic unit that is defined by its focus on a particular world region. In the United States, area studies programs frequently secure federal funding that is designated specifically *for* area studies programs as part of the federal budget. The same is sometimes true in other countries as well: See, for example, the Southeast Asian studies program at the University of Freiburg in Germany. In the case of European studies, many programs will receive founding and sustaining grant money from European institutions, such as the German Academic Exchange Service and the European Commission, through the Erasmus+ funding program. As institutions, area studies programs bring together faculty from disparate disciplines who share a common substantive interest in one or more countries within a world region, to sponsor collective interdisciplinary engagement on area concerns. Area studies programs such as the Southeast Asia Program at Cornell University offer master's-level training, but they normally do not confer PhDs because they are not academic departments employing faculty. In several cases, like the University of California, Berkeley's Institute of European Studies, they may provide a "designated emphasis" for graduate students.

Area studies *departments* differ from area studies programs in that departments directly appoint their own faculty members, with the consequence that faculty normally do not have a separate tenure home in a disciplinary department.[3] They do, however, frequently offer PhD-level degrees awarded

---

[2] One source of confusion is that terminologies like "program" versus "department" can differ across countries. We use "program" here in the common American usage, recognizing that the word translated as "program" may refer to different organizational models in different countries.

[3] Again, terminology varies across countries: Units that are called "programs" often support PhD students in countries like Germany.

in the study of a particular area. Examples in the United States include the Departments of South and Southeast Asian Studies at the UC Berkeley, as well as Asian Languages and Cultures at the University of Michigan, each of which offers a stand-alone PhD degree. Area studies departments can also be found globally, including the Center for Southeast Asian Studies at Kyoto University, the Department of Southeast Asian Studies at the National University of Singapore, and the European Studies Programme at the University of Hong Kong.

The differences between programs and departments, at first glance, come down to tenure homes and PhD training. But it is also worth noting that the general geographic scope of programs and departments differs in subtle but important ways. European studies programs are relatively common in the United States, but "Departments of European Studies" are not. Instead, more common are departments of German, French, Spanish, Russian, and so forth; or alternatively, Germanic versus Romance studies versus Slavic studies departments, and Romance studies will explicitly include the Spanish-, French-, and Portuguese-speaking communities beyond Europe. Generic Asian studies programs are relatively less common than are East Asian, South Asian, and Southeast Asian studies programs,[4] but very rarely will one find a stand-alone department of East Asian studies that coexists with a stand-alone department of South Asian studies in most American universities (Harvard's Department of East Asian Languages and Civilizations and Department of South Asian Studies is an exception). The general tendency for departmentally organized area studies units to divide up Europe into "Germanic" and "Romance" field but lump together half of the world's population as "Asia" will prove important in our discussion below.

A third organizational form for area studies knowledge production is the institute model,[5] in which scholars and researchers are not primarily employed by a university but nevertheless engage in research in the service of area-focused knowledge. Examples include the ISEAS-Yusof Ishak Institute in Singapore, which employs fellows, analysts, and other scholars to study the countries of Southeast Asia, and the Southeast Asia Program at the Brookings Institution. Research produced in institutes tends to respond to

---

[4] Though that is not to say that they are uncommon. For a list, see https://www.asianstudies.org/jobs-professional-resources/asian-studies-centers/general-asia/.

[5] Not to be confused with academic programs that describe themselves as "institutes" (e.g., Berkeley's Institute for European Studies), which employ university faculty.

current events and geopolitical dynamics, often through contracts with governments, multinational corporations, and other stakeholders. Researchers frequently will hold terminal degrees in a social science discipline or a related field, but there are more opportunities for those with nonacademic backgrounds—military, political, diplomatic, and so forth—to hold positions in such institutes. The area-focused research produced in institutes would rarely be identified as "academic" in nature or as attempting to contribute basic conceptual or theoretical knowledge in the service of area studies itself.

The fourth source of area studies knowledge is what we term an area studies community. These communities may be loosely organized (like a mailing list or Facebook group) or formally institutionalized (through a body such as the Council of European Studies or the Southeast Asia Council within the Association of Asian Studies). The lack of institutionalization of most area studies communities—and the infrequent and discontinuous interactions among researchers who are involved with even the most institutionalized of these communities—means that area studies communities produce area knowledge organically and without explicit institutional support at any level aside from a professional organization.

Each of these models exists, in some way, in most countries with robust higher education infrastructures and governments that prioritize area studies in the national interest.[6] The program model for Asian area studies appears to be relatively more common in North America and Europe, whereas the department model of Asian area and European studies is relatively more common in Asia. Countries like Australia and Singapore feature an uneasy mix of both area departments and disciplinary departments, with all of the tensions that follow. And as we have emphasized, differences in academic terminology across countries mean that terms like "program" and "institute" can refer to different institutional forms, an additional source of complexity. But an important takeaway from this discussion is that the way that area studies institutions produce knowledge about world regions—as a

---

[6] There is no example of a robust area studies department, program, or institute that has emerged without consistent support from a national government in some stage in its institutional development. See, for example, the Defense Language Continuing Education Act in the United States, the École Française d'Extrême-Orient, the Royal Netherlands Institute of Southeast Asian and Caribbean Studies, the School of Oriental and African Studies of the University of London, the former Research School of Pacific and Asian Studies at the Australian National University, and the emergence of new Southeast Asian area studies programs and departments in both the People's Republic of China and Taiwan. There are plenty of other examples.

condition of employment (departments, institutes) instead of as a result of common effort (programs, communities)—will surely affect the form and content of area knowledge that they produce.

What Makes Comparative Area Studies Possible?

Which model is most useful for CAS? The answer depends on whether one focuses on the "area" or the "comparative." Speaking in general terms, programs and communities are best suited to infusing country and area knowledge into the disciplines. A Europeanist employed in a political science department with perhaps only one other active Europeanist, but who produces work that draws upon and contributes to European studies as a field,[7] has incentives to introduce European studies insights into the discipline of political science. These incentives, put bluntly, originate in career concerns: to obtain tenure, one might need letters from specialists in the region of interest, but the voting body on hiring, tenure, and promotion is almost always the entire disciplinary department comprised of mostly *not* Europeanists. As a result, the contribution of area studies is to provide background insights about world regions that are fodder for comparison ("Isn't it interesting how the European Union resembles American federalism?")[8] or for empirical testing of theoretical claims ("Carey and Shugart 1995, who worked mostly on Latin America, would not have predicted that Indonesia and the Philippines could be stable multiparty presidential democracies for more than two decades, as Bünte and Thompson 2018 show"). Such endeavors have a natural affinity for our understanding of CAS.

For producing area knowledge itself, by contrast, departments and institutes present a more attractive model. Career concerns (and for institutes, employment contracts) incentivize scholars to work within their area studies community first and foremost, with relatively less attention to disciplinary conventions and entirely different "circles of esteem" (Cribb 2005). Many Southeast Asianists affiliated with Southeast Asia programs view Kyoto University's Center for Southeast Asian Studies and the Australian National University's Coral Bell School of Asia and Pacific Affairs as the pinnacle

---

[7] Of course, there are also Europeanists who employ qualitative and/or quantitative data from one or more European countries, but who are uninterested in the broader European studies community. We hold such examples aside.

[8] Formalized, this type of comparison looks like Goodman 2019.

288 ADVANCING COMPARATIVE AREA STUDIES

of interdisciplinary scholarship on Southeast Asia. Even if scholars in these institutions have not sought to make the kind of general, context-free contributions to the social sciences and the humanities of others working in disciplinary departments have, their knowledge of specific countries and world regions is irreplaceable for area studies—and, viewed from the perspective of Asianists with regular disciplinary homes—refreshingly interdisciplinary in character.

When it comes to the production of area-specific knowledge, the case of European studies and the production of European studies differs from that of (South)(East) Asian studies. Southeast Asian studies departments do exist in some universities, and more general Asian studies departments are more common still. But as we noted above, departments of European studies are comparatively rare in the United States. What departments of German and departments of Slavic studies can produce is knowledge that conceptualizes the Germanic- and Slavic-speaking worlds *as areas themselves*, often in conversation broader European studies concerns, but not designed to make sense of Portugal or Turkey in the same way as they might approach Germany/Austria/Switzerland or Russia/Ukraine/Poland / former Yugoslavia.[9] When Europeans and North Americans produce academic departments that study themselves, they tend to reject the premise that an academic department could cover all of Europe. That European studies programs and communities *do* more frequently cover all of Europe (with the caveat that "all of Europe" is not a well-defined concept; see the discussion below) is an interesting feature of contemporary European studies, showing how the dominant notions of region differ according to institutional form.

As a result of the different affinities of programs/communities and departments/institutes for area-focused versus comparative work, CAS faces an institutional tension. The department/institute model is ideal for incentivizing area knowledge that can produce novel data and informed analyses within one world region. And the program and community models are ideal for infusing area knowledge into the disciplines. CAS requires area studies, but the institutional forms that encourage area studies are different

---

[9] Given the prominence of global communities of Spanish, Portuguese, and French speakers, no Department of Romance Studies could confine itself to the Romance-speaking countries of Europe (France, Italy, Portugal, Romania, Spain, together with parts of Belgium and Switzerland). Even the premise of a Department of Romance Europe seems odd, in a way that a Department of Germanic Studies that covers Austria, Denmark, Germany, Iceland, the Netherlands, Norway, Sweden, and parts of Switzerland, the UK, and Belgium would not.

from those that encourage the cross-regional comparisons that characterize CAS as a distinct mode of inquiry. Even in university communities that are fortunate enough to contain both area studies programs and area studies departments, the former do not align with the latter—there will not be a university with both a Department of Southeast Asian Studies and a Southeast Asian Studies Program, but rather only ones with (at best) both a Department of Asian Studies and a Southeast Asian Studies Program or vice versa.

Thus far, our focus has been on institutional structures and the incentives that they create for academic knowledge production. But incentives and tendencies are not hard constraints and laws. Plainly CAS *does* exist, and scholars who work in the CAS vein *do* thrive in many different university environments. Some scholars may view programs as their intellectual homes rather than their disciplinary departments; some scholars in area departments may seek to contribute to disciplinary conversations while shedding a critical eye on the world region after which their departmental home is named. The growth of CAS is prima facie evidence that institutional structures are not intellectual prisons.

Yet our interest—as scholars of Europe and Southeast Asia who have engaged in comparisons outside of these world regions—is in understanding what sorts of institutional models for area studies can facilitate CAS. Here we see CAS as facing an institutional tension that other qualitative comparative and mixed-methods research strategies do not. This is because CAS considers regions to be meaningful units that are not simply reducible to their component parts, and views area studies as a distinct field of inquiry. The challenges of fitting world regions into the organization chart of the modern university means that CAS also fits awkwardly into the landscape of area studies and the disciplines.

Does Area Studies as Practiced Make CAS Possible?

We turn now to interrogate the state of Southeast Asian studies and European studies in the current moment, to ask whether area studies as actually practiced—in programs, departments, institutes, and in broader communities—is compatible with CAS as its intellectual pioneers have conceptualized it. Our answer is a qualified no, although the qualifications are important and we remain optimistic. Drawing on our experiences working in European and Southeast Asian studies, we can identify two foundational questions about area studies to which CAS as an intellectual project must attend. Do our regions exist? And are there concepts, arguments, findings, and theoretical insights that emerge only from the study of the area rather than of the units that happen to be within it?

To preview our discussion, we use publication data from Google Scholar to examine how scholars understand area studies in the world regions. Specifically, we searched for the strings "southeast asia" "crisis" "area studies" and "europe" "crisis" "area studies," counting the number of publications in each of the five decades beginning 1970–1980 and ending 2010–2020. We then repeated the same searches, but without "crisis." This allows us to calculate, for each decade, the proportion of publications that uses "crisis" as a proportion of publications that use the terms "Europe" and "area studies," and the same for "Southeast Asia" and "area studies." We display trends over time in Figure 12.1.

We infer from Figure 12.1 that "crisis" is more commonly associated with Southeast Asia and area studies than Europe and area studies in published

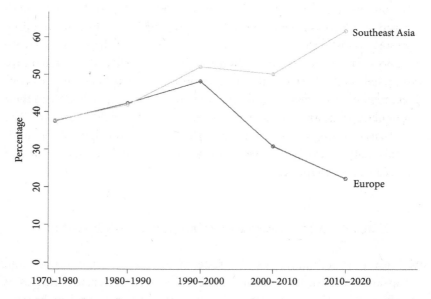

Figure 12.1 "Crisis" and Area Studies, Comparing Europe and Southeast Asia

Note: This figure plots the percentage of all publications mentioning Southeast Asia and area studies or Europe and area studies that also mention crisis. Data available from the authors.

academic research. We think it unlikely that these trends are driven by different types of real-world crises, as both Europe and Southeast Asia have experienced repeated region-wide and country-level crises during this entire time frame. But of course, such a quantitative approach can only provide suggestive evidence of differences in the state of area studies across these two regions. To understand these differences more fully, we examine how intellectual and political developments across the two regions have shaped area studies communities in the past fifty years.

What Is Southeast Asian Studies?

Many Southeast Asianists and Southeast Asian studies program wrestle with the difficult and still-unsettled question of how to define Southeast Asia as world region. The term is a neologism, one that emerged during World War II as part of the Japanese and later Allied conceptualization of the operational theaters of war (Emmerson 1984; McVey 1991). Quite naturally, there were earlier articulations of a general term for some of the lands and waters that today comprise Southeast Asia, including most notably the Chinese term *Nanyang*, which referred roughly to the South China / East Vietnam / West Philippines Sea region. But that term, and others like it, did not refer exactly and exclusively to the eleven sovereign states that comprise the region that the Association of Asian Studies labels as "Southeast Asia": Brunei, Cambodia, Indonesia, Laos, Malaysia, Myanmar, the Philippines, Singapore, Thailand, Timor-Leste, and Vietnam. And this is not surprising, as the peoples and histories of northern Myanmar have very little in common with the peoples and histories of eastern Indonesia aside from their geographical position (and even that is not very close: the distance from Mandalay to Jayapura in eastern Indonesia is about the same as London to Bishkek, or Berlin to Kinshasa). And what they do have in common with one another they also share with neighboring peoples, polities, and histories—all of which are decisively ruled out of the region of Southeast Asia.

The point is not just that it is hard to draw firm natural boundaries around Southeast Asia to find commonalities within the region and distinctions with its neighboring world regions. Rather, it is that Southeast Asian studies is highly conscious of the role of non–Southeast Asians in conceptualizing Southeast Asia as "an area," of the social constructedness of the region, and of the limits to intellectual inquiry that emerge from dividing Vietnam from

292 ADVANCING COMPARATIVE AREA STUDIES

China, Myanmar from India, and the Philippines from Taiwan (or from Latin America, for that matter). Every other world region faces a similar form of boundary trouble—does "the Middle East" properly include the Maghreb, Turkey, or Sudan? Does Latin America include French Guiana? Should the Caribbean be studied separately from Central America? But as Ashley Thompson (2012) eloquently observes, "The existential question—[what] is Southeast Asia?—has been constitutive of and essentially coterminous with the field of Southeast Asian Studies since its emergence after World War II."

Practically, however, Southeast Asia is a social fact. Southeast Asian studies programs in the United States do not cover Papua New Guinea, but political scientists who have never visited Myanmar or Thailand will naturally teach about Aung San Suu Kyi and Thaksin Shinawatra in their Southeast Asian politics courses. The Association for Southeast Asian Nations will someday include Timor-Leste "because it is in Southeast Asia," but it will never include Bangladesh, Sri Lanka, or Australia "because they are not."[10] In this way, Southeast Asia is a concept that does work in the world. In an epistemic sense, Southeast Asia exists, even if every introduction to Southeast Asian studies course probably begins by rehearsing the artificiality of the region, and by politely turning away well-meaning students who had assumed that "Southeast Asia" referred to South Korea or India.

The constructedness of Southeast Asian studies matters because of ongoing debates within critical Asian studies about the essential task of demolishing "colonial" concepts, of which Southeast Asia is one. For many, the question can be posed as "Should scholars of Asia continue to *act as if* Southeast Asia is a natural kind?" The alternative is to decenter Southeast Asia, to embrace different geographies such as the Indian Ocean world or the Sinosphere or the Indo-Pacific, or to encourage work on the countries, peoples, and histories within the region that simply does not require reference to Southeast Asia at all. One of us wrote a dissertation and later book, *Economic Crises and the Breakdown of Authoritarian Regimes: Indonesia and Malaysia in Comparative Perspective* (Pepinsky 2009), that made no reference to Southeast Asia at all even though it dealt almost exclusively with two Southeast Asian countries. As a concept in Southeast Asian studies, "Southeast Asia" *itself* does relatively little intellectual work in modern scholarship, except for as a convenient foil that helps to excite readers at the prospect

---

[10] Wilson (1975) discusses the early expansion of ASEAN, and the question of membership or other relationships between ASEAN and countries like Bangladesh, Sri Lanka, and Australia.

of boundary-crossing, the study of borderlands, and logics of circulation and migration that are currently de rigueur in the humanities and interpretive social sciences. A historian of Southeast Asia might actually find that CAS research that compares Southeast Asia qua Southeast Asia to a world region like Latin America is old-fashioned, even reactionary in its treatment of Southeast Asia as a natural kind worth comparing. Even seemingly banal truisms such as "Southeast Asia is a rice-growing region" are descriptively false if applied to the region as a whole; even anodyne observations such as "Southeast Asia lies between China and India" prove offensive in many professional contexts, because they define Southeast Asia as a residual space between two proper names. We conjecture that the trajectory of Southeast Asian areas studies in crisis, illustrated Figure 12.1, reflects both the crisis of area studies in general and the internal critique of Southeast Asia as an analytical concept in particular.

The picture we have painted of Southeast Asian might seem inconsistent with the observation that several important concepts and ideas have emerged from scholars working comparatively within and beyond Southeast Asian studies, from scholars who are known as Southeast Asianists. Although Southeast Asia is too big and diverse to form a natural kind, scholars working on large portions of what is understood as Southeast Asia have produced what could be understood as Southeast Asian area studies' findings. Some of these, such as the mandala polity (Tambiah 1977), describe state forms that were common in the region prior to the arrival of the Westphalian state system (Chong 2012). Others, such as the plural society (Furnivall 1956; see also the contribution by Erik Martinez Kuhonta to this volume), characterize challenges of late colonialism and early postcolonialism that resonate easily with other world regions within the Global South. "Zomia," coined by Willem van Schendel (2002) and popularized by James Scott (2009), describes an alternative conception of space that replaces flat maps with terrains and topographies that unite and divide portions of Southeast Asia with comparable portions of East and South Asia. Critical social scientists like Tania Li (2007) and Brenda Yeoh (1996) have used Southeast Asian case materials to draw linkages far beyond the region itself. And is there any greater example of CAS in action than Benedict Anderson's *Imagined Communities* (1983), wherein an Irishman born in Kunming uses insights gained from a lifetime of scholarship in three Southeast Asian countries to draw general lessons for nationalism the world over, especially Europe and the United States? No one can doubt that any of this scholarship is both comparative in scope and deeply engaged with the relevant literatures within Southeast Asian area studies.

These examples do indeed show that Southeast Asia contributes meaningfully to CAS—as, indeed, it should. Yet as intellectual trends are leading away from Southeast Asian area studies and in favor of deconstructing Southeast Asia as a concept and analytical category (Chua et al. 2019; Lewis 2010), we hypothesize that none of the scholars listed above would characterize what they are doing as "comparative area studies." Ascendent, instead, are terms like "Inter-Asia" and "Global Asia" and other such regional configurations in which the eleven countries of Southeast Asia occupy no distinct place (see, e.g., the new journal *Verge: Studies in Global Asias*; Chen and Hayot 2015).

The conclusion that we draw from this review of the contestedness of Southeast Asia is that internal debates about the ontological status of world regions matter for CAS. Our point is not to argue that Southeast Asia cannot, or will not, provide a foundation for insightful and generative CAS research that embraces the complexities of Southeast Asian area studies. Rather, we think that Southeast Asia illustrates some of the challenges of area studies as practiced, which have knock-on effects on how CAS conceptualizes the "area." And our experience working in Southeast Asian studies programs in interdisciplinary Southeast Asian studies obliges us to take seriously the internal challenges to the kind of area studies knowledge production that is so essential for making CAS work.

Does European Studies as Practiced Make CAS Possible?

One could characterize European studies as facing a problem that is the opposite of that which Southeast Asian studies faces. Whereas Southeast Asia was constructed and conceptualized as a region first by outsiders, European studies is an ongoing conversation of boundary-drawing among insiders. There are many delineations of "Europe" that conflict with one another; it is an inherently contested region, perhaps even more so than Southeast Asia, even though the idea of Europe (however defined) is older and more established than that of Southeast Asia. In the CAS approach to Europe, we identify at least three different organizational rationales for defining the region.

As with Southeast Asian studies, most European studies programs are interdisciplinary in orientation, organized around languages, literatures, and cultures. The same is true in cases where European studies is organized as a department. And yet the definition of Europe is contested in its own way. For example, is Russia part of Europe? If so, did it become part of Europe through early Swedish settlement, through dynastic intermarriage, or later through the world wars? Are the Baltic states at Europe's center, or on its periphery? Is Algeria, whose territory formerly included three *départements* of France (Oran, Algers, and Constantine), a "former part" of Europe? How European are the United States, Australia, New Caledonia, and the Dutch Antilles? If Israel and Armenia participate in the Eurovision Song Contest, to what extent might we also consider them a part of Europe? The challenge for configuring European studies as a world region is analogous to that of configuring Southeast Asia as a world region, but instead of the Southeast Asian example of non–Southeast Asians projecting a world region onto a heterogeneous mix of peoples and polities, European studies features Europe projecting itself outward.

These are not idle observations, because they delimit the scope of what European studies is. A definition of Europe that includes non-Christian-majority countries in the east rejects any analysis of European politics that locates the essence of Europe in Western Christendom. The political status of New Caledonia and Aruba is constitutive of the architecture of the contemporary French and Dutch states. A meaningful portion of European lawmaking, from the Schengen Agreement to the treaties that evolved toward the European Union, is about specifying the position of Europe's current and former overseas territories within the emerging architecture of a mostly continental Europe. European identity is affirmed, projected, and contested through cultural projects such as Eurovision: what constitutes a national symbol, which peoples may claim a European identity, and what political factors can lead to exclusion from that imagined community? (Spaziante 2021).

During the Cold War, dominant conceptualizations of Europe evolved to reflect geopolitical conditions. Specifically, the Cold War aligned western Europe, the British Isles, and Scandinavia with the United States, and eastern and parts of central Europe with the Soviet Union. The institutional structures of European studies, especially in the United States, evolved along with it. The University of Pittsburgh, for example, features a separate European Studies Center and a Center for Russian, East European, and Eurasian Studies; and Georgetown University has both a BMW Center for German and

European Studies and a Center for Eurasian, Russian, and East European Studies. There is no better illustration of the artificiality of such delineating of world areas than the post-1945 histories of Austria and Hungary, formerly united in a single empire, but subsequently divided as independent states between western and eastern Europe, respectively (as "central Europe" had no separate geopolitical status of its own). And even though the Cold War provided an organizing principle for distinguishing between two parts of the continent of Europe, nagging problems of defining even these world regions remained: neutral Finland, Western-aligned Turkey, and the Caucasus, among others.

Scholars of Southeast Asia can invoke the Association of Southeast Asian Nations as a template for "what Southeast Asia is." ASEAN emerged as a group of five noncommunist countries in the region, but it was seen as self-evident that the association's membership would expand (as it did after the collapse of the Cold War) to include communist Vietnam and nonaligned Myanmar, and it remains self-evident that ASEAN will expand to include Timor-Leste, but no further.[11]

In the European case, however, international organizations create more complexities than they resolve. There is no shortage of international organizations that bind "Europe" together in a variety of permutations. The regional grouping that is maximally inclusive—the Organisation for Security and Cooperation in Europe—reflects countries that *care about* Europe rather than just countries that *comprise* Europe, and hence includes Mongolia and Canada, among others. The Council of Europe (not to be confused with the European Council or the Council of the European Union) has forty-six member states, including Turkey and (until March 2022) Russia. The European Union includes twenty-seven members, but does not include Switzerland, Norway, Serbia, Albania, or the United Kingdom. The European Economic Area (EEA) created the EU's single market and includes non-EU member states like Iceland, Liechtenstein, and Norway. Switzerland participates in the single market not through EEA membership but through cooperation in the European Free Trade Association (EFTA). Turkey is also not part of the single market but does participate in the EU Customs Union. The Schengen Area—which enables free movement within

---

[11] Papua New Guinea, which is culturally and historically linked to Indonesian West Papua, has held ASEAN observer status—which implies that ASEAN membership is possible—for nearly fifty years.

the EU—also includes non-EU member states, like Monaco, Gibraltar, and EFTA members.

These challenges notwithstanding, the European Union Studies Association represents one influential regionally focused institution that stands in for a comprehensive conceptualization of most of western, central, northern, and southern Europe. And yet Brexit has produced an odd problem when delimiting the organization's focus: The UK had been part of EU studies because the UK was a member of the EU, but now EU studies must address the UK as a nonmember. And, for a professional organization centrally occupied with explaining the *institutions* of the EU, Norway or Switzerland are typically not part of the picture beyond their EU membership referendums, while waves of enlargement, for example, the A8 accession wave in 2004 (including Poland, Hungary, and the Baltic states) are treated as semiregions within a larger EU framework, with distinct political and economic characteristics.

Much like Southeast Asia studies, then, European studies faces the challenge of defining Europe as a region. But the challenges are decidedly different in character, a function of the different geopolitical and historical circumstances that led to the two regions' emergence as world regions in the academy. Just as some Southeast Asianists look to dismantle their region to better reflect the complex politics of regionalism in an interconnected world, many Europeanists look to hold their region together despite the many political challenges to pan-European regional that have emerged in recent years. The question for Southeast Asian studies is, *what* is Southeast Asia? The question for European studies is, *which* Europe?

One might respond by saying that European studies is different from Southeast Asia because Southeast Asia is a subregion, whereas Europe is a proper region on its own.[12] According to this line of reasoning, the correct comparison for Europe is Asia, and the correct comparison for Southeast Asian studies would be southern European studies or Scandinavian studies. This argument is unconvincing for two reasons. First, it suggests a political relevance for Asia as a unit that does not exist in global politics: there is no Asian Union, no Asian Economic Area, nor any Asian caucus in any multinational organization. Asia is invariably institutionalized according to its own regions (like ASEAN) or as part of an even larger cross-regional grouping (East Asia Summit, Asia-Pacific Economic

---

[12] We thank an anonymous referee for raising this objection.

Community, Shanghai Cooperation Organisation). Truly *Asian* organizations that encompass Asian countries from Yemen to Japan are rare and nearly irrelevant to global politics. Second, the Association for Asian Studies, the preeminent scholarly organization for Asian studies, is itself internally organized according to four regions within Asia (and does not cover western Asia at all). As a member of the AAS, one's voting rights and substantive representation are tied to a region like "South Asia" or "China and Inner Asia," and governance follows a consociational model in which executive authority rotates across the four area councils. This is entirely different from European studies organizations, whose internal organization is thematic or substantive. Although Western scholars may elide these differences in order to equate Europe with Asia writ large, this does not reflect the actual practice of Asian studies. Europe, like Southeast Asia, is the territories and islands located at one corner of the Eurasian landmass.

With these comparisons between European and Southeast Asian studies in mind, we are now in the position to ask whether European studies—as currently organized and institutionalized—produces "area knowledge" in the strict sense that we have defined it throughout this essay. We are once again skeptical that European studies departments and programs are structured in ways that encourage the production and accumulation of general European studies "area" knowledge. Nevertheless, for some conceptualizations of "Europe"—specifically western Europe, the European Union, and postsocialist Europe—there is cause for optimism.

The challenges for European area studies are analogous to those of Southeast Asia. Most Europeanists are experts in a subset of the countries that comprise Europe, trained to follow politics in a handful of countries (even if teaching responsibilities encompass the entire region). This makes Europe-wide area studies concepts relatively more challenging to identify, for the same reason that general Southeast Asian area studies concepts or patterns can be difficult for scholars trained to focus closely on one or two Southeast Asian countries.

Nevertheless, European area studies in the social sciences faces a relatively less difficult path than does Southeast Asian studies. Due to the relative abundance of primary source materials written in English or other widely spoken European languages, it is more common to find comparative works that cover large swaths of the region. One of us wrote a book, *Immigration and Membership Politics in Western Europe* (Goodman 2014), that identifies genuinely European (note: *not* European Union) policy challenges associated with the changing demography of Europe—alongside within-region variation.[13] Other work has profitably identified patterns in democratization that are common across—but unique to—the postsocialist world (Bunce 2000). And the European Union has presented most of the countries of northern, western, and southern Europe with a common set of institutional challenges and policy problems related to monetary cooperation, agriculture, and so forth. Indeed, the very process of European integration—and resistance to European integration—creates a series of genuinely regional political issues that are unique to the countries of Europe, specifically *because* they are the countries of Europe. And punctuated equilibrium in Europe may also forge new intraregional clusters, for instance, border versus interior countries during the 2015 refugee crisis, or the division between "southern sinners" and "northern saints" during the euro crisis (Matthijs and McNamara 2015). CAS is likely to find firmer empirical ground and a more accommodating institutional environment in the context of European studies than it finds in Southeast Asian studies.

Conclusion

Our application of CAS to CAS itself has identified some useful comparative insights on the intellectual production of area knowledge. Our main conclusion is that CAS encounters a productive dilemma. The institutional models that are best suited to protecting area studies are exactly those that are least amenable to comparisons across areas. And the institutional models that are best suited to encourage border-crossing comparative work are exactly those that are least amenable to deep engagement with the areas themselves. Recognizing that our institutional models for knowledge production play a large role in determining what knowledge is produced, we conclude that existing models may hinder the full development of CAS.

We nevertheless remain optimistic that a careful focus on institutional design, and a pragmatic approach to the continuing challenges facing traditional area studies, present opportunities for CAS to thrive. We believe that one way to resolve the institutional tensions inherent to the CAS enterprise is to design institutions that can support CAS on its own terms. GIGA

---

[13] Books of this form are rare in Southeast Asian studies. One exception is Slater 2010.

300 ADVANCING COMPARATIVE AREA STUDIES

and other institutions like it can play a foundational role in this enterprise by defending the area studies approach to comparative social inquiry, and also by providing the financial support, research infrastructure, and academic community required for CAS to flourish. It is fitting that GIGA hosted our workshop on CAS in a time when area studies continues to face persistence challenges, and it may well be that only institutions that explicitly set out to defend comparisons across area studies domains can produce the appropriate intellectual defense of CAS as a central part of the social scientist's methodological toolkit. We know that CAS is possible under current academic models, and we also know that collaborations among scholars from different regions is not a necessary precondition for CAS in practice. But building up CAS as an intellectual community will mean thinking through the constraints that existing academic structures create.

We offer two additional recommendations by way of conclusion. First, recall our observation that CAS normally is predicated on an already-existing body of area studies knowledge. In addition to defending *comparative* area studies, one constructive implication is that the CAS scholarly community might profit from defending *regular* area studies. And as CAS attempts to defend area studies from the political scientists who continually undermine it in favor of big theory and general inquiry (Bates 1996; Laitin 1995), perhaps it can also help to defend area studies from critical and postcolonial theorists who may wish to dismiss area studies as an inherently colonial project.

CAS might also take a different approach, however, to reconfigure our understanding of world areas along thematic lines. Here we see opportunities for collaboration between critics of traditional area studies and scholars who seek a greater role for CAS in contemporary social science. A flexible approach to areas, conceiving them as situational constructs relative to specific political issues or socioeconomic phenomena that generate particular research questions ("Indo-Pacific," "Theravada Buddhist Asia," "North Atlantic," "Francosphere," "Sahel," etc.), would avoid most of the challenges inherent to traditional conceptualizations of world regions. Much will be lost in de-emphasizing those traditional conceptions of area and region, but much may be gained from adopting new perspectives on how we configure the world around us.

We believe that this is probably the most constructive way for CAS to bend with the winds that are academic trends in area and regional studies. Rather than seeing internal challenges to Southeast Asia as also challenges to CAS,

PROGRAMS, DEPARTMENTS, CONSTRAINTS, OPPORTUNITIES   301

scholars developing CAS further might choose to see concepts like global or inter-Asia as reflecting the same underlying intellectual ambition that CAS does, to explore commonalities across world regions while also identifying flows and circulations among regions rather than seeing them as static and closed entities. Likewise, the profusion of institutional arrangements in Europe represents an opportunity for CAS to think flexibly about what comprises a cross-regional comparison, and how the work of establishing area studies insights can help to constitute the area in question.

Bibliography

Ahram, Ariel I., Patrick Köllner, and Rudra Sil, eds. 2018. *Comparative Area Studies: Methodological Rationales and Cross-Regional Applications*. New York: Oxford University Press.

Anderson, Benedict. 1983. *Imagined Communities: Reflections on the Origin and Spread of Nationalism*. London: Verso.

Bates, Robert H. 1996. Letter from the President: Area Studies and the Discipline. *APSA-CP: Newsletter of the APSA Organized Section in Comparative Politics* 7 (1): 1–2.

Bunce, Valerie. 2000. Comparative Democratization: Big and Bounded Generalizations. *Comparative Political Studies* 33 (6–7): 703–734.

Bünte, Marco, and Mark R. Thompson. 2018. Perilous Presidentialism in Southeast Asia? *Contemporary Politics* 24 (3): 251–265.

Carey, John M., and Matthew Soberg Shugart. 1995. Incentives to Cultivate a Personal Vote: A Rank Ordering of Electoral Formulas. *Electoral Studies* 14 (4): 417–439.

Chen, Tina, and Eric Hayot. 2015. Introducing Verge: What Does It Mean to Study Global Asias? *Verge: Studies in Global Asias* 1 (1): vi–xv.

Chong, Ja Ian. 2012. *External Intervention and the Politics of State Formation: China, Indonesia, and Thailand, 1893–1952*. New York: Cambridge University Press.

Cribb, Robert. 2005. Circles of Esteem, Standard Works, and Euphoric Couplets. *Critical Asian Studies* 37 (2): 289–304.

Emmerson, Donald K. 1984. "Southeast Asia": What's in a Name? *Journal of Southeast Asian Studies* 15 (1): 1–21.

Estévez-Abe, Margarita. 2005. Gender Bias in Skills and Social Policies: The Varieties of Capitalism Perspective on Sex Segregation. *Social Politics: International Studies in Gender, State & Society* 12 (2): 180–215.

Furnivall, J. S. 1956. *Colonial Policy and Practice: A Comparative Study of Burma and Netherlands India*. New York: New York University Press.

Goodman, Sara Wallace. 2014. *Immigration and Membership Politics in Western Europe*. New York: Cambridge University Press.

Goodman, Sara Wallace. 2019. Indexing Immigration and Integration Policy: Lessons from Europe. *Policy Studies Journal* 47 (3): 572–604.

Huat, Chua Beng, Ken Dean, Ho Engseng, Ho Kong Chong, Jonathan Rigg, and Brenda Yeoh. 2019. Area Studies and the Crisis of Legitimacy: A View from South East Asia. *South East Asia Research* 27 (1): 31–48.

Huntington, Samuel P. 1993. The Clash of Civilizations? *Foreign Affairs* 72 (3): 22–49.

Jackson, Peter A. 2003. Space, Theory, and Hegemony: The Dual Crises of Asian Area Studies and Cultural Studies. *Sojourn: Journal of Social Issues in Southeast Asia* 18 (1): 1–41.

Karp, Ivan. 1997. Does Theory Travel? Area Studies and Cultural Studies. *Africa Today* 44 (3): 281–295.

Laitin, David. 1995. Letter from the President: Hiring in Comparative Politics. *APSA-CP: Newsletter of the APSA Organized Section in Comparative Politics* 6 (1): 1–2.

Lewis, Martin W. 2010. Location Asia Pacific: The Politics and Practice of Global Division. In J. D. Goss and T. Wesley-Smith, eds. *Remaking Area Studies: Teaching and Learning Across Asia and the Pacific*. Honolulu: University of Hawai'i Press, 41–65.

Lewis, Martin W., and Karen Wigen. 1999. A Maritime Response to the Crisis in Area Studies. *Geographical Review* 89 (2): 161–168.

Li, Tania. 2007. *The Will to Improve: Governmentality, Development, and the Practice of Politics*. Durham, NC: Duke University Press.

Loriaux, Michael. 1999. The French Developmental State as Myth and Moral Ambition. In Meredith Woo-Cumings, ed. *The Developmental State*. Ithaca, NY: Cornell University Press, 235–275.

Matthijs, Matthias, and Kathleen McNamara. 2015. The Euro Crisis' Theory Effect: Northern Saints, Southern Sinners, and the Demise of the Eurobond. *Journal of European Integration* 37 (2): 229–245.

McVey, Ruth. 1991. Change and Continuity in Southeast Asian Studies. *Journal of Southeast Asian Studies* 26 (1): 1–9.

Mielke, Katja, and Anna-Katharina Hornidge. 2017. Introduction: Knowledge Production, Area Studies and the Mobility Turn. In Katja Mielke and Anna-Katharina Hornidge, eds. *Area Studies at the Crossroads: Knowledge Production after the Mobility Turn*. New York: Palgrave Macmillan US, 3–26.

Pepinsky, Thomas B. 2009. *Economic Crises and the Breakdown of Authoritarian Regimes: Indonesia and Malaysia in Comparative Perspective*. New York: Cambridge University Press.

Pepinsky, Thomas B. 2020. What's the "Area" in Comparative Area Studies? *Qualitative and Multi-Method Research* 17–18 (1): 22–26.

Scott, James C. 2009. *The Art of Not Being Governed: An Anarchist History of Upland Southeast Asia*. New Haven: Yale University Press.

Skocpol, Theda. 1979. *States and Social Revolutions: A Comparative Analysis of France, Russia, and China*. New York: Cambridge University Press.

Slater, Dan. 2010. *Ordering Power: Contentious Politics and Authoritarian Leviathans in Southeast Asia*. New York: Cambridge University Press.

Solingen, Etel. 2007. Pax Asiatica Versus Bella Levantina: The Foundations of War and Peace in East Asia and the Middle East. *American Political Science Review* 101 (4): 757–780.

Spaziante, Lucio. 2021. "So Disarmingly European": Eurovision Song Contest and the European Identity. In Francesco Mangiapane and Tiziana Migliore, eds., *Images of Europe: The Union Between Federation and Separation*. Cham, Switzerland: Springer International Publishing, 185–194.

Szanton, David L., ed. 2002. *The Politics of Knowledge: Area Studies and the Disciplines*. Berkeley: University of California Press.

Tambiah, Stanley J. 1977. The Galactic Polity: The Structure of Traditional Kingdoms in Southeast Asia. *Annals of the New York Academy of Sciences* 293 (1): 69–97.

Thompson, Ashley. 2012. Review of Sheldon Pollock, The Language of the Gods in the World of Men: Sanskrit, Culture, and Power in Premodern India. *Bryn Mawr Review of Comparative Literature* 10 (1): 1–13. https://repository.brynmawr.edu/bmrcl/vol10/iss1/1.

van Schendel, Willem. 2002. Geographies of Knowing, Geographies of Ignorance: Jumping Scale in Southeast Asia. *Environment and Planning D: Society and Space* 20 (6): 647–668.

Wilson, Dick. 1975. Will Southeast Asia Collaborate? The Future of Asean. *Antioch Review* 33 (2): 33–49.

Yeoh, Brenda. 1996. *Contesting Space in Colonial Singapore: Power Relations and the Urban Built Environment*. New York: Oxford University Press.

13

Comparative Area Studies in the Great Brain Race

Institutional Legacies and Programmatic Innovation in the Global Age

Ariel I. Ahram and Connie Stovall

Introduction

The twenty-first century has inaugurated a new era of global competition and engagement in research and higher education. This "great brain race," as Ben Wildavsky (2012) terms it, runs on many tracks. Outwardly, it entails competition to attract students, faculty, and funding from around the world. Inwardly, it means internationalization at home, developing training and research that reflects, explains, and contributes to an increasingly interconnected global system (Beelen and Jones 2015; Knight 2012, 35).

Yet, amid this race, uncertainty looms over area studies, the primary vehicle for social scientific and humanistic inquiry about foreign cultures and societies. On one hand, the crises that beset area studies in the 1980s and 1990s have mercifully abated (Rafael 1999). Friendly critiques have replaced jeremiads, indictments, and obituaries (Clowes and Bromberg 2016; Woods 2016; Anderson 2016; Chansa-Ngavej and Lee 2017; Hutt 2019; Mielke and Hornidge 2017; Milutinovic 2019; Houben 2017; Duller 2015). On the other hand, the epistemological foundations of area studies remain inchoate. Some scholars propose reasserting the linkages between humanities and social sciences through interpretivism (Hodgett and James 2018; Rhodes and Hodgett 2021). Others champion a distinctly social-science-driven model of area studies that furthers the distance with languages and literature (Beissinger 2020). Compounding the intellectual dissensus, administrators charged with leading the internationalization process often treat area studies

---

Ariel I. Ahram and Connie Stovall, *Comparative Area Studies in the Great Brain Race*. In: *Advancing Comparative Area Studies*. Edited by: Ariel I. Ahram, Patrick Köllner, and Rudra Sil, Oxford University Press. © Oxford University Press (2025). DOI: 10.1093/oso/9780197809365.003.0013

304 ADVANCING COMPARATIVE AREA STUDIES

with indifference or skepticism. To them, area studies appears intellectually atavistic and institutionally ill-suited to meet twenty-first-century challenges (Brustein 2007, 384).

This chapter considers the institutional and administrative arrays that support area studies today and that could bolster comparative area studies (CAS) in the future. CAS was first conceived at the German Institute for Global and Area Studies (GIGA) in the mid-2000s (Basedau and Köllner 2007). GIGA consolidated multiple freestanding area studies research centers operating in Hamburg into a unified entity. Since then, CAS has played a key part in the effort to revive area studies, especially modes that center on social sciences. CAS seeks to

(i) balance deep sensitivity to context in each of the locales being examined with the use of some variant of the comparative method to surface causal linkages that are portable across world regions; and (ii) engage ongoing research and scholarly discourse in two or more area studies communities against the backdrop of more general concepts and theoretical debates within a social science discipline. (Köllner et al. 2018, 3)

CAS builds upon the traditional area studies approaches that focus on single country or intraregional comparison. CAS adds consideration of interregional comparisons or larger geographic spans and especially cross-regional comparison, comparing entities across different regional settings. CAS avoids the contextual excision and "flattened" perspectives that are too common in large-N cross-national comparison (Ahram 2011; Ahmed 2022; Kreuzer 2023). It remains focused on core macro-scale social phenomenon of political inquiry, like regimes of representation, political order, economic growth, policy processes, and social movements (Pepinsky 2019). The progress of CAS is bolstered by renewed interest in methodologies that have long been mainstays of the area studies tradition but seemed obsolete in face of quantification and experimental modes of research (Beissinger 2020; Woods 2016). These include single-country studies (Pepinsky 2019), subnational comparison (Snyder 2001; Sellers 2019), and paired comparison (Slater and Ziblatt 2013; Gisselquist 2014). Even sectors of economics, a discipline that seemed to have divorced from area studies long ago, show interest in reconciliation (Ranis 2009; Kuran 2018, 2012). But area studies has always been a collaborative project, not just the work of an individual scholar. CAS, likewise is "often beyond the scope of single researchers and in need of broad institutional agendas to create supportive frameworks" for CAS (Huotari and Rüland 2018, 102). CAS thus provides a blueprint for broader administrative and institutional design, how to organize programs and curricula devoted to global and international affairs.

This chapter examines how different institutional designs enable or inhibit the collaborative pursuit of CAS. Its perspective is admittedly limited. Ironically for a piece about international studies, the chapter's main focus is on the progress of area studies within the United States and interaction of areas studies centers, institutes, and disciplinary departments. These organs do not have the same endowments and experiences as GIGA. Yet CAS offers unique programmatic value for internationalization of higher education. Making this model work requires reimagining and repurposing centers, departments, and other administrative infrastructure interact to new and broader ends.

Area Studies as an American Institutional Project

The internationalization of research and education, John Heyl and Joseph Tullbane argue, necessarily derive from the local history and culture of the initiating institutions. Since *global* and *local* are often housed in distinct disciplines and make competing claims on campus budgets, making links between them often requires a special kind of vision (Heyl and Tullbane 2012, 115). The prospects for CAS on American shores are inevitably bound up in the cycle of growth, crisis, and regression that has characterized area studies in the United States.

The American academy accreted some of the traditions of European orientalists as early as the 1800s. It was not until the post–World War II era that area studies solidified. Cold War competition spurred the US government to train specialists in the histories, cultures, and languages of disparate parts of the developing world. The National Defense Education Act and Title VI, which funded the Foreign Languages Area Studies (FLAS) program, served as the fiscal backbone for area studies centers (ASCs). This was part of a larger democratization and expansion of American higher education (Engerman 2015; Szanton 2004).

A summary of these accomplishments comes from a study by Richard Lambert, conducted on behalf American Academy of Political and Social Sciences in the early 1970s. Lambert, a professor and director the South Asia

Center at University of Pennsylvania and onetime president of the Association for Asian Studies, did a remarkably thorough job of data collection involving questionnaires, site visits, and interviews. Lambert identified some three hundred ASCs across the country. The federal government sought to avoid funding only the august institutions of the East Coast, where area studies-cum-orientalist traditions were already entrenched. Instead, there was a deliberate effort to disperse area studies among a variety of larger, public, and land grant universities across the country. Still, only a fraction of the three hundred ASCs received federal moneys (although many had applied unsuccessfully).

Lambert was cognizant of the tension between area studies and disciplines. As he pointed out, area studies typically involved costly and difficult training in language and culture and extended time abroad. Disciplinary training, in comparison, was often conducted within the physical bounds of university labs and buildings. But Lambert doubted that these differences posed an insurmountable intellectual barrier to individual scholars. He wondered why "scholars become less 'disciplinary' when they add competence with respect to another area of the world and concentrate their research and teaching there" (Lambert 1973, 4).

The tension was less in the minds of scholars than in the administrative and institutional configuration of the universities that employ them. Lambert described two implicit models of area studies programs:

> The first focused on the training of a generalist who was completely familiar with the area he studies from a wide variety of disciplinary perspectives and fully competent in its languages. He was the academic equivalent of the "old hand." The other models saw area and language competences as supplemental skills, difficult and time consuming to acquire, but basically a graft onto a scholar firmly rooted in his discipline. Implicit in the first model is the notion that area studies is a useful way to organize knowledge, and that consequently, permanent organizations need to be built on campus both to conduct instruction in the new fashion and to promote the growth of an interdisciplinary corpus of knowledge. In the second model, language and area studies on the campus are seen as a temporary coalition of scholars struggling to make a place within their disciplines for research and teaching on the areas of the world that interest them and to provide for their common use the language learning, library, overseas fellowships, and other scholarly overhead resources that meet their special needs. As viewed

through this second model, once the needs have been met the coalition may disappear. Some programs have tried to realize both models at once, but ... by and large, the second model fits most naturally into the university context and tends to prevail. (Lambert 1973, 5)

The structure of universities constrains the agency of individual scholars. This is not about the desires, inclinations, or abilities of a single scholar. Some scholars—perhaps our most important (Weiss and McElwee 2021)—manage to contribute significantly to both area studies and to disciplines. But they are, by definition, exceptional. Disciplines, after all, are about establishing and maintaining internal order and cohesion (Jacobs 2014; Abbott 2010). In other words, disciplines set intellectual priorities and values and provided a practical rubric for how to achieve them. Insofar as American universities came to be organized around disciplinary departments, it was the disciplines that held the commanding academic heights. They controlled the workflow and the budget. They conferred doctoral degrees. They decided key questions, such as whether to require students achieve language competency. They held the preponderance of tenure-track lines. And this internal organization of individual universities is extrapolated outward. Studies of peer-review panels for grants highlight how researchers using interdisciplinary approaches have to satisfy multiple standards of excellence at once, a kind of intellectual double jeopardy (Lamont 2009, 202–211). For most scholars, most of the time, the optimal strategy was to stay in your disciplinary lane (Rhoten and Parker 2004).

The situation is more complicated today because the financial precariousness that affects US high education, including—and perhaps especially—area studies. The halcyon days of federal funding are over. Data collected by the National Humanities Alliance show a steady decline in funding for area studies over the last decade (Table 13.1). This decline is especially significant for national resource centers (NRCs) (Table 13.2). NRCs are the main federally funded organs for language training, public outreach, and master's and undergraduate degrees. They also serve as focal points for faculty engagement.

There are some important caveats to these budget data. First, it is important to note that is covers only federal Title VI money. It remains true today, as Lambert noted some half century ago, that many universities adopted area studies without federal support, often with funding from private philanthropies. Second, the impact of these cuts

Table 13.1 Change in US Federal Funding for Area Studies Through Title VI

	2011–13	2014–18	2020 (estimate)	Decade change
No. of NRCs	127	100	96	−24%
NRC budget	$33.7 million	$22.7 million	$22.7 million	−33%
No. of FLAS awarded	126	108	104	−17%
FLAS budget	$25.3 million	$31.0 million	$30.8 million	+21%
Total	$59.1 million	$53.8 Million	$53.6. million	−9%

Table 13.2 US Federal Funding for NRCs, 2011–2021

	2011–13	2014–18	2020 (estimate)	(2011–21)
Africa	$3,200,000	$2,370,000	$2,365,500	−26%
Canada	$541,000	$425,000	$425,000	−21%
East Asia	$5,475,000	$3,467,200	$3,588,482	−34%
International	$2,650,000	$1,655,000	$1,652,000	−38%
Latin America	$5,075,000	$3,482,017	$3,482,017	−31%
Mideast	$5,075,000	$3,375,000	$3,400,800	−33%
Russia/Eurasia	$4,393,875	$2,605,000	$2,491,145	−43%
South Asia	$2,675,000	$1,906,340	$1,921,234	−28%
Southeast Asia	$2,025,000	$1,898,850	$1,858,929	−8%
W. Europe	$2,650,000	$1,558,000	$1,558,000	−41%

was born unevenly in terms of area. Russian and western European studies were the most scathed, Southeast Asia, Canada, and South Asia far less so.

Qualitative examination can help explain how area studies has coped with budget austerity. Mark Beissinger describes how the traditional notion of the area studies center inhabited by Lambert's "old hand" have been eclipsed by more discipline and problem-driven approaches to area studies. These approaches are oriented less toward deepening knowledge of culture and place than using area knowledge to address theoretical or practical puzzles. Beissinger puts it personally: "I am a political scientist who works on the Eurasian region. Or perhaps I am a Eurasianist who works within the grammar of Political Science. I am not exactly sure." This confusion is not debilitating. Rather, it is "a very good thing. It represents the ways in which Area Studies traverses the variety of boundaries by which we organize the production of knowledge and interpenetrates other forms of knowledge" (Beissinger 2020, 130–131).

This uncertainty, although perhaps stimulating for individual scholars, can exacerbate the administrative tensions within area studies communities. The turn to disciplinary and problem-driven area studies in many cases shifts resources away from ASCs and toward new initiatives in international, global, or ethnic/diasporic studies (Ludden 2000; Hu-DeHart 1993). Thus, the challenges of area studies are intrinsic to the deeper crisis in humanities training in the American academia. With less money and attention devoted to the study of languages and literature, the knock-on effects for area studies could be severe (Reitter and Wellmon 2021).

The collaborative work of Mitchell Stevens, Cynthia Miller-Idriss, and Seteny Shami (henceforth, SMS) provide insights into how ASCs in the United States have managed the transition through apparent budgetary stress. SMS and their collaborators retread Lambert's steps. They, too, met with provosts, deans, directors, administrators, and faculty. In some cases, they likely sat in the same offices as Lambert had. Their findings echo Lamberts, especially regarding the relative subordination of ASCs and their financial precarity (Shami and Miller-Idriss 2016; Friedman and Miller-Idriss 2015; Stevens et al. 2018).

Yet this subordination is not necessarily a reason for pessimism. Area studies was never supposed to be a dominant intellectual paradigm akin to the disciplinary pursuits of the social sciences and humanities. ASCs, like other centers, institute, initiatives, and assorted "nondepartments" play an important catalytic role in the university ecosystem (Lattuca 2001; Jacobs 2014). The liminality of ASCs contributes to their dynamism and entrepreneurialism. These centers are "unconstrained by the status and evaluation regimes of disciplines house and convey a wide range of interdisciplinary activity . . . faculty and students participate in disciplinary departments and interdisciplinary not-departments simultaneously. The entire enterprise is predicated on this simultaneity" (Stevens et al. 2018, 81).

ASCs practice the proverbial "stone soup" techniques. The centers alone offer only a handful of cross-listed courses and some non-tenure-track appointments. Their travel funds and fellowship moneys fluctuate. Their most important roles are in convening and co-sponsoring a range of activities that bring otherwise disparate, isolated, and insular units of the university together. ASCs can also quickly adjust their programming,

310 ADVANCING COMPARATIVE AREA STUDIES

curricula, and hiring to remain current and contemporary. ASCs maneuver quicker than inherently conservative, often glacial, disciplinary departments. In this respect, ASCs complement—rather than compete—with disciplinary efforts.

Interestingly, universities often seek to harness the dynamism. Places like Georgetown's School of Foreign Service, Tuft's Fletcher School of Law and Diplomacy, and Johns Hopkins's School of Public and International Affairs remain exemplars of the beneficial relationship between area studies and disciplinary departments housed in the same organizational unit. The universities of Oklahoma and Indiana launched similar interdisciplinary and cross-regional colleges and schools in the early 2010s (King 2015; Juergensmeyer 2018).

A disciplinary-driven approach to area studies concords with what Rudra Sil describes as the division of labor within the social sciences (Sil 2000). Area studies holds a lower status position relative to the nomothetic-oriented disciplines, but this does not render them institutionally moot. Area studies is uniquely situated to respond to policy demands, the need for understanding the politics and society of other countries (Avey and Desch 2014; Avey et al. 2022). This may explain why the US Defense Department has emerged to fill some of the holes left in international education that recent cuts have made (King 2015). Moreover, area studies is essential for collection of new data and observations, providing the ultimate—and crucial—empirical test. As Jorge Dominquez put it:

> Scholars interested in the study of politics somewhere would value the particularities of that "somewhere" as they frame the questions, hypotheses, and research instruments and procedures that they will employ . . . [These scholars] have read, pondered, internalized wherever appropriate, and otherwise learned in various ways from a wide array of fellow scholars who have worked in other "somewhere" with different research instruments and procedures and contrary hypotheses or analytic frameworks. (Cited in Hutt 2019, 24)

Area studies is indispensable because, as economist Robert Solow puts it, data are expensive and theory cheap (Solow 1997, 57).

Administration, Curriculum, and Research: A Foundation for CAS?

Institutional tensions surrounding area studies in the United States have constrained the progress of CAS on American shores. Some of the early adopters of CAS in America testify to the institutional double bind. Amel Ahmed discusses how regional studies organizations like Latin American Studies Association or the Middle East Studies Association and disciplinary training modes establish incentive structures that "silo off" opportunities for cross-regional engagement (Ahmed 2020, 9). Ryan Saylor describes political scientists as too often "sequestered" from valuable opportunities to engage with area studies (Saylor 2020, 2). Roselyn Hsueh describes the difficulty of finding a "thriving, growing community of likeminded academics" (Hsueh 2020, 12). Sara Wallace Goodman and Thomas Pepinsky discuss the divergent goals of humanities and social science scholars within area studies, even if they focus on the same region (Pepinsky and Goodman in this volume).

A granular examination of how area studies and ASCs fit within the broader impetus for higher education internationalization can further detail institutional constraints and possibly elucidate opportunities for CAS. Internationalization has multiple dimensions, encompassing the administration of internationally oriented centers, the introduction of global topics in educational curricula, and the orientation of research toward international or global themes (Beelen and Jones 2015; Godwin and de Wit 2019). The following sections explore how well each of these dimensions might support CAS's model for cross-regional research.

CAS and the Internationalization of Administration

If CAS's key objective is to promote comparisons that transcend traditional area studies boundaries, a key administrative question is whether ASCs are located in close enough proximity to accomplish such research. There is no constructed hierarchy in the relationship between ASCs, unlike the relationship between departments and centers. It makes no sense to argue, for example, that a Middle East center is inherently more valuable than a Latin American center. Yet institutional and bureaucratic agendas still shape the

312 ADVANCING COMPARATIVE AREA STUDIES

Table 13.3 US Universities with Federally Funded Area Centers, 1960

Number of centers	University
3 N = 3	Cornell, Harvard, Michigan
2 N = 7	Berkeley, UCLA, Chicago, Columbia, Hawaii, Univ. of Pennsylvania, Texas, Wisconsin
1 N = 0	Arizona, Colorado, Duquesne, Fordham, Howard, Illinois, Indiana, Iowa State, Johns Hopkins, Kansas, Michigan State, New York Univ., Pittsburgh, Portland State, Princeton, Southern California, Stanford, Utah, Washington, Yale

incentives for scholarly pursuit. The key processes affecting an individual scholar's choice may pertain instead to opportunities for linkage and brokerage. Jonathan Friedman and Elizabeth Anderson Worden describe ASCs at American universities as trading zones. Exchange is a function of proximity, visibility, and access. Spatial layouts turn out to be especially important. One administrator implicitly answered Beissinger's confusion, stating that at her institution "people don't have to choose whether they are a political scientist or a Middle East specialist because all they have to do is run up and down the stairs" (Friedman and Worden 2016, 138). Yet this statement perhaps overestimated the faculty's cardiovascular fitness. In fact, ASCs have resisted relocating to buildings at the edges of campuses, even if these facilities are more expansive and modern.

The co-location of ASCs can facilitate cross-regional research by providing a physical and intellectual venue where area specialists can convene. The more centers cluster, the greater the chance for cross-regional engagement. This clustering, in a sense, relaxes the structural barriers that keep individual scholars in their lane.

In this regard, there is some good news to tell. In 1960, at the beginning of the area studies boom in the United States, thirty universities hosted a federally funded area studies center (Table 13.3). Of these, only Cornell, Harvard, and Michigan had more than two such centers. Most research in area studies was conducted in relative institutional isolation, toggling between department and area studies center.

Things today are much more hospitable to CAS and its vision of interregional and cross-regional research. By 2010 forty universities hosted or cohosted federally funded NRCs. Sixteen of these universities hosted four

COMPARATIVE AREA STUDIES IN THE GREAT BRAIN RACE   313

or more area centers, as shown in Table 13.4. The latest data from 2018 show that this clustering effect is still strong, despite overall budget cuts (Table 13.5). Nine universities host four or more centers. The University of California, Berkeley, and University of Wisconsin are area studies mammoths, each with eight centers.

Table 13.6 shows a correlation matrix of the different area centers. South and Southeast Asian centers, for instance, are strongly correlated and often

Table 13.4 US Universities with NRCs, 2010

Number of centers	University
7–8	Berkeley, Wisconsin
N = 2	
4–6	Chicago, Columbia, Harvard, Illinois, Indiana, Kansas, Michigan, North Carolina, North Carolina / Duke, Ohio State, Univ. of
N = 14	Pennsylvania, Washington, Yale
2–3	Arizona, Cornell, Florida, Georgetown, Hawaii, Michigan State, Minnesota, New York Univ., Pittsburgh, Stanford, Texas, Utah /
N = 12	Brigham Young
1	Boston Univ., Colorado, Florida International / Univ. of Miami, Maine
N=12	/ SUNY Plattsburgh, New Mexico, Oregon, Portland State, Syracuse, Tulane, Vanderbilt, Virginia, Washington / Western Washington

Table 13.5 US Universities with NRCs, 2018

Number of centers	University
7–8	Berkeley, Wisconsin
N = 2	
4–6	Columbia, Illinois, Michigan, North Carolina, Univ. of Pennsylvania, Texas, Washington
N = 7	
2–3	Arizona, Chicago, Cornell, Florida, George Washington, Georgetown, Harvard, Hawaii, Kansas, New York Univ., North Carolina / Duke,
N = 17	Ohio State, Pittsburgh, Stanford, Utah/Brigham Young, Wisconsin at Milwaukee, Yale
1	Arizona State, Boston Univ., Florida International, Georgia Tech /
N = 12	Georgia State, Howard, Maine / SUNY Plattsburgh, Minnesota, Northern Illinois, Penn State, Tulane, Vanderbilt, Western Washington

Table 13.6 Correlation Matrix of NCRs in 2018 (Excluding Canada Centers)

	Africa	Easia	Internl	Lamerica	Mideast	Russia	Sasia	Seasia	Europe
Africa	1								
Easia	.0453	1							
Internl	.138	.1666	1						
Lamerica	.1325	.0237	−.114	1					
Mideast	−.012	.3781*	−.0364	.0214	1				
Russia	.2359	.3475*	.1739	.0749	.1618	1			
Sasia	.138	.2939	.2137	.013	.3509*	.3246*	1		
Seasia	.0314	.2371	.0933	−.0548	.0174	.2196	.5897*	1	
Europe	.3752*	.2254	.1739	.0749	.2855	.4222*	.1739	.061	1

* Correlation > .3.

COMPARATIVE AREA STUDIES IN THE GREAT BRAIN RACE   315

co-located. European and Russian/Eurasia Centers (which suffered the most dramatic cuts in the last decade) were also closely tied. Equally significant is the stark disassociation of Latin American centers from other regional centers. Latin America studies is, at least institutionally, an island unto itself.[1] Also noteworthy is that these data account only for federally funded centers. Universities can and do run ASCs without federal support. Some institutions that host only one or two NRCs may still get the synergistic benefits from the addition of nonfederal centers as well.

CAS and the Internationalization of Curricula

Beside the co-location of ASCs, curricular internationalization is an important component for the progress of CAS. Cross-regional engagement requires opportunities for training. Introductory level courses in regional languages, history, and culture are critical components of area studies training (Morris 1998; MacPherson 2015). In this respect, CAS stands athwart the tendency in nomothetic social sciences, where proper nouns are elided for abstract categories (Katzenstein 2001).

Here again the patterns of curricular internationalization at top American universities favor CAS. Using the Teaching, Research, and International Policy (TRIP) project's definition of the top twenty-five international relations programs (Maliniak 2020), we can examine the extent to which curricula contain area studies content. Data were collected using available online course rosters. Cross-listed courses were included if they were accepted as part of the graduate curriculum in political science. The coding is binary. An institution is coded as offering a particular area if it has at least one course devoted to that area or a country in that area. This means that a university is coded as "1" positive for East Asia if it offers a course on Japan, China, any other Asia Pacific country.

All of these top programs offered at least one graduate-level course dedicated specifically to at least one region, as shown on Table 13.7. The modal number among these top programs was seven area/regions (out of eight area/regions). The most common area studies graduate courses covered the

---

[1] It is worth noting that Pepinsky's survey of single-country studies notes the relative overrepresentation of Latin American (and western European) cases. Pepinsky (2019, 200–201). Contrast with Kurzman (2017) and Martz (1990).

Middle East, western Europe, and East Asia. South Asia and Russia and the former Soviet Union were the least common.

Overall, this shows that area studies remains an embedded component of most international relations graduate programs in the United States. The overlap between these top programs and federally funded NRCs is not coincidental. Yet having an NRC does not necessarily translate into a social science curriculum amendable to area studies. Some universities have robust ASCs without federal funding. Different institutions devote different levels of attention and room in their curricula for area studies. Wisconsin has the second largest number of NCR centers of any university in the United States but offers graduate-level social science courses explicitly covering only western Europe, Africa, Latin America, and the Middle East. Cornell offers graduate-level courses in every region save Russia.

CAS and the Internationalization of Research

Another important role for ASCs is as hubs for research and scholarship. Bibliometric data-tracing publications and grant proposals suggest that researchers affiliated with same centers on campus are more likely to collaborate (Biancani et al. 2018; Yang et al. 2021). If centers are not the brokers per se, they are at least the meeting house where individual researchers can converge to build collaborative research relationships outside the boundaries of normal disciplinary departments. Traditional area studies focuses on catalyzing collaboration among researchers within the same center. This is a kind of bonding capital that occurs within an ASC. CAS requires an additional element of bridging ties that facilitates collaborative researchers *across* different ASCs.

A preliminary probe as to the role of ASCs in internationalizing research comes from examining bibliometric data from Cornell. Cornell is a good case because the university has invested especially heavily in area studies. Cornell has seven ASCs or programs: Institute for European Studies (CIES), Latin American and Caribbean Studies (LACS), Africana Studies and Research Center (ASRC), South Asia Program (SAP), Southeast Asia Program (SEAP), East Asia Program (EAP), and Comparative Muslim Societies Program (CMSP).

Table 13.7 Offering of Graduate Area Studies Courses in Top International Relations Departments in the United States

	ME_grad	Russia_grad	Africa_grad	LA_grad	EA_grad	sEA_grad	Sasia_grad	WEUR_grad	TOTAL
Harvard	1	1	1	1	1	0	0	1	6
Princeton	1	0	1	0	0	0	0	0	2
Stanford	1	1	1	1	1	0	0	1	6
Columbia	1	1	1	1	1	0	1	1	7
Chicago	1	0	1	0	1	0	1	1	5
Yale	1	1	0	1	1	0	1	1	6
UC San Diego	0	0	0	1	0	0	0	1	2
MIT	1	0	0	0	0	0	0	0	2
Michigan	1	1	0	0	0	1	0	0	3
UC Berkeley	0	0	1	1	1	0	1	1	5
Georgetown	1	1	1	1	1	0	1	1	7
Cornell	1	0	1	1	1	1	1	1	7
Ohio State	0	0	0	0	1	0	0	1	2
Johns Hopkins SAIS	1	1	1	1	1	1	1	1	8
George Washington	1	1	1	1	1	1	1	1	8
American Univ.	0	0	0	1	0	0	0	0	1
Duke	1	0	1	0	0	0	0	1	3
NYU	1	0	0	0	1	1	0	0	3
Tufts	1	1	1	1	1	0	1	1	7
Minnesota	1	1	1	1	1	1	0	1	7
Wisconsin	1	0	1	1	0	0	0	1	4
UCLA	1	1	1	1	1	0	1	1	7
Total	18	11	15	15	16	6	10	17	7

We extract citation data from Elsevier Scopus database for all researchers associated with the centers as of 2020 and retrieve citation data covering the years 2010 to 2020. We then export the data to VOSViewer, a visual bibliographic network-mapping software tool. VOSViewer also enables users to see coauthor networks more readily, both at the researcher and institutional level. Network maps are made up of items, in this case the researchers themselves. Each item is connected by links that represent coauthorship collaboration. Only one link can exist between two discrete items, but all links have a strength associated with it. In the case of coauthorship, the strength of the link is indicative of the number of publications coauthored between the two authors. The size of the items can be adjusted to be weighted for number of links, total link strength, documents, and citations. Because the interest here is in coauthorship as a mode of collaboration, weight for item size is attributed to links rather than documents. In other words, the larger the circle, the greater the *collaborative density* per researcher. The distance between items (colored circles with labels) and clusters communicates their relatedness.[2]

Each center is represented in two graphs (Figures 13.1–13.7). The first graph (labeled a) shows the network map for the file for all coauthorship collaborations, regardless of affiliation. A researcher who authored work but did not collaborate is represented by a stand-alone dot, often at the periphery of the map. The second graph (labeled b) shows the network map for the file showing only collaborations within Cornell. The collaborators are listed with ASC affiliation. A visual identification of bonding collaboration (intra-ASC) and bridging collaboration (inter-ASC) comes from the relative density of these figures, as shown in Figures 13.1a and 13.1b, 13.2a and 13.2b, 13.3a and 13.3b, 13.4a and 13.4b, 13.5a and 13.5b, 13.6a and 13.6b, 13.7a and 13.7b. Summary statistics for each center are presented in Table 13.8.

---

[2] While Scopus presents users with the one of the largest proprietary databases and bibliographic data set available with substantial author profile disambiguation, it does not include the entire universe of academic output. Notoriously, databases like Scopus and Web of Science do not cover some humanities and social science publications as well, especially if those publications are smaller, do not have digital content, or do not have digital object identifier (DOI). This limitation naturally then skews visualizations towards researchers who are publishing in STEM or more prestigious publications in the social sciences and humanities. See Martín-Martín et al. (2021).

COMPARATIVE AREA STUDIES IN THE GREAT BRAIN RACE   319

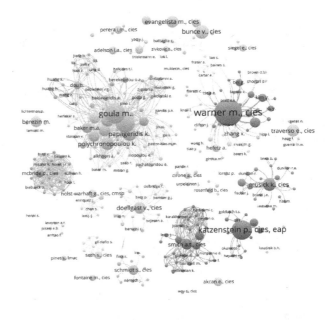

Figure 13.1a All Collaborations, CIES

Figure 13.1b Cornell Collaborations, CIES

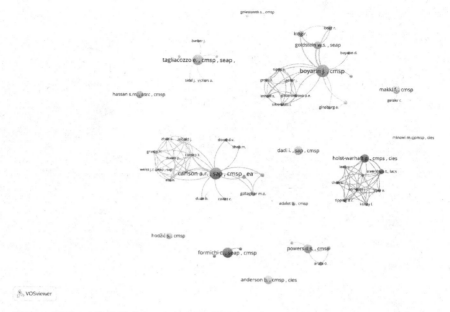

Figure 13.2a All Collaborations, CMSP

Figure 13.2b Cornell Collaborations, CMSP

COMPARATIVE AREA STUDIES IN THE GREAT BRAIN RACE   321

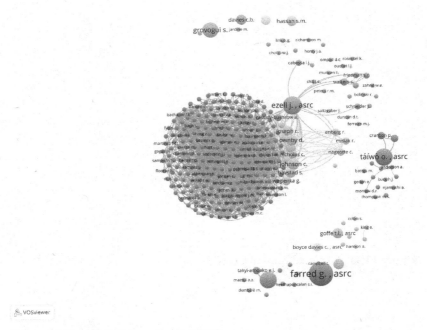

Figure 13.3a All Collaborations, ASRC

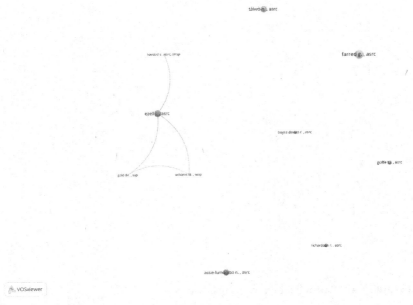

Figure 13.3b Cornell Collaborations, ASRC

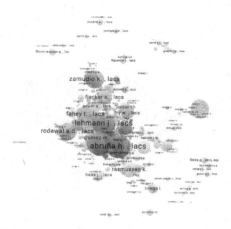

Figure 13.4a All Collaborations, LACS

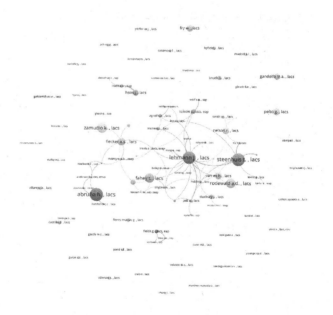

Figure 13.4b Cornell Collaborations, LACS

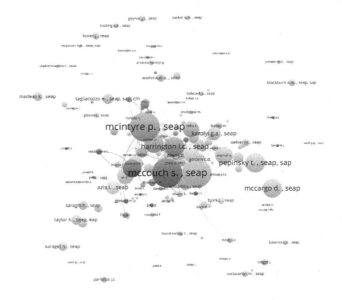

Figure 13.5a All Collaborations, SEAP

Figure 13.5b Cornell Collaborations, SEAP

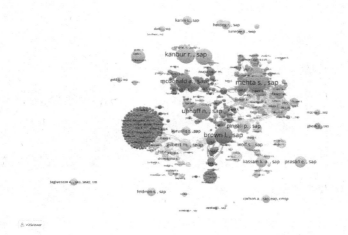

Figure 13.6a All Collaborations, SAP

Figure 13.6b Cornell Collaborations, SAP

COMPARATIVE AREA STUDIES IN THE GREAT BRAIN RACE   325

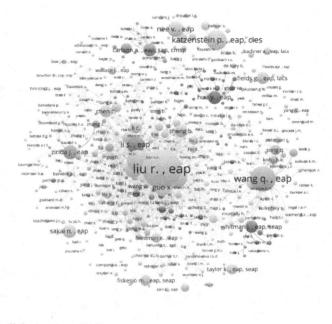

Figure 13.7a All Collaborations, EAP

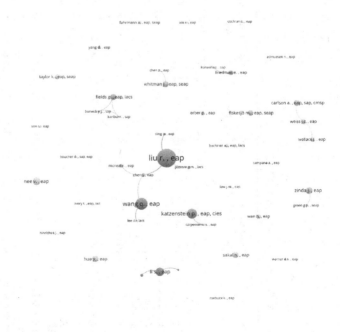

Figure 13.7b Cornell Collaborations, EAP

Table 13.8 Summary of All Cornell ASC

Center	Number of center authors	Total collaborators	Total intracenter collaborators	Intracenter collaborations as % of total	Total intercenter collaborations	Intercenter collaborations as % of total
African studies	11	345	8	2.3	2	0.6
Institute for European Studies	36	340	27	7.8	6	1.8
Comparative Muslim Societies	14	62	13	7.9	5	8.1
East Asian Studies	40	635	40	21.0	5	0.8
Latin American Studies	78	5419	64	6.3	31	0.6
South Asia Studies	46	2000	40	1.2	28	1.4
Southeast Asia Studies	72	3056	64	2.0	22	0.7
Center Average	**47.7**	**1693.9**	**36.6**	**6.9**	**14.1**	**2.0**
Total	**286**	**11,857**	**256**	**2.2**	**99**	**0.8**

The results show significant disparities in the quantity and form of collaboration at Cornell's various centers. EAS, for example, has a very high rate of intracenter collaboration. More than one in five collaborations occurred between center affiliates. This is strong evidence of bonding or intra-ASC collaboration. This is consistent with a strong traditional area studies model, where the focus is on research that is single country or intraregional. On the other hand, though, there was hardly any bridging collaboration between EAS and other ASCs at Cornell in the form of intercenter works. The CMSP is almost the obverse. Scholars in this center collaborate at a much higher rate with colleagues at other ASCs, totaling 8 percent of all coauthorship collaborations. Certainly, the varying features of each center may account for the different types of research collaborations undertaken. Differences in publication culture according to discipline can lead to more or less collaboration. Still, the overall findings suggest that the centers are underwhelming as research catalysts, even though individual faculty associated with ASCs are productive researchers. Looking at total research collaborations, only 2.2 percent involved collaborators within the same center; less than 1 percent involved collaborators at a different ASC.

The data from Cornell offer just a first-cut examination as to how well ASCs facilitating research and collaboration. Different centers at Cornell have different research propensities. Other universities have different organizational models for ASCs and generate different results. Still, it is impossible to overlook the relatively modest yield of these ASCs in terms of building sustained collaborative research agendas, either intraregionally or cross and interregionally. There are several factors possibly at play. ASCs might prioritize teaching and programming on regional affairs, their singular role, while leaving the tasks of stimulating research to the disciplinary departments. Relatedly, individual centers may have little incentive to collaborate with other centers, which are equally resource-poor. But other factors may relate to the wider ecosystem of social science scholarship. Interdisciplinary is valued for its potential to transform fields of inquiry, but scholars that actually engage in cross disciplinary boundaries are often less productive in terms of output volume (Leahey et al. 2017; Jacobs and Frickel 2009). In convening scholars from multiple disciplines, ASCs actually raise the degree of difficulty necessary for publication, as work in this vein must prove proficient in both social scientific techniques and regional language or culture. These challenges compound when researchers wish to engage in cross-regional

328 ADVANCING COMPARATIVE AREA STUDIES

or interregional collaboration—an even higher degree of difficulty. All of this suggests a need to reconsider institutional infrastructure if the next generation of area studies is to proceed.

Conclusion

Area studies had been at the forefront of internationalization and the growth of interdisciplinarity since the mid-twentieth century (Calhoun and Rhoten 2010). Its role in the twenty-first century great brain race remains uncertain. Some inside academia also believe that area studies as a project has run its course. Beissinger, who has both taught and administered area studies program, concedes that "traditional area-driven model of Area Studies as a space for a deepened knowledge of culture and place through multidisciplinary learning is no longer a sufficient basis for the development of Area Studies" (2020, 146). William Brustein, another experienced researcher and administrator, criticizes area studies for "fail[ing] frequently to take advantage of opportunities to generalize from their rich contextual findings to the broader world" (2007, 384). More dire still is the current push to abolish the federal Department of Education, a seemingly deliberate attempt to cripple American high education, area studies included.

CAS offers a promising blueprint for renewal (notwithstanding the possibility of a complete decimation of American universities). CAS reorients and repurposes the intellectual energy of area studies instead of sidelining it. While staying grounded in knowledge of specific regional contexts, CAS leverages this training toward broader comparison and midrange theorizing. Efforts to transition toward global institutions are inevitably constrained by legacies of past experience and the endowments of existing institutions. American institutions will have to find ways to internationalize in their own manner and form, just as the early iterations of CAS built upon the institutions, resources, and intellectual capital available in Hamburg in the 2000s. CAS could be especially valuable for those American institutions already invested in area studies, whether in terms of administration, curriculum, or research.

CAS has never been an orthodoxy but a rubric suggesting forms of research and engagement beyond the standard social scientific mold. Consequently, more than one version of CAS could arise. While scholars individually will make decisions about how to pursue their research, administrators,

COMPARATIVE AREA STUDIES IN THE GREAT BRAIN RACE 329

including deans, provosts, and chief internationalization officers, will certainly play a role in facilitating the venture. So, too, will funding agencies, such as the National Science Foundation. Some institutions could adopt CAS on a contingent bases, convening area studies specialists to work on specific cross-cutting problems or puzzles (Hornidge and Mielke 2017). Others may build a more permanent administrative framework linking ASCs together, akin to GIGA and closer to what Brustein and others recommend. Making CAS work has always required doubly intrepid scholars, willing to venture outside the lanes of disciplinary training and to trespass beyond conventional area boundaries. A conducive institutional setting, though, can make these risks more rewarding.

Bibliography

Abbott, Andrew. 2010. *Chaos of Disciplines*. Chicago: University of Chicago Press.
Ahmed, Amel. 2020. The Utility of Comparative Area Studies for Historical Analysis. *Qualitative & Multi-Method Research* 17–18: 7–10.
Ahmed, Amel. 2022. Crossing the Boundaries of Comparison: Comparative Area Studies and Comparative Historical Analysis. *Polity* 54 (4): 734–763.
Ahram, Ariel. 2011. The Theory and Method of Comparative Area Studies. *Qualitative Research* 11 (1): 69–90.
Anderson, Lisa. 2016. Middle East Studies for the New Millennium: Infrastructures of Knowledge. In Seteney Shami and Cynthia Miller-Idriss, eds. *Middle East Studies for the New Millenium*. New York: NYU Press, 432–446.
Avey, Paul C., and Michael C. Desch. 2014. What Do Policymakers Want from Us? Results of a Survey of Current and Former Senior National Security Decision Makers. *International Studies Quarterly* 58 (2): 227–246.
Avey, Paul C., Michael C. Desch, Eric Parajon, Susan Peterson, Ryan Powers, and Michael J. Tierney. 2022. Does Social Science Inform Foreign Policy? Evidence from a Survey of US National Security, Trade, and Development Officials. *International Studies Quarterly* 66 (1). https://doi.org/10.1093/isq/sqab057.
Basedau, Matthias, and Patrick Köllner. 2007. Area Studies and Comparative Area Studies: A Primer on Recent Debates and Methodological Challenges. *Japan aktuell* 2: 3–34.
Beelen, Jos, and Elspeth Jones. 2015. Redefining Internationalization at Home. In Adrian Curaj, Liviu Matei, Remus Pricopie, Jamil Salmi, and Scott Scott, eds. *The European Higher Education Area*. Cham, Switzerland: Springer, 59–72.
Beissinger, Mark R. 2020. Disciplinarity, Interdisciplinarity and the Plurality of Area Studies: A View from the Social Sciences. In Zoran Milutinovic, ed. *The Rebirth of Area Studies: Challenges for History, Politics and International Relations in the 21st Century*. London: I. B. Tauris, 129–150.
Biancani, Susan, Linus Dahlander, Daniel A. McFarland, and Sanne Smith. 2018. Superstars in the Making? The Broad Effects of Interdisciplinary Centers. *Research Policy* 47 (3): 543–557.
Brustein, William I. 2007. The Global Campus: Challenges and Opportunities for Higher Education in North America. *Journal of Studies in International Education* 11 (3–4): 382–391.

330 ADVANCING COMPARATIVE AREA STUDIES

Calhoun, Craig, and Diana Rhoten. 2010. Integrating the Social Sciences: Theoretical Knowledge, Methodological Tools, and Practical Applications. In Robert Frodeman, Julie Thompson Klein and Roberto C. S. Pacheco, eds. *The Oxford Handbook of Interdisciplinarity*. New York: Oxford University Press, 103–118.

Chansa-Ngavej, Vee, and Kyu Young Lee. 2017. Does Area Studies Need Theory? Revisiting the Debate on the Future of Area Studies. *Korean Journal of International Studies* 15 (1): 85–101.

Clowes, Edith W., and Shelly Jarrett Bromberg, eds. 2016. *Area Studies in the Global Age: Community, Place, Identity*. DeKalb: Northern Illinois University Press.

Duller, Matthias. 2015. History of Area Studies. In James D. Wright, ed. *International Encyclopedia of the Social & Behavioral Sciences*. 2nd ed. Oxford: Elsevier, 949–954.

Engerman, David C. 2015. The Pedagogical Purposes of Interdisciplinary Social Science: A View from Area Studies in the United States. *Journal of the History of the Behavioral Sciences* 51 (1): 78–92.

Friedman, Jonathan, and Cynthia Miller-Idriss. 2015. The International Infrastructure of Area Studies Centers: Lessons for Current Practice from a Prior Wave of Internationalization. *Journal of Studies in International Education* 19 (1): 86–104.

Friedman, Jonathan, and Elizabeth Worden. 2016. Creating Interdisciplinary Space on Campus: Lessons from US Area Studies Centers. *Higher Education Research & Development* 35 (1): 129–141.

Gisselquist, Rachel M. 2014. Paired Comparison and Theory Development: Considerations for Case Selection. *PS: Political Science & Politics* 47 (2): 477–484.

Godwin, Kara A., and Hans de Wit. 2019. *Intelligent Internationalization: The Shape of Things to Come*. Leiden: Brill.

Heyl, John D., and Joseph Tullbane. 2012. Leadership in International Higher Education. In Darla Deardorff, Hans de Wit, John D. Heyl, and Tony Adams, eds. *The Sage Handbook of International Higher Education*. Thousand Oaks, CA: Sage, 113–130.

Hodgett, Susan, and Patrick James, eds. 2018. *Necessary Travel: New Area Studies and Canada in Comparative Perspective*. Lanham, MD: Lexington Books.

Hornidge, Anna-Katharina, and Katja Mielke. 2017. Concluding Reflections: The Art of Science Policy for 21st Century Area Studies. In Katja Mielke and Anna-Katharina Hornidge, eds. *Area Studies at the Crossroads: Knowledge Production after the Mobility Turn*. Cham, Switzerland: Springer, 327–344.

Houben, Vincent. 2017. New Area Studies, Translation and Mid-Range Concepts. In Katja Mielke and Anna-Katharina Hornidge, eds. *Area Studies at the Crossroads: Knowledge Production after the Mobility Turn*. Cham, Switzerland: Springer, 195–211.

Hsueh, Roslyn. 2020. Synergies of CAS: New Inquires, Theory Development, and Community. *Qualitative & Multi-Method Research* 17–18 (1): 10–11.

Hu-DeHart, Evelyn. 1993. The History, Development, and Future of Ethnic Studies. *Phi Delta Kappan* 75 (1): 50–54.

Huotari, Mikko, and Jürgen Rüland. 2018. Context, Concepts, and Comparison in Southeast Asian Studies. In Ariel I. Ahram, Patrick Köllner, and Rudra Sil, eds. *Comparative Area Studies: Methodological Rationales and Cross-Regional Applications*. New York: Oxford University Press, 85–102.

Hutt, Michael. 2019. Area Studies and the Importance of "Somewheres." *South East Asia Research* 27 (1): 21–25.

Jacobs, Jerry A. 2014. *In Defense of Disciplines: Interdisciplinarity and Specialization in the Research University*. Chicago: University of Chicago Press.

Jacobs, Jerry A., and Scott Frickel. 2009. Interdisciplinarity: A Critical Assessment. *Annual Review of Sociology* 35: 43–65.

Juergensmeyer, Mark. 2018. The Evolution of Global Studies. In Mark Juergensmeyer, Manfred B. Steger and Saskia Sassen, eds. *The Oxford Handbook of Global Studies*. New York: Oxford University Press, 21–36.

Katzenstein, Peter J. 2001. Area and Regional Studies in the United States. *PS: Political Science and Politics* 34 (4): 789–791.

Kreuzer, Marcus, 2023. The Grammar of Time: A Toolbox for Comparative Historical Analysis. New York: Cambridge University Press.

King, Charles. 2015. The Decline of International Studies: Why Flying Blind Is Dangerous. *Foreign Affairs*. July 1. https://www.foreignaffairs.com/articles/united-states/decline-international-studies (accessed October 4, 2022).

Knight, Jane. 2012. Concepts, Rationales, and Interpretive Frameworks in the Internationalization of Higher Education. In Darla Deardorff, Hans de Wit, John D Heyl, and Tony Adams, eds. *The Sage Handbook of International Higher Education*. Thousand Oaks, CA: Sage, 27–42.

Köllner, Patrick, Rudra Sil, and Ariel I. Ahram. 2018. Comparative Area Studies: What It Is, What It Can Do. In Ariel I. Ahram, Patrick Köllner, and Rudra Sil, eds. *Comparative Area Studies: Methodological Rationales and Cross-Regional Applications*. New York: Oxford University Press, 3–26.

Kuran, Timur. 2012. Synergies Between Middle Eastern Economic History and the Analytic Social Sciences. *International Journal of Middle East Studies* 44 (3): 542–545.

Kuran, Timur. 2018. Islam and Economic Performance: Historical and Contemporary Links. *Journal of Economic Literature* 56 (4): 1292–1359.

Kurzman, Charles. 2017. Scholarly Attention and the Limited Internationalization of US Social Science. *International Sociology* 32 (6): 775–795.

Lambert, Richard 1973. *Language and Area Studies Review*. Philadelphia: American Academy of Political and Social Sciences.

Lamont, Michèle. 2009. *How Professors Think*. Cambridge, MA: Harvard University Press.

Lattuca, Lisa R. 2001. *Creating Interdisciplinarity: Interdisciplinary Research and Teaching among College and University Faculty*. Nashville: Vanderbilt University Press.

Leahey, Erin, Christine M. Beckman, and Taryn L. Stanko. 2017. Prominent but Less Productive: The Impact of Interdisciplinarity on Scientists' Research. *Administrative Science Quarterly* 62 (1): 105–139.

Ludden, David. 2000. Area Studies in the Age of Globalization. *Frontiers: The Interdisciplinary Journal of Study Abroad* 6 (1): 1–22.

MacPherson, Kristina Ruth. 2015. Decoding Area Studies and Interdisciplinary Majors: Building a Framework for Entry-Level Students. *College Teaching* 63 (2): 40–45.

Maliniak, Daniel, Susan Peterson, Ryan Powers, and Michael J. Tierney. 2020. TRIP Journal Article Database Codebook.

Martín-Martín, Alberto, Mike Thelwall, Enrique Orduna-Malea, and Emilio Delgado López-Cózar. 2021. Google Scholar, Microsoft Academic, Scopus, Dimensions, Web of Science, and OpenCitations' COCI: A Multidisciplinary Comparison of Coverage via Citations. *Scientometrics* 126 (1): 871–906.

Martz, John D. 1990. Political Science and Latin American Studies: Patterns and Asymmetries of Research and Publication. *Latin American Research Review* 25 (1): 67–86.

Mielke, Katja, and Anna-Katharina Hornidge, eds. 2017. *Area Studies at the Crossroads: Knowledge Production After the Mobility Turn*. Cham, Switzerland: Springer.

Milutinovic, Zoran. 2019. *The Rebirth of Area Studies: Challenges for History, Politics and International Relations in the 21st Century*. New York: Bloomsbury Publishing.

Morris, John T. 1998. Introducing Master's Students to Area Studies: An Interdisciplinary Research and Skills Approach. *PS: Political Science & Politics* 31 (2): 204–208.

Pepinsky, Thomas B. 2019. The Return of the Single-Country Study. *Annual Review of Political Science* 22: 187–203.

Rafael, Vicente L. 1999. Regionalism, Area Studies, and the Accidents of Agency. *American Historical Review* 104 (4): 1208–1220.

Ranis, Gustav. 2009. Economics, Area Studies and Human Development. Yale University Economic Growth Center Discussion Paper no. 975.

Reitter, Paul, and Chad Wellmon. 2021. *Permanent Crisis: The Humanities in a Disenchanted Age*. Chicago: University of Chicago Press.

Rhodes, R. A. W., and Susan Hodgett. 2021. *What Political Science Can Learn from the Humanities: Blurring Genres*. Cham, Switzerland: Springer.

Rhoten, Diana, and Andrew Parker. 2004. Risks and Rewards of an Interdisciplinary Research Path. *Science* 306 (5704): 2046–2046.

Saylor, Ryan. 2020. Comparative Area Studies: A Route to New Insights." *Qualitative & Multi-Method Research* 17–18: 1–7.

Sellers, Jefferey M. 2019. From Within to Between Nations: Subnational Comparison Across Borders. *Perspectives on Politics* 17 (1): 85–105.

Shami, Seteney, and Cynthia Miller-Idriss. 2016. *Middle East Studies for the New Millennium: Infrastructures of Knowledge*. New York: NYU Press.

Sil, Rudra. 2000. The Division of Labor in Social Science Research: Unified Methodology or "Organic Solidarity"? *Polity* 32 (4): 499–531.

Slater, Dan, and Daniel Ziblatt. 2013. The Enduring Indispensability of the Controlled Comparison. *Comparative Political Studies* 46 (10): 1301–1327.

Snyder, Richard. 2001. Scaling Down: The Subnational Comparative Method. *Studies in Comparative International Development* 36 (1): 93–110.

Solow, Robert M. 1997. How Did Economics Get That Way and What Way Did It Get? *Daedalus* 126 (1): 39–58.

Stevens, Mitchell L., Cynthia Miller-Idriss, and Seteney Shami. 2018. *Seeing the World: How US Universities Make Knowledge in a Global Era*. Princeton, NJ: Princeton University Press.

Szanton, David L., ed. 2004. *The Politics of Knowledge: Area Studies and the Disciplines*. Berkeley: University of California Press.

Weiss, Meredith L., and Pamela McElwee. 2021. Power and Agency: The Discipline-Shifting Work of James C. Scott. *Journal of Asian Studies* 80 (2): 389–390.

Wildavsky, Ben 2012 The Great Brain Race: How Global Universities Are Reshaping the World, Princeton: *Princeton University Press*.

Woods, Dwayne. 2016. The Future of Comparative Politics Is Its Past. *Chinese Political Science Review* 1 (3): 412–424.

Yang, Liu, Ekaterina Albats, and Henry Etzkowitz. 2021. Interdisciplinary Organization as a Basic Academic Unit? *Industry and Higher Education* 35 (3): 173–187.

Epilogue

Amrita Narlikar

Shall I compare thee to a summer's day?
Thou art more lovely and more temperate
Rough winds do shake the darling buds of May
And summer's lease hath all too short a date . . .

—William Shakespeare, Sonnet 18

Across a variety of fields ranging from poetry and linguistics to anthropology and politics, and sometimes for hundreds of years, the usefulness of comparison has been well recognized. Area studies, however, has been a late bloomer as far as the comparative method was concerned, perhaps with good reason. The richness and depth of knowledge that comes from knowing the history, language, and culture of a region, a country, or indeed a community within a country, should not be underestimated. But there are also costs and trade-offs.

Traditional area studies scholars have tended to be more of Isaiah Berlin's hedgehogs, who may be less tempted to foray into questions of theory and generalization that form the natural terrain of the fox. Stick solely to the area study in a narrow sense, and we risk not knowing whether or how concepts travel, adapt, and change. Intellectual siloization can result from too limited a geographic or temporal focus. Besides, the thick description that characterizes research in area studies "can sometimes be too dense and too specific to be of immediate use to policymakers" (Chafer et al. 2020). But the critique of area studies can go too far, as can the glorification of the theory-building generalist. It is to area-focused political scientists that we owe some powerful theoretical intuitions: the idea of the "developmental state," for instance, derived from studies of East Asian political economy and the concept of consociationalism was born in the study of a single country, the Netherlands (cf. Sil 2018, 230). And models that rely on formal logic and aggregate data can lack the necessary sense of process that comes out of studying phenomena at close range in a more focused way. For a nuanced approach that finds a fruitful middle ground between these two approaches at their best, *comparative* area studies (CAS) can offer some lively and interesting interventions.

CAS promises us a unique advantage: it brings together key disciplinary insights (akin to those offered by comparative political studies and comparative historical studies) and gets them to work hand in hand with the context-sensitivity that is the hallmark of traditional area studies. "The social world is not flattened plane in the CAS perspective. Rather, it is roughly textured by processes that are often big, slow-moving, and invisible"

334   EPILOGUE

(Köllner et al., this volume). This volume, *Advancing Comparative Area Studies*, delivers on this promise in three significant ways. First, it develops an eclectic methodological toolkit for researchers, which draws on the state of the art of not only positivist but also interpretive approaches. Second, it pinpoints the structural and institutional constraints that render academic work in CAS more difficult (in comparison to working primarily with a disciplinary lens or with an area studies focus) and suggests ways in which these challenges might be overcome. Third, it presents us with some fresh illustrations of CAS at work across a range of issue-areas that go beyond those examined in the first volume (Ahram et al. 2018). To the theorist and the empiricist, the intellectual charm of CAS is apparent. Additionally, studies presenting comparative insights offer greater transferability of their findings to the realm of policy, often at relatively little additional effort or resources.

All that said, academic fields are prone to fads, and it would be a mistake to treat the CAS approach as a silver bullet to address all the limitations that have been associated with traditional area studies or with general theoretical models. Besides, CAS too comes with its fair share of challenges. Comparisons have to be well thought out and meticulously executed; casually done, they can result in crude essentialization and reductionism. And much depends on the level of analysis. For instance, the effort to contrast "Asian values" with "universal values" at the macro-regional level has resulted in simplistic and false conflations of some very different (even opposing) traditions on human rights within Asia.[1] The resulting problems are not just "academic"; painting fundamentally different value systems with one broad brush has contributed to a failure to recognize potential allies in the region that share the "liberal" proclivities of the West (Narlikar 2024; Narlikar and Zürn, 2022). A related problem is the application of an inappropriate lens to make the comparison. For instance, attempts to apply insights from theories of European integration to shape regional integration in other parts of the world will only go so far; to make real progress, it may be necessary to tap into the offerings of area studies, taking into account possible sui generis approaches to regionalism that may have had independent origins in anticolonialism, lower levels of development, and different patterns of conflict.

An important way to counter the above problems could involve the adoption of a "Global Approach" to research (Narlikar 2016). Such an approach involves decentering the "West" and studying the world's regions and subregions on their own terms (as well as with reference to each other, when appropriate). Instead of simply applying models and theories developed from empirical work in the Global North, a global approach engages with the traditions and perspectives of actors from the Global South. At the same time, this global approach does not use case studies from the Global South merely for data-mining to reinforce or refute existing theories; rather, it works with cases from the regions to interrogate our assumptions and to generate fresh concepts and theories. Amid the global power shift underway, a global approach enables us to hear the voices of the hitherto marginalized, and also embrace feedback loops into concepts and theories as well as policies and practices.

Get CAS right (working as an integral part of the global approach) and we have a feast of ideas at hand for intellectual debate as well as policy-relevant findings. Ask a scholar who has worked on Brazil, India, and China together, for instance, and we may

---

[1] For a resounding critique of the Asian versus universal/liberal values dichotomy, see Sen 1997.

learn more about not only the phenomenon of rising powers at large but also key differences between their polities, economic development models, foreign policies, and negotiation strategies. CAS allows us a promising intellectual opportunity to consider whether some concepts (such as sovereignty and developmentalism) might be shared across three major players, but also unveils some deep-rooted differences (for instance on state-society relations, human rights, environmentalism, and animal ethics). Take into account the differentiated responses of different countries from the Global South to new forms of economic coercion, and we have the possibility to build more dynamic models of weaponized interdependence (Drezner et al. 2021). Knowing the variegated geopolitical and geoeconomic imperatives facing the diverse actors of the Global South would offer a better understanding of the overtly similar reactions that many countries have given to Russia's invasion of Ukraine (and the sanctions that have followed). The art and science of CAS open up a gamut of previously elusive research breakthroughs as well as encouraging policy choices.

Bibliography

Ahram, Ariel I., Patrick Köllner, and Rudra Sil, eds. 2018. *Comparative Area Studies: Methodological Rationales and Cross-Regional Applications.* New York: Oxford University Press.

Chafer, Tony, Ed Stoddard, and Sorina Toltica. 2020. Overcoming Area Studies' Policy-Relevant Research Problem: The Case of the Sahel. *New Area Studies* 1 (1): 25–40.

Drezner, Daniel W., Henry Farrell, and Abraham L. Newman, eds. 2021. *The Uses and Abuses of Weaponized Interdependence.* Washington, DC: Brookings.

Narlikar, Amrita. 2016. "Because They Matter": Recognise Diversity—Globalise Research. *GIGA Focus Global.* January. https://www.giga-hamburg.de/en/publications/giga-focus/because-they-matter-recognise-diversity-globalise-research (accessed September 12, 2022).

Narlikar, Amrita. 2024. India and the World: Civilizational Narratives in Foreign Policy. In Steve Smith, Tim Dunne, Amelia Hadfield, and Nicolas Kitchen, eds. *Foreign Policy: Theories, Actors, Cases.* 4th edition. Oxford: Oxford University Press, 337–356.

Narlikar, Amrita, and Michael Zürn. 2022. Liberal Scripts in Asia: Ownership, Rejection, Reclamation. Paper presented at Regional Conference on Asian Scripts, Cluster of Excellence, "Contestations of the Liberal Script." February 21–22. https://www.scripts-berlin.eu/explore/reports/Conference-Asian-Scripts/index.html (accessed September 26, 2022).

Sen, Amartya. 1997. Human Rights and Asian Values. Sixteenth Annual Morgenthau Memorial Lecture on Ethics and Foreign Policy, May 25. New York: Carnegie Council for Ethics in International Affairs. www.carnegiecouncil.org/publications/archive/morgenthau/254.html (accessed September 26, 2022).

Sil, Rudra. 2018. Triangulating Area Studies, Not Just Methods: How Cross-Regional Comparison Aids Qualitative and Mixed-Method Research. In Ariel I. Ahram, Patrick Köllner, and Rudra Sil, eds. *Comparative Area Studies: Methodological Rationales and Cross-Regional Applications.* New York: Oxford University Press, 225–246.

Index

For the benefit of digital users, indexed terms that span two pages (e.g., 52–53) may, on occasion, appear on only one of those pages.

Note: Page numbers followed by *f* refer to figures; page numbers followed by *t* refer to tables.

abduction, 51–53
Aceh minorities, 119–120
Acharya, Amitav, 173, 189, 192, 200, 231–233, 237–238, 263–264
Afghanistan, 56–57, 119, 255–256
Africa. *See also* West Africa; *specific African countries by name*
  and African values, 235
  comparative studies, 11, 88, 211–212, 262
  East Africa, 100
  ethnic minorities in, 125
  fieldwork in, 152–153
  history of, 134
  human rights in, 239
  and the ICC, 240
  neo-patrimonialism in, 196
  North Africa, 241–242
  OSGA regional center, xv–xvi
  plural society in, 199–200
  political topographies of, 98–101
  regional and area studies in, 174, 233–234
  regional human rights systems, 242–243
  research in, 131, 134, 135–136
  sovereignty in, 38, 41–42
  state formation in, 37–39, 125
  sub-Saharan, 132, 134, 146–150, 152–153
  taxation systems in, 125
  West Africa, 95, 99, 101–102, 132
Africa Institute of South Africa, 3
African Union (AU), 174, 242
Africana Studies and Research Center (ASRC) (Cornell), 316, 321
Ahmed, Amel, 16, 311
Ahram, Ariel I., 21, 75–76, 129, 159, 173, 174–175, 258, 265
Albania, 296–297
Algeria, 119, 294–295

Ali, Shaheen Sadar, 241
Al-Shabaab, 150
American Academy of Political and Social Sciences, 305–306
American Council of Learned Societies, 188–189
American Political Science Association (APSA), 8
analyticism, 84–85
anarchism, global, 62–63
Anderl, Felix, 232–233
Anderson, Benedict, 47, 62–65, 69–70, 293–294
An-Na'im, Abdullahi Ahmed, 238
Annales school, 16, 159–171, 172–174, 178
  and geohistory, 166–169
  and historical geography, 165–166
  influence of, 172–177
anthropology, 9, 12–13, xv–xvi, 174
  writing style, 66–67
anticolonialism, 334
anti-imperialism, 273
Antweiler, Christopher, 6–7
Appadurai, Arjun, 185
Arab Spring, 241–242
area expertise, 1–2, 4–5
area studies, 3–4, 6, 34–35, 48–49, 53, 105–106, 131–132, 200, 201, 209, 210, 232–234, 257, 290–291, 306, 333. *See also* comparative area studies (CAS)
  communities, 286–290
  and comparative area studies, xv–xvi, xviii, 159, 181–182, 206–207, 281–287, 289–301, 304–305, 328–329
  departments, 284–290
  funding for, 3, 305–310, 312
  future of, 1–2, 8, 20

338 INDEX

area studies (*Continued*)
  institutes, 285–290
  and international relations, 231–232, 262, 316
  programs, 284–290
  research, 208–209, 288, 289–290
  and social sciences, 1–2, 4, 6, 303–304, 316
  vs. specific disciplines, 177, 263–264, 306
  sui generis, 184, 187–188
  in universities, xvi, xvii–xix, 263, 282, 288–299, 305–329
area studies centers (ASCs), 21–22, 305–306, 309–312, 327–329
Argentina, 120
Armenia, 294–295
Aruba, 295
ASEAN Intergovernmental Commission on Human Rights, 243–244
Asia
  and "Asian values," 235–236, 334
  economic crisis, 235
  ethnic minorities in, 125
  human rights in, 232, 239, 242–244
  and the ICC, 241–242
  as region, 188–189, 207
  studies on, 11, 131, 134, 216
Asian Infrastructure Investment Bank, 256, 260–261
Asian studies, xvii, 282–283, 285, 288–289
Asia-Pacific Economic Community, 297–298
Association for Asian Studies, 286, 291, 297–298, 305–306
Association of Southeast Asia (ASA), 189–190
Association of Southeast Asian Nations (ASEAN), 190, 292, 296–298
Australia
  Asian studies in, 286–287
  as European, 294–295
  regional placement, 292
  research on, 118, 125
  and SEATO, 189–190
Australian National University, 287–288
Austria, 95–96, 295–296
authoritarianism, 113–114, 196, 207–208, 214, 222, 235
autonomy
  economic, 98–99
  embedded, 76, 95–98, 196
  state, 208, 270

Balochistan minorities, 119
Baltic states, 294–295, 297

Bandung Conference, 237–238
Bangladesh, 241–242, 292
Bardhan, Pranab, 208
Barnett, Michael, 18, 246, 263–264
Barrington, Jacques, 234–235
Basedau, Matthias, 15, 218
Beissinger, Mark, 308–309, 311–312, 328
Belt and Road Initiative (BRI), 256, 262–263
Bennett, Andrew, 79, 107–109
Berlin, Isaiah, 333
Bhaganan, Manu Belur, 237
Bloch, Marc, 161–165
Boone, Catherine, 76, 98–101
Boswell, John, 48, 66–67
boundary (scope) conditions, 16, 29–30, 42–43, 91–92, 112–113, 115, 137–138, 144–145, 163, 174–175, 206–207, 210, 217–218, 243, 266–267
bounded rationality, 86–87
Braudel, Fernand, 139, 160, 161, 166–171, 173, 178, 191
Brazil, 49, 54–57, 95–98, 208–209, 216
  AIDS policy in, 130
  comparison studies, 117, 274
  human rights in, 232, 244–245
  research in, xvii, 57–59, 63, 65, 67
  taxation systems in, 130
Bretton Woods institutions, 260–261
Brexit, 297
BRICS, 244–246, 260–261, 274
Britain. *See* Great Britain; United Kingdom (UK)
Brookes, Marissa, 15, 118–120, 125
Brookings Institution, 285–286
Brunei, 190, 291
Brustein, William, 328
Burke, Roland, 237–238
Burkina Faso, 119
Burma. *See* Myanmar

Çalı, Başak, 243
Calvinism, 88–89
Cambodia, 118, 190, 291. *See also* Southeast Asia
Cammett, Melani, 215–216
Canada, 296–297. *See also* North America
capitalism, 88–89, 196, 207, 222, 256, 268–269, 282–283
  imperial inheritances of, 269
  Western dominance of, 270–271
Caribbean, 105–106, 199–200, 291–292

INDEX

case studies, 54–61, 77–78, 87–95, 116–125, 140–153, 232–233. *See also* research
and casing, 54–61
and causality, 77–82, 107–110
and cross-case comparison, 62–63, 65, 78–79, 81, 86, 97, 101–102, 106, 109–110, 123, 130–131, 135, 136–137, 141, 142–149, 151, 153, 159, 160, 257, 265, 273–274, 282–283
selection of cases, 54–61, 75, 77–78, 92
Caucasus, 295–296
causal mechanisms, 105–106
in CAS research, 116–125
and case studies, 107–110
generalizability of, 105–107
in Lieberman's comparison of South Africa and Brazil, 117
causal process observations (CPOs), 109–112
cause/causality
adequate, 90–95
causal analysis, 13–15, 29–30, 87, 206
causal theory, 109–110
coincidental, 93–95
historical causation, 170
Center for Southeast Asian Studies (Kyoto University), 287–288
Central America
civil war in, 37
regional human rights systems, 242–243
as research subject, 41, 132, 291–292
Central Europe, 255
Chang, P. C., 237
Chaudhry, Kiren, 211–212
Chavez, Leiry Cornejo, 243
China. *See also* former empires turned revisionist powers (FERPs)
as Asian country, 207–208
Asian Infrastructure Investment Bank, 256, 260–261
Belt and Road Initiative (BRI), 256, 262–263
in BRICS, 244
communist mobilization of, 208–209
comparison studies, 40, 194, 207–209, 222–223, 225–226, 257–258, 291–292
and Eurasia, 255–256
experts on, 261–262
globalization of, 206–209, xvii
growth rate in, 219
human rights in, 235–236, 244–245
and the ICC, 240
imperial inheritances of, 265–266, 272
as international player, 257–258

liberalization in, 214–215
market governance in, 217
multiregional influence of, 256
OSGA regional center, xv–xvi
resemblance to other former empires, 19–20, 268–273
Shanghai, 209
and the Strategic Value Framework, 219
studies on, 132, 208–211, 214, 216–217, 222, 260
and Taiwan, 273
Tiananmen Square incident, 223–224
Warring States, 35
and the WTO, 214, 224–225
Chinese Empire, 255–256, 268–271
Chinese studies, 273–274
clientelism, 197
climate change, 65
Coedès, George, 191
Cold War, 11, 190, 223, 258–259, 272, 295–296, 305
Colombia, 120–122
colonialism, 199, 293–294
comparison study, 208–209
Japanese, 207–208
colonization, 269
commodity chains, 212, 221
comparative analysis. *See* comparison
comparative area studies (CAS), 7–13, 40–43, 200–201, 287–289, 333–335. *See also* area studies
and area studies, xv–xvi, xviii, 131–132, 181–182, 206–209, 281–287, 289–301, 304–305, 328–329
and comparative historical analysis (CHA), 159–161, 178
defined, 131, 265
degree program in, xviii
epistemological flexibility of, 10–11
and Eurasia, 257
and the evolution of global IR, 246–247
and generalization, 32–33, 138–140, 153
and human rights scholarship, 18–19, 133–134, 232–234, 239–247, 334–335
and international relations, 263–266, 273–274
and the internationalization in academia, 311–328
interpretive approaches in, 48, 54, 69–70
research in, 116, 125, 206–208, 266, 300
scope and impact of, 3–7, 20
and social sciences, 40–42

340 INDEX

comparative area studies (CAS) (*Continued*)
theory development in, 105–107
translation in, 43
in universities, 303–305, xviii
and use with MMR, 141–146, 151–153 (*see also under* multi-method research (MMR)
comparative historical analysis (CHA), 1–2, 16, 159–160, 162–163, 165, 167, 169, 172–173, 175, 178, 209
and comparative area studies, 159–161, 178
Comparative Historical Analysis (Mahoney & Rueschemeyer), 172
Comparative Muslim Societies Program (CMSP) (Cornell), 316, 320, 327
comparison. *See also* contextualized comparison; controlled comparison
analytical, 3–4, 61–66, 171, 177–178, 188–196
cross-national/cross-country, 6, 11–12, 17, 151–152, 206, 209, 211–212, 223, 225, 304–305
cross-regional/cross-area, 4–7, 11–14, 16–21, 39, 43, 49, 53–55, 57–58, 63–69, 75, 76, 95–96, 113, 117, 119–120, 129, 130, 139–140, 146, 159, 174–175, 177, 182–184, 206–210, 215–219, 225–226, 232, 239, 243–244, 246–247, 257, 261, 265–267, 273–274, 281–282, 288–289, 297–298, 300–301, 310, 311–313, 315, 327–328
cross-temporal, 64–65, 224
historical, 161–165, 266, 268
interpretive, 14, 47–49, 51–53, 55–56, 58–69, 183–184
interregional, 7, 16–17, 304–305
intertextual, 62
intraregional, 4–5, 17–18, 54–55, 192–196
large-N, 6, 76, 130–131, 133, 137, 139, 149–150, 174–175, 304–305
logic of, 11, 48
medium-N, 139, 217–218
metatheory of, 182
most-different systems, 145–146
most-similar systems, 145–146
multisector, 211
vs. noncomparison, 184–188
and ontology, 16–17, 182–185, 187–189, 200–201
paired, 304–305
regional, 17
site-focused, 12–13

small-N, 7, 12, 54, 78–79, 129–130, 136–137, 139–140, 186, 266–268
structured, 12–13
structured-focused, 145–146
subnational, 6–7, 95, 98–101, 209, 304–305
subregional, 7
translation in, 43
transregional, 2, 211–212
units of, 17
ways of understanding, 12–13, 48
within-case, 62, 65, 108–111, 113, 117, 123, 130–131, 135, 141–142, 218
within-country, 211–212, 217, 224
constructivism, 17–18, 259
context, 48–49, 93–94, 97–98, 105–106, 162.
See also contextualized comparison
application to whole or part of an area, 116
attention to, 81–82
and case selection, 76–77
in causal analysis, 87, 206
in comparative research, 53–55, 75, 183
and contextuality, 51–54, 59–60, 68
and contrast-of-context approach, 222
defined, 93, 115–116
of energy politics, 65
generalization and, 186
global, 171
macro-national, 210, 225–226
micro-sectoral, 225–226
regional, 183
of sectors, 214–215
societal, 48–49
contextualized comparative sector approach (CCSA), 17, 205–211, 217–226. *See also* sectoral analysis
empirical and theoretical puzzles, 218–219
multilevel comparative case research design, 222–225
theoretical framework and hypotheses, 219–221
contextualized comparison, 3–5, 7, 10–11, 14, 16–21, 58–61, 87, 111–112, 118, 121, 123–124, 159, 161, 164, 172, 175, 210–219, 222–223, 225–226, 232, 239, 247, 256–257, 266
controlled comparison, 4–5, 7, 10–11, 14, 47–48, 54–55, 69–70, 111, 122, 136–137, 139–140, 160, 205, 208–209, 215–218, 222, 266, 307
Coral Bell School of Asia and Pacific Affairs (Australian National University), 287–288
Corbett, Jack, 48, 66–67

Cornell Institute for European Studies (CIES), 316, 319
Cornell University, 284, 312, 316, 318
   Africana Studies and Research Center (ASRC), 316, 321
   area studies centers (ASCs), 316, 318–328
   Comparative Muslim Societies Program (CMSP), 316, 320, 327
   East Asia Program (EAP), 316, 325, 327
   Institute for European Studies (CIES), 316, 319
   Latin American and Caribbean Studies (LACS), 316, 322
   South Asia Program (SAP), 316, 324
   Southeast Asia Program (SEAP), 316, 323
corruption, 7, 207, 217
Côte d'Ivoire, 98–101
Council for European Studies, 177
Council of Europe, 242, 296–297
Council of European Studies, 286
Council of the European Union, 296–297
Crimea, 263
Croissant, Aurel, 152–153
cross-case comparison. *See* comparison, cross-case
Crossroads Asia conference, 8
cultural revolutions, 272
cultural rights, 236
cultural studies, 6–7
culture wars, 264–265
Cyprus, 273
czarist empire, 268–271

debt diplomacy, 260–261
decolonization, 232–233, 260–261
Decolonizing Human Rights (An-Na'im), 238
deduction, 135–138, 143
depoliticization, 63
Designing Social Inquiry (*DSI*) (King, Keohane, & Verba), 140–141
developmentalism, techno-security, 224–225
Dian, Matteo, 233–234
diasporic studies, 309
Dimitrov, Martin, 208
diversity
   of approaches in CAS, 48
   civilizational, 235–236
   cultural, 234–236
   ethnic, 198–199
   inclusivity of, 232–233, 241, 246–247
   in IR scholarship, 232–233, 242, 246–247
   power of, 238

in Southeast Asia, 192
Doherty-Sil, Eileen, 18–19, 265
Dominguez, Jorge, 310
Doner, Richard F., 208, 216
Donnelly, Jack, 236
dualism, mind-world, 84–85
Durkheim, Émile, 161–162, 164–165
Dutch Antilles, 294–295

East Africa, 100
East Asia. *See also* former empires turned revisionist powers (FERPs)
   comparative studies, 152–153, 208–209, 211–212
   experts on, 261–262
   newly industrialized countries (NIC), 207–208
   studies on, 196, 208
East Asia Program (EAP) (Cornell), 316, 325, 327
East Asia Summit, 297–298
East Asian studies, 273–274, 285
Eastern Europe, 273, xv–xvi
Eaton, Sarah, 214–215
economic integration, 207–208, 211, 214, 220, 223–226
economic justice, 236
economic rights, 234–235
economics, 11, xv–xvi, 304–305
   2008-9 economic crisis, 256
   behavioral, 11–12, 206
   development, 11
   political, 17–18
   socialist, 223
economies, developing, 225
economy. *See also* political economy
   global, 210, 222–223
   moral, 63–64
Elman, Colin, 79
Embedded Autonomy (Evans), 76, 95–98
embeddedness, 95–98, 122, 192–193
Emmerson, Donald, 189, 192
empires, 19–20, 255, 257–261, 267–274. *See also* Eurasia
   agential family resemblances, 270–271
   family resemblances, 274
   processual family resemblances, 271–273
   structural family resemblances, 268–270
empiricism, 10–11
energy transformations, 49
Enloe, Cynthia, 231
environmental justice, 59–60

342 INDEX

epistemology, xv, 29–30, 42–43, 47–48, 50–52, 54–55, 129–130, 262, 273–274, 303–304
  of area studies, 303–304
  of comparative area studies, 9–14, xv, 129–130, 152
  of international relations, 273–274
  interpretive, 51, 69
  positivist, 14, 48–49, 69
  post-positivist, 12
equifinality, 113–116, 120
Erasmus+ funding program, 284
essentialization, 334
ethnic studies, 309
Ethnogeographic Board, 188–189
ethnographic sensibility, 5, 48, 163–164
ethnography, 29–30, 186
  comparative, 12, 48
  interpretivist, 186
  writing style, 66–68
EU Customs Union, 296–297
Eurasia, 19–20, 255–257, 273–274. *See also* revisionist powers
  CAS approach to, 267–273
  comparative studies, 211–212
  experts on, 261–262
  revisionist former empires, 267–273
Eurasian, Russian, and East European Studies, 295–296
Eurasian studies, 273–274
Eurocentrism, 264–265, 270–271
Europe
  Asian studies in, 286–287
  boundaries of, 174, 176–177
  changing demography of, 298–299
  comparison studies, 11, 32–33, 35, 40
  consociationalism in, 196
  early modern, 34, 41–42, 89
  and Eurasia, 256
  euro crisis, 298–299
  global context of, 171
  human rights in, 232, 239, 242–243
  and the ICC, 240
  and international relations, 259
  political development in, 34–35, 177
  postsocialist, 298–299
  refugee crisis, 298–299
  as region, 188, 294–299
  social cohesion in, 198
  sovereignty in, 38
  state formation in, 125
  studies on, 105–106, 164, 176–177, 207

  on transnational labor alliance campaigns, 118, 125
European Commission, 284
European Consortium for Political Science, 8
European Council, 296–297
European Court of Human Rights, 243
European Economic Area (EEA), 296–297
European Free Trade Association (EFTA), 296–297
European studies, 20–21, 281, 282–285, 287–291, 294–299, 307–308
European Union (EU), 174, 295, 296–299
European Union Studies Association, 297
Eurovision, 294–295
Evans, Allison, 215
Evans, Peter, 76, 95–98
exceptionalism, xviii–xix, 257, 262–264
  cultural, 233–234
explanation
  case-specific, 93
  causal, 75–76, 80–87
  vs. inference, 80
  ingredients of, 80, 86

Falkland Islands, 173
Falleti, Tulia, 5, 93–94, 207
familiarity, 4–5, 175–177
Febvre, Lucien, 162, 165, 166, 173
federalism, 122–125
FERPs. *See* former empires turned revisionist powers (FERPs)
Feudal Society (Bloch), 163–164
field research, 53–54, 56–60, 62, 63, 66–68, xviii
Finland, 295–296
Fisher-Onar, Nora, 19–20, 247
flexibility, 51–54
folk memory, 163–164
Føllesdal, Andreas, 243
Foreign Languages Area Studies (FLAS), 305
Form, William, 97
France, 194, 198, 207–209, 282–283
  and Algeria, 294–295
  and SEATO, 189–190
Frazier, Mark W., 209
French Guiana, 173, 291–292
Friedman, Jonathan, 311–312
Fuller, Doug, 217
Fünfgeld, Anna, 14
Furnivall, John, 63–64, 184, 197–201

Gallagher, Mary, 208–209
game theory, 11

Geertz, Clifford, 186–188
General Agreement on Tariffs and Trade, 223–224
generalizability, 39, 183, 217–218
  of causal mechanisms, 110–111
  of causal theory, 109
  of CCSA, 205–206
  of research, 123–124
generalization, 15, 29–32, 40, 42–43, 129, 130–131, 133–134, 135, 138–140, 143, 150, 153, 163, 186, 196–197
  bridge to individualization, 138–140
  in comparative area studies, 32–33
  goals and characteristics, 139
  mid-range, 187–188
  of theories, 210
geoeconomics, 334–335
geography
  and CAS, 9
  critical approach to, 175
  historical, 160, 165–166, 169, 171–173, 175–177
  open-ended inquiry, 174–175
  physical, 169, 172–173
  political, 174, 176–177
  subnational, 211–212, 217
geohistory, 160–161, 166–171, 173–174, 178
geopolitics, 191–192, 195–196, 240, 244, 256–257, 285–286, 295–296, 334–335
George, Alexander, 77, 79, 107–108
Georgetown University, 295–296, 310
German Academic Exchange Service, 284
German Institute for Global and Area Studies (GIGA), 2–4, 9–10, 21–22, xv–xvi, 299–300, 304, 305, 328–329
German Political Science Association, 8
Germanic studies, 285, 288
Germany, 56–57, 122–124, 176–177, 207
  Weimar Republic, 168–169
Gerring, John, 77–79, 106–107
Gerry, Christopher, xviii
Ghana, 98–101, 120–122, 237–238
Gibraltar, 296–297
Global Asia, 294. See also Southeast Asia
global studies, 309
globalization, xvii–xviii, 206–209, 211, 220
  and development, 218–219
  impacts of, 218–219
  post-neoliberal, 205
globalization studies, 184–185, 187–188
Goertz, Gary, 108–109
Goodin, Robert, 93

Goodman, Sara Wallace, 20–21, 311
Great Britain. See also United Kingdom (UK)
  British Isles, 295–296
  and international relations, 259
  transnational security services (G45), 118
Greece, 273
grounded theory, 53

Haiti, 174, 237
Hall, Peter, 115
Harkness, Kristen, 146–149, 152–153
Harvard University, 285, 312
Heer, Satwant Kaur, 241
Herbst, Jeffrey, 37–39, 41–42
heuristic process, 82–84, 86–99
Heyl, John, 305
historical institutionalism, 169
historical studies, comparative, 333–334
historiography, 3–4
history. See also geohistory
  comparative, 160, 164, 171
  episodic, 166–167
  geographic, 166–170
  global, 173–174, 178
  intellectual, 176
  local, 53
  open-ended, 178
  social, 166–168
  social science, 160, 169, 178
  total, 163, 170
  universal, 163–164
HIV/AIDS, 130
Hochstetler, Kathryn, 216
Hodgson, Marshall, 174
Hoffman, Stanley, 232–233
Hong, Jean, 217
Hopgood, Stephen, 238
Hsueh, Roselyn, 17, 131–140, 210–212, 214, 216–220, 222–223, 225–226, 311
Htun, Mala, 59
Huber, Christopher, 146, 149–150, 152–153
Huber, Evelyne, 105–106
Hui, Victoria Tin-bor, 35–36, 40, 41
human rights
  and "African values," 235
  in Asia, 334
  and "Asian values," 235
  communitarian, 235
  and comparative area studies, 18–19, 133–134, 231–232, 334–335
  contestation in decentering, 237–239

344 INDEX

human rights (*Continued*)
country-specific, 244–246
global, 244
vs. Human Rights, 238
individual-based, 235
international, 18–19, 232, 234–239, 241–242
and the International Criminal Court, 240–242
Islamic framework for, 243–244
and "Islamic values," 235
pluralistic universalism in, 234–236
promise for scholarship, 239–246
regional systems, 242–244
and the "right to subsistence," 235–236
treaty-based, 18–19, 232, 237–239, 243–244
Human Rights Council (HRC), 232, 235–236, 239, 244–246
humanities, 43, 309
interpretive traditions in, 50–51
and social sciences, 303–304
Huneeus, Alexandra, 242
Hungary, 208–209, 295–297
Huotari, Mikko, 48
Husar, Jörg, 245
hydropower, 59–60
hypothesis/hypotheses, 80, 86, 89–90, 94, 96–97, 99, 106–107, 109, 111, 113, 115–117, 120, 122–123, 133, 136–139, 149–150, 219–221

IBSA (India-Brazil-South Africa Dialogue Forum), 239, 244–246
Iceland, 296–297
ideal types, 76–82, 101–102
adjusting, 94–95
building and using, 76, 87–95
and causal explanation, 82–87
and context-sensitive explanations, 85–87
defined, 82–85
heuristic process, 92–94
hypothesizing, 89–92
induction, 88–89
Weberian, 76–77, 95–101
Imagined Communities (Anderson), 293–294
imperialism, 273
Eurasian, 272
European, 270–271
legal, 269
neo-, 273
post-, 10–12, 50–51
Russian, 270–271

Imposing Sanctions on Violent-Non-State Actors to Restore International Peace and Security (Huber), 149–150
India
AIDS policy in, 130
comparison studies, 209, 222–223, 225–226, 274
economic emergency in, 223–224
globalization of, 206–207, 209
growth rate in, 219
human rights in, 232, 237, 244–245
liberalization in, 215
market governance in, 217
Mumbai, 209
studies on, 95–98, 132, 208–211, 222, 291–292
Indiana University, 310
individualization, 15, 129, 130–135, 137–138, 140–153
bridge to generalization, 138–140
goals and characteristics, x 139
Indonesia, 49, 54–57, 111, 189–191, 198, 199, 291
Aceh minorities in, 119–120
research in, 57–59, 63, 65, 67
induction, 88–89, 94–95, 135–138, 143, 145
inferences
causal, 77–82, 109, 140–141, 144, 151–152
descriptive, 140–141, 143–144
empirical, 141
vs. explanations, 75–76, 80
Institute of Southeast Asian Studies, 3
institutionalism, neoliberal, 260–261
Inter-American Court of Human Rights, 243
Inter-Asia, 294. *See also* Southeast Asia
interdisciplinarity, 53, 165, 174, 287–288, 294–295, 307, 309–310, 327–328
International Covenant on Civil and Political Rights, 237–238
International Covenant on Economic Social and Cultural Rights, 237–238
International Criminal Court (ICC), 18–19, 232, 240–242
international financial institutions (IFIs), 260–261
International Institute for Asian Studies, 3
international law, 238, 240, 241, 269–270
international relations (IR)
and area studies, 231–232, 316
and comparative area studies, 9, 13, 17–18, 246–247, 261–267, 273–274
disciplinary, 257

and former empires/revisionist powers
(FERPs), 255–257, 267–274
global, 18–19, 232–239, 245–246, 263–265,
267–274
graduate area studies courses, 317
great debates, 259
hub-and-spokes problem, 257–261
and human rights, 238
and human rights scholarship, 234–239
mainstream, 18–20, 257
mainstream scholarship, 231
pluralistic universalism of, 232–234
top programs, 315–316
Western dominance of, 232–233, 259–261,
265–266, 273–274
international studies, 2, 309
International Studies Association, 8
International Studies Association (ISA), 231
internationalization, 305
of administration, 21, 311–315, 328–329
of curriculum, 311
economics, 210, 223
of education, 303–305, 311, 328–329
of research, 305–311, 316–328
interpretation, 31–32
interpretive analysis, 2, 10–13, 61–68
interpretivism, 12–14, 47–70, 184, 186–188,
303–304
intersubjectivity, 220, 224. See also subjectivity
invariance, 80, 90–91, 107–109, 125
Iran, 19–20, 119, 194–195, 272. See also former
empires turned revisionist powers
(FERPs)
comparison studies, 257–258
and Eurasia, 255–256
imperial inheritances of, 265–266
as international player, 257–258
resemblance to other former empires,
268–273
and Saudi Arabia, 273
studies on, 260
Iranian studies, 273–274
Iraq, 119–120
ISEAS-Yusof Ishak Institute (Singapore),
285–286
Islamic law, 240–241
Israel, 294–295
Italy, 122–123, 171

Jackson, Patrick Thaddeus, 84–85
Jamaica, 237–238
Japan, xvii, 194, 282–283, 297–298

as Asian country, 207
in Eurasia, 271
OSGA regional center, xv–xvi
Java, 62–63, 191, 197–198
Jensen, Steven, 237–238
Jensenius, Francesca, 59
Johns Hopkins University, 310
Johnson, Chalmers, 208–209
Johnson, R. Burke, 140–141
Jordaan, Deuard, 245
Jordan, 241–242
justice
economic, 236
environmental, 59–60
social, 56–57, 59–60
Justice and Equality Movement, 150

Kaplan, Robert D., 255–257, 261
Kayaoğlu, Turan, 269
Kazakhstan, 215
Keddie, Nikki, 184, 193, 194–196, 200–201
Keohane, Robert, 140–141
Kerala (India), 95–96
Khomeini, Ayatollah, 271
Kim, Diana, 186
King, Gary, 140–141
knowledge, 40–43, 50–53, 89–90, 183,
283–284. See also knowledge production
access to, 58–59
accumulation of, 183–184, 259–260
area studies, 181, 200–201, 261–262,
281–284, 300
area-specific, 1–2, 7, 16–17, 20–21, 200,
285–288, 298, 308–309
background, 200–201
causal, 86
conceptual, 285–286
context-specific, 217–218
country-level, 105–106
of culture and place, 308–309, 328
deep, 20–21, 29–30, 131–132, 134, 183, 208,
225–226, 256–257, 281–282
expert, 3
generalizable, 138
historical, 162
immersive, 261–262
international relations (IR), 261
local, 1–2
regional, 183–184, 188–200
social, 12–13
social construction of, 183
theoretical, 285–286

346 INDEX

knowledge (*Continued*)
thick, 260–262
translation of, 33–34
transnational, 15–16
knowledge production, 247, 258–259, 281–282, 284, 286–289, 308–309
academic, 281–282, 289
area-based, 283, 285–286, 294
"hub and spoke," 18–20, 257–261, 265, 273–274
international relations (IR), 258–259, 261, 263–264
logic of, 101–102
models for, 299
processes of, 53
subjectivity in, 82–85
Kohli, Atul, 208–209
Köllner, Patrick, 75–76, 159, 265
Kuehn, David, 15, 218
Kuhonta, Erik Martinez, 16–17, 63–64, 293–294
Kuran, Timur, 11–12
Kurdish minorities, 119–120
Kyoto University, 284–285, 287–288

Lambert, Richard, 305–309
language skills, 57–59
for case studies, 135–136
specific terminology, 64
translation, 64
Laos, 190, 291
Latin America
comparative studies, 211–212, 262
development in, 218–219
human rights in, 232, 237, 239
and the ICC, 240
OSGA regional center, xv–xvi
policymaking in, 215
as region, 173, 188, 291–292
as research subject, 105–106, 132, 196
Latin American and Caribbean Studies (LACS) (Cornell), 316, 322
Latin American Studies Association, 9, 177, 311
Lewis, Martin, 189
Li, Tania, 293–294
liberalism, 17–18, 256
global, 233–234
post-Cold War, 256
liberalization
Big Bang, 215, 224–225
in China, 214–215
in India, 215

macro-, 222–223
in Russia, 215
Liberia, 237–238
Libya, 119, 244–245
Lieberman, Evan, 117, 125, 130
Lieberman, Victor, 184, 193, 194–196, 200–201
Liechtenstein, 296–297
Lijphart, Arend, 78
Locke, Richard, 4–5, 111–112, 208
longue durée, 166–171, 267
Luebbert, Gregory, 105–106, 111
Lula da Silva, Luiz Inácio, 56–57
Lynch, Julia, 93–94, 207

Ma, Xiao, 217
Mackinder, Halford, 255–256
Madsen, Mikael Rask, 242–243
Mahan, Alfred Thayer, 255–256
Mahoney, James, 5, 77, 79, 172
Maidan protests, 263
Malayan peninsula, 191
Malaysia, 187, 189–191, 199–200, 291
Mali, 119
Malvinas, 173
mandala, 191, 293–294
manipulability criterion, 80, 86
Maoism, 271
Maphilindo, 189–190
market governance, 209, 212–214, 217, 218–223, 225
Marx, Karl, 161–164
Marxism, 259
meaning-making, 12, 48–54, 63–67
Mediterranean and the Mediterranean World, The (Braudel), 166–167
Mediterranean region, 191, 255–256, 273
Mehta, Hansa, 237
MENA countries, xvii
Mexico, 208–209
microfoundational mechanisms, 90
Middle East. *See also* former empires turned revisionist powers (FERPs)
as area, 291–292
comparisons and contrasts within, 193–196
ethnic minorities in, 125
experts on, 261–262
human rights in, 232, 239, 242–244
and the ICC, 240–242
OSGA regional center, xv–xvi
plural society in, 199–200
post-9/11 wars, 255–256

INDEX 347

rentier states in, 196
research in, 11, 134, 146, 273
Middle East Studies Association, 177, 311
Middle Eastern studies, 273–274
Middle East/North Africa (MENA) countries, 146, 149–150
Mill, John Stuart, 77–78, 122, 145–146, 174–175
Miller-Idriss, Cynthia, 309
Minawi, Mostafa, 270–271
mind-world dualism/monism, 84–85
Minnich, John, 216
Mohamad, Mahathir, 235
Monaco, 296–297
Mongolia, 296–297
moral economy, 63–64, 197
Morocco, 215–216
Mountbatten, Louis, 189–190
moyenne durée, 166–167
Multifiber Agreement, 223–224
multi-method research (MMR), 15, 130, 131–140, 153
    challenges to, 151–153
    concepts and theory, 145
    examples, 146–151
    methods, 145–146
    objectives and characteristics, 141–146
Murillo, Maria Victoria, 215
Mutua, Makau, 236
Myanmar, 190, 194, 197–199, 291–292

Nahm, Jonas, 217
Narlikar, Amrita, 21–22
narratives
    Asian values, 235
    of ethnic minorities, 119
    idiographic, 138
    postmodern, 79
    single-country, 3–4
    used for comparison, 18, 49, 50–51, 271–272
    writing style, 66–68
National Defense Education Act, 305
National Humanities Alliance, 307
National Research Council, 188–189
national resource centers (NRCs), 307–308, 312–315, 316
national security agencies, 3
National University of Singapore, 284–285
nationalisms
    in China, 224–225
    commonalities of, 64–65
    local, 62–63

resource security, 224
    studies on, 12–13, 62–63, 271–272, 293–294
NATO (North Atlantic Treaty Organization), 256
Nehru, Jawaharlal, 237
neo-imperialism, 273
neoliberalism, 209–211, 217, 219, 222–225, 260–261, 263
neo-patrimonialism, 134, 196, 201
neopositivism, 79, 84–85, 97, 265. *See also* positivism
neorealism, 260
neo-traditionalists, 270
neo-utilitarianism, 95–96
New Area Studies journal, 2–3
New Caledonia, 294–295
New Zealand, 189–191
Nicholas I (czar), 270–271
Niger, 119
Nigeria, 208–209
Noble, Gregory, 216
nomothetic analysis, 10–12, 81–82, 85–86, 89–90, 93–95, 101–102, 132–133, 138, 160, 178, 274, 310, 315
North Africa, 241–242
North America. *See also* Canada; United States
    Asian studies in, 286–287
    and international relations, 259
    regional human rights systems, 242–243
    research on, 118, 125
Norway, 296–297
Nugent, Paul, 100

objectivism, 50–51
On History (Braudel), 171
ontology, 16–17, 50–51, 129–130, 183, 185, 187–188, 192, 200–201
    comparative, 183, 185, 187–188, 192
    comparison as, 16–17, 183, 185, 187–189, 200–201
    constructivist-postpositivist, 50–51
    interpretive, 51
    positivist, 47
Onwuegbuzie, Anthony, 140–141
Organisation for Security and Cooperation in Europe, 296–297
Organization of American States (OAS), 242
Organization of Islamic Cooperation (OIC) Independent Permanent Human Rights Commission, 243–244
Oriental Institutes, 258–259
orientalism, positive, 233–234

348 INDEX

Ottoman Empire, 194–195, 255–256, 268–271
Oxford University School of Global and Area
  Studies (OSGA), 2–3, 21–22, xv–xviii

Pakistan, 119, 189–190
Papua New Guinea, 292
Parsons, Talcott, 186
particularism, 18–19
  regional, 262–263
PED. *See* political economy, of development
  (PED)
People's Friendship University in Russia
  (RUDN), 8
Pepinsky, Thomas B., 6, 20–21, 311
perceived strategic value, 210–211, 216,
  217–218, 220–225
Persian Empire, 255–256, 268–271
phenomena, classes of, 132–133
Philippines, 56–57, 189–191, 237–238,
  291–292
Pierson, Paul, 4–5
plural society, 16–17, 63–64, 184, 197,
  199–201, 293–294
Poland, 297
political economy, 17–18, 49, 185, 205, 206,
  209, 210, 225
  comparative, 211
  critical, 67
  of development (PED), 17, 205, 206,
    208–211, 225
  East Asian, 333
  international, 211
political science, 1, 3–4, 11, 14, 17–18, xv–xvi,
  36–37, 247
  comparative, 48
  and European studies, 287
  generalizability in, 32
  generalization in, 30
  interpretive approach to, 47–50
  research, 43, 47, 48, 52–55
  scientific rigor in, 54–55
  theories of the state, 39
  translation in, 31–32, 37–38, 40–42
Political Topographies of the African State
  (Boone), 76, 98–101
politics. *See also* geopolitics
  academic, xvi
  climate, 55–59
  comparative, 13, 281, 282–283
  energy, 50, 55–59, 65
  global, 256, 297–298
  open-economy, 210–212

populist, 263
Polynesia, 164
population density, 37–38
populism, 263
Portes, Alejandro, 97
positivism, 10–11, 14, xvi, 47, 48–54, 61, 65–69,
  79, 186, 259–260, 263–264, 333–334
  comparative writing styles, 66–68
  neo-, 79, 84–85, 97, 265
  post-, 10–12, 50–51
postcolonialism, 274, 293–294, 300
post-imperialism, 268–269
post-positivism, 10–12, 50–51
Power, Timothy J., 2–3, 9, 21–22
pragmatism, 1–4, 16, 89–90, 110–111, 247, 273,
  299–300
private foundations, 3
process tracing, 1–2, 80–81, 109, 117, 122–123,
  145–146, 150, 151–152, 159, 174–175,
  217–219, 223–226. *See also* analysis
  longitudinal,
property rights, 212–213, 220–221
  intellectual, 215–216
*Protestant Ethic and the Spirit of Capitalism,
  The* (Weber), 88–89
Prussia, 88
Przeworski, Adam, 29
publication, 67–68
Putin, Vladimir, 224

Qualitative and Multi-Method Research, 130
Qualitative Comparative Analysis (QCA), 1–2,
  4–5, 12–13, 136–137, 145–146
qualitative research, 2–7, 11–13, 29–30, 78, 79,
  136–137, 140–141, 143, 145–146, 205, 218
quantitative research, 3–4, 29–30, 78, 140–141,
  143, 205, 266, 290–291

racism, 245, 264–265
Raffles (hotel), 118
rational choice theory, 184–185, 187–188
rationality, 62–63
  bounded, 86–87
Ravenhill, John, 216
realism, 17–18, 50–51, 54, 162, 256
  neo-, 260
reductionism, 334
reflexivity, 51–53, 62
Reformation, 165
regionalism, 274, 334
regions
  in area studies, 208–209, 288, 289–290

Asia, 188–189, 207
comparison withing and beyond, 192–193,
    196–200
and concepts, 201
Europe, 188, 294–299
formation of, 188–196, 201
Latin America, 188, 291–292
meaning of, 129–130
Mediterranean, 191, 255–256, 273
Middle East, 193–196, 291–292
nature of, 184
research design, 222–225
Southeast Asia, 189–193, 291–298
understanding of, 208
regression analysis, 79, 86, 143, 145–146,
    149–153, 305
Reid, Anthony, 191
relativism, 232, 234–239, 246–247
Remington, Thomas, 208
research, 6, 16, 29–30, 43, 47–48, 52–55, 77,
    133, 281–282. *See also* field research;
    knowledge production; multi-method
    research (MMR); qualitative research;
    quantitative research
archival, 262
in area studies, 316–328, 333
collaborative, 21, 316–328
comparative, 281–282
comparative area studies (CAS), 116, 125,
    206–208, 266, 300
experimental, 266, 304–305
funding for, xvii
global approach to, 334
internationalization of, 305, 311–328
mixed-methods, 29–30
multidisciplinary, 261–262
multilevel design, 222–225
positivist, 47, 51–52
produced in institutes, 285–286
regionally focused, 2–3
resources for, 68
single-country, 6, 304–305
statistical analysis, 6
variables, 1–2, 4–5, 29–30, 52–54, 60–61,
    77–78, 93–94, 101, 106–107, 110, 111,
    115–118, 125, 133, 145, 150, 185
research and development (R&D), 221
resource booms, 7, xvii, 120–122, 215–216
resource security nationalism, 224
Return of Marco Polo, The (Kaplan), 255
revisionism, 260, 274

revisionist powers, 19–20, 255, 257–261,
    273–274. *See also* Eurasia
agential family resemblances, 270–271
family resemblances, 274
processual family resemblances, 271–273
structural family resemblances, 268–270
Rhodes, R. A. W., 48, 66–67
Ritchie, Bryan K., 208
Romance studies, 285
Rome Conference, 241
Rome Statute, 240–241
Royal Touch (Bloch), 164
Rueschemeyer, Dietrich, 105–106, 172
Rüland, Jürgen, 48
Russia. *See also* former empires turned
    revisionist powers (FERPs)
in BRICS, 244
comparison studies, 19–20, 194, 207, 209,
    222–223, 225–226, 257–258
and Eastern Europe, 273
and Eurasia, 255
and Europe, 294–297
experts on, 261–262
globalization of, 206–207, 209
human rights in, 244–245
imperial inheritances of, 265–266, 269,
    270–271
as international player, 257–258
invasion of Ukraine by, 256, 263, 273,
    334–335
liberalization in, 215
market governance in, 217
OSGA regional center, xv–xvi
resemblance to other former empires,
    268–273
studies on, 208, 210–211, 222, 224
Russian, East European and Eurasian Studies,
    295–296
Russian Federation, 224
Russian studies, 273–274, 307–308

Safavid Empire, 195
Sartori, Giovanni, 133
Saudi Arabia, 273
Savage, Jesse Dillon, 15
Saylor, Ryan, 14, 108–109, 114, 120–121, 125,
    174–175, 215–216, 267, 311
Scandinavia, 295–296
Schaffer, Frederic, 64
Schatzberg, Michael, 100–101
Schengen Area, 296–297

350 INDEX

School of Oriental and African Studies, 258–259
Schwartz, Rachel, 36–37, 41
scope (boundary) conditions, 16, 29–30, 42–43, 91–92, 112–113, 115, 137–138, 144–145, 163, 174–175, 206–207, 210, 217–218, 243, 266–267
Scott, James C., 47, 63–65, 186, 187–188, 293–294
Seawright, Jason, 78
sectoral analysis, 186, 206, 210–213, 215–221, 225–226. *See also* contextualized comparative sector approach (CCSA)
  and comparative area studies, 205–212–217
  contextualized sectors and value of comparisons, 214–215
  multilevel comparative case research design, 222–225
  national *vs.* sectoral patterns, 215–217
  sectoral organization of institutions, 212–213
  sectoral structural attributes, 212
  and social and political construction of sectors, 206, 213
security, 3, 17–18, 118, 220, 224–225, 256, 257–258, 260–262
Segal, Adam, 216
segmented society, 199–200. *See also* plural society
self-determination, 237–238
self-reliance, neoliberal, 224–225
Sen, Amartya, 236
Senegal, 64, 98–101
Senghor, Léopold, 236
Serbia, 296–297
Shami, Seteny, 309
Shanghai Cooperation Organisation, 256, 297–298
Shari'ah, 240–241
Siam. *See* Thailand
Sikkink, Kathryn, 237
Sil, Rudra, 75–76, 130, 159, 215, 218, 265, 310
Simmons, Erica, 5, 12, 13–14, 48
Singapore, 190, 286–287, 291
single-country studies, 6, 304–305
situatedness, 15, 18, 19–20, 51–52, 61–62, 262, 310
Skinner, Quentin, 175–176
Skocpol, Theda, 222, 282–283
Slater, Dan, 35–37, 41, 89, 105–107, 111, 208
Slavic studies, 285, 288
Sluga, Glenda, 237

Smith, Benjamin, 118–119, 125
Smith, Nicolas Rush, 5, 12, 13–14, 38–39, 42, 48
Smithsonian Institution, 188–189
social justice, 56–57, 59–60
Social Science Research Council, 188–189
social sciences
  area studies and, 1–2, 4, 6, 15
  and comparative area studies, 40–42
  and the humanities, 2–3, 303–304
  influence of the *Annales* school, 161–162, 172–177
  interpretive traditions in, 50–51
  nomothetic, 315
  research in, 6, 16, 77, 133, 281–282
  spatial turn, 6–7
  theory, 7, 107, 196
  translation in, 31–32
  war making (and state making), 33–39 (*see also under* Tilly, Charles)
socialism, 223
socioeconomic rights, 235–236
sociology, 9, 14, xv–xvi
  historical, 12–13
Solinger, Dorothy, 208–209
Solow, Robert, 310
Somers, Margaret, 222
Soss, Joe, 59
South Africa
  AIDS policy in, 130
  apartheid in, 237
  comparison studies, 215–216, 274
  human rights in, 232, 244–245
  research in, 38–39, 42
  state formation in, 38–39
  tax regimes in, 117, 130
South America
  regional human rights systems, 242–243
  state formation in, 125
  studies on, 56–57, 200–201
  taxation systems in, 125
South Asia
  comparative studies, 124–125, 152–153, 194, 211–212
  and the ICC, 241–242
  OSGA regional center, xv–xvi
  plural society in, 199–200
South Asia Program (SAP) (Cornell), 316, 324
South Asian studies, 285
South China Sea, 273, 291
South Korea, 95–97, 208–209, 292
Southeast Asia

comparative studies, 16–17, 152–153, 194, 211–212
compared to Brazil, 117
comparisons and contrasts within, 193–196, 199, 200–201
diversity in, 192
institutional development in, 89
knowledge of, 208
as plural society, 197–200
postcolonial, 35–36, 41
rebel groups in, 124–125
as region, 189–193, 291–298
research in, 56–57, 105–106, 132, 184
on transnational labor alliance campaigns, 118, 125
Southeast Asia Command (SEAC), 189–190
Southeast Asia Council, 286
Southeast Asia Program (SEAP) (Cornell), 316, 323
Southeast Asia Treaty Organization (SEATO), 189–190
Southeast Asian studies, 20–21, 281, 283–294, 296, 298
South-South Human Rights Forum, 235–236
Soviet Union. *See also* Russia
collapse of, 208, 215, 219
communist mobilization of, 208–209
and Europe, 295–296
studies on, 208–209
Sri Lanka, 189, 292
Staniland, Paul, 124–125
Stephens, John, 105–106
Stevens, Mitchell, 309
storytelling, 66–68
Stovall, Connie, 21, 258
Strange Parallels (Lieberman), 194
Strategic Value Framework, 219–221, 223, 225–226
Stroh, Alexander, 174–175, 262, 267
Structuring the State (Ziblatt), 122–125
subjectivity, 82–83, 93, 100–101, 162–165, 172–173, 175, 176–177
SUIN (sufficient but unnecessary part of a condition that is itself an insufficient but necessary condition for an outcome), 114
Sumatra, 191
supercontinent, 255, 257, 261
Switzerland, 296–297
Syria, 56–57, 119

Taiwan, 95–96, 208–209, 273, 291–292
Tambiah, Stanley, 191

Tanzania, 100
Teaching, Research, and International Policy (TRIP), 315
technology transfers, 214–216
telecommunications sectors, 214–215, 220, 222–224
temporality, 165, 172–173
Teune, Henry, 29
textile industry, 215–216, 220, 222–225
Thailand, 111, 189–190, 194, 291–292
Thakur, Ramesh, 244
Thelen, Kathleen, 4–5, 111–112, 208
theory development, 105–107
thick description, 186
Thompson, Ashley, 291–292
Thun, Eric, 216
Tilly, Charles, 32–42, 93, 160, 170, 171
time
geographic, 166–167
historical, 166–167
individual, 166–167
social, 166–167
Timor-Leste, 291–292, 296
Title VI, 305
Tocqueville, Alexis de, 198
translation
in comparative area studies, 33–34, 43
methodological, 13–14, 30–33
in political science, 37–38, 40–4244
war making and state making in, 33–39
transparency, 52–53, 55–56, 58–59, 62, 63, 68
transregional studies, 2, 211–212
Tsai, Kellee, 208
Tufts University, 310
Tullbane, Joseph, 305
Tunisia, 215–216, 241–242
Turareg minorities, 119
Turkey. *See also* former empires turned revisionist powers (FERPs)
comparison studies, 257–258
and Cyprus, 273
and Eurasia, 255–256
and Greece, 273
imperial inheritances of, 265–266
as international player, 257–258
Kurdish minorities in, 119–120
regional association, 174, 295–297

352 INDEX

Turkey (*Continued*)
    resemblance to other former empires, 19–20, 268–273
    studies on, 260
Turkish studies, 273–274
Turner, Lisa, 140–141
typological theory, 145–146

UDHR. *See* Universal Declaration of Human Rights (UDHR)
Ujamaa villagization program, 100
Ukraine, 256, 263, 273, 334–335
understanding
    of areas, 6–7, 175
    of cases, 7
    of comparison, 12–13, 48, 160
    context-sensitive, 52, 66–67, 69–70, 163, 177
    cross-, 61–66
    deep, 31, 49, 132–133
    empathetic, 162–164
    explanatory, 84, 86
    gaps/limits in, 31–32
    grounded, 163–165, 171
    hegemonic, 50
    historical, 162–163, 166–168, 171, 176
    holistic, 53
    interpretive, 52–53
    intersubjective, 213
    local, 38–39, 53
    of place, 132–133, 135, 143–144, 153, 170
    shared, 5
    of space, 165
    subjective, 84–85, 93–94, 162–163, 166, 167–168, 173–174
    Weberian, 135
United Kingdom (UK), 189–190, 296–297
United Nations (UN), 237–238, 273. *See also* Human Rights Council (HRC)
United Nations Educational, Scientific and Cultural Organization (UNESCO), 234–235
United States. *See also* North America
    alignment with Europe, 294–296
    area studies in, 3
    Defense Department, 310
    Department of Education, 328
    and Eurasia, 256–257
    and the ICC, 240
    political development in, 177
    scholarship on, 196, 282–283

and SEATO, 189–190
Universal Declaration of Human Rights (UDHR), 234–235, 237, 238, 240
universalism/universality, xviii–xix, 18–19, 232, 234–236, 238, 241, 246–247, 259
    pluralistic, 232–234, 238, 240, 263–264
    syncretic, 233–234
University of California, Berkeley, 284–285
University of East Anglia, 2–3
University of Freiburg (Germany), 284
University of Hong Kong, 284–285
University of Michigan, 284–285, 312
University of Oklahoma, 310
University of Pennsylvania, 305–306
University of Pittsburgh, 295–296
utilitarianism, neo-, 95–96
utopias, 83–86

value chains, 212–213, 216
van der Veer, Peter, 12–13
van Schendel, Willem, 293–294
variables
    causal, 106, 113–116, 119, 122
    confounding, 78–79
    consequences of, 15
    control, 79
    dependent, 105–107, 109–112, 147–148
    explanatory, 105–107, 117, 118, 124, 136–137, 147–148
    independent, 97, 107, 108–114, 121–122, 135, 147–149, 220, 224
    intervening, 80, 91, 108–109, 267
    mechanisms-as-, 108–109
    organizational, 124–125
    relationship between, 117, 120
    research, 1–2, 4–5, 29–30, 52–54, 60–61, 77–78, 93–94, 101, 106–107, 110, 111, 115–118, 125, 133, 145, 150, 185
    sequential, 108–109
    SUIN, 114
    that reside outside the theory, 93
Verba, Sidney, 140–141
Vienna World Conference on Human Rights, 234–235
Vietnam, 190, 194, 291–292
vigilantism, 38–39
vignettes, 66–68
Viljoen, Frans, 243
Vogel, Steven K., 216
von Soest, Christian, 174–175, 262, 267
Voss, Joel, 245

INDEX 353

Waldner, David, 80, 108–109
Wallace, Alfred Russell, 200–201
Wallerstein, Immanuel, 170
Waltz, Kenneth, 107
Washington Consensus, 219
weapons of the weak, 63–64, 186, 197
Weber, Max, 82–97, 99–102, 135, 161–162, 196, 269
Wengle, Susanne, 215
West Africa, 95, 99, 101–102, 132
Western, educated, industrialized, rich, and democratic (WEIRD) countries, 11
Westernists, 270–271
When Soldiers Rebel (Harkness), 146–149
Whitehead, Lawrence, 173, 182–183
Widodo, Joko, 56–57
Wigen, Kären, 189
Wildavsky, Aaron, 21
Wildavsky, Ben, 303

Witt, Antonia, 232–233
Wittgenstein, Ludwig, 267–268
Wolters, Oliver, 191
Worden, Elizabeth Anderson, 311–312
World Politics (Gallagher), 208–209
World Trade Organization (WTO), 214, 223–224
Wright, Erik Olin, 98
writing style, 66–68
Wu, Yu-Shan, 208–209

Yang, Wenhui, 217
Yasuda, John, 217
Yemen, 297–298
Yeoh, Brenda, 293–294
Yew, Lee Kuan, 235

Zaire, 95–96
Ziblatt, Daniel, 105–107, 111, 122–125, 208
Zomia, 293–294